DISABILITY DEFINITIONS, DIAGNOSES, AND PRACTICE IMPLICATIONS

This introductory text defines and describes disability, while providing concrete practice guidelines and recommendations for students in the fields of counseling, social work, and other helping professions. Various specialty areas are explored in detail, including marriage and family counseling, adolescent counseling, addictions counseling, LGBTQ concerns, multicultural counseling, and career counseling.

The first three chapters lay the foundation by discussing the demand for counseling services by individuals with all types of disabilities; presenting clinical, legal, medical/biological, and personal definitions of disability; and describing physical, cognitive, and psychiatric disabilities. Next, author Julie Smart examines core beliefs about disability using a range of first-person accounts from individuals with disabilities (IWDs). The last seven chapters focus on practice guidelines for various aspects of disability—including ethical considerations, societal issues, social role demands, and individual responses—and explore new possibilities for disability counseling professions.

With rich case studies woven throughout, as well as valuable information on client needs, disability categorizations, and key Models of Disability, this essential textbook will be useful not only to counseling students but also to professional counselors, social workers, and psychologists.

Julie Smart, Ph.D. was Professor in the Department of Special Education and Rehabilitation at Utah State University for twenty-four years. For ten years, she was the Program Director of Graduate Programs in Rehabilitation Counseling. She is also the author of *Disability, Society, and the Individual*.

"Dr. Smart, like all of her other scholarly contributions on disability, has once again written an outstanding book for new and advanced social science students and practicing counselors about working with people with disabilities. This book ties together so many loose ends other similar books do not cover. She explains what disability is for the many professionals who remain unsure and explains various diagnoses using the ICF and DSM-V contemporary classifications. She blends current ethical, legal, and practice guidelines for counselors that crosses practice disciplines in excellent fashion. Finally, she interweaves personal account excerpts across various counseling disciplines, noting attitudes, empathy, societal injustice issues and gender identity concerns, which are exemplary and contemporary matters. This is a must read for undergraduate and graduate students alike across disciplines."
Irmo Marini, PhD, CRC, CLCP, FVE, *certified rehabilitation counselor, certified life care planner, Professor of Rehabilitation Counseling, University of Texas Rio Grande Valley*

"Dr. Smart is, indeed, a disability scholar. The strength of this book is the thorough discussion of the impact that societal attitudes and perceptions have on IWDs. This work integrates various models of research, technological, and medical advances that positively transform the quality of life for IWDs. It comprehensibly defines and interprets complex laws, policies, movements, and disability classification systems that govern programs, services, and systems for IWDs. Dr. Smart's passion for the multicultural nature of humanity drives this work."
Mark A. Stebnicki, PhD, LPC, CRC, CCM, DCMHS, *Professor, Coordinator of Military and Trauma Counseling Program, Department of Addictions & Rehabilitation, East Carolina University*

DISABILITY DEFINITIONS, DIAGNOSES, AND PRACTICE IMPLICATIONS

An Introduction for Counselors

Julie Smart

NEW YORK AND LONDON

First published 2019
by Routledge
711 Third Avenue, New York, NY 10017

and by Routledge
2 Park Square, Milton Park, Abingdon, Oxon, OX14 4RN

Routledge is an imprint of the Taylor & Francis Group, an informa business

© 2019 Taylor & Francis

The right of Julie Smart to be identified as author of this work has been asserted by her in accordance with sections 77 and 78 of the Copyright, Designs and Patents Act 1988.

All rights reserved. No part of this book may be reprinted or reproduced or utilised in any form or by any electronic, mechanical, or other means, now known or hereafter invented, including photocopying and recording, or in any information storage or retrieval system, without permission in writing from the publishers.

Trademark notice: Product or corporate names may be trademarks or registered trademarks, and are used only for identification and explanation without intent to infringe.

Library of Congress Cataloging-in-Publication Data
Names: Smart, Julie, author.
Title: Disability definitions, diagnoses, and practice implications : an introduction for counselors / Julie Smart.
Description: New York : Routledge, 2018. | Includes bibliographical references.
Identifiers: LCCN 2018014241 | ISBN 9781138244689 (hbk : alk. paper) | ISBN 9781138244696 (pbk. : alk. paper) | ISBN 9781315276694 (ebk)
Subjects: | MESH: Counseling—standards | Disabled Persons | Counselors—standards | Counseling—ethics | Disability Evaluation
Classification: LCC RC455.2.C65 | NLM WM 55 | DDC 362.2/04256—dc23
LC record available at https://lccn.loc.gov/2018014241

ISBN: 978-1-138-24468-9 (hbk)
ISBN: 978-1-138-24469-6 (pbk)
ISBN: 978-1-315-27669-4 (ebk)

Typeset in New Baskerville
by Apex CoVantage, LLC

CONTENTS

	Preface	vii
	Introduction to the Chapters	1
1	A New Reality for Counselors	5
2	Defining, Diagnosing, and Measuring Disability	36
3	Models of Disability: Another Way to Describe Disability	76
4	Six Core Beliefs About Disability of Highly Empathetic Counselors	126
5	Ethical Considerations and General Practice Guidelines	163
6	Understanding the Experience of Disability: Counseling Practice Guidelines	199
7	Integrating Counseling Practices with Societal Issues	240
8	Understanding the Individual's Response to Disability: Counseling Practice Guidelines	284
9	Understanding Social Role Demands of Individuals With Disabilities: Counseling Practice Guidelines	332
10	Responding to Some Unique Demands of Disability: Counseling Practice Guidelines	379
11	New Horizons for the Counseling Professions	402
	Case Studies	406
	Index	417

PREFACE

I wanted to write a book that provides basic counseling guidelines for working with individuals with disabilities (IWDs). Throughout 24 years as a professor at Utah State University, I searched for such a book to use in the courses I taught and could not find one. Of course, there were many books on counseling, but these books did not discuss clients with disabilities and there were also books on disability, but these books did not mention counseling practice guidelines. I promised myself that, when I had time, I would write this book. This is the book. Counselors working with IWDs will find their professional and personal lives enriched, strengthened, and expanded.

Counselors, social workers, and psychologists will be working more and more with IWDs. However, ethical principles warn against professionals working outside their areas of competence. This book seeks to begin a reconciliation of these two realities: 1) the need of IWDs for effective and empathic counseling services and 2) the lack of disability training for most counselors, social workers, and psychologists. It is my hope that this book will serve as a starting point to learn about IWDs.

Some counseling professionals might think, "I've already been trained in disability issues." However, much of this disability training is based on unquestioned assumptions and does not reflect the daily lived experience of IWDs. If the most important aspect of counseling is the relationship between professional and client, two concerns must be addressed: 1) counseling professionals will be required to learn about the disability experience, and 2) it is essential for counselors to examine their own feelings and reactions toward disability and the individuals who experience them.

Like everyone else, counseling professionals live in a society that is permeated with media that present unrealistic and demeaning portrayals of IWDs, including the "brave inspiration" and the "pitiful, helpless cripple." Neither is realistic; but these portrayals are often incorporated into public attitudes toward IWDs. Therefore, much of acquiring knowledge and experience of disability and the people who experience them will require a great deal of *unlearning*. It may not be an exaggeration to say that counseling professionals possess little knowledge, skill, and experience with IWDs and most of these are unrealistic and demeaning to IWDs.

Most IWDs consider themselves to be normal people with the same typical concerns and life tasks as anyone else. Their disabilities are a valued part of their self-identity but not the most important aspect. Rather, most IWDs have multiple roles and their self-identities are multifaceted. Counselors, social workers, and psychologists might be inclined to refer clients with disabilities to rehabilitation counselors and other allied health professionals. This may be considered defining the individual by their disability. IWDs will seek out such counseling, social work, and psychological services in the following areas: child and adolescent, marriage and family, military and veterans, career counseling, addictions, LGBT issues, academic, and many other types. Therefore, professionals with training, skill, and experience in these specialties will be required to gain knowledge, skills, and experience in serving IWDs.

Should professionals be "disability blind," ignoring the client's disability? No, but counselors should not define the client by their disability nor think that the client obsesses about their disability 24/7. It will not be possible to build an empathic relationship without understanding the client's disability, including their perceptions and reactions.

This book is intended as an introductory broad overview on disability. Using the analogy of the elephant, I think it is important to gain a picture of the entire elephant, learning how each of part of the elephant fits together. So, rather than learning a great deal of detail about one specific part of the elephant's anatomy, such as the ears, a broad overview of the whole elephant is provided. My hope is that presenting a broad picture of disability, sacrificing detail, will be a helpful, logical start to learning about disability.

Two chapters are devoted to defining and describing disability, including those characteristics that are not disabilities. The clinical, legal, cultural, and personal definitions are discussed. Seven chapters describe practice guidelines. I thought it important that readers gain some introduction to disability before reading about professional guidelines. For example, it worries me when I read articles about disability in the academic literature because I don't think that most readers know what disability is. Therefore, I wrote two chapters that define disabilities. For specific types of disabilities, readers can access information in the *International Classification of Functioning* (ICF) published by the World Health Organization or the *Diagnostic and Statistical Manual of Mental Disorders-5* (DSM-5) published by the American Psychiatric Association.

Finally, I use many first-person accounts because these short excerpts illustrate concepts and, furthermore, it is important to understand the experience of IWDs themselves. I am grateful to these authors for allowing me to use their experiences. Occasionally, I have used the same excerpt in two or three chapters because these particular accounts illustrate two or three important points. I simply thought that re-writing the excerpt would be easier for readers, rather than referring them back to previous chapters.

It is my hope that social workers, counselors, and psychologists will find my book helpful.

Julie Smart
February 9, 2018
Salt Lake City, Utah

INTRODUCTION TO THE CHAPTERS

Chapter One, in a nutshell, presents an argument for the provision of all types of counseling services to IWDs. The concept of "disability" is broadly defined, while the idea of "normalcy" is questioned as an unattainable myth. Except for the disability, most IWDs consider themselves normal people. The unheralded demographic shift of the greater numbers of IWDs is also discussed, including some of the implications for both society and professional service providers, which includes counselors. It may be somewhat disconcerting to learn that the increases in the population of IWDs is progress, considered both a scientific and medical advance. In most cases, the alternative to the acquisition of a disability would be the death of the individual. Therefore, both individuals and the greater society accrue benefits from these increases in the number of individuals with disabilities (IWDs).

Chapter Two defines the medical, biological, organic, mental, and emotional aspects of disability. It may surprise some readers to learn that these aspects are only a *part* of defining and describing disabilities. In fact, most of the general public conceptualizes disabilities as *only* the medical, biological, and emotional symptoms and manifestations. However, most IWDs define themselves as much more than their symptoms and limitations. Does this mean that these biological and mental symptoms should be ignored? Of course not. They are important, simply not as important as most individuals without disabilities (IWODs) think. A brief introduction of two major standardized diagnostic manuals is included. These are the *International Classification of Disease-10* (ICD-10) (2001) published by the World Health Organization and the *Diagnostic and Statistical Manual of Mental Disorders-5* (DSM-5) (2013) published by the American Psychiatric Association.

Chapter Two also includes topics that may be new, including the hierarchy of stigma; low-incidence and high-incidence disabilities; and type of measurement, either categorical or dimensional. At first glance, it may appear unnecessary to dichotomize the method of measurement. However, I do think that this dimensional/categorical dichotomy is important due to several factors, all discussed in Chapter Two.

Chapter Three presents Models of Disability, which are abstract, human-made definitions of disability. While abstract, each of these models directly influences the daily lives of IWDs, even to the point of deciding if they are allowed to live. So, these abstractions are important. Human-made abstractions are open to change. Most of society thinks of disability only in terms of the Biomedical Model of Disability and, adding to this erroneous assumption, most people are not even aware that there are other models. Counselors, embedded in modern society, may also subscribe to these false assumptions. If you were to ask most IWDs which of the models *most* directly affects their daily lives, most would reply the Civil Rights Model of Disability, stating that *most* of the difficulties of their disabilities result from prejudice and discrimination and lack of access.

Does Chapter Three advocate completely dismissing the Biomedical Model of Disability? No, of course not. Even with full civil rights and equal social status with IWODs, there are medical and biological aspects of disability. Further, it is the achievements of medical sciences that have resulted in these greater numbers of IWDs and their longer life spans. Models of Disability can lead to case management and collaboration. One of the practice applications is collaboration between counselors and medical service providers.

Should all of these models be compressed into a single, major model? Some authors have advocated a "bio-social-environmental" model. However, I think that each of the models merits full consideration separately; therefore, I do not support any type of "mega-model." Some sort of a simplistic checklist of boxes to be ticked is not recommended; but rather, by understanding the lives and needs of IWDs in terms of *each* of these models, case conceptualization will be more rich and complete, leading to a greater number of treatment options. Further, the client with a disability (CWD) will appreciate the counselor's greater understanding of their life. Case management becomes more straightforward when each model is considered separately.

Chapter Four is titled "Six Core Beliefs About Disability of Highly Empathetic Counselors" and is very different from the following seven chapters. Its position in the middle of the book seems appropriate because before understanding Chapter Four, it is necessary to understand the definition of disability, and before offering Practice Applications, a foundation of accurate attitudes toward IWDs must be laid. Some of these core beliefs overlap and some may appear counterintuitive. Hopefully, the first-person accounts provided will assist in illustrating and elaborating on these beliefs.

Chapters Five through Ten are composed of practice guidelines. After publishing several textbooks on disabilities, I am aware that everyone, including readers, reviewers, and editors, want concrete, specific guidelines. On the other hand, I understand these chapters may be open to criticisms that these practice guidelines are too concrete, mechanical, and cookbook-ish. To counter, counselors are reminded of two basic foundations of all counseling: the client is an individual and they are the best source of information.

Some of the guidelines overlap, but after great consideration, I decided that the importance of each guideline merited a separate discussion. These guidelines are specific to IWDs, but it is necessary to remember that these practice guidelines should be *added* to the counselor's repertoire of practice in which they are well-trained, experienced, and skilled. Here is an example: A college student comes to the university counseling center for academic and career counseling. The counselor is trained, experienced, and knowledgeable about the various majors and course requirements, matching the individual's aptitudes, desires, and values with various types of occupations and job markets. In addition, the college counselor will need to understand stigma and prejudice toward different types of disabilities; disability laws, including the Americans with Disabilities Act; and assistive technology that could enhance the client's functioning.

I suppose I should identify the four abbreviations used throughout these chapters. They are:

IWD = individual with a disability (singular)
IWDs = individuals with a disability (plural)
IWOD = individual without a disability (singular)
IWODs = individuals without a disability (plural)
CWD = client with a disability (singular)
CWDs = clients with a disability (plural)
CWOD = client without a disability (singular)
CWODs = clients without a disability (plural)

There are other abbreviations throughout and these are explained in the text.

The question of person-first language arises and, as can be seen from the preceding abbreviations, I have chosen to use person-first language. Person-first language places the individual or the role or function of the individual before the disability. The civil rights law for IWDs in the United States is the Americans with Disabilities Act (ADA, 1990), a government usage of person-first language. Generally, in the United States, person-first language is used while the

United Kingdom does not use person-first language. If person-first language were not used, the title would have been the Disabled Americans Act. Generally, in the United States, person-first language is used while the United Kingdom does not use personfirst language. The major premise of this book is that IWDs are more than their disabilities and, accordingly, require the counseling services of all types and, therefore, person-first language is appropriate. Person-first language, and the controversy concerning its used, is discussed at some length later in the book.

Case Studies

The book includes seven case studies, which can be discussed in groups or individuals can work on them. The purpose of these is to allow students to incorporate some of the concepts discussed in the book.

If not used in class discussion, individual students can choose one case study and use it for each of the eleven chapters. If not working on a single case study throughout, students may choose to use all of the case studies, perhaps using a different case study for each of the eleven chapters. All of these case studies are hypothetical.

One
A NEW REALITY FOR COUNSELORS

This chapter consists of three sections. The first section is a general rationale for the need for counselors of all specialties to provide services for individuals with disabilities (IWDs). The second section is entitled, "The Paradox of Disability." The third section is the longest, and it discusses a convergence of factors that has changed the lives of IWDs.

Counselors Providing Services to IWDs

Increasingly, individuals with disabilities (IWDs) are seeking the services of counselors in all specialty areas, including career counseling; marriage and family counseling; child and adolescent counseling; aging and adult development; spiritual and pastoral counseling; lesbian, gay, bisexual, and transgendered issues counseling; college counseling; military veteran counseling; and more. This new demand for counseling services has resulted from the convergence of several factors, all of which are of recent origin, including demographic shifts, the enactment and enforcement of advanced human civil rights laws, more accurate portrayal of IWDs in the media, and the ever-growing group identity of IWDs.

Three Broad Categories of Disabilities
1. Physical disabilities
2. Cognitive disabilities
3. Psychiatric disabilities

Broadly speaking, definitions of disabilities are divided into three major categories, all of which are based on symptoms and not on causes. The first category is physical disabilities and includes sensory loss, such as blindness and deafness, orthopedic impairments, and chronic illnesses. The second broad category is labeled cognitive disabilities and includes intellectual disabilities and developmental disabilities, such as ASD (autism spectrum disorder). The third category is termed psychiatric disabilities and, typically, includes mental disorders, alcoholism, and other chemical and substance abuse conditions.

Chronic illnesses include diabetes; heart conditions; autoimmune diseases, such as lupus, rheumatoid arthritis, and multiple sclerosis; and many others. These chronic illnesses are considered to be disabilities because they limit an individual's functioning, require lifelong management, and individuals with chronic illnesses and conditions are often the target of prejudice and discrimination. When considering the three main categories of disabilities, physical, cognitive, and psychiatric, chronic illnesses are placed in the physical disabilities category.

These categories never precisely and fully reflect the reality of the IWDs. For example, some IWDs experience more than one disability. Nonetheless, to gain a simple introductory explanation and understanding of the disability experience, these three categories provide a framework and a basic overview for all types of disabilities.

In the not-so-distant past, IWDs who desired counseling services were routinely referred to rehabilitation counselors and medical practitioners. The public and the counseling professions, including both practitioners and academicians, considered the disability(ies) of IWDs to be their defining identity or, at minimum, to be the most important self-identity. In this way, IWDs were marginalized or segregated to receive services almost exclusively from the medical professions. However, most IWDs do not consider their disability to be their most defining characteristic although the disability, and the mastery of it, is a valued and important part of the self-identity of most IWDs. As we shall see in this book, most IWDs consider themselves "normal" and as "individuals," albeit with a disability. (This is probably less true of individuals with severe cognitive and psychiatric disabilities, a small minority of all IWDs.) Oliver Sacks (1985), the late neurologist/author explained this difference:

> If a man has lost a leg or an eye, he knows that he has lost a leg or an eye; but if he has lost a sense of self—himself—he cannot know it, because he is no longer there to know it.
>
> (pp. 35–36)

IWDs manage and negotiate the disability, but most view themselves as having the same motivations, emotions, needs, and goals as individuals without disabilities (IWODs). Also, like anyone else, IWDs consider themselves to have multiple identities, roles, and functions, instead of only "being disabled." Additionally, most IWDs deal with the typical developmental demands and life demands as

IWODs do, including education, career development, establishing long-term sexual relations, raising children, and developing a spiritual/philosophical/religious understanding of life. Izak Perlman, the world famous Israeli violinist, remembers when he first started his career, he was known as a "disabled violinist." Now, after decades of success and hard work, the public describes Izak Perlman as a "violinist with a disability." This second description more closely reflects Perlman's self-concept because, while he does not deny or ignore his disability, a more important identity is as a violinist. Perlman contracted polio as a child and, because of lower limb paralysis, uses crutches (Olkin, 1999).

Ways in Which IWDs Consider Themselves "Normal"

IWDs have the same motivations, emotions, and goals as IWODs.
IWDs have the same life tasks.
IWDs do not consider their disability to be their most defining identity.
IWDs claim the right to self-identity, rather than being categorized in a disability group, such as the "blind" or the "mentally ill."

The concept of "normality" also includes the self-identity of the IWD as an individual. In the past, IWDs have been viewed as belonging to categories rather than as individuals. Many IWDs have felt that they were forced to accept stigmatizing diagnoses in order to receive services. These categories included "the disabled" or "the blind" or the "mentally ill," and a myriad of other demeaning, stereotyped labels. It is a short step from categorization to stereotyping, such as "All blind people are musically talented" or "All IWDs must be depressed." Additionally, these categories, mostly defined by diagnostic groups, tend to be negative, pathologizing the entire person and relegating the IWD, regardless of personal resources, to an isolated, inferior status.

Nonetheless, medical services are important to IWDs, especially in the stabilization period after the diagnosis/onset of the disability, in times of relapse, and for medication management. For most IWDs, medical management will be a lifelong process, treating the physical, organic, and biological aspects of the disability, avoiding secondary conditions or complications, and maintaining the highest possible quality of life (QOL). When using medical services, the disability of the individual is rightly the presenting problem. However, thinking in terms of counseling, there is much more to an IWD than their disability and, therefore, IWDs require the same professional services that IWODs seek out.

To clarify the counseling needs of IWDs, we may look at three broad categories.

1. Most often, the IWD is requesting the expertise of the counselor in their specialty or theoretical orientation. In these cases, the disability and the individual's experience of the disability may be of little relevance.
2. Occasionally, the client's experience of their disability, including both medical and social aspects, may have some significance. Nonetheless, the disability is not the presenting problem.
3. The IWD may request counseling services to help with their response to the disability, including the emotional management of the disability (Elliott & Gramling, 1990; Elliott & Warren, 2007).

In all three of these categories, counselors will need both an understanding of and awareness of the disability experience, and based upon this rudimentary knowledge, counselors will be able to understand the client's idiosyncratic response to their disability. Practice applications for these three categories are provided in Chapters 5, 6, 7, 8, 9, and 10.

Although not everyone has a disability, the possibility of acquiring a disability (or being diagnosed with a disability) is universal. The surgeon/author Atul Gawande described this universal possibility by stating, "Life is a preexisting condition" (p. 45). Much like the counseling approach of "successful aging" or "reorientation and coping with major life changes" (Boerner & Jopp, 2007; Grant, 2005), IWDs seek to maintain control of their lives, activate goal optimization, and find alternative methods to reach desired goals. Substitution of goals, maximizing abilities and resources, including civil rights, are effective coping devices for anyone experiencing major life changes, including IWDs. However, in addition to these adaptive strategies, IWDs encounter added needs, including the medical aspects of the disability, managing the disability, reducing relapses, and avoiding secondary conditions or complications. Societal prejudice and discrimination may or may not be a part of many major life changes; however, prejudice and discrimination are almost always a barrier to which the IWD must respond and negotiate. Indeed, many IWDs consider prejudice and discrimination and lack of accommodations to be a greater difficulty than the disability itself (Hahn, 1988). Twenty-five years ago, Madeline Will, former assistant secretary for education and head of the Office of Special Education and Rehabilitation (OSER), explained:

> Most disabled people . . . will tell that despite what everyone thinks, the disability itself is not what makes everything different. What causes the disabilities is the attitude society has about being disabled, attitudes that make a disabled person embarrassed, insecure, uncomfortable, dependent. Of course, disabled people rarely talk about quality of life. But, it has precious little to do with deformity and great deal to do with society's own defects.
>
> (as cited in Weisgerber, 1991, p. 6)

Hopefully, this book will be a start to close the gap between the aspirational directives of ethical codes of the helping professions.

The Paradox of Disability

How can an IWD think of themselves as "normal"? Are not disabilities to be prevented and avoided? There are laws mandating seat belt use, laws against drunk driving, and government-provided prenatal care for pregnant women, all which reflect government/societal actions to decrease the incidence of disability. Also, when an individual is injured, a great number of resources are marshaled to return the individual to pre-injury functioning. Do not disabilities involve impairment and reduced functioning? To use a single example, is it not better to be able to hear than to be d/Deaf? Disabilities are often painful, difficult, require substantial management and treatment, and societal-provided accommodations. Without doubt, most disabilities are expensive and the IWD, or his family, rarely pays the entire sum for the treatment/rehabilitation. Nonetheless, after medical stabilization, most IWDs return to a "new normal," which is life with a disability.

Carol Gill, a psychologist who is paraplegic, noted that most IWDs identify themselves as typical, ordinary people with the usual life concerns, such as family, career, and community life. Nevertheless, often IWDs are unpleasantly reminded that others may not see them as ordinary or typical people.

> Unless they have developed a cultural consciousness that centralizes difference, most disabled people identify as typical. . . . Moreover, most disabled people think of themselves as ordinary because impairments receded in importance as they are integrated into daily routines. It can be repeatedly jolting for individuals who identify as ordinary to be persistently categorized as extraordinary or pathetic by those whom they regard as peers, even intimates.
>
> (Gill, 2000, p. 351)

Legal Aspects

> The Difference Between Civil Rights Laws and Service Laws

American law does recognize the medical/organic aspect of disability. Protection under the law in the United States is provided by the Americans with Disabilities Act (ADA) (1990) Amendments (2008), but to receive this protection, an individual must prove that they have a government-recognized disability. Thus, the IWD is provided legal recourse against prejudice and discrimination based on a well-documented disability. Other laws, such as workers compensation, special education law, and military veterans laws, also provide assistance and benefits based on the medical/organic aspects of disability. However, there are two differences between the ADA and these other laws. First, the ADA is universal for all IWDs and, second, these other laws are service laws. These service laws apply to specific groups to IWDs, such as injured workers (workers compensation), children with disabilities (special education), and military veterans (veterans affairs). Both the ADA and service laws are based on documented disabilities.

The organic, biological, and physical realities of disabilities cannot be denied, nor do most IWDs wish to hide or minimize their disability. They wish to retain their identity as IWDs and, at the same time, enjoy the same civil rights as other Americans. Nonetheless, there are also sociopolitical aspects of disability, such as the provision of government services and acceptance of IWDs in all areas of public life, and medical and scientific advances have greatly improved the disability experience. Laws against discrimination can be enacted and enforced. In contrast, it is impossible to enact laws against prejudice. The ADA addresses discrimination including hiring practices, right of physical access, and entrance requirements for educational institutions. Prejudice, on the other hand, is deeply ingrained beliefs and attitudes that limit the life chances of IWDs.

Social Perceptions

> Civil Rights Laws for IWDs Does Not Require Lowering or Waiving Standards

Most IWDs and disability scholars believe that the social and political position of IWDs have improved—but not as much as predicted. Laws protecting IWDs are often weak, the enforcement spotty, and, until recently, the burden to prove prejudice and discrimination rested with the IWD. The lack of human rights persists today, including the basic right to life, and the unwarranted prejudice and discrimination toward IWDs. Not only does this prejudice and discrimination persists but it is also socially maintained. Defining an IWD as solely their disability is an example of societal-perpetuated prejudice and discrimination and, yet, most IWODs do not consider such a narrow view of an IWD as either prejudicial and discriminating. After all, there *or*, undeniably, negative aspects of disability. Certainly, most people, including IWDS, do not aspire to have a disability nor do most parents hope that their newborn infant will have a disability. It is very difficult to disentangle the organic aspects of disability from the social construction of disability. Here is an example of disentangling the medical aspects from the sociopolitical aspects. Which statement is *most* true?

1. Mr. Smith, a well-qualified applicant, cannot attend law school because he is blind.
2. Mr. Smith, a well-qualified applicant, cannot attend law school because law school requires a great deal of reading and, due to his disability, Mr. Smith will not be able to fulfill one of the most basic requirements of an education in law.
3. Mr. Smith, a well-qualified applicant, cannot attend law school because his civil rights, protected by American law (the ADA) are being violated. Printed materials, in Braille, are not provided.

All three statements are true, but #3 most closely captures reality. First, it should be emphasized that Mr. Smith is not asking for standards to be reduced because he is blind. He is a well-qualified applicant, meeting all the requirements; but he is asking for accommodations, the use of Braille. Asking for accommodations that will help an individual accomplish widely accepted standards and qualifications is not synonymous with asking for requirements to be lowered or altogether waived. First, the ADA does not mandate the lowering of standards for entrance and second, the solution to the "problem" often has nothing to do with the IWD or their disability. Rather, the solution is found in the environment, provision of accommodations. Future applicants and law students could be assisted by "locating" the problem in the environment rather than in the individual. More blind individuals would apply for and finish law school.

A Canadian disability scholar (Bickenbach, 1993) summarized the prejudice and discrimination against IWDs:

> The experience of being disabled is the experience of being treated unfairly because of one's personal attributes and circumstances (perceived and real). Therefore, if policy were to ignore these attributes and circumstances, it would compound the unfairness. This is why it may be profoundly handicapping to treat a person with a disability equally.
>
> (p. 211)

If, as a society, we define disability as *solely* a physical, organic condition, we might take the short leap to believing that IWDs *deserve* societal prejudice and discrimination, including isolation, lowered quality of services, and lack of opportunity. This basic premise states that there is no such thing as the "social construction of disability." In this faulty reasoning, we can reassure ourselves that it is not society who is to blame for disabilities, and, furthermore, it is only the disability that limits the individual. Accordingly, according to this false assumption, society does have not any responsibility to IWODs, and society is relieved of any obligation to view IWDs as complete individuals with multiple identities, roles, and functions (Smart, 2012).

The Combination of Three Realities

As stated, three broad factors have facilitated more accurate views of IWDs and their greater integration into public life as equals to IWODs. These are

1. Increases in both the absolute number of IWDs and the percentage of IWDs in the general population;
2. National laws that protect the human and civil rights of IWDs;
3. Changes in the medical professions.

Increases in the Number of IWDs

The US Census shows that approximately one-fifth (18%) of the American population has a disability. This large number may seem counterintuitive, especially in light of the great scientific, technological, and medical advances of the last few decades. It is true that some disabilities, such as deafness and achondroplasia (a type of dwarfism) have the potential to be entirely eliminated due to the fact that accurate prenatal testing can screen for these conditions, allowing mothers to choose abortion. Note: Abortion of fetuses with known disabilities is a moral choice for each woman. Polio is another example of a disability that, in the past, caused many orthopedic impairments, but since the development of the vaccine, polio has been eliminated in the developed world.

The following subsection describe six reasons for the higher rates of disability. They include:

Medical Causes

1. Advances in neonatal medicine
2. Advances in emergency medicine
3. Greater longevity for everyone
4. Greater longevity for IWDs

Statistical Causes

5. More accurate counting and reporting
6. Liberalization of the definition of disability

Advances in Neonatal Medicine

Today, more newborn infants survive pregnancy and the birth process due to the advances in neonatal medicine (newborn medicine). Most of these newborns do not have a congenital disability (a disability present at birth). Nonetheless, some of these newborns do have congenital disabilities, such as spina bifida, heart problems, intellectual disabilities, and cerebral palsy. The smaller the infant at birth, the greater the probably for a congenital disability. Now, it is possible for a 1.5 pound newborn to survive. *Time* magazine (Kluger, 2014) in a cover article summarized the relationship between birth weight and rate of disability:

> Stanford University researchers recently found that people born prematurely stand a 38% higher risk of dying in young adulthood than full-term (babies), typically from heart problems. University of Rhode Island studies found a 32% greater risk of asthma and vision problems. Overall, about 66% of preemies born before 27 weeks have some kind of disability at age 3, and many may never recover.
>
> (p. 31)

Other factors increase the number of congenital disabilities: 1) In the United States, there has been increasing numbers of teenaged mothers and these younger mothers tend to have larger rates of low weight babies, including more premature infants. 2) There is greater use of fertility treatments which often result in multiple births, such as twins and triplets. Multiple births tend to have a much higher rate of congenital disabilities. 3) Mothers who have smoked, drank large amounts of alcohol, and/or used illicit drugs during pregnancy are more likely to give birth to an infant with a congenital disability.

The infant mortality rate (death at birth or shortly after) is inversely related to the rate of congenital disabilities. Stated differently, as the infant mortality rate *decreases* (fewer newborns die at birth or shortly after) the rate of congenital disability *increases*. For example, there were infants born with severe spina bifida before 1957, but all these infants died days after birth. In 1957, a shunt was developed which drains fluid from the brain, a major indicator of many disabilities, including spina bifida. In the years following 1957, the same number of infants with spina bifida were born; the difference was that almost all survived due to the widespread use of the shunt.

In the past, the United States reported one of the highest infant mortality rates in the developed world. Surgeon/author Atul Gawande (2014) reported that "by the 1950s, one in thirty newborns still died at birth—odds that were scarcely better than they were a century before—and it wasn't clear how it could be changed" (pp. 185–186). Today, in 500 full-term births only one infant dies.

Advances in Emergency Medicine

Many emergency and trauma medicine techniques were developed by military physicians during times of war. "According to a *Christian Scientist Monitor* article (Knickerbocker, 2006) citing a University of Pennsylvania study, 24% of American troops died in Vietnam, compared to 13% in Iraq and Afghanistan" (Smart, 2016, p. 36). Much of these higher survival rates are attributed to better emergency and trauma medical techniques.

These military emergency techniques were subsequently adopted in civilian medicine. Emergency medicine improved during the Vietnam War in which injured soldiers were evacuated quickly, many receiving treatment and stabilization during evacuation. In World War II, transit time was 11 hours for an injured soldier to be transported to medical care; in Vietnam, transit time was one hour. Due to these *medical* advances, fewer soldiers died; but a larger proportion survived with a disability. If the injured individual reaches the hospital alive, they have a much greater chance of survival. Before the Vietnam War, many individuals died at the scene of the accident or while en route to the hospital. Civilian medicine incorporated these military evacuation procedures and civilian survival rates of trauma and injury victims soared. For example, in 1980, only 10% of individuals with traumatic brain injury (TBI) survived while today 90% of these individuals survive. Spinal cord injuries (paralysis) are another disability for which the survival rate has increased greatly due to emergency medicine.

Advances in prostheses (artificial arms and legs) is one of the technological improvements of the Afghanistan and Iraqi wars. Not only are there more types of prostheses available but they are far more functional, allowing the user much more flexibility. In these recent wars, the innovation of body armor protected soldiers from injuries to the central core of their bodies, injuries which previously led to death. Due to body armor, the survival rates of combat soldiers increased. Instead, soldiers sustained injuries to their limbs which required prostheses and designers and engineers responded to this need. These improved, advanced prostheses became available to civilians with disabilities.

Greater Longevity for Everyone

Medicine and science have greatly increased the life spans of individuals in the developed countries. These greater numbers of elderly individuals have resulted in higher disability rates. Indeed, it is a truism that "rate of disability is positively correlated with age." Stated differently, for both individuals and large populations, individuals who are elderly are more likely to have more disabilities. Demographers (Galambos & Rosen, 2000) have illustrated these increasing numbers: "In the 20th century, the percentage of Americans ages 65 and older . . . more than tripled in number and (eventually) increased 11 times" (p. 13). Health demographers (Cheak-Zamora et al., 2012) described the rising number of elderly Americans and some probable results:

> In the United States, the number of people age 65 or older is expected to increase from approximately 40 million in 2012 to 72 million by 2030. The prevalence of activity limitations from chronic illnesses rises rapidly from age 55 to age 85. Approximately 28% of those aged 85 years and older experience activity limitations from arthritis and musculoskeletal conditions, heart and circulatory conditions, visons and hearing limitation and progressive dementia. Another study revealed that 26% of adults aged 65–74 years old had significant activity limitations (National Center for Health Statistics, 2010). The baby boom generation's size and its anticipated health care needs threatens the financial solvency of the Medicare and strain the health care systems in the United States and Europe.
>
> (p. 512)

This increase in older populations is also seen in the United Kingdom, paralleling the demographics of the United States and the rest of Europe.

> There were 1.7 million more adults over the age of 65 living in the United Kingdom in 2009 than in 1984 (Office for National Statistics, 2009). This represents an increase from 15% to 16% of the total population, and this increase is expected to grow by 23% by 2034. Older adults over the age of 65 represent the fastest growing segment of the population.
>
> (Office for National Statistics, 2009)

This does not mean, however, that all elderly individuals experience disabilities; it simply means that they are more likely to have a disability. Indeed, in the United States, the rate of disability among elderly Americans has not been as high as predicted. It is thought that these lower rates are due to the healthier lifestyles of elderly individuals, including the use of medication for heart disease and blood pressure and lower rates of smoking and alcohol use. The US Census, using 2010 data, summarized:

> At 70.5 percent, people in the oldest age group (people 80 years and older) were about 8 times as likely to have a disability as the youngest age group (children less than 15 years old), at 8.4 percent. Between 2005–2010, disability rates *decreased* for people 55 to 64 years old and for people 65 to 69 years old.
>
> Severe disability and the need for personal assistance also increased with age. The probability of severe disability was 1-in-20 for people aged 15–24, while 1-in-4 for those aged 65–69.
>
> (Brault, 2012, p. 5)

Greater Longevity for IWDs

For the first time in history, there is a large cohort of IWDs who are in midlife or old age. Some of this cohort have acquired disabilities in old age while others are IWDs with congenital disabilities who have survived into old age. IWDs do not live as long as those without disabilities, but the lifespans of IWDs has greatly increased due to medical advances including antibiotics that treat secondary infections, typical of many types of disabilities. For example, those with spinal cord injuries (SCI) have some level of paralysis and contract many respiratory and bladder infections, which are successfully treated with antibiotics. Before the advent of antibiotics, most individuals with SCI died of secondary infections. The longer lifespans of those with Down syndrome is, in part, due to antibiotics since respiratory infections are common secondary conditions of Down syndrome. These respiratory infections, before antibiotics, used to cause death (at a typically young age).

The deinstitutionalization movement accelerated increases in longevity for IWDs. Simply stated, IWDs who are institutionalized do not live as long as those who live at home. In the past, many parents of infants with severe congenital disabilities were often advised to place their children in institutions. Parents were often told, "Why don't you have a healthy baby, and we'll forget about this one. It's going to ruin your marriage and any kids you have subsequently will suffer" (Solomon, 2012, p. 188). In the past, the lifespan was 20 years for infants institutionalized after birth. Crowded conditions, leading to infections, often resulted in early death. Those who experience mobility impairments in addition to psychiatric disabilities or intellectual disabilities have always had shorter life spans. In the 1930s, the average age of death for institutionalized males with intellectual disabilities was about 15 years of age and for females the average was 22. The age of death for these individuals gradually increased. In the 1980s, the average age of death for males was 58 and, for females, 60. Today, more than 60% of individuals with intellectual disabilities and 40% of those with psychiatric disabilities live with their families (Harris et al., 2012). Living outside institutions, in group homes or the family home, is more humane, moral, and cost-effective, and it increases lifespans.

Deinstitutionalization, especially for those with psychiatric disabilities, has presented problems and is discussed later when we learn about medical advances that have led to societal structural lags.

Fifty years ago, parents of an infant with a severe disability were told that their child would never reach adulthood. Down syndrome, a genetic condition that results in intellectual disability, provides a good example to describe the longer lifespans of IWDs. In the past, most individuals with Down syndrome died in their 20s, while in 2007, the average lifespan was 56 years. For the first time in history there are elderly individuals with Down syndrome. IWDs also benefit from universal medical advances, such as medication for heart disease, and better dental care.

These longer lifespans, for both IWDs and IWODs, present never-before-asked questions of personal meaning. What should an elderly individual do and be? It is probably easier for the IWOD because they tend to have a greater number of societal resources and more role models. For elderly IWDs, many of whom have never been employed, are socially isolated, and lack necessary care and accommodations, it is more difficult to ascribe purpose and meaning to their lives. A widely used method for IWODs to ascribe a sense meaning and purposefulness is the use of a life review. For IWODs, their life review is often narrow and incomplete due to the unnecessary circumscribed lives society has forced upon them.

More Accurate Counting and Reporting

More accurate counting of the number of IWDs is considered a statistical cause for the increase in the number of IWDs because the actual number of IWDs did not increase, simply more IWDs reported their disability. There is no truly accurate count. People may be reluctant to report having a disability and there are others who do not realize that their condition is defined as a disability. In the past, IWDs did not want to be identified because of the unwarranted societal stigma against disability and many IWDs were kept hidden at home. But, today, with more civil rights and more opportunities to access disability services, greater numbers of IWDs report their disabilities; thus, reporting rates have increased.

Accurately counting and reporting disability presents difficulties for demographers. First, there is no uniform definition of disability among the various agencies and programs that provide services to IWDs. These agencies and programs, such as the national Social Security Disability Insurance (SSDI), define disability differently than other government agencies, such as the federal rehabilitation agency or special education laws. It is common to be declared eligible for services on the basis of a disability in one government program but to be denied services in another program because the same condition is not defined as a disability in their service law. It should be remembered that there are two broad types of disability law: service law and civil rights law. SSDI, workers compensation, and special education laws are service laws and the Americans with Disabilities Act (ADA) is a civil rights law.

Also, there is a great deal of overlap in clinical definitions of disability; there is no one universal definition. For example, the *Diagnostic and Statistical Manual of Mental Disorders-5* (DSM-5) lists almost 600 codable conditions (Morrison, 2014), but not all DSM-5 disorders are defined as disabilities by government service agencies. There are also discrepancies in disability definitions found in the other large diagnostic systems, such as the *International Classification of Disease* and the *International Classification of Functioning*, both published by the World Health Organization (WHO, 2001). Nonetheless, among these government programs and clinical diagnostic systems, there is a great deal of agreement. The broadest definition of disability is the Americans with Disabilities Act (ADA).

There is a difference between the *actual* number of disabilities and the number of *reported* disabilities. For example, during times of economic recession and depression, the number of reported disabilities rises. Much of this increase is simply the result of individuals reporting their disability to apply for disability financial benefits or services. In times of economic prosperity, these individuals could find work and, therefore, it was not necessary to report their disability. Differences in reported rates of disability are also related to the objectives of various entities. Essentially, advocacy groups and service providers for individuals with designated disabilities tend to report the higher estimates of incidence to gain government or other large institutional support. Government and other large institutional support is often based on need and, so, the tendency is to report the largest estimate of prevalence. On the other hand, if an agency wished to prove its effectiveness in decreasing the number of a designated disability, the agency might use the lowest estimate of prevalence.

Liberalization of the Definition of Disability

Until the 1970s, learning disabilities, some types of developmental disabilities, and alcohol and chemical abuse were not legally defined as disabilities. Not recognizing these neurocognitive conditions as disabilities resulted in lack of services and greater degrees of societal stigma. For example, school children with learning disabilities were often labeled and considered to be lazy, oppositional, and not very bright. Even worse, many of these children internalized these false judgments into their self-concepts. In addition to the stigma, these types of judgments precluded services, which could have helped these often-bright students succeed in school. Alcohol abuse and drug use were considered to be the result of weak character and moral failing. Many developmental disabilities, including Autism Spectrum Disorder (ASD), were thought to be the result of another moral and character failing, resulting from poor parenting. Decades of research opportunities were wasted simply because professionals were very sure that ASD was a moral failing of the parents, especially the mother.

Once again, there is a corresponding difficulty in enlarging and expanding the definition of disability. If diagnostic criteria are lowered, more individuals will be diagnosed as having that disability. Diabetes is an example that demonstrates this relationship. Diabetes is diagnosed when the amount of sugar in the blood is measured and, therefore, a reliable (same results, or number, each time), objective (the same result regardless of the clinician), and quantifiable (a number) measure is used. The American Medical Association made a deliberate decision to lower the number of the amount of sugar in the blood required to be diagnosed as having diabetes and, therefore, many more people received a diagnosis of diabetes. This decision was based on three factors: 1) diabetes is a very serious disability, which can result in blindness and lower limb amputation; 2) diabetes is a subclinical or asymptomatic condition—the individual has no symptoms and often does not seek routine, preventive medical care; and 3) diabetes is treatable and, if diagnosed early, secondary conditions, such as blindness and amputations, can be avoided. Therefore, the AMA could explain and defend its choice to lower the diagnostic criteria for diabetes.

The DSM-5, published by the American Psychiatric Association, provides another example of liberalization and expansion of the diagnosis of disability. Each edition of the DSM includes more diagnoses and lower diagnostic criteria. The possibility that there may large increases in the number of diagnoses may become an issue in future editions. Therefore, while it is generally agreed that liberalizing the definition of disability has been an advance; today, however, further liberation and expansion of diagnoses of disability is being questioned.

Outcomes of the Medical Causes of Higher Rates of Disability

Outcomes

1. Have led to societal structural lags.
2. New professions have been developed.
3. Training and education programs have expanded to train these professionals.

With all four medical advances—neonatal medicine, emergency medicine, longevity of the general population, and longevity of IWDs—the alternative to acquiring a disability has been death of the individual. Once again, it is important to make the point that avoiding a disability altogether is the best alternative. However, when death is the alternative, acquisition of a disability is likely to be viewed as a better outcome. We also know that most IWDs do not consider themselves or their disabilities to be unbearable tragedies. Therefore, these higher number of disabilities (when death is the alternative) are considered societal progress. These medical advances will continue to result in still larger numbers of IWDs.

It is possible to quantify (or estimate) each of these gains. One quantifiable measure is the number of individuals who survived trauma and injury. Another measure is the number of newborn infants who survived pregnancy and the birth process and the increase in congenital disability rates, and the number of military personnel who survive combat injuries. All of these survival rates result in higher disability rates. Another quantifiable measure is the number of added years of life for everyone, with or without a disability.

The second outcome of these medical advances (and demographic changes) relates to "structural lags," which is the gap between the development and widespread use of these new medical technologies and society's moral and ethical response. The longer lifespan of individuals with Down syndrome is an example of a structural lag. Science and medicine has greatly increased their lifespans, but there are no societal and government-sponsored old-age programs for elderly individuals with Down syndrome or for IWDs with any type of disability. The small number of IWDs served by counselors in the various specialties also may be considered a structural lag. A disability scholar (Trieschmann, 1987) noted a structural lag when he wrote that "our entire health system" was "caught by surprise." This was more than 30 years ago:

> Aging is synonymous with living.... The issue of aging with a disability is a new problem for western societies, one that has caught our health care system by surprise. Currently, individuals who have lived with spinal cord injury, polio, and other disabilities for 30, 40, and 50 years are arriving in physicians' offices with a variety of complaints that the physicians have not been taught to handle.
>
> (p. 1)

Except for the aging of IWDs, each of these causes of higher rates of disability have resulted in the development of new professions, with new training and education programs, academic accreditation guidelines, continuing education requirements, and licensing and certifying laws. The greater survival rates of newborns resulted in the profession of neonatal medicine; the longer lifespans of IWODs resulted in the specialties of geriatrics and gerontology, and the higher survival rate of trauma victims resulted in specialists in emergency medicine.

The Americans With Disabilities Act (ADA)

For the first time in history, the American people are facing serious challenges from Americans with disabilities. This mass movement to ensure that Americans with disabilities are provided basic civil rights and to provide legal protection under federal law is considered, by many, to have begun with the signing of the Americans with Disabilities Act (ADA) in 1990. The ADA is composed of five sections, called titles. These titles prohibit discrimination in these areas:

- Title I: Employment (equal opportunity for IWDs with the necessary job qualifications);
- Title II: Transportation (public transportation must provide services to IWDs);
- Title III: Public Accommodations and Services (such as hotels, movie theaters, libraries, shopping malls, and professional offices, including counseling offices);
- Title IV: Telecommunications (telephone companies must provide emergency communications for D/deaf individuals to ensure their safety);
- Title V: Miscellaneous—National parks and historical sites must be accessible to IWDs, providing wheelchair ramps, materials in Braille, and other accommodations.

The ADA was strengthened by the Amendments to the Americans with Disabilities Act (ADAAA) which were signed into law in 2008. Under the original ADA of 1990, the Supreme Court of the United States defined disability very narrowly, thereby refusing to hear cases brought by IWDs, stating that, according to the ADA, they did not have a disability. Essentially, the Supreme Court was undermining the original intent of the ADA by making it difficult for IWDs to gain federal protection and redress under the law. By explicitly broadening the definition of disability, the Amendments of 2008 facilitated stronger enforcement. Robert Burgdorf (2002), who wrote the original draft of the ADA, adapting much of the language of the 1964 Civil Rights Law, expressed surprise at the way in which the American court system undermined the rights of Americans with disabilities:

> As I drafted the original version of the Americans with Disabilities Act, I never dreamed that this landmark civil rights law would become so widely misunderstood and my words so badly misinterpreted, particularly by the body meant to protect the very rights guaranteed by the law.
>
> (para. 1)

There are many disability laws, such as special education, vocational rehabilitation, veterans affairs, and workers compensation, all of which are *service* (or entitlement or eligibility) laws, defining eligibility for services and funding. In contrast, the ADA is a *civil rights* law, which defines disability broadly and protects all Americans with disabilities, and places responsibility on institutional changes and resource allocation. For the first time, disability became a public issue rather than an individual, private problem. In the past, all the responsibility for the "solution" to disability was placed on the IWD.

Why the Widespread Resistance to Civil Rights for IWDs?

1. Are thought to be too expensive to implement and enforce.
2. Since IWDs receive government financial benefits and other resources, they should not ask for civil rights.
3. Civil rights for IWDs is falsely considered to be preferential treatment.
4. The false belief that society should be "disability blind." However, civil rights for IWDs are based on documented disabilities.

Why the widespread public resistance to the ADA? It was thought that the ADA was too expensive to implement and enforce. Another way in which funding might have become an issue is the fact that many IWDs receive government resources in rehabilitation, medical services, and financial benefits (which are expensive) and, subsequently many in the general public have thought that IWDS have no justification to demand civil rights (which are also expensive). When IWDs receive services and financial benefits, without perceived repayment to society, IWDs are forced to assume a permanent position of long-term dependence and indebtedness. In this twisted logic, to ask for civil rights is to display ingratitude.

Civil rights are not dependent on available funding or even the appropriation of funds (Percy, 1989). "It is a matter of privilege based on race, class, gender, and disability" (Pfeiffer, 2005, p. 38).

One scholar (Wildman, 1996) specializing in societal advantages (privilege) viewed the major difference between privileged groups and non-privileged groups in this way: privileged groups are *automatically given* their privileges (including civil rights) while non-privileged groups are *required to fight* for their privileges (including civil rights). Wildman (1996) shows how some persons receive benefits while other people—such as people with disabilities—are told it costs too much. Among the many obstacles of fighting and advocating for one's privileges and civil rights are these 1) it adds another "job" to being an IWD, 2) some IWDs are socialized to believe that their lack of privilege is well-deserved, and 3) many IWDs are not inclined to engage in fighting for their privilege and rights.

Many IWODs consider the ADA to be "preferential treatment" for IWDs, lowering all sorts of widely held standards and requirements for IWDs. Comments such as "I didn't get the job because a disabled person got the job" or "You're so lucky! You're a black woman in a wheelchair; you can get any job you want!" illustrate the false, but widespread perception, that IWDs receive preferential treatment. The ADA provides for equal treatment for IWDs, with the use of accommodations.

The ADA and the ADAAA are not "disability blind"; instead, Americans are guaranteed their civil rights based on a documented disability. The question can be asked: Aren't the ADA and disability identity politics simply a different way of defining the individual as their disability? No, IWDs want first-class citizenship and still retain their identity as IWDs, in much the same way as racial and ethnic groups, women, and sexual minorities claim their civil rights as Americans. The ADA is based on the concept of justice and fairness in which everyone receives what they *need*. This type of justice is different from standardization in which everyone receives the same and equal resources and services. For example, applying the principle of standardization to a classroom of 20 children, including one child who is blind, there would be two types of responses: 1) all 20 children receive printed materials in Braille or 2) none of the children, including the blind child, receives Braille materials. Either solution would be unworkable.

A Canadian disability scholar (Bickenbach, 1993) summarized the prejudice and discrimination against IWDs:

> The experience of being disabled is the experience of being treated unfairly because of one's personal attributes and circumstances (perceived and real). Therefore, if policy were to ignore these attributes and circumstances, it would compound the unfairness. This is why it may be profoundly handicapping to treat a person with a disability equally.
>
> (p. 211)

Disability rights movement is a type of identity politics and, as with all types of identity politics, is based on common experiences of oppression. Identity politics has been defined as: "political mobilization organized around group characteristics such as race, gender, and sexuality as opposed to party, ideology, or pecuniary (financial) interest" (Rauch, 2017, p. 10). Large numbers of IWDs are required to raise public awareness of their experiences and needs before government and society can be changed. The right to self-definition is another significant aspect of identity politics. Leonard Kriegel described the way in which IWDs were not allowed to define themselves.

> The world of the crippled and disabled is strange and dark, and it is held up to judgment by those who live in fear of it. The cripple is the creature who has been deprived of his ability to create a self. . . . He is the other, if for no other reason than that only by being the other will he be allowed to presume upon the "normal." He must accept definition from outside the boundaries of his existence.
>
> (Kriegel, 1997, p. 66)

Both requirements, large numbers and the right of self-definition, have been denied to IWDs and both were given a strong impetus by the ADA. For the first time, IWDs with all types of disabilities, including physical, cognitive, and psychiatric disabilities, coalesced to demand their rights, no longer factionalized by diagnostic groups. We have seen that the US Census states that almost one-fifth of the population has a disability, giving disability rights movement power to assert their rights. In addition, the increasing numbers of IWDs and the de-institutionalization movement has increased both the absolute number of IWDs and their percentage of the population. IWDs are no longer hidden away, marginalized, or segregated.

The right to self-definition and pride drives identity politics. In the past, IWDs were defined by others and given stigmatizing labels and diagnoses. Occasionally, society has effectively instilled in IWDs a sense that they should not ask for accommodations and accept their segregated status. A woman with a disability demonstrated this:

> When are we ever going to believe, in our hearts—truly believe—that our problems are not things we are given by God to solve ourselves, but are things that we have a right to require our society to change—because the problem isn't our disabilities but the inaccessible environment which society built in the first place.
>
> ("The Problem with 'Challenge'," 1985, para 12, http://www.raggededgemagazine.com/blogs/edgecentric/media/003033.html)

Another commentary on the need for identity politics was provide by Bowe, a disability scholar and activist who observed:

> It is a tremendously tragic commentary that . . . disabled people came to have hope to protest. It took two hundred years after this country was formed—*two hundred years*—for these people (IWDs) to begin to have hope (author's emphasis).
>
> (Bowe, 1993, p. xi)

Identity politics of any group leads to a better and richer (figuratively and literally) society for everyone.

The Generational Effect of the ADA and the ADAAA

Counselors are very aware of the developmental impact of the historical time in which individuals live, recognizing that people of the same generation not only have experienced the same historical events but also tend to have similar values, attitudes, behaviors, and expectations. Labels, such as "baby-boomers," "Generation X," or "Millennials" convey a great deal of information about a group of individuals. Common to all generations, is the increased range of choices and greater individual freedoms.

Presently, IWDs born after 1990 are considered part of the "post-ADA generation" (Smart, 2012a). Most adults today have not experienced pre-ADA history. For Americans with disabilities, the ADA was a "watershed event" in their lives. These IWDs (and their parents and families) know and understand their rights and the services available, making them very different from IWDs of older generations who believed that they were not to make demands on society and to keep their aspirations modest. Older, pre-ADA IWDs remember experiences of not being allowed to fly on commercial airlines because of their wheelchairs or, not being allowed a public education, or, tragically, D/deaf individuals dying because emergency telephone services were not available for individuals with hearing and speech impairments. One IWD summarized, "I think back to all the time I've been thrown off busses, trains, and planes for being a person with a disability" (McCarthy, 2003, p. 217).

One woman with a spinal cord injury told of her difficulty in paying for disability-related expenses:

> Unfortunately, I have found it hard to get a home loan due to the doctor bill I have been unable to pay. Unfortunately, I had to choose whether to feed my children or pay a doctor. There are a lot of bills that come along with being disabled but very little assistance. I have been told I make too much for help through Social Services. . . . Where is the help financially for the disabled?
> (Graf, Marini, & Blankenship, 2009, p. 30)

The post-ADA generation view themselves as assertive individuals with many positive qualities who want to participate fully and contribute to American life. One of the societal resources IWDs wish to access is counseling services from a wide variety of agencies, specialties.

The Self-Transformation of the Medical Profession

Two radical changes to the practice of medicine in the developed world are: 1) universal health care coverage and 2) a shift from acute care to long-term care. We have discussed that the higher rates of disability both cause and result in changes in the way in which medical professionals are trained, supervised, and practice.

Universal health care coverage impacts the rate of disability and helps to "humanize" the experience of disability. Greater health care coverage will result in increased prenatal screening and routine health monitoring. With widespread preventive care, more disabilities will be diagnosed, such as congenital disabilities and disabilities that are asymptomatic, including diabetes. To use the example of diabetes: The only way in which to diagnose diabetes is standardized medical testing, usually blood tests. Diabetes is invisible to others and to the individual, but it has devastating side effects such as blindness and lower limb amputation due to vascular damage. Untreated diabetes can be fatal. Successful management of diabetes includes preventing secondary disabilities or complications, such as blindness and amputation, which often (unnecessarily) accompany diabetes. Diabetes has been termed a "gateway disability" (Smart, 2012b). Seventy-five percent of all therapeutic amputations in the United States are performed on people older than the age of 65, mostly as a secondary condition of diabetes. Regular medical care reduces these secondary conditions and other complications.

The second shift in the way in which medical care is provided is a result of scientific and medical advances. Medicine has transformed itself in the ability to sustain life which has often led to the need for providing care for those with lifelong conditions (disabilities and chronic illness). Acute care is expensive, requires highly specialized skills, such as surgery, and will always be necessary; however medical care and surveillance of chronic conditions, much of it due to the increasing rate of disabilities, is required more and more. After medical stabilization, including emergency medicine and surgery, most IWDs require long-term care. In the past, most medical care resulted in two outcomes: total cure or death. Both these outcomes were easily diagnosed and measured and neither required any after care. Chronic conditions (and disabilities) were not very common. Today, the opposite is more common. Chronic, long-term care will become increasingly important. Atul Gawande (2017) suggested that the current system of health care has not changed enough.

> Our health care system is not designed for the future—or, indeed, for this present. We have built it at a time . . . when illness was experienced as a random catastrophe and medicine discoveries focused on rescue, insurance for unanticipated, episodic needs was what we needed. Hospitals and heroic interventions got the large investments; incrementalists were scanted.
>
> (p. 44)

Providing Counseling Services to IWDs

Providing counseling services to IWDs requires a wide range of knowledge and skills and yet most counselors have not been trained in disability issues and have not completed supervised practica and internships counseling with IWDs. This lack of knowledge and supervised experience can be considered an environmental or sociopolitical aspect of disability, an aspect that has nothing to do with IWDs or with disabilities. At its extreme, this lack of training in disability issues could be considered a type of prejudice and discrimination and services from all types of counselors may be considered an opportunity structure that has not been available to IWDs. From the earliest written history, we know that there have been IWDs; however, the counseling professions have not addressed the needs of these individuals. In addition to the larger numbers of IWDs asking for counseling services, the following broad influences will impact the counseling professions:

1. Academic accreditation requirements for educational programs are requiring course work on IWDs;
2. State licensing laws and national professional certifications will require disability course work on university transcripts;
3. Codes of ethics compel counseling professionals to practice within the boundaries of their competences and to do no harm to clients;
4. Federal laws mandate "reasonable accommodations" for counseling clients with disabilities, such as written materials in Braille, American Sign Language (ASL) interpreters, and physically accessible counseling offices, including public bathrooms;
5. Insurance coverage which is sensitive to disability issues;
6. More demands from IWDs themselves for appropriate services.

Counselor Training Programs Have Failed to Adequately Prepare Counselors to Work With Clients With Disabilities

Some counselors mistakenly think that they have been trained in disability issues. However, much of this training has been based on the Biomedical Model in which the entire responsibility of dealing with a disability lies with the individual, seldom taking into account factors in a social and culture environment, which can even question IWDs' humanity. Training has tended to be organized around different types of disability, such as a chapter on blindness, another chapter on paralysis, and another on intellectual disabilities, thus consigning IWDs to categories based on a single characteristic of their disability. Finally, especially in course work on individuals with psychiatric disabilities, the focus remains on the pathology and deviance of these types of disabilities, including course titles such as "abnormal psychology," or "psychopathology."

Limitations of Outmoded Disability Training in Counseling

1. Is based on the Biomedical Model of Disability in which responding to a disability is the entire responsibility of the IWD.
2. Is based on the Biomedical Model of Disability, which studies various disability types, such as blindness, paralysis, or psychiatric disabilities, thereby categorizing IWDs on a single characteristic, their disability.

> 3. Uses simulation exercises, which, in most cases, increase prejudice and discrimination toward IWDs.
> 4. Uses demeaning and pathologizing course titles.

The use of simulation exercises for allowing students without disabilities to gain some sort of insight into the experience of disabilities is not only useless, but is actually counterproductive (Brew-Parris 2004; Kiger, 1992; Olkin, 1999; Pfeiffer, 1989; Smart, 2012, 2016; B. A. Wright, 1983). Most important, the use of simulation exercises is unethical because these types of simulations demean IWDs and trivialize the disability experience. Students wear blindfolds to simulate blindness, earphones to simulate deafness, wear bulky mittens to simulate cerebral palsy, or use wheelchairs to simulate orthopedic impairments. Sometimes the duration of these exercises is as short as one hour while other exercises required a full day. In the past, students in courses on drug or alcohol abuse were required to abstain from a favorite food or drink for the duration of the course. The most common choices included chocolate, coffee, or beer.

There is no way to simulate a disability and, yet, simulation exercises continue to be part of many psychology, counseling, and special education courses. First, it is not possible to simulate a congenital disability; second, it is not possible to simulate a chronic, day-to-day disability; students understand that the exercises are time limited. Last, the management of a disability cannot be simulated because the use of Braille, or American Sign Language, or assistive technology such as wheelchairs, all require years to become fluent and skilled in. Blind people learn orientation and mobility skills at national specialized training centers. Simulators often complete the exercise feeling frustrated, dependent, and demeaned, and often conclude that living with a disability is frustrating, demeaning, and requires total dependence on others. Moreover, simulators falsely think that they have some sort of knowledge about the disability experience. Kiger (1992) undertook a review of 60 simulation exercises and found that none had any positive effects on the attitudes of IWODs toward IWDs. Following is a quote from an article in *The Disability Rag* (Brew-Parrish, 2004) written by a mother who is a polio survivor and her husband who is blind. Their daughter, Tara, is a high school student with two parents with disabilities.

> My daughter Tara had come home from school in tears. It was Disability Simulation Day at Greenwood High [School]. Blindfolded students were being led around by sighted students, others were bumping into walls.

The students were terrified of their newly created disabilities. Some had told Tara they thought persons with disabilities had horrible lives; a few thought they might be better off dead.

(para. 8)

I contacted the school's psychology teacher once and tried to get Disability Simulation Day stopped. It was a lost cause. She [the teacher] liked having Disability Simulation Day featured in the local newspaper, and saw no need for me or my husband . . . to come to her classroom to talk with students.

(para. 11)

I am baffled as to why nondisabled people sees a need to simulate a disability. Across our nation in February, we celebrate Black History Month. Is it necessary for people with white skin to paint their faces black to better understand this minority?

(para. 21)

The daughter is in tears because she anticipates that her classmates will feel that a disability is a horrible experience and these misconceptions invalidate her parents' successful and happy lives. Students in programs that train counselors, and other helping professionals, have a great deal to learn about disabilities and individuals with disabilities. Moreover, some "unlearning" of outdated, prejudicial, and disrespectful concepts is necessary.

Counselors, like other trained and credentialed professionals, are the product of their training and education. However, there is little disability-awareness training in most graduate counseling programs. Moreover, codes of ethics direct counselors to provide only those services for which they are trained and have developed competence. These codes of ethics also warn against doing harm to clients. The six core beliefs discussed in Chapter Four have shown that the results of well-intentioned people often causes harm to IWDs. In summary, three conclusions may be drawn: 1) most counselors are not trained and educated to serve IWDs; 2) nonetheless, ethical guidelines mandate that counselors provide services only for which they are trained and competent; and 3) codes of ethics also mandate that counselors do no harm to clients, yet a great deal of limiting, stereotypical, paternalistic, harmful attitudes and behaviors are unrecognized and unacknowledged. How are counselors to avoid these types of behaviors and attitudes, if they themselves are not aware of them?

Another complicating factor is that the lack of disability training available to students in counseling programs has been patronizing, condescending, and simplistic. The modicum of disability training available in counselor training in disability has been based on the Biomedical Model in which the focus is on a pathology located solely within the individual. In the Biomedical Model, the goal of treatment is the rehabilitation of the individual; in this way, placing the entire responsibility on IWDs themselves. Training based on the Biomedical Model is appropriate for medical and health professionals but not for counselors who are committed to providing services for and with empowered clients who function in varied environments. The focus in counselor training programs should be on interactional models of disability, which view disabilities and IWDs as living within various environments and, at times, it is these environments which must be rehabilitated, or changed. Disability training based on the Biomedical Model typically does not include the experience of prejudice, discrimination, and lack of access to societal resources in spite of the fact that many IWDs report that these societal limitations are more difficult problems than managing the demands of their disability. The Biomedical Model often organizes training and education around diagnostic groups. For example, there are chapters on blindness, deafness, psychiatric disabilities, chronic illness, and many more. Individuals in disability rights movements refer to this type of education as "factionalizing disability groups." Many of the names of courses reflect the pathological emphasis on the biomedical, such as "abnormal psychology," "psychopathology," and "mental illness." Furthermore, in most counseling and psychology programs there is little training on physical disabilities; the emphasis is placed on psychiatric and intellectual disabilities.

In the following excerpt, Linton (1998) describes two problems with disability-awareness university training: 1) the little available training consists solely of "patronizing and distorted representations of disability" and 2) small, incremental changes, "minor housecleaning," will not be sufficient to develop a more accurate view of disability:

> Even a cursory review of the [university] curricula reveals only patronizing and distorted representations of disability, and these are left largely unexamined and unchallenged. But minor housecleaning will not rid out the deeper structural elements, the scholarly conventions, and theoretical underpinnings within these representations are deemed valid and useful. A closer look reveals problems in both the structure and content of the curriculum, predicated on a narrowly conceived interpretation of disability.
>
> (p. 4)

Are there not physical and organic realities to disabilities? Should not counselors have some training in these aspects in order to better understand the experiences of clients? The answer is "yes" to both questions. Nonetheless, training in the sociological aspects of disability is of greater value to counselors. In summary, training in the biomedical aspects of disability is necessary but not sufficient for counselors-in-training.

There is no definition or description of counselor disability-awareness training. Therefore, the first step would require efforts at defining disability awareness. This is important because the definition of any competence is multifaceted and perhaps a place to start would include a review of the various Models of Disability. Further, disability-awareness training should be on a level of parity with other types of therapeutic skills, such as multicultural counseling or gender counseling. Supervised practica and internship should be provided, and, after graduation, supervised practice with IWDs should be provided. The definition of disability itself is an elastic concept and demographic and medical advances will also influence the development of a disability-awareness curriculum.

Why not simply include a chapter or two on disability awareness in multicultural counseling or gender issues courses? Disability-awareness training merits its own curriculum with a cross disability focus that includes all types of disabilities—physical, developmental, intellectual, and psychiatric disabilities. Factionalizing IWDs into diagnostic groups is both necessary and constructive for medical and health professionals, but a cross-disability focus would provide counselors with a greater range of disability definitions and guidelines for professional practice.

Conclusion

A new reality for counselors of all theoretical orientations and agency settings was described in this chapter. Individuals with disabilities (IWDs) will ask for counseling services, and most often, the disability will not be the presenting problem or the focus of the counseling process. IWDs will seek marriage counseling, LBGTQ counseling, academic counseling, pastoral counseling, family counseling, adolescent counseling, and many other types of counseling services because IWDs have the same life tasks as IWODs, the same emotions and motivations, and while they consider their disabilities to be a valued and important part of their self-identity, in most cases, they do not consider their disabilities to be their only self-identity nor the most important part of their self-identity.

Nonetheless, most counselors have had little training or experience in counseling IWDs, and the little training they might have received is of little use and may have contributed to misperceptions and prejudicial attitudes. Therefore, this chapter advocated for well-informed training in disability issues.

References

American Psychiatric Association. (2013). *Diagnostic and statistical manual of mental disorders 5*. Washington, DC: Author.

Americans with Disabilities Act Amendments of 2008, 42 U.S.C. 12101 *et seq.* Retrieved from www.adaaa.gov/ Retrieved 02–26–2018

Americans with Disabilities Act of 1990, 42 U.S.C. 12101 *et seq.* Retrieved from www.ada.gov/ada_archive.htm www.justice.gov/crt/disability-rights-section Retrieved 02–26–2018

Bickenbach, J. E. (1993). *Physical disability and social policy*. Toronto, ON: University of Toronto.

Boerner, K., & Jopp, D. (2007). Improvement/maintenance and reorientation as central features of coping with major life change and loss: Contributions of three life-span theories. *Human Development, 50,* 171–195.

Bowe, F. (1993). Preface. In M. J. Scherer (Ed.), *Living in the state of stuck: How technology impacts the lives of people with disabilities* (pp. xi-xvi). Cambridge, MA: Brookline.

Brault, M. W. (2012). *Americans with disabilities: 2010*. Retrieved from www.census.gov/prod/2012pubs/p70-131.pdf Retrieved 02–26–2018

Brew-Parrish, V. (2004, August 9). The wrong message still. *Ragged Edge Magazine*. Retrieved from www.raggededgemagazine.com/focus/wrong message04html Retrieved 02–24–2018

Burgdorf, R. (2002). *Americans with Disabilities Act: Supreme court decisions thwart intent of ADA*. San Diego, CA: Center for an Accessible Society. Retrieved from www.accessiblesociety.org/topics/ada/index.html Retrieved 02–26–2018.

Cheak-Zamora, N., Reid-Arndt, S. A., Hagglund, K. J., & Frank, R. G. (2012). Health legislation and public policies. In P. Kennedy (Ed.), *Oxford handbook of rehabilitation psychology* (pp. 511–524). Oxford, UK: University of Oxford.

Elliott, T. R., & Gramling, S. E. (1990). Psychologists and rehabilitation: New roles and old training models. *American Psychologist, 45,* 762–765.

Elliott, T. R., & Warren, A. M. (2007). Why psychology is important in rehabilitation. In P. Kennedy (Ed.), *Psychological management of physical disabilities* (pp. 16–39). New York, NY: Routledge.

Galambos, C. M., & Rosen, A. (2000). The aging are coming and they are us. In S. M. Keigher, A. E. Fortune, & S. L. Witkin (Eds.), *Aging and social work: The changing landscapes* (pp. 13–19). Washington, DC: NASW Press.

Gawande, A. (2014). *Being mortal: Medicine and what matters in the end*. New York, NY: Metropolitan Books and Henry Holt.

Gawande, A. (2017, January 23). Tell me where it hurts: The power of incrementalism. *New Yorker,* 36–45.

Gill, C. (2000). Health professionals, disability, and assisted suicide: An examination of relevant empirical evidence and reply to Batavia. *Psychology, Public Policy, & Law, 6*(2), 526–545.

Graf, N. M., & Marini, I., & Blankenship, C. J. (2009). One hundred words about disability. *Journal of Rehabilitation, 75,* 25–34.

Grant, G. (2005). Healthy and successful ageing. In G. Grant, P. Howard, M. Richardson, & P. Ram Charan (Eds.), *Learning disability: A life cycle approach to valuing people.* New York, NY: Open University Press.

Hahn, H. (1988b). The politics of physical differences: Disability and discrimination. *Journal of Social Issues, 44,* 39–47.

Hahn, H. (1993). Can disability be beautiful? In M. Nagler (Ed.), *Perspectives on disability* (2nd ed.) (pp. 213–216). Palo Alto, CA: Health Markets Research.

Harris, S. P., Heller, T., Schindler, A., & van Heumen, L. (2012). Current issues, controversies, and solutions. In T. Heller & S. Harris (Eds.), *Disability through the life course* (pp. 39–102). Thousand Oaks, CA: Sage.

Kiger, G. (1992). Disability simulations: Logical, methodological, and ethical issues. *Disability, Handicap, & Society, 7,* 71–78.

Kluger, J. (2014). A preemie revolution: Cutting edge medicine and dedicated caregivers are helping the tiniest babies survive and thrive. *Time, 183*(21), 24–31.

Knickerbocker, B. (2006, August 29). In Iraq, fewer killed, more are wounded. *The Christian scientist monitor.* Retrieved from http://csmonitor.com/2006/0829/p03s02-usmi.html

Kriegel, L. (1997). Falling down. In K. Fries (Ed.), *Staring back: The disability experience from the inside out* (pp. 41–49). New York, NY: Plume.

Linton, S. (1998). *Claiming disability: Knowledge and identity.* New York: New York University.

McCarthy, H. E. (2003). The disability rights movement: Experiences and perspectives of selected leaders in the disability community. *Rehabilitation Counseling Bulletin, 46,* 209–223.

Morrison, J. (2014). *Diagnosis made easier: Principles and techniques for mental health clinicians* (2nd ed.). New York, NY: Guilford.

Office for National Statistics. (2009). Mid-year population estimates. Retrieved from www.statistics.gov.uk/nugget.asp?=949

Olkin, R. (1999). *What psychotherapists should know about disability.* New York, NY: Guilford.

Percy, S. L. (1989). *Disability, civil rights, and public policy: The politics of implementation.* Tuscaloosa, AL: University of Alabama.

Pfeiffer, D. (1989). Disability simulation using a wheelchair simulation. *Journal of Post Secondary Education & Disability, 7,* 53–60.

Pfeiffer, D. (2005). The conceptualization of disability. In G. E. May & M. B. Raske (Eds.), *Ending disability discrimination: Strategies for social workers* (pp. 25–44). Boston, MA: Pearson.

Ragged Edge Online. (1985). *The problem with "challenge."* Retrieved from www.raggededge-magazine.com/archive/challenge.htm

Rauch, J. (2017, November 9). Speaking as a. . . . *New York Review of Books, 10,* 12–13.

Sacks, O. (1985). *The man who mistook his wife for a hat and other clinical tales.* New York, NY: Simon and Schuster.

Smart, J. F. (2012a). Counseling individuals with physical, cognitive, and psychiatric disabilities. In C. C. Lee (Ed.), *Multicultural counseling: New approaches to diversity* (4th ed.) (pp. 221–234). Washington, DC: American Counseling Association.

Smart, J. F. (2012b). *Disability across the developmental lifespan.* New York, NY: Springer.

Smart, J. F. (2016). *Disability, society, and individual* (3rd ed.). Austin, TX: PRO-ED.

Solomon, A. (2012). *Far from the tree: Parents, children, and the search for identity.* New York, NY: Scribner.

Trieschmann, R. B. (1987). *Aging with a disability.* New York, NY: Demos.

Weisgerber, R. A. (1991). *Quality of life for persons with disabilities: Skill development and transitions across life stages*. Gaithersburg, MD: Aspen.

Wildman, S. M. (1996). *Privilege revealed: How invisible privilege undermines America*. New York, NY: New York University.

World Health Organization. (2001). *International classification of functioning, disability and health*. Geneva: Author.

Wright, B. A. (1983). *Physical disability—A psychosocial approach*. New York, NY: Harper & Row.

Two

DEFINING, DIAGNOSING, AND MEASURING DISABILITY

Defining disability is complex and covers a broad range of aspects. The purpose of this chapter is twofold: 1) to provide a basic understanding of the wide range of disabilities and 2) to describe two large diagnostic manuals that define and describe hundreds of disabilities, the *Classification of Functioning* (ICD), published by the World Health Organization (WHO) (2001), and the *Diagnostic and Statistical Manual of Mental Disorders-5* (DSM-5) (2013), published by the American Psychiatric Association.

In addition, we also describe disabilities in four ways that are typically not found in these large diagnostic systems. These include the degree of stigma directed toward the various categories of disabilities and the way in which the disability is measured, either on a spectrum or in categories. Low incidence disabilities (disabilities which occur very rarely) and high incidence disabilities (disabilities which occur frequently) are described. Finally, the balance between under-diagnosis and over-diagnosis of disabilities is explained.

In this chapter, we use the term "the general public." Who are the general public? First, they are people with whom IWDs and their families associate, including, friends, neighbors, teachers, church or synagogue members, job interviewers, and admission officers. When IWDs enter school or the workplace, the general public expands to include supervisors, professors, coworkers, customers, and clients. The general public also includes people whom most IWDs never meet, such as members of national lawmaking bodies, judges and attorneys who consider protection under the law for IWDs, and movie producers who portray prejudicial and inaccurate views of disability to millions. For some IWDs, they will not find support and understanding in their own families. One IWD stated, "I was hidden in the closet when my family had guests." Finally, IWDs may be prejudiced and discriminating against IWDs with different types of disability, although the factionalization of disability groups has been reduced with the passage of the ADA.

We can see that the general public includes many individuals, groups, and institutions, and they all determine the quality of life of IWDs. In a few extreme examples, the general public determines if IWDs will be allowed to live at all.

Before we begin, it is important to emphasize four important points.

1. **Does everyone have a disability?** The answer is no. The universality of the possibility of acquiring a disability does not mean that everybody has a disability. Nor is disadvantage a disability. Everyone has challenges, weaknesses, and shortcomings, such as fear of public speaking or lack of athletic ability or limited education. These are disadvantages and are not legally or medically documented as disabilities. To state that everyone has some type of a disability or to refer to someone with a disability as "physically challenged" devalues and diminishes the experience of living with a disability.
2. **The most important definition of disability is the client's subjective, idiosyncratic meaning of their disability**, a self-evident statement to counselors. All counseling orientations understand the importance of the counselor–client relationship, especially as a therapeutic tool. Relationship building and developing a working alliance will facilitate a deeper understanding of the client's unique experience of disability.
3. **Clients with the same disability have very different experiences.** Since everyone has multiple roles, self-identities, and differing resources, needs, and values, clients with the same disability will ascribe differing meanings to their disabilities. Therefore, it is important to actively listen. Most individual counseling is based on a one-on-one relationship, and group counseling is based on relationships with a small number of people, and it is the individual nature of these types of relationships that drives the therapeutic alliance. IWDs have common experiences of prejudice and discrimination and limited life choices circumscribed by society and lack of civil rights, because this history is common to all IWDs throughout centuries. The solution for these types of problems is political advocacy and strong identity politics, which require large numbers of IWDs with all types of disabilities working together.
4. **For those without disabilities, it will be impossible to completely understand the disability experience.** Having a severe case of the flu is different from having a chronic illness/disability and, likewise, sustaining a broken leg from a skiing accident, which completely heals, is not the same as paralysis nor would either situation result in a medical or clinical definition of disability. Furthermore, some training methods, in misguided efforts to give IWODs some idea of the disability experience, have failed and may have *increased* prejudice and stigma toward IWDs. Simulation exercises, such as using a blindfold to simulate blindness or using a wheelchair, have been found to increase prejudice. These types of exercises are demeaning to IWDs and cannot lead to any sort of understanding of the lifelong, day-to-day experience of disability.

Defining Disability

Disability is a multifaceted experience which includes various types of definitions with differing levels of detail. This chapter considers disability according to three broad categories: 1) physical disabilities, 2) cognitive disabilities, and 3) psychiatric disabilities.

> **Categorizing Disabilities**
>
> There is no one universal system of categorization. The categories listed here are the most commonly used
> Categories are based on symptoms, not causes.
> Categories are necessary for treatment plans.
> Categories are necessary for payment systems.

There is no one universally accepted categorization of disabilities, but for the purposes of this book, the entire range of disabilities has been divided into three categories, each based on a disability's *symptoms* and not on its cause. Diagnoses and categorization of disabilities are necessary to develop treatment and management plans, to provide documentation for eligibility for services and benefits, and to provide a starting point for data gathering and epidemiology estimates of prevalence. Diagnoses and categorization of disabilities also exert a powerful influence of the self-concepts of the individuals who are diagnosed and categorized and also affect (or influence) the degree of prejudice and stigma society directs toward individuals. Therefore, a simple categorization presented in a textbook has many complex interactions between medical treatments, governmental systems, IWDs' self-concepts, and societal reactions. This oversimplification does not depict reality because many IWDs have more than one disability, often in different categories.

Physical disabilities include

- Sensory loss, such as blindness or deafness, or dual sensory loss, e.g., blindness and deafness (in a single individual);
- Mobility impairments and paralysis;
- Neurological impairments such as strokes, cerebral palsy, seizure disorders, and traumatic brain injuries;
- Musculoskeletal conditions such as muscular dystrophy, multiple sclerosis;
- Chronic illnesses, such as diabetes, heart disease, and autoimmune diseases such as lupus and rheumatoid arthritis.

Cognitive disabilities typically impair perception, memory, information processing, reasoning, sensory discrimination (auditory and visual). They include

- Intellectual impairments (previously referred to as mental retardation);
- Learning disabilities, such as dyslexia and dyscalculia;
- Developmental disorders, such as ASD (autism spectrum disorder);
- Neurocognitive disabilities, such as dementia and Alzheimer's.

Psychiatric disabilities include

- Mental illnesses, such as schizophrenia, anxiety disorders, or depression;
- Chemical and substance abuse, including alcohol dependence.

Does disability always include loss?

Most disabilities do include loss or deficiency or absence of a sensory process or functioning.

Newly recognized disabilities (such as ASD) include superabundance of a sensory process or functioning.

Common to the first two categories, physical and cognitive disabilities, is the idea of loss or deficit, meaning that something (such a part of the body) is missing or a part of the body is not functioning (such as the eyes, or the ears, or the legs, or the pancreas). Deficit, loss, and impairment are part of most physical disabilities. In contrast, Oliver Sacks (1985) described the way in which many neurological disabilities, such as ASD or Tourette's syndrome, are due to an *overabundance or excess* of one or more functions. Further clouding the picture is neurology's lack of a concept to describe this overabundance due to the long-accepted understanding that all impairments and disabilities included loss and deficit. Sacks pointed out that many of the words of neurology's diagnostic criteria often begin with the prefix "a" or "an," meaning lack or absence.

> What is the opposite of deficit? An excess or superabundance of function? Neurology has not a word for this—because it has no concept. A functional or dysfunctional works—or it does not; these are the only possibilities it allows. Thus, a disease which is "ebullient" or "productive" in character challenges the basic mechanistic concepts of neurology, and this is doubtless one reason why such disorders—common, important, and intriguing as they are—have never received the attention they deserve.
>
> (Sacks, 1985, p. 87)

> Neurology's favourite word is "deficit." Denoting an impairment or incapacity loss of neurological function: loss of speech, loss of language, loss of memory, loss of vision, loss of dexterity and myriad other lacks and losses of specific functions (or faculties). For all these dysfunctions (another favourite term) we have privative words of every sort—Aphina, Aphemia, Aphasia, Alexia, Aphraxia, Agnosia, Amnesia, Ataxia—a word for every specific neutral or mental function of which patients, through disease, or injury, or failure to develop, may find themselves partly or wholly deprived.
>
> (Sacks, 1985, p. 3)

Physical disabilities, more than cognitive or psychiatric disabilities, are diagnosed with standardized measurements, which leads to great interrater reliability. An example of this is diabetes. Testing for amounts of sugar in an individual's blood is a standardized diagnostic process; most physicians would render the same diagnosis. Furthermore, diabetes is conceptualized as deficit in the functioning of an organ of the body, the pancreas.

Psychiatric disabilities tend to be more closely related to social factors and individuals with cognitive/developmental disabilities, such as intellectual disabilities, are at a greater risk for psychiatric disabilities (when compared to the general population). Disability scholars (Harris, Heller, & Schindler, 2012) explained:

> The increased prevalence of psychiatric disorders in this population is associated with social, biological, and medical factors, life events, and specific syndromes. Among social factors are lack of education, institutionalization at an early age, limited social networks, loss of close and confiding relationships, bereavement, lack of valued roles, low incomes and relative poverty, service breaks and transitions, and shifting patterns of interdependence with parents during the life course.
>
> (p. 72)

Diagnostic Masking

Occurs when one disability prevents the diagnosis of another disability.
Most often occurs when an individual's intellectual disability (ID) masks their psychiatric disability.
Occurs because both training programs and funding agencies do not consider the possibility of co-occurring IDs and psychiatric disabilities.
Results in individuals being shuffled between services for IDs and the mental health system.

The term "diagnostic masking" most often refers to individuals with IDs who also experience psychiatric disabilities but, technically, diagnostic masking occurs when the presence of any disability is overlooked due to the diagnostic significance of another disability. Often, psychiatric disabilities are not properly diagnosed and treated in individuals with intellectual disabilities (ID) due to "diagnostic masking." In this case, diagnostic masking means that many psychiatrists and psychologists are unable to render a diagnosis because the symptoms and signs of many psychiatric disabilities are not easily detected due to the individual's lack of intellectual and verbal ability. Those with intellectual abilities are not always able to describe and elaborate on their feelings or motivations. Nonetheless, people with IDs experience higher rates of psychiatric disabilities than any other disability groups, some estimates suggest that 20% to 60% of individuals with ID experience this combination of disabilities. However, separate funding for these two types of services is based on the false assumption that there are few individuals with both types of disabilities—intellectual and psychiatric disabilities. This results in individuals being ping-ponged between the mental health system and services for psychiatric disabilities. Further compounding the problem is the lack of professional training in these concurrent disabilities, and the lack of experienced therapists.

Problems in diagnosing psychiatric disabilities in people with IDs include the lack of verbal fluency; inability to understand their emotions; they often appear to have a bland affect when, in reality, their blandness and flat affect is due to the fact they have fewer life experiences; and many clinicians misattribute behaviors which, appear due to the ID, but are, in reality, psychiatric symptoms. Stress is a common cause of psychiatric symptoms and the stress tolerance threshold of individuals with IDs is lower, making it difficult to differentiate the source or cause. In order to avoid diagnostic overshadowing in individuals with IDs, it is important to gain some idea of the individual's baseline functioning, and to use family members and others to gather collateral information.

Diagnostic overshadowing, of all types, can be reduced if counselors, psychologists, and psychiatrist are trained in co-occurring disabilities and if funding sources can be co-located.

Other Characteristics of Disability

There are many factors that affect the experience of disability. Some of these factors are specific to the individual, including their available resources, and other factors are the result of the response of the societal environment, including the degree of treatment and number of services available. Often, the general public has reacted to the disability and the individual with the disability with marginalization, stereotyping, pity, lowered expectations, and other types of prejudice and discrimination. The section that follows focuses only on aspects of disabilities and not on the IWD or societal responses.

1. Type of onset
2. Time of onset
3. Course of the disability
4. Functions impaired
5. Severity of the disability
6. Visibility of the disability

Type of Onset

Typically, there are two broad types of onset:

1. Acute, which is sharp and sudden and the date is referenced;
2. Insidious, which is subtle, at times, invisible, and the date of diagnosis is referenced.

With deafness, the two main types of onset are based on the acquisition of spoken language abilities: either prelingual or postlingual.

Type of Onset. There are two broad categories of type onset, *acute* or *insidious*. Acute onset refers to a disability that has a sharp, sudden, definite beginning point. Occasionally acute onsets are also described as traumatic, such as accidents and injuries. Acute onset disabilities are considered medical emergencies and require immediate hospitalization. The individual who experiences an acute onset disability is required to disengage entirely from their life and focus all attention on the disability. Examples include bacterial infections, the birth of a child with a congenital disability, or a spinal cord injury. Disabilities with an acute onset can present an individual and their family with simultaneous, multiple, and overwhelming demands. Acute onsets are often unanticipated and represents a sharp turning point in the individual's life. Often months or years of hospitalization or physical rehabilitation are required. Both the demands of the disability and the changes in self-identity are a "turning point." One young man told of his acute, traumatic onset of a spinal cord injury, emphasizing that he did not understand his diagnosis: "I was 22, a recent college graduate, and all of a sudden, I'm a T8 bilateral paraplegic, whatever the hell that is!" (Crewe, 1997, p. 382). Perhaps surprising, some IWDs with an acute onset have disability "birthday" parties, such as "The Day I Broke My Neck" party. These disability birthday parties are often more a rite of passage for the IWD than their birthdays; the IWD views their life as divided between pre-disability and post-disability.

The other type of onset is an insidious onset, in which the time of diagnosis is referenced because no one, neither the individual nor medical professionals, can determine the exact time of onset. Insidious onsets are subtle and stealthy; however, the individual often feels that "something hasn't been quite right for a long time." Examples of insidious onset disabilities include diabetes, autoimmune diseases, and multiple sclerosis. Often, years of misdiagnosis and seeking the services of various types of medical professions has preceded a definitive diagnosis. Many of the symptoms of insidious onset disabilities appear ambiguous and are unacknowledged, and have no standardized, objective test. Moreover, many of the symptoms are difficult to measure, including loss of energy, sleep disturbances, vision problems, fatigue, and problems with balance and, moreover, are seen by others as character failings of the individuals rather than as symptoms. Both before the definitive diagnosis and, occasionally, after the individual is accused of malingering (faking). Long pre-diagnosis periods and wrong diagnoses can result in a great deal of stress for the individual. Typically, individuals with acute onset disabilities receive more social support than those with insidious onset disabilities.

Time of Onset

Two general categories are used:

1. Congenital—present at birth or shortly after. The correct term is "congenital disabilities," rather than "birth defects";
2. Acquired—onset or diagnosis at any other time.

Time of Onset. Time of onset is typically considered to be either *congenital* or *acquired*. Congenital disabilities are present at birth, or shortly after, whereas acquired disabilities occur later in life. There are two important aspects of congenital disabilities: First, it is the parents who must adjust to the disability, and, second, the IWD has no pre-disability identity since they have "always been this way." Congenital disabilities include intellectual disabilities, cerebral palsy, some types of blindness and deafness, and achondroplasia (a type of dwarfism). Time of onset is defined differently in deafness. Prelingual deafness refers to deafness that occurs before the individual learns to speak and postlingual deafness is deafness which occurs after the individual has learned to speak. There is also a third type of onset for hearing impairments and deafness, late-life deafness and hard of hearing. With prelingual deafness, the small child or infant must learn Sign Language immediately, which requires the parents, family members, and other caregivers to learn Sign Language. Therefore, infants and small children have access to language in the same way that hearing infants do, only not *spoken* language but *signed* language. Late-onset hearing impairments typically refer to older people who have developed these impairments as part of the aging process.

Acquired disabilities are those disabilities that are acquired or diagnosed at any other time of life. Typically, early onset disabilities require fewer emotional responses than later onset disabilities. There are three explanations for this ease of response: 1) the young child has not yet acquired society's prejudice and stigma toward disability and IWDs; 2) the child has not fully developed their body image; and 3) young children are generally more flexible and adaptable.

Developmental Stage of Individual at Time of Onset or Diagnosis

Disabilities acquired or diagnosed during adolescence are difficult in two ways:

1. Disfiguring disabilities (including the assistive technology) are difficult because adolescence is the time of life when body image and appearance are most important to individuals;
2. Adolescence is the period when individuals undertake education and career exploration, and disabilities with a typical onset of the late teen years and early twenties, such as schizophrenia, often cause the individual to miss out on these important life tasks.

Disabilities acquired or diagnosed during midlife are difficult because midlife is typically the time of the greatest family, professional, and financial success.

Another type of "time of onset" relates to the developmental stage of the individual who acquires or is diagnosed with a disability. The only developmental period in which disability is considered "normative" or "expected" is old age. We have learned that late-onset hearing impairments are very much different from prelingual deafness simply due to the different developmental stages. Individuals with late-onset hearing impairments rarely learn Sign Language. Although the possibility of acquiring or being diagnosed with a disability can occur at any stage of life, most of us do not consider (or prepare for) this possibility. It is only in old age that we actually consider that we might acquire a disability. Therefore, because old age onset disabilities are normative there is less prejudice and discrimination directed toward aging individuals with disabilities; older individuals respond and adjust to their disabilities better due to a combination of having few functional demands, such as work and career or raising children, and having had a lifetime of responding to difficulties, giving them both experience, practice, and self-images of successful problem solvers. Finally, in old age, body image become less important and elderly individuals invest less of their self-identities in their appearance and physical capabilities; rather they see themselves as "more" than their bodies.

The onset of a disability can interact with the developmental stage of the individual; however, none of the developmental theorists, including Freud; Erikson; the cognitive theorists; and behavioral theorists such as Skinner, Pavlov, and Bandura, considered IWDs in their theories. Also, the "humanist" theorists, such as Maslow, were silent on the development of IWDs (Smart, 2012). Nonetheless, a few examples may help to explain the interaction of the time of onset of a disability with the developmental stage of the individual. Disfiguring disabilities tend to present more adjustment demands when they occur during adolescence, the period of life in which one's appearance is of utmost importance and the establishment of long-term romantic sexual relationships is a critical developmental task. The disability of schizophrenia is unique due to the combination of the time of onset and the severe functional impairments. Typical time of onset is during the late teens or early twenties. During these years, individuals are making significant decisions, including educational and career options. Schizophrenia, therefore, renders a demanding period of life difficult, or impossible, to negotiate. Middle age is typically the period of greatest achievement, as families have been established, careers are flourishing, and finances are at a lifetime high. Individuals have planned, sacrificed, and worked to reach these successes and are saving for retirement. Those in middle-age feel, justifiably, that they have earned the right to enjoy their successes. Middle age is a time in which the individual has developed a well-defined identity, which the occurrence of a disability may disrupt, since many chronic illnesses are diagnosed during middle age. Careers must often be abandoned, financial stability is lost, and well-established families are presented with demands and role changes. With this brief explanation, we have learned that the same disability may be experienced very differently based on the developmental stage of the individual.

Neurodevelopmental disabilities, including Autism Spectrum Disorders, are lifelong disabilities and, therefore, the largest number of individuals with ASD are adults. In this case, the word "developmental" refers to the time of life in which the symptoms of ASD appear and are diagnosed. It does not mean that the ASD disappears when individuals complete the developmental period. The chapters of the DSM-5 are arranged in chronological order of time of onset. Therefore, the first chapter is Neurodevelopmental Disorders since these disorders have the earlier onset, and one of the final chapters is Neurocognitive Disorders since these disorders typically appear in old age.

Disabilities Acquired in Old Age

Present fewer emotional response demands for three reasons:

1. Old age is the only developmental period in which disability is normative (or expected).
2. Old age disabilities tend to be high incidence disabilities (e.g., many elderly individuals have hearing and vision impairments).
3. Individuals in this developmental stage typically have fewer life tasks, such as employment or care of children.

Thinking in terms of large groups of populations, or demographics, and in individual terms, the following statement is true: Rate of disability is positively correlated with age. In statistical terms, this means that the older the individual, or the older the population, the rate of disability increases. Conversely, the younger the individual or the population, the rate of disability decreases. This is a strong positive correlation, but it does not imply that it is 100% true. Not every elderly individual will have a disability; however, the majority will experience a disability. Nonetheless, this strong correlation has positive results: Most individuals and society, as a whole, consider old-disability to be "normative," or expected, and therefore, less stigmatizing. Another advantage of old-age disabilities is related to the fact that these disabilities tend to be high-incidence disabilities, resulting in a greater number of resources and benefits provided by society and more role models. Further, disabilities acquired or diagnosed in the later years of life do not conflict with the functional demands of a job or child care.

> **Course of the Disability**
> 1. Stable
> 2. Episodic
> 3. Degenerating
> 4. Degenerating and episodic

Course of the Disability. Following diagnosis, medical stabilization, and physical rehabilitation, day-to-day life with a disability and the course of the disability begins. Course of the disability is defined as the progression, advancement, or the trajectory and includes three aspects: the direction (stays the same, improves, or deteriorates), the pace or the rate of change, and finally the degree of predictability. There are four general types of courses: stable, episodic, degenerating, and episodic degenerating.

In stable course disabilities, such as intellectual disabilities, spinal cord injuries, and deafness, the symptoms are permanent and they do not vary. The individual whose disability has a stable course knows what they are dealing with and, therefore, of all the types of courses, this may make for the easiest adjustment.

Episodic disabilities are also referred to as relapsing disabilities and the symptoms come and go, alternating with periods of remission. Seizure disorders, many types of mental illnesses, and multiple sclerosis are examples of disorders with episodic courses. These types of disabilities are much more ambiguous to both the IWD and to others, due to the unpredictability of the relapses or episodes of symptom flare-up. The goal in episodic disabilities is to reduce the number of episodes, and to reduce their intensity and duration. With some types of disabilities, individuals, and their families, become skilled in discerning prodromal or warning signs of episodes. Nonetheless, each episode, symptom flare-up, or relapse requires treatment and, perhaps more important, an emotional response.

Degenerating disabilities become steadily worse over time, often leading to the individual's death. With each level of loss, the individual encounters additional emotional response demands. In degenerating course disabilities, the pace of the course assumes great importance. For example, 50% of those diagnosed with amyotrophic lateral sclerosis (ASL) die within three years of onset. In most cases, the only medical treatments are symptom relief and pain management.

Degenerating episodic course disabilities include many autoimmune diseases and have downward trajectories, although instead of a steady downward course there are periods of remission. Nonetheless, the general direction is downward. Of all four types of courses, the degenerating episodic type is the most difficult to respond to. With each relapse, the level of symptom reduction becomes lower. Thus, the unpredictability and lack of control of episodic course disabilities is combined with the fearful prognosis of a degenerating disability. For some, the individual does not know if an episode is a symptom flare-up or could lead to death. Richard Cohen, author and journalist who has an episodic, degenerating disability, multiple sclerosis, described the experience: "I felt powerless, a passenger in a speeding car" (2004, p. 26).

All disabilities, with all four types of courses, include ambiguity. Ambiguity is stressful; we feel out of control and our capacity to plan and organize our lives is reduced. Most people try to reduce ambiguity in their lives and no one has total control over their life course. Nonetheless, the ability to control our lives (to the fullest extent possible) is a very important part of quality of life. For IWDs, the challenge of dealing with ambiguity looms as more of a factor than is the case for IWODs.

Medically, the goal of responding to disability is management and care rather than cure. Medical professionals focus on controlling symptoms, reducing the number of secondary conditions and complications (such as bladder infections in spinal cord injuries) and retaining the highest quality of life. This focus on long-term care for the medical professions, rather than the two-outcome paradigm of total cure or the death of the individual, has created widespread and radical changes in the medical system, including academic training, practice of medicine, and insurance and other payment systems. Moreover, the focus on long-term care has required a deep philosophical shift for medicine and, as we have seen, the medical profession is transforming itself.

We have discussed the effects of various types of courses on the IWD and on medical professions. The stable course disability presents less ambiguity and, therefore, presents fewer emotional demands on the IWD and renders medical treatments more straightforward. Stable-course disabilities also elicit less prejudice and discrimination from the general public, because of this reduced ambiguity. Society regards IWDs with stable-course disabilities to have a disability, while with the other types of episodic disabilities, it is unclear to others if the IWD is disabled or not. A legal disability scholar Stefan (2001) explained: "Society is most comfortable with disabilities that are permanent and chronic: either one is disabled or not. Even with people who sometimes have to use a wheelchair find themselves regarded with skepticism and suspicion bordering on hostility" (p. 10). Individuals with episodic disabilities face the same prejudice and discrimination in the larger legal and economic structures:

> The economic, mental health, and legal structures, however, cannot accommodate the central truth of alternating or concurrent crisis and functioning at all. The U.S. legal system, mental health system, and labor market are marked by a static and dichotomous vision: One is either disabled or not, and once identified as disabled, residence in the category is presumed permanent. There is no place for the complexities and contradictions of people's real lives. . . . Defeats . . . are also not seen as temporary, but as permanent. One bad episode can mean the termination of parental rights, an involuntary commitment or involuntary medication. It is all or nothing in American society.
>
> (p. 59)

As an aside, the "skepticism and suspicion" of IWODs toward IWDs with episodic course disabilities has nothing to do with the IWD or the disability. The fault and responsibility for this "skepticism and suspicion" is due to the lack of awareness of IWODs. However, these are strong emotions and most IWODs think the fault lies with the IWD and the disability.

Nonetheless, it can be stated that there are no stable course disabilities. Secondary conditions or complications are extremely common. For example, blindness or lower limb amputations are common secondary conditions of diabetes. Stephen Hawking, the astrophysicist, had a progressive neuromuscular disease and he could not speak; instead, he used a communication board (with an American accent!). His inability to speak was due to an emergency tracheotomy that was once required to restore breathing and save his life. The tracheotomy was a complication of his neuromuscular disability. As can be seen, even with stable course disabilities, secondary conditions and complications can require emergency care and can result in the individual's death. The effects of the "normal" aging process also interacts with the effects of the disability.

Functions Impaired

Capitalizing on residual functions—for example, individuals with physical disabilities often "escape into their minds."
Functions are also defined culturally, politically, and idiosyncratically.
Assistive technology has increased the functioning of IWDs.

Functions Impaired. When an IWD loses a function in one area, the solution is to develop and capitalize on their residual skills. For example, there are many collections of first-person accounts of survivors of the polio epidemics in the United States, the United Kingdom, Canada, Australia, and Scandinavia. For these survivors, polio resulted in orthopedic impairments. Throughout these accounts, a single phrase is often repeated, for men and women, regardless of nationality, "I escaped into my mind." Even pre-polio academic failures and goof-offs took learning and education more seriously and became physicians, academics, authors, and journalists. Due to the fact that polio does not result in cognitive or intellectual disabilities, they were capable of capitalizing on their intellectual capabilities. For individuals with all types of disabilities the wider range of options available to the IWD, such as intellectual abilities, educational attainment, a strong occupational identity, and a supportive family, the greater the number of choices accessible.

Functions are defined idiosyncratically, culturally, and politically. Although receding in importance, functions have also been defined by gender. Idiosyncratically defined functioning is based on individual preference, choice, and experience. For visual learners, a vision impairment would be more difficult, while a hearing impairment would present more difficulties for an oral learner. Jenny Morris, lives in the United Kingdom and is an author and member of Parliament. She is paraplegic as a result of injuries sustained in an accident. In her book *Pride Against Prejudice* (1991), Morris summarized the functional results of her disability: "Most of my life was spent sitting down anyway (not least in Parliament meetings) so being in a wheelchair wouldn't make that much difference" (p. 3). In contrast, there are many individuals with orthopedic impairments who enjoy physical activities, athletics, competitive sports, and the outdoors. The development and widespread introduction of athletic wheelchairs, improved prostheses, and a host of other adaptive technology (AT) devices allowed these activities.

Assistive technology, or adaptive technology (AT), has changed the meaning of functioning for most IWDs. In the past, wheelchairs and other assistive devices were mechanical and homemade by a family member. For example, President Franklin D. Roosevelt's "favorite" wheelchair was a kitchen chair to which wheels had been attached. Because kitchen chairs are typically very narrow, this "homemade" wheelchair allowed the President to pass through the doorways of the White House. Today, AT is computerized, customized for the individual and their activities and preferences, and very often government agencies and insurance policies pay for these devices. For example, wheelchair sports began in the 1980s because the sports wheelchair was not developed until the 1980s. Therefore, World War II veterans with disabilities did not participate in wheelchair sports and this lack of participation had nothing to do with the veteran or their disability; it was simply the lack of technology. Today, a power wheelchair costs as much as some cars.

AT also provides both privacy and social interaction for many IWDs. Privacy is facilitated when IWDs use computer technology to manage their finances and pay their bills and as environmental controls to lock doors, open windows, or regulate the heat or, as emergency and safety measures, to call the police or the hospital. Neurologist Oliver Sacks wrote a book entitled, *The Mind's Eye* (2010), which related an account of the way in which AT (audio books) returned a very important function and solved a "devastating problem."

> (Charles Scribner) presided over the publishing house established by his great-grandfather in the 1840s. In his sixties, he developed visual alexia (inability to read)—probably as a result of a degenerative process in the visual parts of the brain. It was a devastating problem for a man who had published the work of Hemingway and others, a man whose life was centered on reading and writing.
>
> (p. 64)

It took some time and practice, but Scribner was able to switch to audio books and, consequently, was able to resume his career. Before the AT of audio books, Scribner could have hired a person to read to him. Thus, AT replaced a paid individual who would have read to him. AT has given Scribner more privacy and flexibility.

A great deal of assistive technology has been designed only for PWDs, such as wheelchairs, communication boards, and hearing aids. However, IWDs have adopted many of the technological advances designed for the general public. Computers, especially the internet, also facilitate social support and understanding, allowing IWDs to communicate with others, including IWDs. Silberman (2015) illustrated the importance of the internet: "The impact of the internet on autistics may one day be compared in magnitude to the spread of Sign Language among the deaf" (p. 433).

Severity of the Disability

For disabilities that are defined in categories, such as blindness or intellectual disabilities, the level of severity is typically measured as profound, severe, moderate, or mild.

For disabilities that are defined on a spectrum, the cut-off points are less clear.

Severity of the Disability. For many disabilities, typically physical disabilities, there are levels of severity with well-defined, standardized cut-offs. These levels are often labeled, mild, moderate, and severe. Examples of these standardized cut-off points include levels of visual impairments and hearing loss. For other types of disabilities, the level of severity is based on the number of functions impaired or by the number of disabilities experienced by a single individual. In psychiatric disabilities, levels of severity and their measurement are more complex and idiosyncratic (specific to the individual). Medications can also contribute to the complexity of diagnosis, including the efficacy to reduce symptoms and the degree of compliance. In depression, for example, the efficacy of antidepressants to control the symptoms of depression and the lack of unpleasant side effects in an individual renders the experience of depression very different than for someone who is refractory to antidepressants or who will not take the medications because of severe side effects.

For intellectual disabilities (formerly termed "mental retardation"), level of severity was determined by a combination of a range of IQ points and the level of adaptive abilities of the individual. IQ scores, or measures of intelligence, were derived from testing instruments and level of adaptation was determined by behavioral observations. The *Diagnostic and Statistical Manual of Mental Disorders-5* (DSM-5) (American Psychiatric Association, 2013) has changed the measurement of levels of severity for individuals with intellectual disabilities. Presently, the fifth edition of the DSM determines level of severity by including the amount of support the individual requires, thus providing more descriptive information for treatment and educational plans. This also subtly shifts part of the responsibility for the treatment of the intellectual disability from the individual to public institutions, such as schools.

Ironically, the degree of stigma and prejudice toward the different categories of disabilities is never included in determining the level of severity of the disability. However, many IWDs consider the greatest obstacle and difficulty in their disability is not the disability itself but rather the prejudice and discrimination of society.

Visibility of the Disability

Two broad categories:

1. Visible
2. Invisible

> Typically, there is more prejudice and discrimination toward individuals with invisible disabilities.
>
> With invisible disabilities, the individual must choose the "point of disclosure."
>
> Individuals with invisible disabilities must disclose their disability in order to receive accommodations and protection under the ADA.

Visibility of the Disability. In the broadest terms, disabilities can be considered as either visible or invisible. Visible disabilities include disabilities such as blindness and various forms of paralysis. Assistive technology, such as hearing aids, insulin pumps, or a wheelchair, can make a disability visible. Invisible disabilities cannot be immediately discerned by others. Examples of invisible disabilities include learning disabilities, seizure disorders, mild intellectual disabilities, chemical and substance abuse, and many types of mental illness. Interestingly, many IWDs can "pick up" on another individual with the same disability simply because they know what to look for. The expectation that others have disabilities (which most IWODs do not have) alerts other IWDs to the adaptations and behaviors in others. Much like those who wear contact lenses are aware of others who wear contact lenses, adaptations and assistive technology are noticed and understood by IWDs. Individuals with learning disabilities can often recognize others with learning disabilities, because they are aware of common mistakes and the accommodations. As an example: A candidate for governor of a western state brought his wife to a campaign cocktail party. The wife was unstable on her feet, leaned on her husband for support, and her speech was slurred. The next day, the newspaper headline read: "Do We Want a Governor Whose Wife Gets Falling Down Drunk?" The wife had a neuromuscular disability with an unpredictable episodic course and did not drink any type of alcohol because alcohol exacerbates these types of neuromuscular disabilities. Others, with no expectation of a disability, automatically assumed that she was drunk. Her husband was elected governor. Years later, after her husband had died, a reporter from the same newspaper conducted an extensive interview with her, asking her about high points and low points of the couple's public life. She recalled a single disappointment: the campaign cocktail party and the resulting newspaper headline. Especially hurtful to her was the lack of a retraction in the newspaper and an apology.

It is often thought that visible disabilities are more severe than invisible disabilities. This is not necessarily true as explained by this maxim: Level of severity is not correlated with degree of visibility. This does not mean that invisible disabilities are always more severe than visible disabilities, only that they can be and often are more severe. Generally speaking, there is more prejudice and discrimination directed toward individuals with invisible disabilities. Often, as in the example of the governor's wife, IWODs ascribe negative motivations to behaviors when they do not understand disabilities. For example, during a meeting, when a man in a wheelchair falls asleep, his colleagues might think him inconsiderate, uninterested, and unmotivated. In reality, the man takes strong medication to prevent spasms and the medication has the side effect of sleepiness. Another example is the lawyer who is late to work. Her colleagues do not understand that the single bus with a wheelchair lift was late.

Low-Incidence or High-Incidence Disabilities

Low-incidence disabilities typically are more difficult to adapt to.
High-incidence disabilities are typically easier to adapt to.
Most congenital disabilities are low-incidence disabilities.
Most disabilities acquired in old age are high-incidence disabilities.

Low-Incidence Disabilities and High-Incidence Disabilities. Low-incidence disabilities are relatively rare and only a small percentage of the population has low-incidence disabilities (hence the term), whereas high-incidence disabilities are fairly common, comprising a large percentage of the population of IWDs. These two designations of disability say nothing about the type (such as physical, cognitive, or psychiatric), nor about level of severity or degree of visibility. Nonetheless, the incidence of the disability, whether high or low, greatly impacts the IWD and their experience.

Low-Incidence Disabilities:

Characteristics of Low-Incidence Disabilities

- They tend to be congenital disabilities, which in earlier times, would have resulted in death.
- Both diagnosis and prognosis are difficult, occasionally wrong, and often corrected or changed as more knowledge and experience is acquired.
- Treatment, management, and other service provision are often available only in large training hospitals, found in metropolitan areas.

- There are few role models and less social support.
- There is more stigma and prejudice because others think of the disability as ambiguous.

Low-incidence disabilities are much more difficult to deal with for the IWD, their family, and for medical professionals. These types of disabilities are difficult because diagnosis and prognosis are problematic, decisions for treatment are unclear or treatments are nonexistent, there are fewer available accommodations, and finally there are fewer role models (individuals with the same type of disability) to provide support and share experiences. Physicians (including highly specialized ones) may occasionally state, "I've never seen this before." Congenital disabilities are often low-incidence disabilities because these are found in less than 1% of children. We have learned that with the reduction in the infant mortality rate, many of these infants survive, but some have disabilities, many of which are very rare. Patterson (1988) summarized:

> Unlike adults, where the type of chronic illnesses (disabilities) are few in number but are prevalent, each of the hundreds of different conditions in children is relatively rare. . . . Except for the common disorders such as mild asthma, the prevalence of any single condition is less than 1 per 100 children.
>
> (p. 70)

Low-incidence disabilities are often so rare that most medical professionals have not treated anyone with this type of disability and the family must travel to a large training hospital, typically located in a metropolitan area. Even in these large hospitals, with the highest level of neonatal care, it may be difficult to arrive at a definitive diagnosis, much less determine a prognosis. Often, the diagnosis changes as doctors acquire more information. Questions such as: "What does my baby have?" "What types of treatment should we seek?" "Will they be able to attend school?" or "How long will they live?" are stressful for both parents and doctors. Solomon (2012) interviewed a family, the Haddens, whose sons, Jamie and Sam, were born with disabilities that physicians could not diagnose. Focus on the link between diagnosis and prognosis and, then, consider their attempts to find a diagnosis.

> With diagnosis, you have prognosis and with prognosis, you have greater peace of mind. The Haddens have run advertisements in hospital journals and *Exceptional Children*. They've had workups done on the boys at NYU (New York University) and Mass (Massachusetts) Eye and Ear. They've

corresponded with doctors at Johns Hopkins. The constellation of symptoms experienced by Jamie and Sam seems to be unique, so no one has been able to predict how the boys would best be treated, how much they might deteriorate, or how long they might live.

(p. 359)

There is far more anxiety with low-incidence disabilities because there is no "role guidance" available. An example of this low-incidence/high-incidence dichotomy is infants born with a relatively high incidence disability, Down syndrome (DS), a type of intellectual disability. Today, many parents of children with DS are grateful to the previous generations of families with DS because these parents advocated for their children, resulting in free public education for children with DS. Moreover, most of the general public know people with DS because earlier generations of parents insisted that their children remain at home and be integrated, rather than be sent to a special care facility. These parents are considered "pioneers," having fought battles that the present generation of parents of children with DS are no longer required to fight.

Two parents of a child with a low-incidence disability came to one of my graduate-level classes to speak about their experience. They brought their 7-year-old son, John, with them. They met while both were university students, married, and within a year had their first baby, named John. Immediately after John's birth, he was life-flighted to a children's hospital in a large city. John could not breathe, could not move, nor could he eat. None of the physicians had seen a newborn with such severe disabilities, and they did not have a diagnosis. The prognosis was a peaceful death within a few days. Nonetheless, with surgeries and treatments, John lived to go home. He has never breathed on his own, eaten any type of food, nor moved. He is in a wheelchair and is tube-fed. His respirator is fitted with an alarm, in case of an electricity outage. John goes to school and uses a communication board that is manipulated by eye movements, showing him to be a bright boy with a fun sense of humor. When John's grandmother first volunteered to babysit, she told the parents, "I'm afraid that John will die while he is in my care." The parents told her, "He could die while he's in our care." Every summer John attends an Easter Seals camp for children in wheelchairs. John loves this camp, telling his family, "At camp I'm with children like me, but none of the kids are as bad as me. They can eat and breathe on their own." John's disability is so rare that it is doubtful he will ever meet someone "like me."

John's story illustrates two points. First, the relationship between lower infant mortality rates and higher infant disability rates: In the past, John would have died at birth or shortly after. Second, in the past, John would have been institutionalized for his entire life, not knowing his family, which grew to include several brothers and sisters. Nor would his family have known and loved John, their son and brother. Many friends of John's family assume that the family must feel "relieved" when John goes to summer camp and are amazed that the family misses John. The family has painstakingly developed a "new normal," in which John's care is integrated into their daily family life.

High-Incidence Disabilities

Benefits of High-Incidence Disabilities

- They tend to occur in old age.
- Due to the combination of the high numbers of individuals with these disabilities and the normative age at which they occur, there is less prejudice and discrimination.
- More accommodations and treatments are available.
- There is a great deal of social support and many role models.

There are only a few types of disabilities in old age, such as vision loss, hearing loss, diabetes, and other chronic illnesses. Nonetheless, these are considered high-incidence disabilities because so many individuals experience this small number of disabilities. High-incidence disabilities are much less stressful simply because they are so commonplace. Many of these high-incidence disabilities have been recognized for centuries and, therefore, the disabilities are less ambiguous to others; there is a great deal of role guidance because the IWD has friends and family with the same disability; society, including the government, provides services and accommodations; and in any senior citizen's center, there will be a great many people with the same disability. In any group in which everyone has the same disability, the disability becomes irrelevant, which is a welcome and relaxing relief. In most other environments, however, the individual's disability becomes their most salient characteristic to others. In most other environments, IWDs are required to explain themselves, their disability, its cause, and the accommodations necessary. Discussing the disability becomes a burden and a nuisance and, further, the IWD understands that others are not interested in them, but in the disability. For example, in many senior centers, deafness almost becomes irrelevant because so many elderly individuals experience hearing impairments.

> **Hierarchy of Stigma of Categories of Disability**
>
> From less stigma to more stigma, the hierarchy is
>
> Physical disabilities;
> Cognitive disabilities (including developmental disabilities and intellectual disabilities);
> Psychiatric disabilities.

Hierarchy of Stigma. The next aspect of disability to be discussed is stigma and has nothing to do with the disability itself, or with the treatment/management of the disability or the individual who has the disability. No large, standardized diagnostic manuals will discuss this aspect of the disability experience. However, many IWDs consider this aspect of the disability to be more difficult than the disability itself or its treatment and management. The stigma, prejudice, and discrimination of society that is targeted toward IWDs affects their lives, unnecessarily limiting their independence, and keeping them isolated. Perhaps the most devastating result of such stigma is the lowered self-esteem of IWDs because society has taught them that they are inferior. In the following excerpt, George Covington felt immune from prejudice and discrimination. Covington graduated from law school at the University of Texas, became special assistant for disability policy in the office of the Vice President of the United States and wrote the regulations for section 504 of the Rehabilitation Act of 1973. (Section 504 is considered the forerunner of the Americans with Disabilities Act.) He is legally blind, which he described as "a combination of what we've come to know as astigmatism, nystagmus, eccentric fixation, and myopia—all of which were acute—and probably even further back, a degenerating retina." His blindness included the lack of vision and the surprising prejudice and discrimination.

> As a white southern male, I never thought I would have to worry about my civil rights. But as I wrote the 504 regs (regulations) for the Department of Interior—the Handicapped Civil Rights law—I realized that there is a lot of discrimination against those with disabilities.
> (Covington, 1997, p. 41, cf. Pelka, 1997)

A mother with two deaf children worked very hard to encourage her children's self-confidence and aspirations. As a hearing mother, she learned

American Sign Language so that she could work as a secretary at the school, a school for deaf children. Slowly, she became aware that for deaf people, self-confidence and high aspirations may not be enough. She became aware of stigma.

> The whole time they were growing up, I said, "You can do anything you want to do. This (the deafness) doesn't limit you." Then it started to hit me. It's got nothing to do with them. It's got to do with that hearing person across from them at an interview.
>
> (Solomon, 2012, p. 104)

In a way, the mother was right, the prejudice and lowered expectations of hearing people had nothing to do with D/deafness; the stigma was due to ill-informed prejudice. Nonetheless, this stigma would limit her children's lives. Furthermore, the "hearing person across from them at an interview" probably would not think of herself as prejudiced and discriminating.

Broadly speaking, this is the hierarchy of stigma: Individuals with psychiatric disabilities experience the most stigma, those with cognitive disabilities experience less stigma, and those with physical disabilities have the least degree of societal stigma directed toward them. IWODs believe that they understand the experience of the physical disability and are less likely to blame the individual for the disability while IWODs understand cognitive disabilities less, which results in more stigma. Illustrating this hierarchy of stigma is a remark made by a mother of a child with achondroplasia (a type of dwarfism). She described the hierarchy of stigma when she stated: "I wish my daughter were blind or paralyzed, but not a dwarf!" (Solomon, 2012, p. 116).

The category of disabilities toward which the greatest degree of stigma is directed is psychiatric disabilities. Individuals with psychiatric disabilities often appear ambiguous, frightening, and unpredictable. The popular media has exaggerated these images, allowing viewers to infer that most IWDs with psychiatric disabilities are dangerous and unpredictable. A psychiatrist (Paris, 2015) illustrated the role that ambiguity plays in the diagnosis of psychiatric disabilities and illustrates the hierarchy of stigma when he compared psychiatric disabilities with physical disabilities. Specifically, citing the disabilities of blindness or paraplegia, Paris noted that, among medical professionals, there is little cross-national debate about these diagnoses. Professionals around the world define blindness and paraplegia in much the same way. Furthermore, most nonprofessionals (the general public) understand the physical disabilities of blindness or paraplegia. However, in addition to the lack of clarity in diagnosis, the media exaggeration of individuals with psychiatric disabilities, Paris stated that no one would debate the existence of physical disabilities such as blindness or paraplegia, while there has been debate if psychiatric disabilities actually exist.

Also, those with psychiatric disabilities (which includes chemical and substance abuse and alcoholism) are widely thought to have caused their own disability. This mistaken view elicits less understanding and this often translates in a reduced number of resources allocated to individuals with psychiatric disabilities. Further, the symptoms of psychiatric disabilities often appear to be character and moral failings. In no other category of disability are the symptoms thought to be personal failings. The degree of stigma toward any disability is rooted in fear; those disabilities that elicit the greatest amount of fear are the most stigmatized. Encountering an IWD reminds others of the universal possibility of acquiring a disability or chronic illness and we often go to great lengths to avoid being reminded. A psychiatrist (Paris, 2015) succinctly stated, "Fear of losing control of one's own mind is the main cause of the stigma associated with mental disorder" (p. 13).

Many psychiatric disabilities are diagnosed and measured by spectra whereas most physical disabilities are measured in categories, often dichotomous categories, or either-or. For example, an individual is blind or not blind. Spectrum, dimension, and continuum are considered to be synonymous terms.

Disabilities That Are Measured on a Continuum (or Spectrum)

1. There tends to be more existential angst and discrimination against individuals with disabilities measured on a dimension, spectrum, or continuum.
2. Second, disabilities measured on a dimension or spectrum (rather than in categories) lend themselves more easily to adjustment. A simple change in the cut-off point between disability and normalcy could result in fewer diagnoses or more diagnoses.
3. Disabilities measured dimensionally illustrate the human influence on diagnoses, which are often erroneously thought to be solely biological and medical.
4. To the general public, the disability is typically represented by individuals on the higher end of the continuum.

Not all continua, spectra, or dimensions are the same. Some dimensions start at the extreme end of the disability and end at the mild or borderline end, such as Autism Spectrum Disorder (ASD) and an individual diagnosed on any point of the spectrum has the disability. Another type of spectra shows normality at one polar end and pathology at the opposite polar end, such as Obsessive Compulsive Disorder (OCD). So, not all spectra and dimensions are measured in quite the same way. At first glance, it may appear unnecessary to dichotomize the method of measurement. However, this dimensional/categorical dichotomy is important due to four factors: First, there tends to be more existential angst and discrimination against individuals with disabilities measured on a dimension, spectrum, or continuum. Disabilities measured on a dimension are thought to be more ambiguous than disabilities measured categorically, and ambiguity results in prejudice and discrimination. Second, disabilities measured on a dimension or spectrum (rather than in categories) lend themselves more easily to modification. For example, in times of economic downturns, governments could make the determination that disabilities at the polar ends of these continua would not qualify as a disability. This would be more difficult to do with categorical disabilities, such as blindness or deafness. Third, disabilities measured dimensionally illustrate the human influence on diagnoses, which are often erroneously thought to be solely biological and medical. A large medical organization could simply move the cut-off point (between normalcy and disability) higher or lower. Raising the diagnostic threshold results in fewer IWDs and lowering the diagnostic threshold results in more IWDs. Nothing changed in the disabilities or the individuals; a human-made judgment was made. Fourth, to the general public, the disability is typically represented by individuals on the higher end of the continuum. Differing degrees of severity of varying symptoms are presented on a spectrum, typically with individuals with more severe symptoms represented on the low end and those with less severe symptoms (and often demonstrate extraordinary strengths and talents in other areas) are represented on the high end of the spectrum. Ask for a name of someone with ASD and most people would answer "Temple Grandin," an individual who has accomplished a great deal and has achieved fame, more than most IWDs or IWODs. For the general public, Temple Grandin represents the entire autism spectrum. Dr. Grandin is a university professor, the author of several books, and has developed more humane methods of cattle production. Nonetheless, Dr. Grandin is at the very high end of the autism spectrum and certainly has little in common with those on the lower end who are often not toilet trained, display self-stimulating behavior such as arm-flapping, and have very poor verbal skills.

> **Hierarchy of Stigma by Perceived Cause From Lowest to Highest**
> Disabilities acquired for "noble" causes, such as war injuries or work accidents, or injuries caused by lifesaving attempts
> Congenital disabilities
> Acquired disabilities
> Disabilities perceived to be caused by the individual's recklessness

Perceived cause of the disability also can be thought of as another type of hierarchy of stigma. Individuals with disabilities thought to have been acquired for "noble causes," such as combat and industrial accidents, experience the least degree of societal stigma; those with congenital disabilities experience more stigma, and those who are perceived to have caused their own disability experience the greatest degree of stigma. In congenital disability, any stigma (and often there is none) is directed toward the parents. Individuals who are thought to have caused their own disability include drunk driving or other reckless and unnecessary activities, are the target of the greatest degree of stigma. The word "perceived" is very important because often, when the true cause is not known, IWODs invent a cause. Here's an example: A young man with two lower limb prostheses enters a bar and immediately everyone wants to pay for this combat veteran's drinks. However, the young man incurred his amputations while driving under the influence of drugs. Often, unless the IWD reveals the cause of the disability, others may "fill in the gaps." This example is rather rare because when others "fill in the gap" about the cause of the disability, it typically is not a positive one.

The perceived social class, gender, race, or sexual orientation can also interact with the disability to increase or decrease societal stigma. A president of the United States with a disability, such as Franklin Roosevelt with polio, is judged much more positively than a young black girl in the American south during the Jim Crow period. Wilma Rudolph, an African American girl, contracted polio as a child and went on to win an Olympic Gold Medal. She was not allowed to be treated at a "white" hospital and for her physical rehabilitation sessions, she and her mother took a long bus ride (which included eating a packed lunch) to a rehabilitation center for African Americans. The bus passed a "whites only" polio rehabilitation center in Memphis, Tennessee. Therefore, a severe disability was needlessly made more difficult due to the institutionalized prejudice and discrimination of the Jim Crow American South.

The effect of the hierarchy of stigma has far-reaching effects for IWDs. One physician told his patient with a psychiatric disability to compare herself to someone with diabetes. In the same way that the individual with diabetes has a non-functioning organ, the pancreas, the woman with a psychiatric disability has a malfunctioning organ, the brain. Furthermore, neither condition can be cured, only managed and controlled with daily medicine, insulin for diabetes and psychoactive drugs for the psychiatric disability. This is an excellent analogy which will help in medication compliance and assisting those with psychiatric disabilities to view their disability more accurately. Nonetheless, the analogy does not extend to the degree of stigma. There is much less stigma toward individuals with diabetes and much more stigma toward those with psychiatric disabilities.

The Need for a Cause of Disability

The Need for a Cause

Most IWODs want a cause that is clear cut, unitary, and physical.
For many disabilities, none of these is possible.
However, there are organic (physical) causes for all disabilities, including psychiatric disabilities, and this is the reason that disabilities are not categorized by cause but rather by symptoms.

We introduced the three categories of disabilities; we emphasized that none of these categories were based on cause. The reasons for disregarding the cause of disabilities are 1) often the cause is not known; 2) often there are multiple causes; 3) often hypotheses of causes change; and 4) for some disabilities, the same treatments may apply, regardless of cause. Also, there are organic causes for all disabilities, including psychiatric disabilities. So, if disabilities were categorized according to cause, there would only be one category, physical disabilities. Nonetheless, most everyone *wants* to know the cause of disabilities. The presence of disability in the modern world questions the twin fallacies of a fair world and the idea that everyone is in total control of their body. In a chapter entitled, "Walking the Edge of Tragedy and Transformation," a woman professor of English expressed her shock at the diagnosis of disability, in part, to her long-held belief in a fair world.

> For so long I believed that if I followed the rules, gave my best, or did the "right" thing, I might accomplish something or at least escape some painful fate. Now, I know if there ever were any rules, they have been broken.
> (Toombs, 1995, p. 24)

In a fair world, only bad people would have disabilities; but we know it is *not* a fair world, regardless of how much we might want the world to be fair, predictable, without randomness, and under our personal control. Bacterial infections, random gene mutations, and accidents happen and often result in lifelong disability.

Another motive to ascribe false causes concerns our need to distance ourselves from the possibility of acquiring a disability. This need can be expressed as, "This would never happen to me! So, I'm safe." The English member of Parliament, Jenny Morris, discovered very quickly that IWODs needed to "separate themselves from me."

> These defense mechanisms all took the form of people separating themselves from me. Sometimes this was achieved by believing that I had somehow brought my own paralysis on myself—as when the hospital nurses said that I had attempted suicide and thrown myself off the wall.
> (Morris, 1991, p. 2)

Actually, Ms. Morris had jumped over a garden wall to rescue a small child.

The unbearability of not knowing is strong, often overwhelming. Occasionally, individuals may "fill in the gap," inventing negative stories that include blaming someone. Women who give birth to an infant with a congenital disability are often asked, "What did you do during your pregnancy?" Another example of finding one individual responsible for his daughter's disability concerns a young woman who has a displaced hip which causes a severe limp. This was a congenital disability and, as a child, she endured many surgeries to ameliorate the displacement. Her father was a pastor of a small Christian church and, although her parents were open about the disability and its cause, rumors circulated among church members that her father had severely beat her and this abuse resulted in the hip displacement. In this case, the true cause was openly discussed; but perhaps the need to blame *someone* overwhelmed church members' acceptance and belief in the real cause.

Most individuals want a cause that is both organic and unitary, but a disability often has many causes and not all are organic. Perhaps, this is part of the strength of the false idea for the "vaccine scare" when thousands of parents refused to vaccinate their children, believing that vaccines caused autism. The vaccine hypothesis was both unitary and physical and, therefore, very plausible. Plausible theories of disability causation are often reductionist and either-or, meaning that the cause must either be organic or psychological.

Autism Spectrum Disorders (ASD) and to some extent, schizophrenia, were thought to be caused by poor parenting, and two generations of psychiatrists, psychologists, and counselors were trained to accept this false concept. It is now known that the causes of ASD and a psychiatric disability, schizophrenia, have an organic basis and demonstrate strong genetic links. Nonetheless, a combination of the overwhelming need to understand the causality coupled with the prevailing theories of psychology and psychiatry resulted in well-recognized and authoritative psychologists and psychiatrists publishing their (false) theories. It seems, that authoritative sources also feel the need to fill the uncertainty gaps and further, the history of these theories showed remarkable resistance to consideration of other types of causality. It is very human to set up beliefs that we want to believe.

Freudian theories often postulated causes for mental illness in families. An introduction to a textbook, *Disability Through the Lifecourse* (2012) described this:

> Freud's theories have had many implications for people with mental illness and their families. These theories tend to blame parents for the mental illness of offspring and have guided treatment interventions. More recently, researchers have recognized that biological factors play a large causative role in mental illness.
>
> (Harris, Heller, & Schindler, 2012, p. 16)

Freudian psychoanalyst Frieda Fromm Reichman introduced the term, the "schizophrenogenic mother" in 1948. Schizophrenogenic mother means that the mother causes schizophrenia in her children. In his book, *Far From the Tree* (2012), Andrew Solomon wrote about a mother of a child who had been diagnosed as schizophrenic. The mother, a bioethicist, expressed her public shame: "I sometimes felt as though I wore a scarlet letter 'S' emblazoned on my chest" (p. 308).

Autism was also thought to be caused by poor parenting. Bruno Bettelheim, a well published professor and psychologist, who was later discredited, stated, "The precipitating factor in infantile autism is the parent's wish that his child should not exist" (Solomon, 2012, p. 231). Belief that parents caused mental illness and autism resulted in 1) these disabilities becoming very stigmatizing for the entire family and, because of this, it is unknown the number of families who did not seek services because of this stigma; 2) families, especially mothers, were not given support for raising a child with a severe disability; and 3) research into the organic and biological origins was delayed for decades.

Large Standardized Systems of Clinical Diagnostic Criteria

> **Two Large Standardized Systems of Diagnostic Criteria**
> 1. The *International Classification of Diseases and Health Related Problems*
> 2. The *Diagnostic and Statistical Manual of Mental Disorders*

Two large standardized systems of clinical diagnostic criteria are used to provide services to IWDs. The first is the *International Classification Statistical Classification of Diseases and Related Health Problems-Tenth Revision, Clinical Modification* (ICD-11) published by the World Health Organization (WHO) in Geneva, Switzerland in 2015. The second large system is the *Diagnostic and Statistical Manual of Mental Disorders-5* (DSM-5) (2013) published by the American Psychiatric Association.

• The ICD-10-CM, used by medical practitioners, includes biological conditions, organized by the various body systems. The categorical numbers are often referred to as codes and are often used for billing purposes. For example, F00-F90 is Mental and Behavioral Disorders, G00-G99 is Diseases of the Nervous System, and M00-M00 is Diseases of the Musculoskeletal System and Connective Tissue. Level of severity is included in the coding number given to each diagnosis. It has been translated into 15 languages and is used by 43 countries. The *International Classification of Functioning* (ICF) is considered an adjunct to the ICD and divides functions into various areas, such as learning; activities of daily living; and community, civic life, and social activities. In this way, rather than emphasizing the disorder, the functions of the individual are considered. As would be imagined, the ICF presents greater difficulty in transcending cultural differences since functioning is culturally defined (Smart, 2005). The ICD-10-CM is considered to be more universal since biological conditions are not as influenced by culture and gender, as are functions. Not all countries accept the use of ICF (Raveloot & Seekins, 2012, p. 143).

The *Diagnostic and Statistical Manual of Mental Disorders-5* (DSM-5) is considered the world's standard diagnostic manual for mental disorders, in spite of the fact that it is developed and published by a national professional organization, the American Psychiatric Association. (Smart & Smart, 1997) There are 947 pages with 12 sections in the DSM, each describing various disorders, such as Neurodevelopmental Disorders, Schizophrenia Spectrum and Other Psychoses and Neurocognitive Disorders. To render a diagnosis, the practitioner must use the "diagnostic criteria," which are narrative descriptions of the symptoms. These criteria also include the duration and intensity of the symptoms and the number of "criteria" necessary for a disorder to be diagnosed; therefore, the diagnosis is only as good as the diagnostician. In order to describe the individual's symptoms as meeting these diagnostic criteria, the diagnostician must include descriptions of the client's symptoms, including duration and intensity, and the way in which these symptoms match the DSM diagnostic criteria. These diagnostic criteria provide a common language for psychologists, psychiatrists, counselors, schools, prisoners, and other agency providers.

A frequent criticism of the DSM is that it is pathology oriented rather than wellness oriented. Pathology orientation means that the diagnostician is looking *only* for a diagnosis and, being human, eventually finds pathology. However, one of the stated purposes of the DSM is to differentiate those with mental disorders from those without mental disorders. Often, a diagnosis of "no disorder" is rendered, but the diagnostician must provide documentation that all of the diagnostic criteria were considered and ruled out and, furthermore, list the various methods of decision making, such as clinical interview, history-taking, record review, collaboration from family and other service providers, and paper-and-pencil testing. When a "no disorder found" diagnosis is made, the diagnostician is stating that they have "looked everywhere the DSM suggested" and found no disorder. The DSM-5 lists ICD codes with each diagnosis, thus providing some coordination between the two systems. Physician/author Jerome Groopman explained the importance of diagnosis, including the *way* in which doctors explain diagnoses to patients.

> Language is as vital to the physician's art as the stethoscope or the scalpel. Of all the words the doctor uses, the name he gives the illness has the greatest weight. The name of the illness becomes part of the identity of the sufferer.
>
> (2000, p. 366)

All three systems serve three purposes: 1) provide standardized diagnoses, 2) assist in epidemiological studies, and 3) help with research by providing standardized definitions of diagnoses. All three of these purposes require a common language, making it possible to share and compare data. These last two purposes are included in the title of the DSM, meaning statistical causes. Epidemiological studies seek to estimate the prevalence (or number of) of disabilities in order to allocate resources for treatment. Such resources include determining the number of hospitals and treatment facilities needed and the provision of university training programs which will eventually result in more professionals. Therefore, it is important that each diagnostic category is defined in operationalized terms or diagnostic criteria. Imagine that we wanted to compare the rates of intellectual disability in Canada and in the United States. A common standardized definition of intellectual disability would be the starting point.

Research studies use the DSM and ICD to ensure that groups of participants are homogeneous. For example, imagine that we want to know if a certain medication is effective in treating depression. How would we define depression? We would state that each of the participants meets the diagnostic criteria for depression as defined by the DSM-5. Also, if other researchers wished to repeat our study, these researchers would be able to define the participants by using the diagnostic criteria of the DSM-5. In this way, future researchers build upon our research, using the same criteria for the participants and the same medication, adding another piece to the "body of research on depression."

A final note about both the ICD, ICF, and the DSM: All of them are serial enterprises, meaning that there are various editions, each edition reflecting the time in which it was developed. The ICD is in its 10th edition and the DSM is in its 5th edition. Task groups, comprised of practitioners and researchers in each of the various diagnostic sections, spend years of practice, study, deliberation, and debate to create each new edition. The fifth edition of the DSM, according to the American Psychiatric Association, is the most radical revision to date, taking 14 years to create, and it is comprised of the largest numbers of diagnoses to date. As expected, there has been more debate and disagreement with the DSM-5, simply because, as the APA stated, this edition includes the most radical (big) changes in contrast to all the earlier editions whose changes were incremental (small). While no standardized diagnostic manual is totally inclusive or free of error, these manuals are developed by experts, are expensive to compile, and they are, as stated, serial enterprises, meaning that when one edition is published, development on the next edition begins. When the APA stated that the DSM-5 is not "inclusive," it means that there are some valid diagnoses which are not included in the DSM-5 and when the APA stated that the DSM-5 is "atheoretical," it means that there is no information of possible causes included. There is a section at the front of the DSM-5, entitled, which describes the changes to the DSM-5.

Not all the disorders found in the DSM-5 are regarded as disabilities. For example, individuals with most behavioral addictions and personality disorders would not be deemed eligible for government services and benefits. Also, the DSM-5 makes clear that "unpleasant" does not equal "pathology," stating that many experiences are unpleasant, but in order to be considered a disorder, the symptoms must be of clinical concern, out of the ordinary, and substantially impair the individual's functioning.

Diagnosis and Self Concept

The diagnosis of a disability changes the individual's self-concept. Changing diagnoses from one edition to another is very rare, but such changes occasionally occur. In an article in the *Atlantic*, a popular magazine (Rosin, 2014), John Elder Robison was reported to have been diagnosed with Asperger's syndrome, but the 5th edition of the DSM eliminated this diagnosis (simply dropping the name "Asperger's" and including it as "high-functioning autism" on the ASD spectrum). The following is Robison's reaction:

> For John Elder Robison, the revision is an abrupt and unwelcome assault on an all-important identity. "Just like that, Asperger's was gone," he wrote in an essay on the *New York magazine's* Web site. "You can do things like that when you publish the rules. Like corrupt referees at a rigged college football team, the APA removed Asperger's from the field of play and banished the term to the locker room of psychiatric oblivion." Robison, who grew up feeling under siege in a deeply dysfunctional family in the 1960s, champions the label and the tribal protection it offers in a "neurotypical" world that he is sure will always stigmatize and misunderstand people like him—and his son.
>
> (Rosin, 2014, para. 1)

Elimination of a diagnostic label, such as Asperger's, is rare, but it does not illustrate that the diagnostic criteria for a condition did not change, only the way in which it is labeled and categorized. It appears that Robison feels mistreated by both the DSM-5 (who are like corrupt referees who cheat) and the "neurotypical" world that stigmatizes and misunderstands people like him, including his son. Robison's situation illustrates that changes in nomenclature can have serious effects for individuals. In Robison's case, the change in self-identity also includes his son.

Moreover, the type of measurement used to render the diagnosis also affects the individual. Two types of measurement are used in the DSM, categorical and dimensional. One of the most radical changes to the fifth edition was that a greater number of diagnoses were diagnosed on dimensions, continuums, or spectrum rather than as discrete categories. Many other disabilities listed in the ICD are measured categorically.

Categorical Measurement

- Diagnoses are qualitatively different.
- Assumes that all individuals diagnosed with the same disability have little variation in symptoms.
- Assumes that diagnoses are objective.
- Are more understandable to the general public.

Categorical measurement assumes that all individuals diagnosed with a disability have similar symptoms and attributes and the difference between categories is *qualitative*. Many physical disorders/disabilities (which are not included in the DSM-5), such as blindness and deafness, are listed as two types of categories because each is very different from the other. Categorical measurement is based on the ideas that mental disorders have little variation, populations are homogeneous, and that diagnoses are objective phenomena (Dailey, Gill, Karl, & Minton, 2014; Morrison, 2014a, 2014b). Generally, individuals with disabilities measured and defined as categories are less stigmatized. To the general public, categories appear familiar and understandable and, furthermore, most categorically measured disabilities have long histories.

Dimensional Measurement

- Assumes that diagnoses differ quantitatively.
- Individuals with diagnoses measured dimensionally often consider their disability ego-syntonic, which leads to more social support and higher self-esteem for those receiving these types of diagnoses. Individuals of the high end of spectrums often "celebrate" their disability.
- Appears more ambiguous to the general public and thus, elicits more prejudice and discrimination.
- Individuals diagnosed at the higher end of the spectrum often represent all individuals on the spectrum.
- Can lead to diagnostic inflation.

Dimensional measurement means that differences among difference diagnoses are *quantitative*. Different individuals have varying amounts of the same diagnosis. For ASD, one end of the spectrum is severe autism and the other end is high-functioning autism and symptoms fall at some point between these two ends. For other disabilities, one end of the spectrum is "normal" and the other end is "pathology." For most IWODs, individuals diagnosed at the higher end of the spectrum (when the higher end represents higher functioning) tend to represent the entire group. Dr. Temple Grandin often represents the entire spectrum of autism because she is high functioning, has achieved remarkable professional success, and is famous. By thinking that Dr. Grandin, and other high functioning individuals, represent the entire spectrum, those with low-functioning autism are often ignored for services and benefits. Typically, disabilities measured on dimensions appear more ambiguous to others. Interestingly, dimensionally measured disorders in the DSM are more ego-syntonic, meaning the individual does not find the symptoms foreign or alien. This seems to be true of those diagnosed on the ASD spectrum, often referring to themselves in positive terms and using the somewhat derisive term of "neurotypicals" for those not diagnosed with ASD. They refuse the "disabled role" of inferiority and deviance and often think of themselves not as "disabled or disordered" but only outnumbered. If a derisive, inferior term is used, it is applied to IWODs, such as "neurotypical." Silberman (2015) published a best-selling book entitled, *NeuroTribes: The Legacy of Autism and the Future of Neurodiversity*. For this book, Silberman interviewed individuals with ASD and their families and, at the end of the book, came to this conclusion:

> Not all the features of atypical human operating systems are bugs. By autistic standards, the "normal" brain is easily distracted, is obsessively social, and suffers from a deficit of attention to detail and routine. Thus people on the spectrum experience the neurotypical world as relentlessly unpredictable and chaotic, perpetually turned up too loud, and full of people who have little respect for personal space.
>
> (p. 471)

There are problems with both types of measurement, categorical and dimensional, but dimensional diagnoses present more problems. Categorical diagnoses assume that all individuals diagnosed with a specific disorder have similar symptoms. Dimensional diagnoses have the potential for diagnostic inflation since there are no definitive cut-off points. At what point do the symptoms indicate a disorder? When services and benefits are tied to a specific diagnosis, medical practitioners and psychologists may be tempted to diagnose an individual who does not actually reach the diagnostic threshold. The "cut-off" point or the diagnostic threshold often leads to diagnostic inflation, but, less often, it can misdiagnose individuals as not having the disorder when they actually do.

> **Diagnostic Inflation**
>
> Occurs when diagnostic criteria are lowered.
>
> Diagnostic inflation results in more individuals being diagnosed with a disability.
>
> Examples of diagnostic inflation include raising the IQ score at which intellectual disabilities are diagnosed or lowering the amount of blood sugar at which diabetes is diagnosed.
>
> The benefit of diagnostic inflation is that fewer disabilities are undiagnosed and untreated.

What's So Bad About Diagnostic Inflation? There are problems for the individual and for medical and government systems of service provision. Diagnostic inflation means that "normal" behavior is pathologized. There are some children who are annoying, some people who are weird or eccentric, and others who are scattered, disorganized, and forgetful. None of these people are easy to live with, but neither do they merit the diagnosis of pathology. Not all annoying children meet the criteria for ASD, not all eccentric people are schizophrenic and not all forgetful people qualify for a diagnosis of intellectual disability or dementia. When "normal" people receive a false diagnosis, their life opportunities may be reduced, and, moreover, their self-identity is needlessly changed. Diagnosticians may be pressured by parents and families to render a diagnosis, especially in the case of ASD, so that children whose symptoms do not quite meet the diagnostic cut-off point may receive services. Further, diagnostic inflation may divert attention from environmental and social causes and all treatment options focus on the individual.

> **Ways in Which the DSM-5 Has Lowered Diagnostic Thresholds**
>
> Reducing the length of duration for symptoms in order to render a diagnosis.
>
> Reducing the number of diagnostic criteria required in order to render a diagnosis.
>
> For Post-Traumatic Stress Disorder (PTSD) the diagnostic criteria has been changed to include individuals who have not personally experienced the trauma. Now, family members of individuals who have experienced the trauma can be diagnosed with PTSD.

Diagnostic inflation also increases epidemiological estimates, leading to large numbers and quantities of public resources allocated to a disability/disorder which, in reality, is not as big as thought. Harris Heller & Schindler (2012) described the increases in prevalence of mental disorders in the United States based on a previous edition of the DSM.

> Depression and other types of mental illness—like anxiety disorders, alcohol and drug dependence, and impulse control disorders—are more prevalent than previously thought and often result in disability (Kessler & Wang, 2008). The prevalence of mental disorders in the United States is high, with about half of the population meeting criteria.
> (as measured by the *Diagnostic and Statistical Manual of Mental Disorders* or DSM-IV)

We can see that there is a balance between under-diagnosis and over-diagnosis. In Chapter One, we learned about under-diagnosis. In the past, many learning disabilities and psychiatric disabilities were falsely thought to be moral and character failings rather than disabilities and this under-diagnosis led to a prejudice and stigma and lack of treatment. Society effectively "taught" individuals with these disabilities that they were, in fact, morally weak, lazy, or lacking intellectual abilities. In this chapter, we have learned about the risks of over-diagnosis. If diagnostic criteria were lowered and/or enlarged, the numbers of people diagnosed with disabilities would greatly expand. This over-diagnosis could lead to lifetimes of lowered expectations, unnecessary medication regimens, and a lifetime of unnecessary treatment. It is true that under-diagnosis results in more prejudice and discrimination and over-diagnosis would probably lead to less prejudice and discrimination.

Summary

In this chapter, we have presented a brief overview of the three broad categories of disabilities and followed this with a discussion of seven important aspects of experiencing a disability. Two other aspects of disabilities were considered, the incidence of disabilities (high or low) and the hierarchy of stigma directed toward individuals diagnosed with these various categories of disabilities.

The two most important large diagnostic and statistical manuals, the ICD-10 and the DSM-5, were briefly introduced. The measurement, description, and diagnosis of disabilities were reviewed, focusing on the differences between categorical measurement and dimensional measurement. Finally, the ways in which both under-diagnosis and over-diagnosis can result and the consequences of each were discussed.

The first sentence of this chapter stated that disability is a very complex and multifaceted experience and this chapter provides explanation of this complexity and a plethora of circumstances, values, and needs. The following matrix may assist in understanding disability. Choose one or two disabilities and answer each of the questions posed in the matrix that follows:

Characteristics of Disabilities

Disability:

(Broad category)
Physical, cognitive, or psychiatric?
Type of onset
Time of onset
Course
Functions impaired
Severity
Visibility
Hierarchy of stigma
High or low incidence?
Categorical or dimensional measurement?

References

Brew-Parrish, V. (2004, August 9). The wrong message still. *Ragged Edge Magazine.* Retrieved 02-24-2018 www.raggededgemagazine.com/focus/wrong message04html Retrieved 02-26-2018

Cohen, R. M. (2004). *Blindsided: Living a life above illness: A reluctant memoir.* New York, NY: Harper Collins.

Crewe, N. (1997). Life stories of people with long-term spinal cord injury. *Rehabilitation Counseling Bulletin, 41,* 377–391.

Covington, G. (1997). The Americans with Disabilities Act. In F. Pelka, (Ed.) (1997). *The ABC-CLIO companion to the disability rights movement.* Santa Barbara, CA: ABC-CLIO.

Dailey, S. F., Gill, C. S., Karl, S. L., & Minton, C. A. B. (2014). *DSM-5: Learning companion for counselors.* Alexandria, VA: American Counseling Association.

Groopman, J. (2000, November 13). Hurting all over. *New Yorker.*

Harris, S. P., Heller, T., & Schindler, A. (2012). Introduction, background, and history. In R. Heller & S. P. Harris, & G. L. Albrecht (Eds.), *Disability through the life course* (pp. 1–37). Thousand Oaks, CA: Sage.

Kessler, R. C., & Wang, P. S. (2008). The descriptive epidemiology of commonly occurring mental disorders in the United States. *Annual Review of Public Health, 29,* 115–129.

Morris, J. (1991). *Pride against prejudice: Transforming attitudes towards disability.* London: The Women's Press.

Morrison, J. (2014a). *Diagnosis made easier: Principles and techniques for mental health clinicians* (2nd ed.). New York, NY: Guilford.

Morrison, J. (2014b). *DSM-5 made easy: The clinician's guide to diagnosis.* New York, NY: Guilford.

Paris, J. (2015). *A concise guide to personality disorders.* Washington, DC: American Psychological Association.

Patterson, J. M. (1988). Chronic illness in children and the impact upon families. In C. S. Chilman, E. W. Nunnally, & F. M. Cox (Eds.), *Chronic illness and disability* (pp. 69–107). Thousand Oaks, CA: Sage Publications.

Pelka, F. (1997). *The ABC-CLIO companion to the disability rights movement.* Santa Barbara, CA: ABC-CLIO.

Raveloot, C., & Seekins, T. (2012). An emerging role for the rehabilitation psychologist in community rehabilitation service delivery. In P. Kennedy (Ed.), *The Oxford handbook of rehabilitation psychology* (pp. 143–159). New York, NY: Oxford University.

Rosin, H. (2014, March). Letting go of Asperger's. *The Atlantic.* Retrieved from www.the altantic.com/magazine/archive/2014/03/letting-go-of-asperger's/357563/

Sacks, O. (1985). *The man who mistook his wife for a hat and other clinical tales.* New York, NY: Simon and Schuster.

Sacks, O. (2010). *The mind's eye.* New York, NY: Knopf.

Silberman, S. (2015). *NeuroTribes: The legacy of autism and the future of neurodiversity.* New York, NY: Penguin Random House.

Smart, D. W., & Smart, J. F. (1997). DSM-IV and culturally sensitive diagnosis: Some observations for counselors. *Journal of Counseling and Development, 75,* 392–398.

Smart, J. F. (2005). The promise of the *International Classification of Functioning, Disability, and Health (ICF). Rehabilitation Education, 19,* 191–199.

Smart, J. F. (2012). *Disability across the developmental lifespan.* New York, NY: Springer.

Solomon, A. (2012). *Far from the tree: Parents, children, and the search for identity.* New York, NY: Scribner.

Stefan, S. (2001). *Unequal rights: Discrimination against people with mental disabilities and the Americans with Disabilities Act.* Washington, DC: American Psychological Association.

Toombs, S. K. (1995). Sufficient unto the day. In S. K. Toombs, D. Barnard, & R. A. Carson (Eds.), *Chronic illness from experience to policy* (pp. 2–23). Bloomington, IN: University of Indiana.

World Health Organization. (2001). *International classification of functioning, disability and health.* Geneva: Author.

Three

MODELS OF DISABILITY

Another Way to Describe Disability

We have learned a great deal about disability in the first two chapters of this book. Much of the information may be new to us, but it makes sense and is fairly easy to understand. Models of Disability are more difficult to understand, perhaps because they are abstractions, human-made abstractions. Disability scholars (Rath & Elliott, 2012) explained the purpose of models: "Models are organizing tools that can help understand, explain, and predict related phenomenon" (p. 32). Why describe any human experience, including disability, using abstractions? It may appear that a long, detailed explanation of the various models creates unnecessary complexity and minutia. However, throughout this chapter, the words, "unspoken notions," and "unchallenged beliefs," often describe the basis for much of the societal response to disability and IWDs. Therefore, it is essential to dig deep to show that unquestioned, unchallenged, and unspoken beliefs are neither realistic nor true.

To understand these models, some basic understandings are necessary. First, these abstractions, Models of Disability, determine the daily lives of IWDs. Moreover, in times past, these abstractions determined *if* IWDs lived. Therefore, these abstractions are not harmless. Second, everyone subscribes to one or more of these models but, most of the time, the general public are not aware that there is more than one model to describe the disability experience. Without realizing, most of us think of disability in terms of the Biomedical Model, without understanding that there are other models. All models of disability are products of the historical period in which they were constructed, reflecting wider cultural and political values. Finally, understanding and acknowledging that these models are human-made constructions allows options for deconstructing some aspects of the various models. Nonetheless, all of these models, with the exception of the Moral/Religious Model, are necessary and valuable in describing the lives of IWDs.

> **Ten Functions of Models of Disability (Smart, 2016)**
>
> 1. To provide definitions of disability
> 2. To identify the location of the "problem"
> 3. To determine causal attribution
> 4. To determine responsibility attribution
> 5. To determine the needs of IWDs
> 6. To determine the professional(s) who serve IWDs
> 7. To determine which academic disciplines study the disability experience
> 8. To serve as a "starting point" for government laws, policies, and regulations
> 9. To serve as a starting point for research on disability and the development of theories and psychometric instruments
> 10. To determine the cultural interpreters of the disability experience. Who tells the story of disability—professional service providers or the individuals who experience disability? (Smart, 2016, pp. 50–51)

Each model serves these ten functions; but regardless of common functions, all models have important differences, differences that affect the lives of IWDs. The Models of Disability are:

- Moral/Religious Model
- Biomedical Model
- Environmental Model
- Social Model
- Functional Model
- Economic Model
- Civil Rights Model

We shall discuss each of these models and, by considering each, a more complete picture of the way disability is experienced and perceived, for both IWDs and IWODs, may be obtained. For counselors, gaining a complete understanding of disability and the client's perception of their disability, is foundational to establishing rapport and to developing a therapeutic relationship. Seven considerations merit discussion: 1) Each of these models is incomplete, leaving some questions unanswered, rendering each model "reductionist," and "simplistic"; nonetheless each model merits full consideration on its own. For example, some authors propose a "bio-social-functional" model, merging three dissimilar models (biomedical, social, and functional) into a single model, which may lead to important aspects being ignore or deemphasized. Typically, the major focus on these concatenated models has remained on the Biomedical Model with less attention on the other models listed. 2) During an IWD's experience, some models take precedence; for example, during medical stabilization or at times of relapse, the Biomedical Model is the most important. At most other times, the Civil Rights Model may take precedence. 3) These models are not "competing," but rather are complementary; each has something to contribute to the lives of IWDs and to the counseling relationship. 4) Related to number 3, the use of these models is a very practical guide to case management among various types of practitioners. 5) Some components of various models overlap; for example, the functioning of IWDs is included in three models. 6) Each model has advantages and disadvantages. 7) All models are subject to change, since models are human-made abstractions, influenced by both history and values. Nonetheless, most of these changes are small, incremental changes, rather than large, comprehensive changes and, occasionally, vestiges of outmoded models may be found in other models. Whenever a human experience is both multifaceted and complex, the services of experts in many different professions are necessary.

In clinical and service provision terms, these various models can facilitate case management practices among various types of professionals. In academic terms, these models can facilitate an interdisciplinary approach to studying the experience of disability and the individuals who have disabilities.

We shall discuss each of these models, starting with the two models with the longest history.

The Moral/Religious Model, or Biology Is Morality

The Moral/Religious Model of Disability

- Disability is defined as the result of sin and immorality. The IWD has *chosen* to violate religious laws and, therefore, *deserves* prejudice, discrimination, shame, enforced isolation.
- Disability is located within the individual.

- The individual, or his family or ancestors, caused the disability, rendering disability shameful.
- The responsibility for dealing with the disability lies with the individual, or their family.
- The needs of the IWD are spiritual and religious, such as prayer and repentance.
- The professionals/authorities with the power of definition and who "serve" IWDs are religious/spiritual leaders.
- Religious/spiritual leaders "tell the disability story" to the general public.

The Moral/Religious Model of disability has the longest history of all the models, having been in force for thousands of years. Most religious systems, in the past, considered disability to be the result of sin or evil and, because of this causal attribution, disability was considered a divine punishment from God. IWDs were often shunned or avoided because they were thought to be dangerous, frightening, unclean, considered to be contagious and sinister. Disability was stigmatized because an act of God is fearsome. On the other hand, IWDs were sometimes publicly displayed as morality lessons, showing the results of wickedness. Those with psychiatric disabilities or seizure disorders were often thought to be the embodiment of the devil, rendering these IWDs as very frightening. Conversely, IWODs were considered morally superior while IWDs were viewed as wicked and unclean. This idea that IWODs would never choose to break religious laws also helped to quell the fear that anyone, at any time, could acquire a disability. In this model, disability was often thought to be morally contagious (or, at minimum, unclean) and IWDs were hidden and segregated. If God conferred disability upon evil individuals, then it seemed reasonable to believe that IWDs, and their families, deserved their shame and stigma. Biology became associated with morality.

Much of the shame and stigma surrounding disabilities, especially psychiatric disabilities, is due to the enduring effects of the Moral/Religious Model. Invoking deity and scripture, aided by the unquestioned authority of religious leaders, taught IWDs to be ashamed of their disabilities. Indeed, shame was considered part of the repentance process. Adding to the strength and persistence of this model was the lack of any other model to explain disability. A schoolgirl, a survivor of the American polio epidemics of the 1940s, stated: "being in a wheelchair carried a fair amount of shame" and, after her parents took her to a local concert, one of their neighbors reprimanded them for "taking a child like that out in public" (Wilson, 1990, pp. 178–179). One of strongest vestiges of the Moral/Religious Model are stigma and shame accorded to IWDs. Further, most of the people who hold these stigmatizing beliefs do not consider themselves as prejudiced and discriminating because they consider it clearly self-evident that it is the disability that causes prejudice and discrimination. Ironically, people who are not prejudiced against racial and ethnic groups, women, or those of differing sexual orientations, often do not view themselves as prejudiced and discriminating against IWDs.

As with all models, the *perceived* cause of the disability determines both the "treatment" and the group of professionals who defines disability, who determines which individuals had disabilities, and were tasked with serving IWDs. If the causes of disability are thought to be spiritual sin, then prayer and repentance are the prescribed treatments and spiritual leaders, such as shamans, priests, and ministers, direct this "treatment." These spiritual leaders were endowed with their authority over disability by their societies, and thus, became the cultural interpreters of disability, providing their societies with explanations for disability. In the Moral/Religious Model IWDs did not have the power of self-definition.

At this point in history, most of us would consider the Moral/Religious Model laughable and not of merit for consideration, other than as an historical artifact. However, many vestiges of the Moral/Religious Model remain in the way society views and treats IWDs and can be found today (Braddock & Parrish, 2003). Much of the "great" literature, including fairy tales, portrayed villains and "unfortunates" as IWDs, thus conflating disability with morality. Shakespeare's Richard III, Melville's Captain Ahab, and J. M. Barrie's Captain Hook all experienced visible disabilities and communicated to the audience that their disability was somehow related to their "warped souls." Fairy tales with characters such as Rumpelstiltskin, the Wicked Witch, and many others in the stories of the Brothers Grimm taught children that IWDs were wicked, frightening, dangerous, weak, and tortured people. In more modern times, Disney created animated films of these wicked characters who also had a visible disability.

Charles Dickens inverted the idea that disability is a manifestation of immorality in that most of his characters with disabilities were portrayed as impossibly kind, good, and virtuous. Remember Tiny Tim in *The Christmas Carol* who wished everyone well and acted as a foil to Mr. Scrooge, who did not have a disability and was mean and miserly? Dickens used IWDs as morality lessons. He wrote 16 major literary works, 14 of which featured at least one IWD (Byrd & Elliott, 1988). Print media have been transformed into visual, electronic media, thus exponentially increasing the audience for the idea that disability is related to morality, most often in a negative way. Therefore, the

Moral/Religious Model of disability is constantly reinforced albeit unrecognized by most. Moral failing (or the false perception of it) can bring stigma, isolation, punishment, abuse, and even death. Today, the media are changing, portraying IWDs as normal people with jobs, families, and personalities unrelated to the disability.

Another vestige of the Moral/Religious Model is the widespread idea that charity is both an ethical and constructive way to help IWDs. In many religious systems, IWDs were beggars and IWODs were directed to give to these unfortunate IWDs. In this model, it was very clear who the moral person was—the generous, magnanimous giver. However, it is known that the giver, although they may act from the highest intentions, produces prejudice and discrimination against PWDs. Pity is prejudice and discrimination and comes from a position of superiority and reduces the range of choices open to the beneficiary. The recipient, the IWD, is put on public display to elicit pity and charity. The benefactor can feel good about giving. Today's charity telethons are an outgrowth of the Moral/Religious Model. Many IWDs report being given money by strangers on the street. The National Public Radio Disability History series (1998a) featured a man who uses a wheelchair:

> I was in Kansas City, doing Christmas shopping. This old man came up to me and looked at me and said, "Do you need money for Christmas?" I'm a lawyer and I'm working for the government EPA (Environmental Protection Agency). Nearly every adult with a disability that I knew had a story about being given unsolicited money as donations.

Another little boy with a visible disability showed his mother the dollar bills that strangers in the mall had given him—out of sight of his mother. The little boy thought it was wonderful to receive free money and could not understand why his mother told him he was never to accept money from strangers simply because they felt sorry for him. The little boy learned to hide the money from his mother. It was years before the grown man understood what his mother was trying to communicate. Instead of pity, most IWDs desire government-guaranteed civil rights and access to opportunity structures, such as educational opportunities and the workplace. Charity is a type of prejudice and discrimination and any type of charity diverts society's attention from the real problems that IWDS encounter. It is safe to say that charity comes at a very high price, both economically and emotionally. Charity is economically expensive because it has allowed society to think that private charity, instead of public government funding, is the solution to disability. Many in the disability rights movement (Fleischer & Zames, 2001, 2009) believe that many IWODs would prefer to write a check to charity, rather than hire an IWD, admit an IWD to an educational institution, or allow their children to date and marry IWDs. In addition, charity, although well-intentioned, has resulted in limited opportunities for IWDs. Further, and more important, it is fair to ask, what do charity telethons communicate to children with the same disabilities? Telethons and other types of charity may be communicating that IWDs are inferior and require pity to survive.

With today's scientific knowledge and humanistic views, it is difficult to understand how the Moral/Religious Model could have been believed and enforced by almost everyone, for thousands of years. Nonetheless, society believed in this model, just as we accept the DSM and the ICD as valid systems of definition and classification.

Many IWDs find meaning, strength, and support in their personal religious/ spiritual orientations and this positive response and adaptation has very little to do with the Moral/Religious Model of Disability. Rather than viewing their disability as a *punishment* from God, IWDs consider their disability to be a *gift* from God. For these IWDs, their spirituality and beliefs allows them to confer meaning on the experience of disability.

The Biomedical Model of Disability: Biology Is Identity

The Biomedical Model of Disability

- Disability is defined as biological, mental, and emotional pathology.
- The location of disability is totally within the individual.
- Most of the time, the IWD is not held personally responsible for the cause of the disability.
- IWDs are responsible for their own rehabilitation and should not make demands on society.
- Physicians have the power of definition and are the professionals who treat IWDs.
- Physicians determine the needs of IWDs.
- Medical education is the primary academic discipline which studies the disability experience.
- Government services or laws are not necessary for IWDs since physicians attend to all the needs of IWDs.
- Psychometric instruments are developed from the premise that disability is individual pathology and deviance.
- Physicians tell the stories of IWDs to society, often using IWDs as case studies.

The Biomedical Model of Disability supplanted the Moral/Religious Model and, while we will pose and list criticisms of this model, the Biomedical Model was an advance for IWDs; but, nonetheless, both models maintain the individual should not take pride in their disability. In both the Moral/Religious and Biomedical Models, disability is shameful, individual pathology and deviance, and the best response is to try hard to find a cure, hide or minimize the disability, or to self-isolate. These three responses were thought to be well-deserved. Disability scholars have summarized the relationship between these two models, showing that there are some remnants of the Moral/Religious Model in the Biomedical Model.

> The roots of understanding bodily and cognitive differences within our Western Judeo-Christian society are biblical texts and religious traditions (2001). During the period of the Enlightenment, these religious values were challenged by a surge of interest in reason and rationality, which in turn, caused medical and scientific knowledge to dominate our understanding of disability. Both of these historical traditions continue to profoundly influence our current understanding of disability within Western societies. These shifts in worldview have been and remain incomplete, with remnants of each combining with a more recent worldview of rights-based understanding of disability.
>
> (Harris, Heller, & Schindler, 2012, p. 13)

Physicians became the professional authorities of disability, both documenting the presence of a disability defining IWDs, and their lives. Physicians also became the "cultural interpreters" of disability, telling the story of disability to the public. In the Biomedical Model, at its most extreme, no other characteristic of the IWD merits attention. Therefore, individuals with the same type of disability are considered interchangeable. Using clear-cut, standardized, and objective diagnostic procedures (especially with physical disabilities, less so with psychiatric disabilities) the Biomedical Model makes a great deal of sense to the general public. The *International Classification of Disease* (ICD) and the *Diagnostic and Statistical Manual of Mental Disorders* (DSM) replaced scripture and holy texts in defining prognosis and treatment following diagnosis. Physicians become increasingly specialized and highly trained. Today, diagnosis and treatment require high levels of training and skill. Many IWDs have felt that they were not allowed a voice or choices in their treatment, feeling that to receive services, they had to submit to the power and authority of doctors. This situation parallels the authority-in-charge of the Moral/Religious Model, but with medical professionals replacing religious authorities. Some in the disability rights community assert that the paternalism of religious and medical professionals has contributed to the infantilization and lack of boundaries experienced by IWDs throughout society.

To their credit, the medical and scientific communities saved and prolonged lives, leading to the societal advance of the largest numbers of IWDs ever experienced. The profession developed rapidly, creating enormous changes within a single generation. However, until recently, medical practice focused on acute care with a clear two-outcome paradigm—total cure or death. Sensory loss (blindness and deafness) and psychiatric disabilities were the only exceptions to the "cure or death" choice. It took some time for medicine and science to advance to long-term care of lifelong disabilities and chronic illnesses. The widespread introduction of antibiotics, such as penicillin, cured many bacterial diseases; new vaccines conquered polio, diphtheria, rubella, and measles. Surgeons transplanted organs, performed open heart surgery, and removed cancerous tumors. An American surgeon/physician/author Atul Gawande, summarized, "A single generation experienced a transformation in the treatment of human illness as no generation had before. It was like discovering that water could put out fire. . . . Doctors became saviors" (2017, p. 39). Gawande is stating that medicine changed in a very short period of time ("one generation") and the change was both radical and valuable ("like discovering that water could put out fire").

Gawande continued describing the Biomedical Model (including the practice of medicine) using the analogy of fire.

> But the model (acute care) wasn't quite right. If an illness (or disability) is a fire, many of them (fires) require months or years to extinguish, or can be reduced only to low-level smolder. The treatments may have side effects and complications that require yet more attention. Chronic illness (and disability) has become commonplace, and we have been poorly prepared to deal with it. Much of what ails us requires a more patient kind of skill.
> (p. 39)

Gawande concluded the article by stating: "We can give up an antiquated set of priorities and shift our focus from rescue medicine to lifelong incremental care" (2017, p. 45).

The polio epidemics, which affected North America, Europe, and the British Commonwealth nations, provide an illustration of these changes. Unlike other disease epidemics, such as typhus or diphtheria, in which individuals either died or were completely cured, polio left some patients with lifelong orthopedic impairments, most often affecting the lower limbs. For most individuals, the polio virus did not invade the spinal cord and, therefore, they recovered with no residual effects, and in a small percentage the virus reached the spinal cord and brain stem causing their deaths. Epidemics occurred in developed nations because, with the advent of public sanitation, large populations were left without a natural immunity to polio. Physicians could do nothing to stop the epidemics nor were they able to predict the course of the disease in patients. Scientists did not know how polio spread; they simply knew that it was highly contagious. Nor did scientists or physicians understand why, in some individuals the polio virus did not invade the spinal column, but rather, was simply excreted from the body. In 1955, the polio vaccine became widely available, polio was eradicated, and polio and polio survivors were forgotten. Wilson (1990), a polio survivor who collected first-person accounts of surviving polio, summarized:

> While physicians, surgeons, physical therapists, and nurses focused on rehabilitating the body, the polio survivors of whatever age were largely left to deal with significant emotional and psychological responses to physical crippling and extended rehabilitation hospitalization. The cost was tremendous.
>
> (p. 67)

Gawande discussed the medical solution to medicine's remarkable advances. "Medicine has been slow to confront very changes that it has been responsible for—or to apply the knowledge we have" (2017, p. 36). Gawande used the term, "incremental care," to describe long-term care for lifelong disabilities. Disabilities often include secondary conditions and complications, and other disabilities require numerous surgeries and treatments throughout the lifespan. A simple cold or urinary tract infection for some IWDs requires immediate hospitalization to save their lives. The medical care and management of disabilities will improve with medicine's "shift from rescue medicine to lifelong incremental care" and physicians are becoming more skilled in providing incremental (and lifesaving) care to IWDs. In Graf's (Graf et al., 2009) study, the authors concluded: "Only one participant (of 78) noted the quality of initial care following injury as good but they also noted poor follow-up care" (p. 31).

Health insurance practices, policies, and payment have been closely related to the medical professions, including the now-outdated attitudes of the acute-care paradigm of total cure or, at minimum, returning the individual to the highest possible functioning. The idea of incremental care, as used by Gawande (2017), or of medical long-term care of chronic disabilities, is only now becoming a standard of care. Health insurance must update and upgrade their payment reimbursements to include chronic, long-term care. Bickenbach (1993) explained:

> To some extent, this medical bias goes back to the original social predilection to look at medicine as an acute intervention that takes a fully functioning person with a short-term, acute problem and repairs that person so he or she can resume functioning. Insurance payments for health care have always tended to be keyed to rehabilitative potential with the assumption that treatment should be withdrawn when progress toward full recovery stops.
>
> (p. 89)

Health insurance policies, medical care, and long-term care of IWDs are becoming more interrelated and, it seems reasonable to suppose that as medicine changes and improves, health insurance policies will also change and improve, paying for long-term services after medical stabilization has been reached. For example, health insurance policies might pay for marriage and family counseling when an individual in the family acquires a disability or is born with a disability. Counseling and social work services will be reimbursable within the advanced type of incremental care. To cite a single example of marriage and family counseling services: If such services could be provided (with an informed view of the disability) and paid with insurance funds, a great deal of personal stress will be ameliorated and will also contribute to lower divorce rates and other types of family break-ups. This approach does not hold that the acquisition of a disability *causes* divorce; rather, that the lack of counseling and social work services *contributes* to divorce.

The contributions of medicine cannot be understated, but there are deficiencies in the Biomedical Model (as there are in all models). First, although medicine is changing to a focus on wellness, most medical diagnosis is focused on deficit, pathology, and defect. A Canadian disability scholar, Bickenbach, summarized this focus on deficit:

> The most commonly held belief about [this model of] disablement is that it involves a defect, deficiency, dysfunction, abnormality, failing or medical "problem" that is located within the individual. We think it is so obvious to be beyond serious dispute that disablement is a characteristic of a *defective person*, someone who is functionally limited or anatomically abnormal, diseased, or pathoanatomical, someone who is neither whole nor healthy, fit nor flourishing, someone who is biologically inferior or subnormal. The

essence of disablement, in this view, is that there are things *wrong* with people with disabilities.

(1993, p. 61)

Physicians understand that a diagnosis describes only a condition and not the individual, nor are diagnoses moral failings. Typically, holding the individual responsible for the disability because of moral failings confers some type of judgment. However, often society views disabilities, and the individuals who experience disabilities, as socially inferior, because they are thought to be physically or cognitively or mentally or emotionally inferior. Reflecting on this this last statement, it seems an incomprehensible leap to associate physical attributes with moral and social worth. Nonetheless, the social inferiority of IWDs is widely accepted and rarely questioned.

Consequently, IWDs, regardless of their characteristics and resources, become aware that they are part of a devalued group. Often, IWDs are made to feel unwelcome in their communities or welcome only on certain conditions. The Biomedical Model typically has not focused on the psychosocial factors in the treatment of their patients. This narrow focus is termed "medical reductionism," and it is society at large which has given medicine such power. The answer to this narrow focus is the concept of *case management*, allowing a wide array of professionals to serve IWDs. Wilson's excerpt underscores the total lack of psychological and emotional support for polio survivors, focusing only on the contribution of physicians, physical therapists, and nurses. Rather than considering only the work of medical professionals (medical reductionism), the role of social workers, and counselors who provide counseling and family support, and could have collaborated with doctors, were left out. Ultimately, society at large bears responsibility for placing too much responsibility on one profession, medicine. In both the Moral/Religious and Biomedical Models, one authority (priest or physician) served IWDs; however, it is society who endowed both spiritual and medical professions with such power and it is society who also maintained and prolonged this power structure. Today, medical practice involves more information sharing and patient involvement in decision making, often termed "informed choice."

This deficit orientation of disability also places the location of the "problem" of disability within the individual, requiring the IWD to deal with the disability privately, not making any demands on society. Placing the problem—and the solution—solely within the individual absolves society of any responsibility to accommodate IWDs, and physical, mental, or emotional inferiority often translates into civic inferiority. Society may like to think that every individual is equal; but we often believe that some lives are worthy of investment and others, such as the lives of IWDs, are not worthy of civil rights and societal resources. IWDs were often told, "The world isn't going to change for you." The reasoning was often, "It's bad luck you have a disability, but it's *your* bad luck." Historically, this statement appeared both reasonable and moral. Taken to an extreme, however, it could lead to the IWD's death.

Critics of the Biomedical Model have claimed that medicine reduced individuals to their disabilities, ignoring or, at minimum, devaluing other attributes. If only this aspect of the individual is acknowledged and if that single aspect is interpreted as pathology and deficit, it may be said that the individual becomes the disability. The IWD is the disability and nothing more. Biological inferiority then automatically translates to social inferiority. Such a conflation of a seemingly negative, pathological attribute with an individual's entire identity is at the root of many bioethical issues. It follows that, whether in the womb or in old-age, the individual's talents, resources, environment, or civil rights are ignored because the disability becomes the paramount, and sole, definition. Therefore, the automatic abortion of fetuses with disabilities, infanticide, allowing newborns with multiple and severe disabilities to die, and automatic assisted suicide for IWDs (without the safeguards that are in place for IWODs) might appear to be sensible, humane, and ethical. The disability rights community has a strong and derisive term for these automatic solutions to disability, "Cure 'em or Kill 'em!"

Health insurance policies and practices have been closely allied to medicine, and as we learned, as the medical profession advocates for more long-term, incremental care for patients, health insurance payments will fund these types of care. Current trends indicate that long-term care will be recognized to be economically feasible, important for insurance businesses; as well as ethical, humane, and will become professionally satisfying for physicians. Insurance reimbursement systems will also include a broader range of professionals, including social workers and the counselors, recognizing that adding these services will reduce medical care costs. The concept of incremental care may be applied to counseling IWDs. For example, for individuals with all disabilities, including those with stable courses, it is essential to complete developmental tasks throughout their lifetimes. The different types of developmental milestones and the resulting changes in self-identity interact with the disability. Disabilities with episodic or degenerating courses typically make greater demands upon the individual's self-identity. A man with degenerating vision loss explained:

> As my disability becomes worse, I am becoming less and less at home in the world. The world is the world of the normal. The world of the normal is the background against which disability stands out.
>
> (Michalko, 2002, p. 38)

Counseling provided at each major development stage might be considered a type of "incrementalism." Nonetheless, none of the developmental theorists have included IWDs in their theories (Smart, 2012).

One of the purposes of models of disability is to serve as a starting point or provide the underlying assumptions of laws and policies. As we have learned, the specialties of medicine have experienced exponential leaps in a very short period of time in the ability to treat disability. Moreover, new medical specializations have been developed. We have also learned that the Biomedical Model of Disability conceptualized disability as pathology and deviance for which the IWD was solely responsible, both for the cause and the solution. The American federal programs of Social Security Disability Insurance (SSDI) and the Supplemental Security Income (SSI) were enacted during the Great Depression, in 1935, before the great scientific and medical advances Gawande has discussed, when the Biomedical Model was the only model of disability available. Social Security Disability Insurance (SSDI) provided subsistence payments to Americans with documented disabilities, predicated on the idea that they could not financially support themselves by employment in the competitive workplace. Since 1935, antibiotics, psychotropic medications, computerized and individualized assistive technology, the increasing lifespans of IWDs and a host of other advances have been developed, rendering the Social Security Disability Insurance (SSDI) outdated (Batavia & Schriner, 2001). Both the societal and financial foundations for SSDI are largely outdated. The words to describe the advances in medicine are "radical" and "exponential" while the words typically used to describe change in federal legislation is "incremental."

It is important to clearly delineate the boundaries and limitations of the professions who work within each of these models. Obviously, it is absurd to imagine that a single profession can or should serve all the needs of all IWDs. Medicine is no exception. Who has placed these great responsibilities in the hands of physicians? We have, or society has. The profession of medicine simply follows the mandates of the broader society. For example, abortion, life-saving techniques, and assisted suicides are all medical and scientific *procedures*. The decisions that drive these procedures have originated in the general society. More difficult to understand is the concept that governments can, and have, legislated normalcy. Physicians render diagnoses of disabilities, but it is society, including governments, that define abnormality. The murder of 200,000 Germans with disabilities by the Nazis before the start of the World War II and the practice of eugenics and forced sterilization of IWDs in the United States are reminders that normalcy/abnormalcy or disability/no disability has been defined, legislated, and enforced by governments in seemingly advanced nations (Friedlander, 1995).

Interactional Models of Disability

Describing Interactional Models of Disability

- These models take the emphasis off cure and the rehabilitation of the IWD.
- Interactional models posit that disability is a collective concern.
- Interactional models have the power to change the experience of disability in relation to other factors.
- Interactional models have a greater flexibility to change.
- Interactional models allow IWDs to define themselves.
- Interactional models acknowledge and respond to other identities of the IWD, such as gender, racial/ethnic identity or LBGTQ identities.
- Interactional models more closely represent the daily, lived-life of IWDs.
- Interactional models "normalize" IWDs because their motivations and life tasks are viewed as natural and ordinary.
- Interactional models are more complex and, because of this, no single profession is tasked with serving IWDs. Case management, of a wide range of professions, is an important component of interactional models.
- Interactional models task a large number of professionals to serve IWDs, thus reducing paternalism and authoritarianism.
- Disability and IWDs are more likely to be integrated rather than marginalized
- Interactional models allow IWDs to describe and interpret the disability experience to the public.

The Moral/Religious and Biomedical Models of Disability are considered to be non-interactional since both the "problem" and "solution" are considered the responsibility of the IWD or their family. A teenaged polio survivor's father told him, "The world is not going to change for you" (Mee, 1999). Mee's father was trying to help him by warning him not to expect too much and it would be his own responsibility to negotiate the world.

Mee's father based his opinion of his teenaged son's future on the Biomedical Model, rather than an interactional model which would have assumed that the world *should* and *would* change for Mee, and the tens of thousands of polio survivors with disabilities. Interactional models view disability as a collective responsibility, an idea which has historically been met with unease and skepticism. A disability scholar (Michalko, 2002) explained this reluctance:

> The idea that disability is a collective issue, however, is not easy to grasp. It seems to run counter to the traditional Western social political philosophies, influenced by the Enlightenment, that place tremendous importance on the individual. Combine this emphasis with belief in the superiority of reason and mind over the passions and vicissitudes of the body, also a legacy of the Enlightenment, and we can begin to understand why disability has long been conceived of only as an individual issue.
>
> (Michalko, 2002, p. 6)

The Canadian disability scholar, Bickenbach (1993) succinctly stated the collective responsibility for the solution to disability when he quoted the Canadian Bill of Human Rights: "All Canadians are responsible for the necessary changes which will give disabled persons the same choices of participation that are enjoyed by those who are not disabled."

One of the basic premises of the interactional models is that while disability is inevitable, the limiting, discriminating, and prejudicial societal responses are not inevitable nor immutable. It may make us uneasy or uncomfortable when reading the quotations of IWDs who state that it is society who has *chosen* to erect, enact, and maintain these prejudicial responses.

The remaining models of disability to be discussed, the Environmental, the Functional, and the Civil Rights Models, have the potential to be more powerful than non-interactional models. None of these models "compete" with each other; each of the six current models (Biomedical, Functional, Economic,

Social, Environmental, and Civil Rights) all have a role to play in providing a full array of services.

Interactional models define disability in a more complete manner, in relation to other factors and, therefore, it is not possible to define an individual's disability without understanding all the factors working together in mutual interaction with each other. As these factors change, the disability changes, for better or worse. In the Functional Model, functions are related to disability; in the Environmental Model, environments are related to disability; and in the Civil Rights Model, societal attitudes and government-conferred civil rights change the experience of disability. It can be seen that these related factors are imposed upon the individual or their disability.

While the definitions of disabilities and their treatments are far more elastic and changing in the interactional models, there have been changes in the definition and treatment of disabilities in the non-interactional Biomedical Model. For example, each of the editions of the *Diagnostic and Statistical Manual of Mental Disorders* has included more types of disabilities than the previous edition.

Interactional models include both macro and micro factors. Micro factors, unique to the individual, such as idiosyncratic and specific cultural definitions of role functioning; while macro factors of functioning include the worldwide labor market and the economic climate. The power of these interactional models creates a good deal of complexity while the non-interactional models are much simpler and, therefore, easier to understand.

The long history of the non-interactional models (the Moral/Religious in the past and currently the Biomedical Model), combined with their monolithic nature has led to their unchallenged position in society. Perhaps some of the resistance to these newer models also lies in the complexity and limitless array of possible solutions to disability. Not only are the non-interactional models simple to understand, these models allow "society" to forfeit responsibility for both the cause and the solution to disability, surrendering these responsibilities to expert authorities, such as religious leaders or physicians. Assigning only one profession to "serve" IWDs (spiritual leaders in the Moral/Religious Model and physicians in the Biomedical Model), paternalism often results. After all, both spiritual leaders and physicians are designated by society as authoritarian experts. In the interactional models, the disability experience encompasses a strong social dimension, placing some of the responsibility upon society for both the cause and solution for disability.

Most research on disability has been based on the Biomedical Model, including the definitions, diagnoses, and proposed solution to disability. Research requires precise, operationalized definitions of variables and control over the variables in order to establish that A causes B. Therefore, non-interactional models are the basis of much of the research completed on disability. Stated differently, variables and hypotheses, based on the Biomedical Model, are easier to control. This is not to state that research based on the Biomedical Model is unnecessary. Rather, in addition to Biomedical Model research, research based on the other models should also be undertaken. Moreover, new statistical methods, often termed "multivariate statistics" allow investigation of many different variables simultaneously, variables which could be defined by models of disability, *in addition to* biomedical variables. For example, a study of a new medical treatment or drug could also include the environment, functions, and employment of subjects.

Survey questions that ask, "If there were a surgery or a magic pill available to completely cure your disability, would you take it?" are insulting to many IWDs and reflects the (extreme form) of the Biomedical Model in which disability is to be prevented or cured.

The Functional Model of Disability: Functions Define Disability

The Functional Model of Disability
- Disability is defined as impairment in functioning.
- The location of disability is within the individual's functions.
- IWDs determine which functions are important to them.
- The cause of the disability is the lack of accommodations and assistive/adaptive technology (AT).
- The responsibility for "treating" the disability includes society (to remove barriers and fund AT).
- The needs of the IWD are removal of barriers and provision of AT.
- IWODs appear to not have functional needs or accommodating physical environment, simply because the world has been designed to meet these needs.
- Today, AT is used to increase and substitute for "normal" abilities.
- In the future, the AT used by IWDs may surpass the abilities of IWODs.
- Some of the professionals who serve IWDs are city planners, engineers, and architects.
- The academic disciplines of urban planning, engineering, and architects would include disability issues.

In the Functional Model, the individual's functions influence the definition of the disability. We saw an idiosyncratic (meaning specific to the individual) example of this in Chapter Two when we learned about the UK Member of Parliament, Jenny Morris, who uses a wheelchair because of her lower limb paralysis sustained in an accident. Morris (1991) summarized: "Most of my life (before the accident) involved sitting down. So, using the wheelchair was not that difficult" (p. 3). Chapter Two defined functions in the individual, or the environment with which individuals are most directly involved, such as home, family, school, and friends. Idiosyncratically defined functions also include the individual's values and previous experience.

In the Functional Model, it is the *idiosyncratic* functioning of the IWD, considering both needs and values, that drives the need for *customized* assistive/adaptive technology (AT). The rapid development and advances of AT have mirrored both the speed and extent of the improvements in medicine.

Until the invention of the computer, the design and use

> for IWDs changed little for hundreds of years. Before computers, these devices were simple mechanical equipment that were most often homemade. These included prosthetic devices such as (plastic and wooden) artificial arms or legs, orthotic (straightening) devices such as braces, and mechanical wheelchairs without power (Weisgerber, 1991). Now, most assistive technology is either computerized or electromechanical.
>
> (Smart, 2016, p. 334)

Today, some assistive technology allows IWDs to become "supernormal." Hugh Herr, the head of biomechanics at the Massachusetts Institute of Technology, lost both legs at age 17 due to a mountain climbing accident. With his double prostheses, Herr participates in mountain climbing competitions; however, the other climbers want him disqualified, stating that Herr's prostheses give him an unfair advantage. In the book entitled *Design Meets Disability* (Pullin, 2009), Herr's prostheses are described. Note that before the fitting of the prostheses, Herr "came to terms with his disability."

> As he came to terms with his disability, his prostheses became an important part of his self-image. But he still thought of himself as a climber, not an amputee. He fashioned himself climbing prostheses that gave him a foothold, and telescopic legs that could be extended during a climb to any length, shorter or longer than his original legs—even each leg a different

length. Then he witnessed the reaction of his fellow climbers turn from pity to calls for him to be disqualified from competitive free climbing for having an unfair advantage.

(p. 33)

Obviously, following his accident and amputations, Herr continued to think of himself in terms of his functioning "as a climber." Herr's experiences are an excellent illustration of the Functional Model of Disability. The prostheses also changed the way in which others viewed him—from pity to viewing his functioning as "an unfair advantage."

Conceptualizing the individual's functional improvement as the "treatment" or "solution" to the disability reduces any perceived individual blame. The definition of disability in the Functional Model typically does not include symptoms or possible causes. Rather, disability is defined as a lack of specific functions, making assistance/adaptive technology (AT) the necessary treatment. Allocating societal resources to the development of advanced AT shifts the responsibility for a solution to society, most often governments. AT also changes the *perception* of disability. Wheelchair athletics demonstrates these ideas (which were briefly discussed in Chapter Two). There were no wheelchair athletics before the 1980s, simply because athletic wheelchairs were not yet developed. Today, there are wheelchairs (and prostheses) for many different types of sports. For IWDs for whom athletics is a major component of quality of life, their disability experience would have been much different before the 1980s (not due to any aspect of the disability or to anything about themselves). In addition, both self-images and societal perceptions of wheelchair athletes have changed. In the movie *Murderball*, a movie about wheelchair athletes, one competitor states, "I didn't come here to give hugs." In the past, IWDs, both men and women, were considered to be loving, nice, and sweet. This comment from the film succinctly captures the competitive nature of all athletes, including those in wheelchairs.

Eric Weihenmayer (2001), who is blind, has successfully summited Mount Everest and has also climbed the highest peaks on each of the seven continents. Born with juvenile retinoschisis, an inherited condition which caused his retinas to disintegrate completely by the time Weihenmayer entered high school, Weinhenmayer was introduced to mountain climbing at a summer camp for the blind. His experiences show that everyone, including IWDs, have very specific goals and functions. Reading about Weihenmayer's use of new electronic assistive technology provides insight into how the technology was developed and the way in which it is used to compensate for sight at high altitudes (Twilley, 2017).

Weihenmayer's story about how AT was developed for and used by IWDs presents the perhaps startling possibilities that IWDs may someday surpass the "natural" abilities of IWODs. The AT Weihenmayer used is termed "sensory substitution." Sensory substitution has been used for centuries and has, until recently, been very simple. White canes and Braille are sensory substitution devices, replacing sight with touch. However, Dr. Paul Bach-y-Rita is considered "the father of sensory substitution," having invented the BrainPort in which tactile information is used as a replacement for visual information. A magazine article (Twilley, 2017) described the way in which an AT device for the blind has changed the science of brain organization and development.

> He has used it (BrainPort) on challenging outdoor climbs in Utah and around Colorado, and he loves the way it restores his lost hand-eye coordination. "I can see the hold, I reach up, and I'm like, Pow!" he said, "It's in space, and I just grabbed it in space. It sounds so simple when you have eyes, but that's a really cool feeling."
>
> The BrainPort, which uses the sense of touch as a substitute for sight, is one of a growing number of so-called sensory-substitution devices. Another voice, turns visual information into sounds. Others translate auditory information into tactile sensation for the deaf or use sounds to supply missing haptic information for burn victims and leprosy patients. While these devices were designed with the goal of restoring lost sensation, in the past decade they have begun to revise our understanding of brain organization and development. The idea that underlies sensory substitution is a radical one: that the brain is capable of processing perceptual information in much the same way, no matter which organ delivers it.
>
> (Twilley, 2017, pp. 38–39)

Functions are also considered more broadly in the Functional Model. We also consider the general public, with which most individuals do not have personal contacts or experience, consisting of widely held values, laws, and the resources of each society at a historical period. It might be tempting to think of individual functions as more self-defining and affecting individuals on a daily basis, but the public view of the functioning of IWDs regulates the broader government-supported opportunity structures, such as educational prospects, employment choices, and, on a social basis, if IWDs are accorded equal social status. Frequently, it is not the disability that limits IWDs, but rather, the illogical public prejudice and discrimination against disability that results in withholding of resources and privileges. Further, withholding resources and privileges is prejudice and discrimination. A businessowner asked, "Wouldn't it be cheaper to carry someone and his or her wheelchair up a few stairs rather than to install a ramp, which would hardly be used at all?" Without equal social status, many types of relationships, including friends, family, and long-term romantic partnerships, may be denied to IWDs.

Accommodations, as mandated by the Americans with Disabilities Act (ADA), are an important part of the Functional Model. Physical accommodations such as ramps for wheelchairs, elevators, signs in Braille, transportation, and accessible bathrooms are perhaps easier to understand. Emotional accommodations such as flexibility in work schedules, the opportunity to take medications and injections at school or work, and other less tangible accommodations are as important as easily seen physical accommodations. Nonetheless, when these public accommodations are not provided, most IWODs do not notice; however, most IWDs and their families *do* notice. IWODs often mistakenly think that the absence of accommodations is the "natural world," and not human-made constructions. Additionally, IWODs often attribute IWDs' lack of participation (especially in the workplace) as due to personal moral failings in IWDs, but rarely consider that perhaps the accommodations are not in place that would allow the IWD to get to work and work productively.

It may appear that IWODs do not have functional needs or require accommodations. However, on a closer look, we see that IWODs do have functional needs; but these needs are hidden because the physical environment is automatically built to accommodate their needs. A British disability scholar (Marks, 1999) explained this:

> No person is completely self-reliant. Those people who are identified as being particularly dependent are *made* (author's emphasis) this way because social organization and distribution of resources are arranged in such a way that discriminates against them. For example, if steps rather than ramps are built at the entrance of buildings, then wheelchair users (or parents pushing prams) are made dependent on the assistance of others to carry them into the building.

(p. 96)

> [T]heorists have argued that people's level of independence should relate to their autonomy and control over their own lives, rather than on the ability to perform particular technical activities. Consequently, they argue, their "needs" are not located in a relationship between those whose needs are met automatically *and therefore seen as having no needs* (author's emphasis)—and those whose needs are not met and who must make a *special* plea for assistance and support.
>
> (p. 97)

Regardless of the capabilities of any AT device, the physical environment can render AT less useful, or useless, or even dangerous. A *New York Times* article (Mattlin, 2016, Oct. 5) describes the accidental, and unnecessary, death of Laurie Hoirup. Ms. Hoirup's death resulted from a physical environment that did not accommodate her AT, an extremely heavy motorized wheelchair. Ms. Hoirup's disability was spinal muscular atrophy (S.M.A.). The *New York Times* article explained the disability.

> S.M.A. is a congenital and progressive neuromuscular weakness akin to muscular dystrophy. Until recently, half the babies born with it would die before their second birthday. Their hearts and lungs become too weak to continue. Medical care and understanding have improved the odds somewhat.
>
> (para. 4)

> I learned of the death of Laurie Hoirup, a prominent 60-year-old disability rights advocate in California. Laurie drowned in the Sacramento River after a July 4 celebration. She was well-loved and accomplished. She'd served as a chief deputy director of the State Council on Developmental Disabilities for five years and wrote books about living with a disability.
>
> (para. 1)

> Laurie's sudden and tragic death was not directly caused by her S.M.A., but it is the stark reminder of the vulnerability of disabled lives. She was deboarding a pleasure boat when the ramp to the dock shifted. The weight of her motorized wheelchair—and the fact that she was strapped into it—pulled her down into the water too rapidly for rescue.
>
> (para. 2)

The title of this article is, "A Disabled Life Is a Life Worth Living," which, of course, is true. Nonetheless, it is surprising that the author (and the editors) could consider it necessary to state such an obvious fact. Perhaps a better title is "The Vulnerability of Disabled Lives."

One of the purposes of Models of Disability is the determination of which academic disciplines train professionals to serve IWDs. In a *New York Times* article (Anrieff, 2017), entitled "Designing for Access," the opening of an exhibit at the Cooper Hewitt Design Museum was announced (https://www.nytimes.com/2017/12/14/opinion/design-disability-accessibility-cooper-hewitt.html). The exhibit featured assistive technology for IWDs. Other museums and art schools have featured assistive technology exhibits, including the Museum of Modern Art, the University of Dundee, and the Institute of Making at University College London. At the conclusion of the article, the author summarized, "It's so encouraging that more people are interest in pursuing this area of design." While the first purpose of the assistive technology is to increase function, independence, and mobility, museum curators and designers saw larger purposes:

> The show also reveals the challenge of bringing empathy to the marketplace. . . . "Many of these are consciousness-raising products," the exhibition's co-curator, Cara McCarty, said. "They put the magnifying glass up to something others might experience every day. We take moving around for granted, but if you find yourself on crutches one day, or you have a baby, and then have to navigate getting into the subway with a stroller, you become aware."
>
> (para. 2)

> There's another major shift in approach. . . . In earlier generations, hiding disability was always a high priority. Today, there's a lot more emphasis on fashion, glamour, choice. For so long, many of these programs looked clunky and clinical. . . "young people may not be so concerned about concealing it [a hearing aid]. They want something that looks nice," possibly one they can decorate.
>
> (para. 9)

So the hearing aids on view here, like the one designed by Elana Langer, are "bedazzled and bejeweled" with Swarovski crystals or metal, or metal minimalist, like the Zon designed by Stuart Karten Design.

The Sabi Roam cane may not reinvent the form, but it certainly upgrades it; it comes in several colors and uses the same Baltic birch wood used in skateboards.

(para. 10)

The Economic Model of Disability: Disability Is the Inability to Work and Produce

> - In some societies, the worth of individuals is based on their ability to work.
> - Most consider the high unemployment rates of IWDs as due to their disabilities rather than a prejudicial and discriminating labor market.
> - Nazi Germany murdered more than 200,000 Germans with disabilities, deeming the cost of their care to be too expensive.
> - IWDs, especially those with severe and multiple disabilities, are considered to be "burdens," "drains," or "luxuries."
> - Large businesses, including insurance companies and nursing homes, make large profits from IWDs, at times directly receiving government payments.
> - Labor market conditions change the definition of disability.
> - World War II is regarded as the "Golden Age of Employment for IWDs."

The Economic Model of Disability is often considered as part of the Functional Model, with employment and financial self-sufficiency as the functions considered. We discuss it here as a complete model, separating economics from functions. For some, employment and financial self-sufficiency are not only the defining factors of disability but may also define humanity.

While often not clearly stated, in many individualistic and modern societies, an individual's worth is determined by their level of intelligence, occupation, and financial status. With this often-unstated belief, it is difficult to maintain that everyone is equal. Many resources and services for IWDs are often thought to be "gifts" or "charity" of a generous society and government rather than rights as citizens. Provision of civil rights to IWDs, because they receive government resources, may appear to many as unnecessary. The choice, then, is artificially reduced to medical and financial resources *or* civil rights.

To the extent that society measures a person's worth by their earning capacity may reflect "the often explicit religious syndrome of work, social value, and moral worth" (Liachowitz, 1988, p. 46). There are some IWDs who will never be able to work, due to the nature and severity of their disabilities. However, the number of these IWDs is much smaller than thought. Most PWODs ascribe the low employment rates of IWDs as due to the disability, rather than an unaccommodating physical environment and prejudicial social environment. The National Organization of Disability (NOD, Kessler, 2010) has tracked ten indicators of quality of life over time. Therefore, surveys were completed in 1986, 1994, 1998, 2000, 2004, and 2010 thus tracking changes four years before the passage of the ADA in 1986 and continuing beyond the passage of the 2008 ADA Amendments. These surveys produce *relative* rankings, comparing IWDs to IWODs. Many of the results on the ten indicators of quality of life have *increased* for IWDs, but they have *increased more* for IWODs. Therefore, the *gap* between IWDs and IWODs continues to increase in spite of advances in civil rights laws, medicine, and assistive technology. For example, in 2010, 21% of IWDs were working full time or part time, compared to 59% of IWODs. The two largest gaps were employment (a gap of 38% in favor of IWODs) and use of technology (a gap of 31% in favor of IWDs).

Silberman (2015), in his bestselling book, *NeuroTribes: The Legacy of Autism and the Future of Neurodiversity*, described some societies and the way in which IWDs were perceived.

> They argued that food and medical care are not everyone's birthright, but are properly earned by doing productive labor. Their life is absolutely pointless but they do not regard it as being unbearable.
>
> (p. 116)

The first step in the Nazi murder of more than 200,000 Germans with disabilities at the beginning of World War II was to embark upon a public campaign that labeled Germans with disabilities as "life unworthy of life," (or "lebensunwerten Lebens" in German). In mass media, such as newspapers and films, those in institutions that cared for individuals with disabilities such as intellectual disabilities, psychiatric disabilities, deafness, and polio survivors were shown as pitiful, helpless, miserable individuals (Friedlander, 1995). According to the Nazis, the "compassionate" treatment would be to release them from their pathetic, useless lives. The second step was to calculate, to the penny, the cost of caring for these IWDs, showing that IWDs not only did not contribute to society, but they also consumed scarce resources. The third step was to reduce costs, by decreasing their food and medical care. The last step was to murder Germans with disabilities, sometimes by starvation or beatings, but most often by mass gassing.

The Nazi mass murder of 200,000 German citizens with disabilities in a Western European 20th-century nation shocks us, but many IWDs, and their families, are aware of the economic threat. A university professor who is the father of James, a child with Down syndrome expressed his deepest fear:

> Among the many things I fear coming to pass in my children's lifetime, I fear this above all: that children like James will eventually be seen as "luxuries" employers or insurance companies cannot afford, or as "luxuries" the nation or the planet cannot afford. I do not want to see a world in which human life is judged by the kind of cost-benefit analysis that weeds out those least likely to attain self-sufficiency and to provide adequate "returns" on social investments.
>
> (Berube, 1998, p. 52)

Until recently, much of the academic literature on IWDs, used the words "burdens" or "drains" in their titles or as keywords (used to index the work). The disability rights community label this type of scholarly work as "the burden literature." Thus, on a very scholarly and academic level, prejudice and discrimination against IWDs is disseminated. Both professionals in practice and students who are preparing for the workplace are unquestioningly "taught" these demeaning and dehumanizing attitudes. Rather than considering every life worthy of social investment, including counseling and social work services, the ingrained, unquestioned idea that IWDs are not as valuable as IWODs, often precludes them from receiving services which could enhance their quality of life.

Many IWDs believe that the Economic Model of Disability holds the public and government funding structures to be responsible to fund only the basic resources and services, communicating to IWDs to keep their demands at the lowest level. Linton (1998) explained in more explicit terms, asking "How dare we crippled, blind, and crazy folks ask for parity?"

> Society's choice, and I see it as a choice, to exclude disabled people from social and cultural events that afford pleasure, or deny them sex education, sexual health care and, at times, marriage, privacy, and friendship

are indications of the belief that pleasure is less consequential to disabled people than to nondisabled people. Yet that belief is likely a rationalization for more virulent impulses. Are disabled people denied access to pleasure by the unspoken notion that they are not entitled to it because they cause displeasure to others. . . . How dare we crippled, blind, and crazy folks ask for parity? Shouldn't we be satisfied with the provision of medical care and sustenance, and leave the luxuries for those who are thought to drain fewer resources from society?

(p. 111)

Governor Lamm of Colorado was very clear in his concern for medical cost containment measures, specifically concerning both elderly individuals and IWDs. A disability activist (Longmore, 2003) summarized:

Applauding those who reject life-sustaining treatment, he said, "You've got a duty to die and get out of the way. Let the others in society, our kids, build a reasonable life." It is not a coincidence that he has also resisted integrating public transportation by making it accessible to persons with disabilities and has criticized special education as a waste of money because after years of getting, all mentally retarded (sic) people can do is "roll over."

(p. 155)

Powerful, large government institutions in the United States have struggled with the question: Is there a relationship between the ability to financially support oneself and the provision of civil rights? Stefan, a legal disability scholar (2001) told of an US Supreme Court ruling:

In 1985, the U.S. Supreme Court heard its first case raising the claim that discrimination against people on the basis of disability in a civil settlement violated their constitutional rights to equal protection under the 14th Amendment.

Because the Supreme Court identified "the ability to perform or contribute to society" as a central organizing value in this country, differences in the ability to perform or contribute to society justify differential and disadvantageous treatment. Therefore, the Supreme Court held because "those who are mentally retarded have a reduced ability to cope with and function in the everyday world . . . they are thus, different, immutably so, in relevant aspects."

(p. 74)

A physician asked why so few doctors were IWDs and then answered her own question. The small number of physicians with disabilities was not due to anything in the individual or their disability; instead, the dual reality of lack of experience with IWDs on the part of medical school admissions committees and the lack of reasonable accommodations were responsible.

> Over the years, I've thought a lot about situations like this (in which others "equated my wheelchair with illness, rather than empowerment") and I do not believe they come so much from direct prejudice as from people's lack of experience with doctors who are also wheelchair users. A recent study revealed that less than 3 percent of medical school trainees are people are individuals with mobility impairment. How can we expect our patients or colleagues to know about the perspectives and needs of physicians with disabilities when we remain invisible to them?
> The reason for this underrepresentation is complicated. Most physicians with mobility disabilities will tell you that the problem is not that we lack the ability to do our job competently. As with many other educated, skilled professionals, we know how to choose a path that suits our talents and abilities. Reasonable accommodations, such as the use of standing wheelchairs in the operating room, give us the access we need to do our work. The larger barrier to entry for prospective doctors with disabilities, however, is bias, both overt and hidden.
> A colleague who is quadriplegic recounted a medical school admissions officer telling him, "I'm afraid that you will not meet the technical standards for admission. . . ." Dr. Lisa Iezzoni, a professor of medicine at Harvard Medical School recounted her experience as a medical student at Harvard in the early 1980s. . . . At a student-faculty dinner, an influential professor told her: "There are too many doctors in this country right now for us to worry about training a handicapped physician. If that means someone gets left by the wayside, that's too bad."
>
> (Blauwet, 2017, December 6)

If large opportunity structures, many of which are government funded, are closed to well-qualified individuals simply because of personal characteristics, such as disability, race, or gender, and relevant qualities such as initiative, intelligence, and hard work become worthless. Dr. Iezzoni's experiences and treatment of bias and prejudice occurred in the 1980s, before the passage of the Americans with Disabilities Act in 1990.

In addition to considering the costs of disability, it is important to remember that there are large fiscal interests who are interested in IWDs as a source of profit (Fleischer & Zames, 2001, 2009). Large businesses and insurance companies are in the "disability business," and therefore, government funding and laws could increase or decrease their business profits. Two examples illustrate this point: If US Medicaid and Medicare funds were paid directly to IWDs, rather than to the nursing homes, beds in nursing homes would quickly empty. Most people, including IWDs, prefer to live at home. Presently, Medicare and Medicaid send these long-term funds directly to the nursing homes, albeit in the individual's name. If these government funds were sent directly to the individual, IWDs (and others) could for arrange assistive services and monitoring, home care assistants in their homes. Naturally, some IWDs would continue to need or want to live in nursing homes. There is a large nursing home lobby in Washington, DC, that works to maintain the status quo. Another example of businesses endeavoring to keep profits high is the failure of large insurance companies to provide medical coverage for individuals with "preexisting conditions," which describes IWDs. As would be expected, large insurance companies are against any legal changes that would mandate coverage for preexisting conditions because these changes would, invariably, lead to large expenses. Nonetheless, IWDs, often highly educated and qualified, report that they are not able to go to work because in order to do so they would be required to surrender their government health insurance and their employers' group plan does not cover their disability costs, or preexisting conditions. In a twisted logic, these potential taxpayers cannot afford to work. In this way, a large opportunity structure, the workplace, is closed to many IWDs.

Worldwide labor market conditions and economic conditions affect IWDs, perhaps to a greater extent than IWODs. IWDs are often the last to be hired and the first to experience "downsizing." Often, when IWDs are both qualified and experienced, they are not hired nor promoted. Finally, IWDs experience a high unemployment rate and when they are employed, they are more likely to have jobs, rather than long-term, fulfilling careers. Nonetheless, when there are acute labor shortages, IWDs are hired, do well in a competitive environment, and when the labor shortage ends, these IWDs are fired. An example of this is termed "the Golden Age of Employment for IWDs." This Golden Age occurred during World War II when large numbers of young men were mobilized to fight, while at the same time, factories and manufacturing greatly increased to produce munitions and other military needs. Thus, an acute labor shortage was combined with greatly increased labor needs. In unprecedented numbers, women entered the labor force, doing work that was formerly accomplished by men. Physical exams for IWDs were often waived and IWDs also entered the labor force in great numbers. Both women and IWDs proved their capabilities on the job, notwithstanding that both groups had been disenfranchised from the labor market. When World War II ended, women and IWDs were encouraged to quit their jobs to allow military veterans to return to their jobs.

If disability is defined as the inability to work, the world labor market plays a part in the definition of disability. Broadly speaking, when the labor market is based on physical labor, then a physical disability would be more impairing. In the developed world, until the 1920s, the labor market was based on the physical labor of farming, mining, building railroads, and logging. Today, the labor market is based on industries in technology, knowledge, and service, all of which require a great deal of intelligence, education, and well-developed social skills. Consequently, intellectual, cognitive, and emotional disabilities would adversely affect an individual's ability to work while those with physical disabilities (and the proper qualifications, accommodations, and AT) would be able to work.

However, much of disability law, including the American SSDI and SSI, was based upon a labor market based on physical labor. These outmoded characterizations of work contribute to the difficulty in joining the competitive workforce while at the same time surrendering government financial benefits. In the United States, it estimated that only a fraction of a percent of IWDs leave Social Security programs for paid work. Much like the medical professions, the labor market has radically changed in the last century while the laws and policies affecting IWDs has only partially, slowly, and incrementally changed.

The Environmental Model of Disability

Disability Can Be Caused by Barriers in the Physical Environment

- Disability is defined as an unaccommodating physical environment.
- The location of the problem of disability is within the built environment.
- Often, it is falsely thought that it is the disability that disadvantages IWDs, when it is the built environment that puts IWDs at a disadvantage.
- The solution to disability is the removal of these barriers. If these are removed, the disability disappears.

- Most IWODs do not recognize the presence of barriers or the lack of accommodations.
- In social support groups composed of individuals with the same type of disability, the disability "disappears."
- Academic disciplines that would study disability include architects, engineers, and urban planners.

In the past, the phrase describing the environmental needs of IWDs was "the least restrictive environment." Today, the phrase used is "the most accommodating environment," which holds society to a higher standard. The widespread societal bias against IWDs may be considered a structural lag in which society and government have not kept pace with the demographic changes in the number of IWDs or the scientific and medical advances in technology and medicine. Environments can be disabling.

There are environmental factors in all types of disabilities, environmental factors may play a greater role in psychiatric disabilities. Stefan (2001), a legal scholar, explained psychiatric disabilities as:

> Episodic, highly responsive to context and environment, and exist along a spectrum, which theoretically can be cause of hope—people with mental disabilities are frequently strong, talented, competent, and capable, and their environments can be structured in a way to support and increase their strengths, talents, competence, and capabilities.
>
> (p. 10)

The developmental psychologist, Urie Bronfenbrenner, recognized even as a small child that environment played a role in defining intellectual disabilities. Bronfenbrenner grew up in the rather isolated setting of a residential state facility for individuals with intellectual disabilities (ID). At that time, intellectual disabilities were labeled mental retardation. Notice the other terminology used to describe individuals with ID, which were considered clinically accurate at that time, each label ("morons," "imbeciles," and "idiots") referring to individuals with IQs that fell within a specified range. Anne Levine (Scarr, Weinberg, & Levine, 1986) interviewed Bronfenbrenner and some excerpts are included here:

> I grew up on the grounds of what was called an institution for the "feeble-minded" in the 1920s: 3,600 morons, imbeciles, idiots—and me. They were my friends and companions. My father was a physician, a

neuropathologist. In those days, it was hard for a Russian immigrant to establish a private practice. You got a job at a state institution. We lived at Letchworth Village in upstate New York—a marvelous place, really.... Two things that happened at Letchworth stand out in my mind. Some of the kids who were sent there didn't belong in a home for the mentally retarded.... My father would examine them when they arrived and see that they were not mentally retarded. His problem was to get them tested before the institution had its effect, for then they would be stuck there for life. The Binet was the hand of God. It was the only way he could get them out. [The Binet was the first intelligence test.]

The second thing that happened was that the inmates worked in the physicians' homes as maids and helpers. I was brought up by Hilda and Anna and Marilyn. They were my caregivers. They were supposed to be mentally retarded. But, when they worked in our homes, their IQs would go up. So you can see the beginnings of an interest in development right there.

(p. 45)

From this short account, it can be seen that Bronfenbrenner lived with these individuals with ID, had daily contact, and enjoyed their company. Moreover, he viewed them as individuals, with specific names. Even as a child, Bronfenbrenner understood that their intelligence increased when they were out of the institution, working in a family home. Also of interest, the elder Dr. Bronfenbrenner recognized that many of the incoming residents did not belong in a residential facility and he used scores on the *Binet Intelligence Test* to convince a state judge to release them from Letchworth. Therefore, he considered the Binet to be "the hand of God" because it released the "inmates" from a lifetime of institutionalization. Dr. Bronfenbrenner also understood that time spent in a low-demand and low-stimulating environment, institutionalization at Letchworth, would act to lower their measured IQ and, therefore, he needed to act quickly. The rationale and administration of state residential institutions illustrate the phrase, "Disability is clinically defined and normality is legally enforced." Physicians, such as Bronfenbrenner's father, examined incoming residents and referred them for testing, using psychometric instruments such as the *Binet*, thus clinically defining disability. But, it was a judge, a legal authority, who determined the residential placement of IWDs, thus legally enforcing normality.

Interestingly, the highly successful developmental psychologist looked back at his childhood home as a beginning of his pursuit of developmental psychology. He had learned early that environments can and do change the definition of intellectual disabilities. Bronfenbrenner's theory is called the Ecological Systems Theory and his research led to the development of the government-sponsored Head Start program, a preschool intervention which would give young children early academic development and enrichment. Part of a federal initiative, the War on Poverty, Head Start has served millions of American children.

Jonathan Mooney (2017, October 12) grew up with dyslexia and attention deficit disorder. As an adult, he now understands that it was school (the environment) that disabled him.

> Research shows that learning and attention differences correlate with enhanced problem solving, creativity, and entrepreneurship. What disabled me were limitations not in myself but in the environment: the passive learning experience where students sit at a desk most of the day; a narrow definition of intelligence conflated with reading and other right-brain skills; and a medicalization of difference that reduced my brain to a set of deficits and go hand in hand with many brain differences.

The first paragraphs of Mooney's *New York Times* article described sitting at the desks at school as a type of torture. Note that he describes his school day in terms of seconds.

> Let me tell you about my relationship with the school desk. From my first day at Penny Camp Elementary School in 1982, it was fraught.
>
> This is how it went down: Five seconds into class, the foot starts bouncing; 10 seconds in, both feet; 15 seconds, I bust out the drums! After a few minutes, it's all over. I'm trying to put my leg behind my neck. No, that desk and I didn't get along. For some kids, it was just school furniture, but for me was a form of enhanced interrogation.

School children with learning disabilities, both diagnosed and undiagnosed, were often referred to as "six-hour retardates." After the six-hour school day was over, these children suddenly became intelligent, adaptive kids.

Environments change throughout history. In rural, pre-industrial times, families worked together, forming an economic unit. People rarely traveled far from their birthplace and everyone in a small agricultural village knew each other from birth to death. In this type of environment, most people knew an IWD, interacting with the IWD daily, but probably not understanding the disability very well. The Industrial Revolution brought people to cities and required these individuals to work standardized hours in anonymous factories. IWDs disappeared from daily work life, unable to work in manufacturing and industry. Hahn (1997) summarized: "Deviant or atypical impersonal characteristics that may have become familiar in a small community seemed bizarre or disturbing in the urban milieu" (pp. 177–178). Others have also written the absence of IWDs when the labor market changed from rural agricultural labor to industrial labor, but considered the loss greater for IWODs than IWDs: "Americans have lost familiarity with disabled people in small-scale societies" (Scherer & Groce, 1988, p. 33).

Support groups of individuals with the same type of disability provide an environment in which the disability disappears. Most disability support groups are composed of individuals with the same type of disability. There are support groups for children, teens, and adults with disabilities and groups for partners, parents, and siblings of IWDs. In support groups, the disability is openly discussed and, indeed, the entire purpose of these types of groups is to discuss the disability, providing role models and providing useful information about available resources, practical suggestions for managing the disability, and coping with emotional resources. How then, does the disability disappear? The disability disappears because, in addition to alleviating social isolation, these groups normalize disability, showing that disability is not pathology, inferiority, or deviance. Often, an IWD with a newly acquired or diagnosed disability, has internalized society's prejudices and discrimination about disability. One woman with a congenital disability had accepted society's stigmatization of disability as a self-identifier:

> After a lifetime of isolating myself from other disabled people, it was an awakening to be surrounded by them. For the first time in my life, I felt like a real adult member of the human community. Finally, identifying myself as a disabled person was an enormous healing. It was about recognizing, allowing, and acknowledging something that I had been trying to deny, and finding that disability does not equal ugliness, incompetence, and misery.
>
> (Tollifson, 1997, p. 107)

Tollifson's disability disappeared because she was *surrounded* by others with disabilities, allowing her to feel normal. The word *normal* as it is used here, simply means that the disability does not "stand out," and the individual is not viewed as her disability. Actually, in a support group of individuals with the same type of disability, it would be impossible to identify a single individual only by their disability! The group thinks of the disability as ordinary, natural, and commonplace and, because of this, the IWD is allowed to shed the primary social identification of an IWD or as only a disability. Therefore, the IWD feels accepted as an individual, with many different types of identities *in addition* to the disability. As a result, they feel comfortable and relaxed, understanding that they can discuss their disabilities without elaborate explanation. Further, the group members are not required to deal with the stress of dealing with the reactions of PWODs. Often, the discussion centers on the shared experiences of undeserved prejudice and stigmatizing attitudes. In this way, group members learn that the attitudes of others are not their fault. If everyone in the group has experienced prejudice, individual members begin to learn self-definition, self-worth, and empowerment. Tollifson described:

> They shared so many of what I had always thought were my own isolated experiences that I began to realize that my supposedly private hell was a social phenomenon. We had eye-opening, healing conversations. We discovered, for example, that we had all had the experience of being patronized and treated like children even though we were adults. It wasn't simply some horrible flaw in my own character that provoked such reaction, as I had always believed, but rather, this was part of a collective pattern that was much larger than any one of us. It was a stereotype that existed in the culture at large. Suddenly, disability became not just my personal problem, but a social and political issue as well.
>
> (p. 107)

In the past, institutions or long-term care facilities were one of the few living arrangements available to IWDs, especially those with multiple and severe disabilities. Today, there are some IWDs who require the round-the-clock care provided by institutions, but most IWDs do not require such care and would prefer, like most anyone, to live at home with family, rather than in a facility with strangers. However, in the past, institutionalization was the *only* living environment available to IWDs and was automatically accepted. Without oversight or accountability, many of these so-called care facilities subjected the residents to neglect, abuse, and cruelty. The lifespan of IWDs in institutions was much shorter, perhaps due, in part, to crowded living conditions and the resulting infections. The disability rights movement refers to institutionalization as "incarceration," comparing IWDs to prisoners who are imprisoned but have not committed a crime. Note that in Bronfenbrenner's excerpt, he refers to the residents of Letchworth as "inmates."

The Deaf culture is another type of disability group refusing the self-identity as IWDs, viewing Deaf people as a separate cultural group defined, as other cultural groups, by the language used. The Deaf culture argues that if an accommodation in the environment, Sign Language, is available, then Deaf people are fully functional. For the Deaf culture, there is no individual disability (deafness); instead, it is the environment that is impaired. In this way, the Deaf culture rejects the pathological deviant construction of deafness.

In the Deaf culture, the language is Sign Language, a complete language that serves as the repository of culture, including, art, theater, and literature. Therefore, in an example often used, the Deaf culture sees themselves as another linguistic group, such as Hispanic Americans who speak Spanish. Deaf babies learn their native language, Sign Language, becoming "native" signers. The history of Deaf people includes residential schools, with inferior and non-academic education and physical and sexual abuse. Most harmful was the institutionalized, long-standing, and systematic repression of their natural language, Sign Language. Most of the Deaf children were forced to learn lip reading and oral speech and were physically punished if "caught" using Sign Language. This centuries-long history contributed to the rise of the Deaf culture, a culture which has provided mutual support and solidarity.

New technology such as cochlear implants, electrodes which are surgically implanted in the inner ear and create a pathway to the auditory part of the brain, may greatly affect the Deaf culture, and, historically, the Deaf culture has not been in favor of cochlear implants.

Title IV of the Americans with Disabilities Act mandates that citizens with speech and hearing disabilities have access to emergency services. For those who can speak and hear, the capability to summon life-saving help from emergency services is rarely considered. However, countless Deaf people have died because they had no way to get help quickly.

The Social Model of Disability: The Disability Role Is Socially Constructed

- There are a few disabilities which are entirely socially constructed.
- Societies and cultures interpret disability differently.
- The "disability role" is defined by the IWD's culture, societal conditions, and historical time in which the IWD lives.
- The prejudice and discrimination against IWDs is socially learned.
- Most IWDs refuse the societal construction of the disability role.
- Social and political conditions can contribute to higher rates of disabilities.

One of the few examples of a disability that is entirely socially constructed is the crippling foot-binding practices of young upper-class Chinese girls. Up until the advent of the Manchurian dynasty in the early 20th century, young girls' feet were wrapped tightly, a very painful procedure that resulted in the inability to walk and in what most would regard as a deformity since the foot was essentially bent back upon itself and the bones permanently broken. Therefore, according to both the Biomedical and Functional Models of Disability, these girls would be considered to have a disability. However, in upper-class Chinese culture, female bound feet were considered beautiful and sexually alluring, thus ensuring excellent marriage prospects. Bound feet were a status system, communicating that these women were not expected to work or even walk. In the Environmental Model, obviously, these girls would not be judged to have a disability. In this social construction of disability, it was loving and conscientious mothers who bound their daughters' feet. The Manchu dynasty outlawed this practice.

It is difficult to find another example of a disability that is totally socially constructed. However, it is true that cultures and political entities throughout history have *socially interpreted* disability. It is safe to say that with a few notable examples, most IWDs were thought to be inferior and deviant. Today, in the developed Western world, it is safe to state that an individual with a severe psychiatric illness is more stigmatized than an individual with a visible physical disability, such as blindness or paralysis.

Many IWDs feel that the greatest "problem" in dealing with their disabilities is society's ill-informed prejudice and discrimination. Madeline Will (as cited in Weisgerber, 1991), former assistant Secretary for Education and head of the Office of Special Education and Rehabilitation (OSERS), explained:

> Most disabled people . . . will tell you that despite what everyone thinks, the disability itself is not what makes everything different. What causes the disabilities is the attitudes society has about being disabled, attitudes that make a disabled person embarrassed, insecure, uncomfortable, dependent. Of course, disabled people rarely talk about the quality of life. But it has precious little to do with deformity and a great deal to do with society's own defect.
>
> (p. 6)

Society often believes that the prejudice and discrimination against IWDs is an inherent part of the disability, rarely considering that there is nothing in the disability, or the IWD, that warrants such prejudice. Perhaps more troubling is the results of these thoughtless attitudes. Many "nice" IWODs do not recognize the absence of IWDs in schools, the workplace, public accommodations, such as hotels, or in public transportation, restaurants, and entertainment venues. This type of unawareness may be considered harmful to IWDs. Further, many IWODs attribute the absence of IWDs in public, daily life as caused only by their disability. For example, it is difficult to understand the reluctance with which many theater and restaurant owners complied with the ADA in making their facilities physically accessible to IWDs. It seems to make sense that these businessowners would consider IWDs, and their families, as an additional source of income. This reluctance may have been due to fear or stigmatization of IWDs. Theater and restaurant owners may not have wanted IWDs as customers, fearing that they would lose other customers who would not want to be confronted with the "spectacle" of disability.

As with other types of prejudice and discrimination, the stigmatizing attitudes toward disability and the people who experience them are taught to children. Many children with disabilities experience "stigma recognition" for the first time when they enter kindergarten. Of course, these children understand that they have a disability and, often, are very skilled at managing the disability; however, they have not yet encountered prejudice and discrimination due to their disability.

The "disability role" is defined as one of pathology, deviance, inferiority, and private tragedy. Many IWDs believe that this role is imposed upon them by IWODs in the general public. According to this social role "guidance," the IWD is expected to manage the disability as well as possible, be cheerful and grateful, keep their aspirations low, and above all, not be assertive or make demands upon society. This description of the social role of IWDs may seem exaggerated or out-of-date. Nonetheless, this disability role is continuously maintained and reinforced and, worse, it is not often noticed by IWODs. Media, including television and movies, which portrays IWDs as pathetic, tragic figures without personal characteristics or social roles, other than the disability, are rarely questioned by anyone, other than IWDs. The character thus becomes a tragic, pathetic symbol for disability rather than a fully developed individual (with a disability). (Johnson, 2012)

Most IWDs do not deny the presence of their disability; however, most deny the socially constructed role enforced upon them, and when IWODs do not conform to these roles, occasionally others interpret these behaviors as negative, oppositional, and ungrateful. Occasionally, IWDs will take on this role of inferiority and deviance when gatekeepers to resources, such as services and other resources, demand compliance to this role. IWDs understand that they may be medically abandoned or refused for services or denied eligibility for funds if they do not act appropriately compliant, respectful, and accepting of a role of inferiority and deviance.

If IWDs were given their full civil rights, if there were no prejudice and discrimination, complete integration into the community were achieved, the appropriate medical care and technology provided, they would still have a disability that would require medical care and lifelong surveillance. In an effort to combat the societal stigmatizing discrimination and to "normalize" disability, some IWODs have used euphemisms to describe disability, such as "human variation" or "physically challenged." Although well-intentioned, these euphemisms are insulting for two reasons: 1) they imply that the IWDs are (and should be) ashamed of their disability and 2) these descriptors minimize the disability and its effect on the individual. A disability is not a minor inconvenience. It is true that IWDs want to be considered normal, ordinary people, just like anyone else, but, at the same time, IWDs *also* want their disability to be acknowledged. IWDs do not think their acceptance and normalization should be dependent upon relinquishing a valued and important part of their self-identity, their disabilities.

Social factors do contribute (not cause) to disability and this relationship is most evident in viewing large numbers of IWDs, rather than individual IWDs. Health demographers have known social inequalities raise the probability of disability including such inequalities as lack of education, lack of insurance coverage, employment in physically dangerous work, lack of prenatal care, low incomes, and transient lifestyles. The higher rates of disability found in racial and ethnic minorities in the United States are due to these social circumstances. Social circumstances are human-made and, therefore, have the possibility of improvement. While it may not be possible in the near future to eliminate the disability gap between majority and minority races, this gap could be greatly reduced, if society made the choice to do so.

The Civil Rights Model of Disability: Disability is a Lack of Civil Rights

- The solution to disability is a radical change in the social, political, and physical infrastructure.
- The Civil Rights Model asks the questions: Are IWDs citizens? Does disability make them ineligible for full citizenship?
- IWDs want their basic civil rights as citizens and, at the same time, IWDs want to be contributing citizens.
- Civil rights for IWDs is an issue for everyone.

- IWDs, as a group, have experienced political disenfranchisement.
- The Civil Rights Model is the model with the greatest input from IWDs.
- The Civil Rights Model is the model with the greatest accountability to IWDs.
- The Civil Rights Model believes that government and societal resources should be paid directly to IWDs rather than to large businesses, such nursing homes.

The Civil Rights Model (sometimes referred to as the Sociopolitical Model or the Minority Group Model) considers disability to be the creation of law and policy, having little to do with the physical and mental aspects of disabilities. In a book, *Privilege, Power, and Difference*, A. G. Johnson (2001), in addition to many other minority groups, described IWDs:

> Privilege exists when one group has something of value that is denied to others simply because of the groups they belong to, rather than because of anything they've done or failed to do. . . . For people with disabilities, the disability is the liability that make it less likely that their talents, abilities, and aspirations will be recognized and rewarded.
>
> (p. 24)

A textbook titled, *Rethinking Disability in Social Work* (May & Raske, 2005) recognized the relationship between disability and political concerns:

> Welfare capitalism leads to new forms of domination and subordination as the world becomes increasingly colonized under the control of bureaucracies. . . . Although cast in biomedical terms, the determination of disability involves political decisions about the distribution of social goods. The ongoing debate is that "objective criteria" and measurement of incapacity leads to the perception that the state is distributing "scarce" goods in a "fair" and systematic way.
>
> (Hiranandani, 2005, p. 74)

For centuries, IWDs have been given inferior public services, such as education, transportation, housing, and medical care. Their range of choices has been limited, reduced, or nonexistent. IWDs have been segregated, isolated, and, at times, killed simply because of their disability. Most IWDs understand that their basic civil rights as citizens are protected by weak laws, which often places the burden of proof on IWDs, as plaintiffs.

IWDs have become increasingly involved in organized politics, advocating for equal access, community integration, and independent living (not in institutions). National political and advocacy groups include the British Council of Organizations of Disabled Peoples, the American Coalition of Citizens with Disabilities, and the Coalition of Citizens with Disabilities in Canada. Cross-national groups include Disabled Peoples International (DPI) of more than 110 organizations from Europe, the Americas, Africa, and Asia. Disability rights activists adopted many strategies of the American Civil Rights Movement and much of the language of the Americans with Disabilities Act was taken almost word-for-word from the 1964 American Civil Rights Bill. However, unlike racial/ethnic minority Americans, the disability rights movement involves a large financial investment. Disability is expensive but civil rights are never guaranteed on the basis of cost.

While it is true that many of the problems and disenfranchisement of IWDs in the United States parallels the disenfranchisement of racial and ethnic groups, there is a basic difference between these two groups. It was legal to isolate, segregate, and provide inferior services to IWDs and, moreover, IWDs had no legal redress against these practices. However, for other minority groups, including racial/ethnic groups, women, and LBGTQ groups, there is nothing inherently negative in their status or personal identification. For IWDs, the disability poses a question: If IWDs were to receive full civil rights, would the disability disappear? No, the disability would not entirely disappear, but many IWDs believe that the lack of civil rights, rather than their disability, is their greatest problem. IWDs believe that they have mastered the management of their disability and are often proud of this mastery and control, but in terms of their daily lives, they consider their biggest "problem" to be the laws, policies, and underlying attitudes that limit their lives.

Disability civil rights is often considered marginal to IWODs. Nonetheless, most everyone (including IWODs and IWDs) understand that civil rights for other disenfranchised groups, including racial/ethnic minorities, immigrants, women, and LBGTQ groups, literally the pays the entire nation in contributions to the economy and the tax base. National economies are strengthened when formerly disenfranchised groups are given societal resources, including civil rights. Allowing any group to fulfill their potential has all the advantages of diversity and, also, results in a larger tax base for everyone. For example, individuals without children pay education taxes, recognizing that an educated citizenry helps everyone. Perhaps the idea of the Biomedical Model that disability is deviance, rather than diversity, is part of the reluctance to accord rights to IWDs. A disability scholar described her dawning awareness that civil rights for IWDs were personally important to IWODs. She described, in spite of understanding that provision of civil rights for other disenfranchised groups were essential for the entire nation, the idea that IWDs were somehow ineligible for civil rights due to their deviance and pathology.

> I now believe that my resistance to disability studies is of a piece with a larger and more insidious cultural form of resistance whereby nondisabled people find it difficult or undesirable to imagine law is central to civil rights legislation. Here's what I mean. Just as I was "liberal" with regard to disability, so was I "liberal" with regard to gender and race: I supported (and I continue to support) equal pay for equal work and initiatives such as affirmative action *regardless of whether those initiatives would ever benefit me*. I did not feel that I would become black or Hispanic someday: I was not reserving the right to sex-change operation: I simply supported civil rights with regard to race and gender because I regarded these as long overdue attempts to make good on the promise of universal human rights. . . . But, for some reason, *even though disability law might someday pertain to me*, I could imagine it as central to the project of establishing egalitarian civil rights in a social democracy.
>
> (Linton, 1998, pp. ix–xi)

There are both laws and organizations, composed mostly of IWDs, that seek government protection for IWDs and methods of redress when prejudice and discrimination. Nonetheless, it is not only the law itself that is important. Strong enforcement guidelines must be in place and often they are not. In the United States, the public and judicial response to the ADA was unexpected and damaging. The intent of the US Congress was undermined by the US Supreme Court who refused to hear many cases brought by plaintiffs with disabilities, finding ways in which to determine that the plaintiffs did not have disabilities and therefore were not eligible for protection under the Americans with Disabilities Act. These courts never considered if there were violations of the ADA; defendant attorneys argued that the plaintiff did not have a disability as defined by the ADA, and therefore was not protected by the ADA.

In the United States, on National Public Radio's "This American Life," a podcast by Brittany Wilson (2017) entitled "Expect Delays," speaks of the (supposedly) accessible transportation available in New York City for IWDs. Ms. Wilson is a law graduate of the University of Pennsylvania, is an African American, and has cerebral palsy, which requires the use of leg braces and crutches. She has used the Access-Ride system for IWDs since she was 11 years old and, currently, she uses it to get to work. Before becoming an attorney, she protested and complained about the inferior, demeaning, and unreliable Access-Ride system. After her graduation from law school, she started petitions, filed formal complains, attended board meetings, stating that she wants the Access-Ride system changed for all the riders. Advocating for changes and improvements for everybody confused the Access-Ride administrators. When they did respond to Ms. Wilson's specific complaints, they thought that the problem was solved. Often, these complaints and protests are met by the sentence: "You people (meaning IWDs) are spoiled and entitled." Complaints include: the bus is often late, but considered to be "on-time" if no more than 30 minutes late; drivers will wait five minutes for riders and then leave; riders are expected to wait outside in all weathers; riders are allowed a maximum of two bags; and riders are required to call the evening before to make a reservation. Ms. Wilson was advised by a bus driver to refrain from directly confronting other drivers, regardless of their insensitivity and rudeness, because "these drivers know where you live." One day returning home from work Ms. Wilson was the last passenger to be dropped off at her home. Stopping in front of her house, the driver said, "I have to pee." He took a Styrofoam cup and walked to the back of the bus, sitting in the seat across from Ms. Wilson. He urinated into the cup. Ms. Wilson recounted, "This was inappropriate and disgusting. I was 10 feet from my house, but without my crutches, I couldn't get off the bus alone. I wonder if he would have done this if I had been white. As if nothing had happened, he helped me off the bus." She was relieved that the driver did not sexually assault her. Ms. Wilson went inside and immediately telephoned Access-Ride, lodging a complaint. The driver was fired the next day.

Another time, when Ms. Wilson was riding, she saw a 70-year-old black woman who used a walker, hurrying out of a McDonald's restaurant, hailing the Access-Ride bus. The woman had three large black garbage bags draped over her walker. The driver told she was over the limit of two bags and, furthermore, she was supposed to wait outside. The woman replied that she had been waiting for more than three hours in the cold and had stepped inside McDonald's to wait and, further, that she didn't need help with her bags. She told the driver that she was able to go to the grocery store only once a month and the garbage bags were stuffed with grocery bags. Responding to the driver's resistance to helping her on the bus, the woman tried to appeal to his sense of decency by asking: "Don't you have a mother? Would you like someone treating her as you've been treating me?"

From Ms. Wilson's contribution to the podcast, it becomes apparent that most IWDs state that the Civil Rights Model describes both the difficulties of their disability and, more important, outlines the "treatment" or intervention needed. Most IWDs medically manage and treat their disabilities, but a lack of civil rights presents obstacles. Which of the following statements is most true? Ms. Wilson cannot get to work on time because of her disability or Ms. Wilson cannot get to work on time because her civil rights are being violated. Her experience illustrates the main point of disability rights activists: Providing government-funded supports and accommodations to IWDs, which allows IWDs to work and pay taxes, is more cost-effective than financial disability benefits. (The provision of civil rights is also more humane and ethical.) At the end of the podcast, Ms. Wilson concluded: "Years ago, I thought that education would be answer to all my problems. I'm still a woman, black, and disabled. It's as if nothing had changed."

Attitudes may be widespread, maintained by the media, and institutionalized in government, education, the workplace, and in general society. Physical barriers may be found in almost every environment. None of this, however, is immutable or unending. Attitudes, civil rights laws, and physical barriers are human-made, most historical artifacts of times when medicine and the workforce had not been radically improved. IWDs often hear, "Now is the best time to have a disability." A physician described the perception of IWDs is gradually improving due to the increased experience and familiarity of younger patients or, as she related, "I find that these reactions are somewhat generational."

> I have been a wheelchair user since early childhood, when I sustained spinal cord injury in a farming accident. I am now a practicing physician in the field of rehabilitation and sports medicine.
>
> In my busy outpatient clinical practice, I witness the spectrum of patients' reactions when they find out that their doctor is, herself, disabled. Typically those first few seconds after entering an exam room—before the patient's guard goes up—are the most informative.
>
> I find that these reactions are somewhat generational. Younger patients, having grown up amid a growing awareness of disability in society, typically do not react at all. They have clearly encountered empowered people with disabilities working in various professional roles. Older patients often seem confused, curious, or in rare circumstances, dismayed.
>
> Several months ago, I wheeled into the room of an elderly woman. She looked at me, placed her hand on mine and with a kind look asked, "Are you an invalid?" More recently, a jovial older man exclaimed, "You've got

to me kidding me!" A few times, patients will hesitate to tell me their concerns, indicating, "Well, doc, I feel bad about complaining about this to you, when clearly your problems are bigger than mine."

(Blauwet, 2017, December 6)

The elderly woman thought she was being kind (when in reality she was expressing prejudice and discrimination) and the patient who tells the doctor that her problems must be worse than theirs is demonstrating a sensationalized and exaggerated view of disability. Nonetheless, these patients are convinced that they understand the physician's disability.

Conclusion

To those without disabilities, it a human tendency to seek simplicity when attempting to understand the disability experience. Viewing disability as both a multidimensional and subjective experience with physical, emotional, social, functional, and environmental aspects may seem overwhelmingly complex. At the same time most individuals, with or without a disability, want to be viewed and treated as multidimensional, whose lives are embedded in physical, emotional, social, functional, and environmental aspects.

Speaking about psychiatric disabilities, a psychiatrist summarized the way in which a large, standardized diagnostic manual, the DSM, has radically changed in order to describe diagnoses that "embrace more aspects of client functioning." Thus, the DSM is moving away from the non-interactional Biomedical Model and moving toward more interactional models, which cannot only render more complete diagnoses but also reduce the stigma of these diagnoses.

> [D]ifferentiation among emotional, behavioral, physiological, psychosocial and contextual factors is misleading and conveys a message that mental illness is unrelated to physical, biological, and medical problems. Combining these axes (of the DSM) has the potential to be more inclusive, embracing more aspects of client functioning. If used intentionally, (considering all these factors) they may remind counselors that medical and psychosocial issues are just as important to mental health diagnoses and reduces stigma.
>
> (Paris, 2015)

Two conflicting views of disability, each view held by an IWD who is both author and disability activist provide a conclusion. Longmore, an American described: "(Disability) is an elastic social category shaped by cultural values, societal arrangements, public policies, and professional practices. It is always an array of culturally constructed identities and highly mutable social roles" (Longmore, 2003, p. 58). In contrast, Morris, UK Member of Parliament, considered the Social, Environmental, and Civil Rights Models of disability as incomplete:

> There is a tendency within the social model of disability to deny the experience of our bodies, insisting that our physical differences and restrictions are *entirely* socially created. While environmental barriers and social attitudes are a crucial part of our experience of disability—and do indeed disable us—to suggest that this is all there is to it is to deny the personal experience of physical or intellectual restriction, of illness, of the fear of dying.
> (J. Morris, 1991, p. 10)

Both Longmore and Morris are correct. Disability is an elastic category, not only in the interactional models, which makes sense because the definitions of disability interact with societal attitudes, functions required, and advances in technology. However, in the single non-interactional model, the Biomedical Model, the concept of disability, including its definitions and treatments, is also elastic. For example, we have learned that many human conditions with long histories have only recently been defined as disabilities, including learning disabilities, alcohol and substance abuse, and autism spectrum disorder (ASD). In addition to these changes in definition, there are many diagnoses/disabilities that most physicians have never observed or treated. For example, physicians, including neonatal doctors, report previously unknown conditions of various low-incidence congenital disabilities, often changing the diagnoses when new information becomes available or using long descriptions of symptoms to substitute for a specific diagnosis. Physicians are also treating large numbers of IWDs who, in the past, would have died, thus illustrating that although these disability diagnoses were known but not treated due to the fact that these individuals died, either at birth, or upon sustaining the disability. Severe spina bifida (hole in the spine with a congenital onset) provides a good example. It was not until 1957, when a shunt was developed, that babies born with SB survived and physicians began treating these infants and saving their lives. This shunt drains excess spinal cord fluid from the brain. Today, most newborns with SB survive and many adults with SB live and thrive. Emergency medicine has resulted in the survival of large numbers of individuals with traumatic onset disabilities, such as spinal cord injuries and traumatic brain injury. Without these medical advances, many injury victims died before they arrived at the hospital. It might *appear* that there are more people who use a wheelchair, but it is true that there *are* more people in wheelchairs because they have survived their traumatic injuries.

The definition of disability is elastic and, furthermore, this elasticity applies to both scientific advances and social progress for humankind. Allowing the definition of disability to change will lead to great flexibility in society's view of IWDs.

Counseling and Models of Disability

> **The Importance of Models for Counselors**
> - Examination of the various models will lead to more ethical counseling services.
> - Consideration of these models will lead to more positive counseling outcomes.
> - Because there are emotional aspects to all the models of disability, each model has counseling implications.

Why should counselors interest themselves in models of disability? There are emotional aspects of all the models of disability and, therefore, counselors have the opportunity to provide effective services to IWDs. However, positive counseling outcomes are not possible if services are not ethical and empathic. It is difficult, if not impossible, to be empathic with IWDs, if counselors do not incorporate aspects of all these models in the therapeutic relationship.

Conceptualizing disability, and the individual client's experience and perception of their disability, with each of these models in mind will increase counselors' empathy, guard against ethical violations, and communicate that counselors do not define clients solely on their disabilities. Is it necessary to refer to each of these models by name? Of course not. In the same way that counselors understand that there are various theoretical foundations and therapeutic techniques in the practice of counseling. Moreover, counseling training, licensing standards, in-service education, and supervised practice require counselors to demonstrate working knowledge of these theories and techniques. Simple awareness of differing counseling orientations and skills enhances each counseling relationship. Awareness and understanding of the various models of disability also enhances each counseling relationship.

References

Anrieff, A. (2017, December 14). Designing for access. *New York Times.* https://www.nytimes.com/2017/12/14/opinion/design-disability-accessibility-cooper-hewitt.html

Batavia, A. I., & Schriner, K. (2001). The Americans with disabilities act as an engine of social change: Models of disability and the potential of a civil rights approach. *Disability Policy Studies, 29,* 690–702.

Berube, M. (1998). *Life as we know it: A father, a family, and an exceptional child.* New York, NY: Pantheon.

Bickenbach, J. E. (1993). *Physical disability and social policy.* Toronto, ON: University of Toronto.

Blauwet, C. A. (2017, December 6). I use a wheelchair, and yes, I'm your doctor. *New York Times.* Retrieved from https://nyti.ms/2AXVlcy Retrieved 02-26-2018

Braddock, D. L., & Parrish, S. L. (2001). An institutional history of disability. In G. L. Albrecht, K. D. Seelman, & M. Bury. (Eds.), *Handbook of disability studies* (pp. 11–68). Thousand Oaks, CA: Sage.

Byrd, E. K., & Elliott, T. R. (1988). Media and disability: A discussion of the research. In H. E. Yuker (Ed.), *Attitudes toward persons with disabilities* (pp. 82–95). New York, NY: Springer.

Fleischer, D. Z., & Zames, F. (2001). *The disability rights movement: From charity to confrontation.* Philadelphia, PA: Temple University.

Fleischer, D. Z., & Zames, F. (2009). *The disability rights movement: From charity to confrontation.* (2nd ed.). Philadelphia, PA: Temple University.

Friedlander, H. (1995). *The origins of Nazi genocide: From euthanasia to the final solution.* Chapel Hill: University of North Carolina.

Gawande, A. (2017, January 23). Tell me where it hurts: The power of incrementalism. *New Yorker,* 36–45.

Graf, N. M., Marini, I., & Blankenship, C. J. (2009). One hundred words about disability. *Journal of Rehabilitation, 75,* 25–34.

Hahn, H. (1997). Advertising the acceptable employment image: Disability and capitalism. In L. J. Davis (Ed.), *The disability studies reader* (pp. 172–186). New York, NY: Routledge.

Harris, S. P., Heller, T., & Schindler, A. (2012). Introduction, background, and history. In R. Heller & S. P. Harris (Eds.), *Disability through the life course* (pp. 1–37). Thousand Oaks, CA: Sage.

Hiranandani, V. (2005). Rethinking disability in social work: Interdisciplinary perspectives. In G. E. May & M. B. Raske (Eds.), *Ending discrimination in social work: Strategies for social workers* (pp. 71–81). Boston, MA: Allyn & Bacon.

Johnson, A. G. (2001). *Privilege, power, and difference.* Boston, MA: McGraw-Hill.

Johnson, M. (2012). *Politics of popcorn save me from Clint Eastwood.* Retrieved from www.ragged-edgemagazine.com/departments/closerlook/000947.html Retrieved 02-26-2018

Kessler Foundation/National Organization on Disability. (2010). *The ADA 20 years later: Survey of Americans with disabilities.* Retrieved from www.2010disabilitysurveys.org/pdfs/surveyresults.pdf

Linton, S. (1998). *Claiming disability: Knowledge and identity.* New York, NY: New York University.

Longmore, P. K. (2003). *Why I burned my book and other essays on disability.* Philadelphia, PA: Temple University.

Marks, D. (1999). *Disability: Controversial debates and psychosocial perspectives.* London: Routledge.

Mattlin, B. (2016, October 5). A disabled life is a life worth living. *New York Times.*

May, G. E., & Raske, M. B. (Eds.) (2005). *Ending discrimination in social work: Strategies for social workers* (pp. 71–81). Boston, MA: Allyn & Bacon.

Mee, C. (1999). *A nearly normal life: A memoir.* Boston, MA: Little, Brown.

Michalko, R. (2002). *The difference that disability makes.* Philadelphia, PA: Temple University.

Mooney, J. (2017, October 12). You are special! Now stop being different. *New York Times.* Retrieved from www.nytimes.com/2017/10/12/opinion/learning-disabilities-attention-deficit.html Retrieved 02-26-2018

Morris, J. (1991). *Pride against prejudice: Transforming attitudes towards disability.* London: The Women's Press.

National Public Radio. (1998a, May). Inventing the poster child. In *The disability history project* [Radio documentary]. Retrieved from www.npr./org/programs/disability/ba_shows.dir/index_sh.html Retrieved 02-26-2016

Paris, J. (2015). *A concise guide to personality disorders.* Washington, DC: American Psychological Association.

Pullin, G. (2009). *Disability meets design.* Cambridge, MA: Massachusetts Institute of Technology.

Rath, J. F., & Elliott, T. R. (2012). Psychological models in rehabilitation psychology. In P. Kennedy (Ed.), *The Oxford handbook of rehabilitation psychology* (pp. 32–46). New York, NY: Oxford University.

Scarr, S., Weinberg, R. A., & Levine, A. (1986). *Understanding development.* Orland, FL: Harcourt Brace Jovanovich.

Scherer, M. J., & Groce, N. (1988). Impairment as human constraint: Cross cultural and historical perspectives on variation. *Journal of Social Issues, 44,* 23–37.

Silberman, S. (2015). *NeuroTribes: The legacy of autism and the future of neurodiversity.* New York, NY: Penguin Random House.

Smart, J. F. (2012). *Disability across the developmental lifespan.* New York, NY: Springer.

Smart, J. F. (2016). *Disability, society, and individual* (3rd ed.). Austin, TX: PRO-ED.

Solomon, A. (2012). *Far from the tree: Parents, children, and the search for identity.* New York, NY: Scribner.

Stefan, S. (2001). *Unequal rights: Discrimination against people with mental disabilities and the Americans with Disabilities Act.* Washington, DC: American Psychological Association.

Tollifson, J. (1997). Imperfection is a beautiful thing. In K. Fries (Ed.), *Staring back: The disability experience from the inside out* (pp. 104–112). New York, NY: Plume.

Twilley, N. (2017, May 15). Sight unseen: Seeing with your tongue and other surprises of sensory-substitution. *New Yorker,* New York.

Weihenmayer, E. (2001). *Touch the top of the world: A blind man's journey to climb farther than the eye can see.* New York, NY: Dutton.

Weisgerber, R. A. (1991). *Quality of life for persons with disabilities: Skill development and transitions across life stages.* Gaithersburg, MD: Aspen.

Wilson, B. (2017). National public radio: This American life #629. "Expect delays." Retrieved from www.thisamericanlife.org/629/expect-delays Retrieved on 02-26-2018

Wilson, D. J. (1990). *Living with polio: The epidemics and its survivors.* Chicago, IL: University of Chicago.

Four

SIX CORE BELIEFS ABOUT DISABILITY OF HIGHLY EMPATHETIC COUNSELORS

Twenty-five years ago, two counselors/educators explained the ways in which counselors bring themselves to counseling relationships by stating,

> Helpers bring unique ways of viewing the world to the helping process. They contribute their personalities, beliefs, assumptions about the world, values, experiences and cultural and demographic characteristics. In addition, helpers bring their theoretical orientations (beliefs how to help) and their previous experiences in helping (both informal and formal).
> (Hill & O'Brien, 1999, p. 32)

Hopefully, this chapter will cause counselors to reevaluate some of their long-held "beliefs, assumptions about the world, values, and experiences."

Important Aspects of Counseling
- The relationship between counselor and client
- The counselor's deep understanding of the client's worldview
- A safe environment for the client
- Ethical guidelines that mandate that counselors provide only those services for which they are trained and are competent

---

The process of becoming an empathetic, skilled, and effective counselor takes many years of study and practice. However, most counselors have had little training and few clients presenting with disabilities (Parritt & O'Callaghan, 2000). Nonetheless, many counseling practitioners, researchers, and scholars consider the relationship between the counselor and client as one of the most significant sources of counseling success. Corey (1996) considered the counselor–client relationship as the *most* critical aspect of counseling successes, stating, "the quality of the client/counselor relationship seems to be the most important factor fostering growth" (p. 15). Before counselors can develop empathy for their clients, a deep understanding of the basic worldview, values, motivations, and experiences of their clients is necessary. For clients, including clients with disabilities, to experience success in counseling, it is essential that counselors create a safe climate in which clients feel understood, accepted, and respected.

Professional counseling codes of ethics require counselors to provide services for which they have been trained, have had supervised clinical supervision, and have developed competence. Therefore, counseling clients with disabilities, in addition to being unsuccessful, may be at risk for being an ethical infraction.

In addition to unsuccessful outcomes and ethical violations, counselors untrained and inexperienced in disability may cause harm to clients with disabilities. Counselors often subtly communicate their values and assumptions. It is true that disabilities are physical and emotional realities; however, the assumptions or beliefs about disability, and the individuals who experience them, are socially created and maintained. (Disabilities themselves are physical, mental, and emotional realities; assumptions and beliefs are human-made judgments about disabilities.) These assumptions are almost always negative, communicating a lack of respect for IWDs, and, whether intended or not, often result in limited life choices for IWDs. Many of the false beliefs about disability appear to be common sense, which most everyone, including many counselors, believes. Counselors are subjected to the ill-informed and prejudicial attitudes of society and, with neither training nor professional experiences with IWDs, often unquestioningly (and unconsciously) accept these demeaning attitudes toward IWDs. Otherwise, ethically sensitive and empathically skilled counselors may not be aware that they may perpetuate these false values and beliefs about disability in their counseling relationships with IWDs. Of course, to some extent, all counseling relationships reveal the counselor's beliefs and values and this is especially crucial in working with clients with disabilities. In summary, a counseling relationship, regardless of the counselor's skill and techniques and years of professional practice, will be more likely to fail if the counselor does not understand the fundamental and essential realities about disability. An empathic and respectful counseling relationship cannot be established when counselors fail to incorporate and communicate more accurate and complete views of disability.

Therefore, before beginning a discussion of specific practice guidelines, this short chapter discusses six basic beliefs concerning disability. The following core beliefs are not comprehensive, but they do serve as a starting point and can be considered "preemptory training." Some of these six core beliefs overlap; however, they provide general awareness training, which precedes skill training. It is hoped that these six core beliefs can serve as an introduction to awareness training for working with clients with disabilities. In the next six chapters, we shall discuss the client's perception of their disability.

Six Core Beliefs

1. The individual is not the disability.
2. Many individuals with disabilities (IWDs) do not constantly long to be normal or cured.
3. Individuals without disabilities (IWODs) are responsible for their own discomfort when interacting with IWDs.
4. A great deal of the prejudice and discrimination against IWDs comes from well-intentioned, nice people.
5. IWDs experience frequent "little acts of degradation" (of which most IWODs are unaware).
6. The little training and education about the experiences of IWDs have been of little value and, indeed, often resulted in *more* prejudice and discrimination.

1. The Individual Is Not the Disability

Thinking that the IWD is their disability results in:

- The IWD is denied the right of self-definition.
- It distances IWDs from IWODs.
- It robs the IWD of their individuality and humanity.
- It reduces the IWD to a single role and function—to be a disability.
- The IWD's potential is limited.
- The disability is falsely considered to be the motivator of the IWD's every thought and behavior.
- It communicates the idea that IWDs are very different from IWODs.
- It communicates that individuals with the same types of disability should only associate with each other. "All quads over there and all blind people (blinks) over here."
- It ultimately reduces the range of choices for IWDs.

No one wants to be known only as a single aspect of their identity. Nonetheless, many IWDs state, "People meet my disability before they meet me" or "IWODs attribute much more importance to my disability than I do!" or "People ask me to be my disability when I want to be me." Disabilities, and the people who have them, often appear unusual and ambiguous, and both of these false perceptions arouse strong feelings in others. Unaware of their lack of awareness,

IWODS see only a disability, rather than an individual with a disability. Very often, the IWD feels compelled to discuss the disability in order to allow a relationship to develop. Wanting to be viewed as individuals first does not mean that IWDs are attempting to hide, minimize, or deny their disabilities. Being defined or recognized *only* as their disability deprives IWDs of their humanity, their uniqueness, and clearly communicates "you're different from me!" and "your disability is freaking me out." Defining IWDs as only their disability communicates that there is nothing generalizable or important about their experience, since not only is the disability the most salient (important) characteristic of the IWD, the disability is typically viewed (by others) as a negative characteristic (Pfeiffer, 2005).

In an online forum for IWDs, a woman describes another pitfall of thinking of the individual as their disability:

> [T]he mere fact of having a disability is still believed to convey important information about a person's potential and limitation beyond the particular disability itself. When a person's entire being is thus reduced to what is perceived as a negative characteristic—her physical or mental impairment—attitudes about the individual's capabilities in other areas also tend to become negative.
> (www.raggededge magazine.com/garrett/causes.htm)

Regarding IWDs as only their disability takes away their right of self-definition, a right that most people claim for themselves. Self-definition simply means that individuals decide who they are, who they want to be, and how they present themselves to the world. Those with disabilities have had little right of self-definition. IWDs have a long history of being defined by others, not only in medical or diagnostic terms, but in terms of their entire character. Moreover, seeing an IWD only as the disability, an identity that is almost always considered to be tragic and inferior, leads to a negative and limited view of the IWD's potential. Also, in this limited view of the IWD, the disability is often erroneously believed to the motivator of every thought and action of the IWD.

Ways in which to view IWDs as *more* than their disability have been discussed in Chapters One and Two. In Chapter One, we learned that most IWDs consider themselves "normal," because they have multiple identities, characteristics, talents, skills, and life tasks. We also cautioned counselors that they should not automatically assume that the client's disability is the presenting problem. These attitudes of the general public are also present in encounters with professional service providers. In an article on the health and well-being of people with disabilities, one woman described the result of physicians seeing only her disability:

> No matter what I go in for, they look at the disability first and forget about whatever I'm talking about, whether it has to do with the disability or not. Everybody just stops and says I have to go to a specialist for this or that.
> (Putnam et al., 2003, p. 41)

This excerpt illustrates the point that physicians have *unnecessarily* complicated the IWD's access to services and reduced her range of choices. By seeing this IWD as only her disability, doctors have sent her to specialists for minor complaints such as colds and sore throats, which have nothing to do with her disability. Counselors who automatically consider referring all clients with disabilities to rehabilitation counselors are defining potential clients by their disabilities. Often, however, these IWDs want marriage counseling, gender issue counseling, career counseling, adolescent counseling, or some other specialty area in which rehabilitation counselors are neither trained for nor have had experience.

A young boy growing up in Brooklyn, New York, in the 1950s (Uhlberg, 2008) described the way in which his parents' deafness defined the entire family.

> It was one thing to be singled out on my street as the son of the "deafies" in 3A, which is all my parents were ever known as on our block. Not as Louis and Sarah; not as Mr. and Mrs. Uhlberg, but rather as the "deaf and dumb mutes in 3A." The unthinking consignment as objects of curiosity and even pity, was something I had adapted to.
> (p. 58)

Another way in which to avoid thinking of the IWD as only their disability was discussed in Chapter Two when we discussed the various large, multinational, standardized diagnostic systems, such as the ICD-10 and the DSM-5. Rather than stating, "He is schizophrenic," the most accurate way to describe someone is: "He has been diagnosed with schizophrenia," or "His symptoms meet the diagnostic criteria of the DSM-5 for schizophrenia." At first glance, these sentences may appear synonymous, or semantic wordplay; however, the way in which the individual is described, diagnosed, and labeled has a profound influence on their self-identity. The second and third statements separate the symptoms from the individual and the third sentence references the diagnostic system. Although diagnostic systems have the advantage of providing general objective categories, they often fail to provide sensitivity to individual differences.

Naturally, IWDs are aware of the salience IWODs ascribe to their disability. In an article entitled, "It's Not All About My Legs" (Oldenburg, March 16, 2014, *USA Today*, pp. 7B, 8B) spoke of her experience competing on the national television program, "Dancing With the Stars." To counter the expected (and unwanted) focus on her prosthetic legs, Purdy stated, "The media make it sound so tragic and it was extremely traumatic at the time, but I'm so beyond that. I've done so much with my life." Purdy is a 34-year-old model, massage therapist, and bronze medal winner in the Paralympics in Sochi, Russia. At age 19, Purdy had both her legs amputated just below the knee to save her life because she had contracted bacterial meningitis. One day, she thought she had the flu and the next day she was hospitalized and on life support. Her legs were amputated to save her life. The title of the newspaper article skillfully communicates the main point of the interview with Ms. Purdy, "It's Not All About My Legs" or "I don't want to be defined by my disability."

2. Many IWDs Do Not Wish to Be "Normal" or "Cured"

> **Results of Thinking That IWDs Want to Be Cured**
> - Communicates to IWDs that "normality" is more valued than having a disability.
> - Forces IWDs to justify and defend their existence.
> - Difficult does not mean tragic inferiority.
> - For those with congenital disabilities, they have no memory of not having a disability. They humorously explain: "For us, abnormal is normal."
> - Many IWDs are proud of their mastery of the disability.
> - Many IWDs feel that their disability is an important and valued part of their self-identity.
> - Many IWDs think that society's focus on a cure removes attention from improving the quality of life of IWDs.
> - The desire to shed "the social role of being disabled" is not the same as wanting to be cured of the disability.

It is often surprising to many IWODS when they discover that many IWDs do not constantly long for a cure. It seems counterintuitive to those who have not experienced a disability that many IWDs do not wish to have their disability eliminated. Linton (1998) described this surprise as "startling" and further stated that in most cases, a cure is not possible, but there are other possibilities, provided by society, that could make their lives better.

It is often startling to nondisabled people that many disabled do not pine for the nondisabled experience, nor do they conceptualize disability as a potent determinant. What IWDs do "pine" for is equal social status, opportunity structures.

Jenny Morris, an Englishwoman with paraplegia described this ill-informed (and insulting) idea as prejudicial:

> One of the most oppressive features of the prejudice which disabled people experience is the assumption that we want to be other than what we are: that is, we want to be normal. Yet, as Pam Evans says, "Do we only have value, even to ourselves, in direct relation to how closely we can imitate 'normal' appearance, function, belief, and behavior?" The only way in which it seems we can gain acceptance is to emulate normality . . . the pressures on us to aspire to be "normal" are huge—friends and family all conspire from the kindest and highest of intentions to ensure that we make the wrong choice. Better to betray ourselves than them!
>   Thrown on the defensive of trying to prove that their lives are worth living by denying that disability sometimes involves being sick, in pain, or generally experiencing an awful time.
>
> (J. Morris, 1991, p. 35)

Morris also described the cost to IWDs of this false belief of IWODs, by use of words "Better to betray ourselves than them." Stated differently, IWDs often feel that they must minimize and hide their disability so that IWODs can maintain these false, but comforting, beliefs.

Even young children are able to discern the (unwanted) pity of others. As a young girl in South Carolina, Harriet McBryde Johnson was annoyed when adults told her that they felt sorry for her when she couldn't play on the beach. Johnson was born with a neuromuscular disease, a progressive degenerating disability which made her unable walk.

> As a little girl playing on the beach, I was already aware that people felt sorry for me that I wasn't frolicking with the same level of frenzy as the other children. This annoyed me and still does. I took the time to write a detailed description of how I, in fact, had fun playing on the beach without the need of standing, walking, or running.
>
> (H. M. Johnson, 2003)

A woman with a congenital limb deficiency, does not wish to eliminate her disability. Instead, she imagines her relief if society would change:

> I used to dream about being in a world where being disabled was no big deal, where no one considered it a tragedy. No one thought you were inspiring or felt sorry for you. No one stared at you. I imagined what a relief it would be to have been to be seen in every way as perfectly ordinary.
>
> I am missing my right hand and half of my right arm. They were amputated in the uterus, before I was born, by a floating fiber.
>
> (Tollifson, 1997, p. 104)

It is noteworthy that Tollifson uses the words "perfectly ordinary" instead of "normal."

Stating that many IWDs do not aspire to be "cured" of their disability, does not mean that *other* IWDs would not gladly be cured of their disabilities, with their functional limitations, occasionally pain, frequent treatments and hospitalizations, and huge expenses. There are, without doubt, negative aspects of disabilities; however, many IWODs believe that those without disabilities consider the lives of IWDs to be one unending, continuous misfortune. One IWD summarized, "Difficult does not mean tragic."

In the *New York Times* bestselling book *Far From the Tree* (Solomon, 2012), the author told of a young woman with congenital blindness, Deborah Kent. Kent compared the desire to have wings to her desire to have sight.

> Deborah Kent is a congenitally blind woman who has written about the pain that society's prejudice against blindness has caused her. Describing a level of self-acceptance that was almost unheard of before the disability rights movement came into its own, Kent has said that her blindness is, to her a neutral trait like her brown hair. "I didn't long for sight any more than I yearned for a pair of wings. Blindness presented occasional complications, but it seldom kept me from anything I wanted to do. I believe that my life could not have turned out any better if I had been fully sighted. My parents raised all three of children, including my blind brother and me, with sensitivity and unwavering love. In all of us, they tried to nurture confidence, ambition, and self-respect."
>
> (pp. 30-31)

A polio survivor described the negative, difficult aspects of living with a disability, yet values her disability. She compares her disability with her ethnic and gender identification:

> I'm proud of being Italian. There are things I am ashamed of, like the existence of the Mafia—but these things do not stop me from embracing my Italian-ness. I love being a woman, but I hate going through menopause. But I wouldn't want a sex-change operation, just because of menopause. Certainly the pain and physical limitations of disability are not wonderful, yet that identity is who I am. And I am proud of it.
>
> (Fleischer & Zames, 2001, p. 202)

There are several unintended, and negative, results in thinking that all IWDs want to be cured of their disability. This narrow and inaccurate worldview 1) reinforces the automatic and unthinking prejudice toward IWDs by implying that it is better *not* to have a disability; 2) places the focus on the cure or prevention of the disability, rather than concentrating on quality of life issues for IWDs, 3) ignores the fact that some IWDs consider their disability to be an asset, feeling that their lives are better *because* they have a disability; and 4) IWDs who wish to refuse the socially constructed "disabled role" are often thought to be denying the disability itself. The "disabled role" has little to do with the disability itself (the Biomedical Model) but is a socially constructed role of pathology, deviance, dependence, and inferiority. Often, when encountering IWDs who refuse to think of themselves in this negative way, IWODs mistakenly conclude that "they have just not accepted their disability" or "they have a chip on their shoulder."

Normalcy, or lack of a disability, is enshrined within our culture and, therefore, it is often difficult to understand that there are some IWDs who do not constantly wish for a cure. Moreover, most IWODs rarely consider the costs of these beliefs for IWDs. Michalko (2002) explained:

> Contemporary culture, particularly Western culture, since the Industrial Revolution, represents disability as something that should be prevented or cured and sees disability as a tragedy that befalls some people. No one aspires to be that type, a disabled person. Being a person who is not welcome, who is feared, pitied, and looked upon as a type that no one would aspire to be is often difficult to bear.
>
> (Michalko, 2002, p. 1)

Whether on a societal level, as the preceding excerpt describes, or on an individual level, the single focus on a cure impacts the IWD's self-perception. Everyone, including IWDs, internalize and believe these widely held negative assumptions about disability. To struggle against the focus on a cure, IWDs often feel that they need to justify or defend their existence. IWDs may interpret the need for a cure as implying that their lives have no value. Finally, the focus on cure diverts both attention and resources from improving the quality of life for IWDs and providing and enforcing civil rights for IWDs.

In the following statement, a woman who uses a wheelchair refuses the role of inferiority and uses a humorous term to describe individuals who can walk, "wobblies." "I do believe I am as good as all those wobblies who walk around on two legs, and I think that everyone should have that attitude" (Faull et al., 2004, p. 136).

In summary, the results of a single focus on curing disability include:

- Enshrines the ideals of normality and health. To be "normal" is always better than to be "disabled."
- Some IWDs may internalize the idea that "people like them" shouldn't exist.
- Ignores the fact that many IWDs consider their lives fulfilling *because of* the disability and they have had many positive experiences *because* of the disability.
- Ignores the fact that many IWDs are proud of their mastery of their disabilities.
- Diverts attention and resources from improving the quality of life for IWDs and providing them with resources and benefits.

3. IWODS Are Responsible for Their Own Discomfort

Results of falsely thinking that IWDs are responsible for our discomfort:

- Many IWODs do not understand that their discomfort is caused by a combination of:
  1. Their lack of experience, knowledge, and education about disability
  2. Their existential angst of acquiring a disability
- Places an unwanted and undeserved burden upon IWDs. They are placed in the position of "comforting" and "explaining" their disabilities to people who should know better.
- Blames the victim—or the IWD who is the recipient of others' discomfort.
- Allows IWODs to continue to ignore the disability experience.
- Contributes to IWODs' fear of acquiring a disability.
- Separates IWODs from IWDs and thus limits the range of choice available to IWODs.
- Considering IWDs to be "inspirational" distances IWDs from IWODs and is often thought to be burdensome.

Many IWODs are uncomfortable around IWDs, feeling stressed, threatened, vaguely sad, and not quite sure how to interact. A woman with a disability not only described the reactions of "many people," but also her reaction to this unwanted and unexpected response from others.

> So many people will become highly nervous around people with obvious disabilities, and that's what bugs me most. I can't tell you how many times I've been out for dinner and had the waitress avoid eye contact; too shy for the job. It's not like I'm hideous to look at, the wheelchair can be just very, very intimidating. Nobody told me this in rehab.
>
> (Karuth, 1998, p. 46)

Another woman tells IWODs that her disability does not warrant their grief by stating, "Put your handkerchiefs away."

> I would like to be able to sit people down and say, "Look, I appreciate your concern, but my life isn't that bad. Sure, it's not quite uninterrupted bliss, but whose life is? It's a good life. I work and play and have friends and make love and mistakes and get bored now and again just like you. So, put your handkerchiefs away. First impressions aside, I'm a lot more like you than you probably imagine."
>
> (Karuth, 1998, p. 46)

Another IWD stated, "one is forced to deal with the meaning that the diagnosis has for others" (Toombs, 1995, p. 6). Notice the word, "forced," suggesting that dealing with the reactions of others is unwanted and unwarranted.

There are several reasons for this discomfort around IWDs. First, someone with a visible disability is an unpleasant and unwanted reminder of IWODs' potential to acquire a disability and everyone's failure to completely control their bodies. Second, many IWODs believe in the fallacy that the world is fair and someone with a disability causes them to question this long-held, cherished (but false) belief. Third, disability is experienced as ambiguity and the perception of ambiguity often leads to feeling stressed. Finally, seeing someone with a disability often makes others question their philosophical or religious beliefs. One author (Smart, 2016) termed this discomfort around IWDs as "existential angst."

Fear of acquiring a disability is sometimes referred to as the *existential angst of disability*. *Angst* is the German word for *fear*, and existentialism is a school of philosophy that holds that human life is fraught with peril, to which everyone is subject. The human condition, according to existential philosophers, is full of unexpected and unwanted circumstances that have the potential to threaten our well-being. Disability is one of these unexpected circumstances.

(p. 108)

The way in which IWODs respond to this discomfort actually *increases* their discomfort. Avoiding IWDs and distancing themselves from IWDs increases the stress and ambiguity in IWODs. In the National Public Radio *Disability History Project* (1998), a mother of a child with Down syndrome stated, "It just doesn't make sense to make us part of a metaphysical puzzle." Many IWDs report experiences in which strangers have prayed over them, or quoted bible scriptures, and one man in a wheelchair was told by a stranger in the street that he would walk in heaven.

A professor of English describes the way in which others often mistakenly think her disability is contagious, eliciting fear. The professor also describes the effect of others' fears, "It forces me to dig for deep waters of self-love."

Anne Kaier teaches Shakespeare at a university in Philadelphia. She was born with lamellar ichthyosis, "a (noncontagious) genetic disorder which manifests itself in scales not just on my face, arms, hands, but over my whole body. My skin is perpetually red and itchy." "What's it like to be the object of such fear? It forces me to dig for deep waters of self-love. It also makes me angry." Even a person who scares some people has to make her way in the world. Ms. Kaier gave an example of this fear: "A checkout lady's panic surged as she held the coins six inches above my hand and dropped them into my palm. "What's wrong with you?" she asked, her voice rising to a higher pitch. "Just dry skin," I murmur.

(Kaier, 2016)

A feminist disability scholar summarized that most IWODs rarely think about their bodies:

The body is usually unobtrusive and taken for granted; all of this is changed seeing an individual with a disability. (The) physically disabled body becomes the repository for social anxieties about such troubling concerns as vulnerability, control, and identity.

(Thomson, 1997, p. 297)

Another way in which IWODs distance themselves from IWDs is to think of IWDs as "inspirations." Often, it is difficult for IWODs to understand that judging IWDs as inspirational is prejudicial, unwanted, and distancing. It is also difficult for IWODs to see these attitudes as self-protective myths. There is a cultural tendency to regard anything that threatens our sense of self as alien. Solomon (2012) explained, "When a disability is viewed as inexplicable and impenetrable, people tend to react with one or two extremes, either they stigmatize or romanticize. It's hard to know which is worse" (p. 347).

Many disability advocates have expressed distain for being viewed as "inspirational" and reject the premise that this emotion adds any positive status to IWDs. This often-used description associated with able-bodied individuals' emotions in connection with accomplishments or just daily living of those with disabilities is seen by some in the community as separating, objectifying, condescending, and regressive in terms of equality and inclusion. A very good description of this point of view is reflected by Australian activist/comedian Stella Young. In a TED talk entitled, "I Am Not Your Inspiration," Ms. Young explained:

> I can't help but wonder whether the source of this strange assumption that living our lives takes some particular kind of courage is in the news media, an incredibly powerful tool in shaping the way we think about disability. Most journalists seem utterly incapable of writing or talking about a person with a disability without using phrases like, "overcoming disability," "brave," "suffers from," "defying the odds," "wheelchair bound," or my personal favourite, "inspirational."

By acknowledging this discomfort and stress often felt when interacting with IWDs, IWODs can begin learning more accurate understandings of IWDs. The second step is recognizing that IWODs are responsible for their own discomfort and existential angst. Recognizing this is more difficult and, perhaps, harder to understand and accept. Contributing to this discomfort are lack of experience with IWDs, exaggerated and emotional responses to the disability, and the inability to view the IWD as an individual who, except for the disability, is a normal person. Everyone is responsible for their own feelings and reactions, including the powerful emotional reactions due to lack of experience and knowledge. Knowledge about disability includes an awareness of prejudice and discrimination. By keeping IWDs out of sight, IWODs ignore them but also pay a price for this deliberate, self-inflicted ignorance.

IWODs are responsible for their "existential angst" and can take steps to reduce it. It is not the responsibility of IWDs to make IWODs feel comfortable, nor are IWDs responsible for the distress and discomfort felt by IWODs. As the number of IWDs grows and the deinstitutionalization movement continues, greater integration into the educational, social, and occupational roles, and government-protected and enforced civil rights will contribute to a more accurate understanding of the disability and the people who experience disabilities. Nonetheless, it is a personal responsibility to acknowledge discomfort around IWDs, see this discomfort as having nothing to do with the IWD, but rather as a result of our emotional, irrational, and uninformed responses, and finally to take steps to reduce this discomfort.

4. A Great Deal of the Prejudice and Discrimination Against IWDs Comes From Well-Intentioned, Nice People

Results of these well-intentioned attitudes and behaviors:
- Allows IWODs to feel beneficent and generous.
- Can lead to paternalism and possessive feelings toward IWDs.
- Maintains the power differential—the IWOD is superior to the IWD.
- Objectifies IWDs.
- Promotes *unnecessary* dependence.
- The IWD is aware that such "kindnesses" are actually patronizing and demeaning.
- Denies the IWD the right of self-definition.
- Makes equal social status relationships more difficult.
- Limits the range of choices of IWDs or "I know what's best for you."
- Absolves governments and societies of the responsibility to accord civil rights. IWDs want civil rights and opportunities rather than charity.

Paternalism, positive stereotypes, charity, pity, reducing or waiving requirements, and lowered expectations are rooted in the actions and attitudes of "nice" people who want to "help." Misguided kindness is the prime *motivator* of all these behaviors and attitudes and, therefore, it is difficult to understand that its *results* negatively affect the self-image of IWDs, does not allow IWDs equal social status with IWODs, absolves governments and societies of responsibility to provide civil rights, and often limits the range of choices available to them. Further, these types of well-intentioned behaviors and attitudes objectify IWDs. But, the IWOD may ask, "don't IWDs want help, at times?" Yes, IWDs do want help occasionally; however, they want to determine which types of help they receive. Behaviors and attitudes that *unnecessarily* result in dependence for

IWDs are prejudicial and discriminating. Many IWDs question if charity telethons solve "the right problem," since IWDs typically have not been included in organizational decision making.

Anne Emerman, former director of the New York Office of People with Disabilities, described the pervasive nature of paternalism, terming it as a "residue."

> Our issues are always being discussed by people who are experts about us—politicians, policymakers, doctors, social workers—but not us. It's as if they thought, what do we know about ourselves? With all the enlightened thinking about disability, there's still that residue of paternalism.
> (Fleischer & Zames, 2001, p. 211)

More importantly, most IWDs want to be respected, accorded equal social status with IWODs, and given access to public opportunity structures such as health care, education, and employment opportunities. Stated differently, IWDs want opportunities to earn respect and financial independence. Moreover, IWDs want to be contributors to others, most of whom are IWODs.

An American disability scholar summarized:

> We, like all Americans, have talents to use, work to do, our contribution to our communities and country. We want the chance to work and marry without jeopardizing our lives. We want access to opportunity. We want access to work. We want access to the American dream.
> (Longmore, 2003, p. 258)

Respect, civil rights, and opportunity are not congruent with charity telethons, lowered expectations, pity, or positive stereotypes, all misguided concepts of effective support. An English disability scholar described the effects of organized charity:

> The disabled movement has been particularly critical of charities run by non-disabled people who claim to attend to the needs of disabled people, yet who in practice demean and devalue them. Charity plays a key role in perpetuating dependency by constructing images of disabled people as helpless.
> (Marks, 1999, p. 96)

Examples of misguided positive stereotypes include: "All blind people are musically talented" or "All IWDs are compassionate." Another "compliment" is the idea of IWODs conferring "honorary normal status" on an IWD by stating,

"I never think of you as disabled." These types of "compliments" ignore the disability, which often is a valued and important part of the IWD's identity. A feminist disability scholar, Rosemarie Garland-Thomson summarized: "This impulse to rescue people with disabilities from a discredited status, while usually well meaning, is decidedly at odds with the various pride movements we've come to know in recent decades" (2016, August 19, *New York Times*). The speaker often feels benevolent and tolerant when, in actuality, they have robbed IWDs of their individuality and the right to self-definition.

IWDs do not want pity, however kindly offered, nor do they want to be viewed as something that others do not want to be. If others consider disability to be a burden, they are inclined to view the IWD as a "victim," and therefore engage in "enabling" and accepting of behaviors that would not be accepted in IWODs. One clear-cut example of this enabling behavior is substance and alcohol abuse. Helwig and Holicky (1994) explained,

> In an effort to ease their own pain, well-meaning professionals, care givers, family members, and friends often help the individual who is disabled continue his or her chemical dependence. Through enabling, the individual who is disabled can continue to "mood alter" and escape both the reality of the disability and the necessity to deal with it on an honest emotional level.
>
> (p. 228)

Lowered expectations include expressions such as "Let's give these poor disabled people a break." Or the teacher who says, "I will give this student with a disability a 'mercy C,' so that they can pass my class." Lowered expectations are difficult to understand because they may solve a short-term problem, but eventually standards are upheld and the IWD understands that they have not been adequately prepared. Moreover, IWDs realize that the lowered expectations communicate, "You're not quite good enough, so we're lowering expectations and giving you mercy perks." Brenda Premo was director of the California Department of Rehabilitation and is legally blind. In the following excerpt, she illustrates the relationship between high expectations and the accommodations provided to meet these standards:

> I really appreciated the teachers in high school who would accommodate me but who had high expectations. They would ask me, "What can I do that would make this better for you?" but they wouldn't let me slide at all academically. There was a math teacher, an old gruff guy. He would accommodate me, but I had to achieve and I had to earn my grade. I always got

Bs from him but I respected him so much more than some college teachers who gave me easy As. The same thing happened in college. I always appreciated the teachers who expected the most out of me out of me and I worked my hardest in their classes. I got the most out of them.

(Mackelprang & Salsgiver, 1999, p. 142)

Ms. Premo's account tells of a high school math teacher, and other teachers, who asked which types of accommodations would work best but, at the same time, upheld standards, both of which uphold the tenets of the ADA. It is standards that are standardized, meaning that standards are identical for everyone; it is accommodations that are need-based. Ill-informed IWODs often assume that the ADA mandates lowered standards or some sort of hiring or admission quotas. In reality, the ADA mandates accommodations but does not require standards to be waived or lowered. In Ms. Premo's account, we can see that the teachers who required her to meet the standards and who gave her grades she had earned, asked Ms. Premo what accommodations she needed. Notice that in the account, neither Ms. Premo or the teachers uses the word, "accommodations," but rather, "What can I do to make this better for you?" In this simple question, there are two basic and important assumptions, first, the teachers asked (rather than told) Ms. Premo which accommodations she needed, understanding that accommodations are highly individualized, and, second, the teachers said, "What can I do?" understanding that providing the accommodations was the teachers' responsibility and not Ms. Premo's obligation. The other teachers who gave Ms. Premo unearned, easy As probably did not ask which accommodations were necessary. These teachers probably found it easier to give the unearned grade, probably thinking: "This kid is blind; she can't learn math (or any subject)." Lowered expectations freed these teachers from providing accommodations and, perhaps, these teachers thought they were being kind. However, in due course, Ms. Premo learned that she had been disadvantaged by that easy A. Everyone, with or without a disability, performs better in a high-demand environment. However, different types of disabilities, such as severe intellectual disabilities, would prevent some students from succeeding in some environments.

Another type of well-intentioned behavior has been termed "inspiration porn" by the late Stella Young, an Australian comedian and disability activist. Young used a wheelchair, due to a congenital disability. She related that throughout her life she was considered "inspirational" because "I got out of bed in the morning and remembered my name," and she hated being used as someone else's source of inspiration. The use of the word "porn" is strong and somewhat shocking; however Young's definition of pornography is "to objectify one group of people for the benefit of another group of people" (Young, 2014). In her TED talk, Young derides inspirational posters of IWDs, pointing out these being regarded as "inspirations" relegates IWDs to positions of inferiority and separates IWDs from society. The demeaning stereotypes, which include inspirational posters, communicates 1) IWDs have not been allowed in society, such as becoming professionals who, in reality, accomplish things that are inspirational; 2) IWODs "exceptionalize" IWDs, assigning IWDs the master status of disabled and expecting very little of them; and 3) IWODs can feel better about their own problems and shortcomings, because by social comparison, their lives are (falsely) thought to be better than the lives of IWDs.

Young told about teaching high school history and in the middle of lectures (on history) students would interrupt her to ask her when she would be giving her disability inspirational speech, demonstrating that her students viewed her as only a disabled person. Young stated, "I want to live in a world where people don't have so low expectations of disabled persons." Finally, she explained the Social Model of Disability, or the sociopolitical model, in which many of the difficulties of disability are created and maintained by "society," which cheerfulness and a good attitude on the part of IWDs will not solve, stating, "No amount of smiling at a flight of stairs will make it turn into a ramp." Her clear message, humorously related, is: "I'm here to tell you that you've been lied to about disability. Disabled people don't do anything out of the ordinary."

5. IWDs Experience Frequent "Little Acts of" Degradation" (of Which Most IWODs Are Unaware)

Results of "little acts of degradation":
- Remind IWDs of their inferior status.
- Make life an unending public performance.
- Violate boundaries and the privacy of IWDs.
- Reinforce the power differential.

"Daily large and small events that, whether or not by design, remind us our place in American society. It is an endless struggle with humiliation, depression, and rage" (M. Johnson, 2003, p. 24). These "little acts of degradation" include intrusive questioning by strangers and staring and other types of hypervisibility. Often, IWDs report that they have felt like children stripped of boundaries, rather than regarded as adults. All of these intrusions violate boundaries, result in less privacy, and make life for IWDs an unending public performance. IWDs consider staring and intrusive questioning to be reminders of their inferior position in society.

Surprisingly, many IWODs are not aware that IWDs consider the staring and intrusive questioning to be demeaning. The following description of insensitive questioning also describes his wife's reaction, "suppressed psychotic rage."

> Not a day passes that I am in public where I am not approached by a child, a student, parent, or random creepy person in the mall. Why do they approach me? Curiosity has gotten the better of them and I resemble Mr. Ask Me. Many people are not acquainted with people who live in a wheelchair. I don't usually mind, especially the children. The questions range from children asking how I tie my shoes to adults asking about my sex life. . . . When those people approach us, my wife's face shows a mix of embarrassment and suppressed psychotic rage. It can be difficult to distinguish the two of them.
>
> How do I pee?
> In a toilet. How do you pee?
> Do I have sex with my wife?
> Yes, on a daily basis. High five creepy random mall guy!
> The point I try to make during these encounters is that I am Mr. Average Joe. Am I special? Only in ways that annoy my wife. I put my pants on the same way as you. One leg at a time. I live a normal life. I cook my daughter breakfast and take her to school. I coach soccer. I love playing basketball. I'm crude. I play video games. I wrestle my dogs on the floor. I travel. I teach high school. I get enjoyment from embarrassing my child in every social setting possible, "Hey, Bella, is that the boy you said was soooo cute?" I am happily married. I'm involved with my church. How much more average can I possibly be in this life? I lead an active life like any married guy with kids in his 30s.
>
> https://dredf.org/healthcare-www.raggededgemagazine.com/departments/closerlook/00713.html

Note the types of questions that are asked, questions about areas of life that are typically considered to be private, which most adults without disabilities would not be asked. Also notice the lengthy description of his "normal" life.

This man in a wheelchair describes his wife's reaction to these intrusive questions as "a mix of embarrassment and psychotic rage." Other family members of IWDs, including young children, also notice these minor acts of degradation.

Lee Martin's father wore double hooks because both his hands were amputated in a farm accident. Lee was a very young child at the time of the accident and, therefore, could not remember his father without the double hooks. Lee became accustomed to the hooks; but he never did become inured to the staring: "I had never gotten used to the attention those hooks drew, the furtive glances from people trying not to be rude, the out-and-out stares from others who were so surprised to see the prostheses they couldn't begin to mask their curiosity" (Lee, 2000, p. 114).

Amazingly, many IWODs do not consider the effects of their insensitivity. Martha Undercoffer, a little person, found a way to inform insensitive IWODs of the harm they have inflicted.

> I have developed a safe and easy system to use. It's a business card. On the front, "Yes, I noticed your behavior towards me. (For some reason, the public seems to think we don't notice their treatment of us.) On the back of the card: I realize that you probably mean no harm by yours actions and/or comments: However they did cause harm and were not appreciated.
> (Solomon, 2012, p. 145)

Staring and other acts of intrusion serve to reinforce the power differential between IWDs and IWODs. Garland-Thomson (1997) perceptively noted: the person staring, the IWOD, is the "spectator," and the person who is being stared at, the IWD, is "the spectacle." Garland-Thomson explained: "One role is to look, judge, and act while the other role is to be gazed upon, measured, and passive" (p. 300). The following excerpt describes the way in which a polio survivor, although "flat on his back," reversed the power differential.

> There was Leroy who must spend the rest of his life flat on his back. Sometimes the curious ones would make so bold as to stand directly above him. Without a word, they would stand and stare.
>
> Photography has long been Leroy's hobby and he decided that a splendid opportunity has come to get unusual shots. Slightly concealed in his clothing so that no one would suspect, he planted his candid camera. Now, let the curious ones come!
>
> Slowly as before, they approached his cot. Now they stood beside him. Now they were bending over to *really* get a look. Eyes were opened wide. The jaw had dropped. Then *click* went the camera. And bewildered, nonplussed onlookers fled speedily away.
>
> What a collection Leroy must have now.
> (Lee, cf. Wilson, 1990)

Family members of IWDs, including young children, also notice these minor acts of degradation. Two disability scholars (Cate & Loots, 2000), in an empirical study, interviewed the siblings of Dutch children with physical disabilities, including 18 with spina bifida, 11 with cerebral palsy, and 14 with multiple disabilities. Cate and Loots found that young siblings found the behaviors of "strangers" to be disrespectful and specifically mentioned "staring."

> The siblings took the view that the behavior of strangers was certainly open to improvement. They thought that people should be better informed, should behave more "naturally," show more respect, and certainly refrain from staring.
>
> (p. 408)

These little acts of degradation and intrusions are exhausting for IWDs, emotionally, mentally, and physically. The cumulative effects of being defined negatively by strangers, scrutinized, and judged are difficult to imagine.

> Every few hours I run up against people who feel free to remind me that I am inferior and I should conform to whatever they've decided "people like me" are supposed to be like. . . . We should drop everything to satisfy other people's curiosity about us, and we should do it in a manner that is pleasant and convenient for them even if it is physically impossible for us. . . . Every few hours I run up against people who are so convinced that this is true that they are mystified that I'm not grateful for the experience.
>
> (Montgomery, 2006, para. 12)

The disability rights lawyer, Harriet McBryde Johnson, told of the intrusions she experienced. "Some people call me the Good Luck Lady; they consider it propitious to cross my path when a hurricane is coming and to kiss my head just before voting" (2003). Johnson was born with a progressive neuromuscular disease which necessitated the use of a wheelchair. She gained national fame when she told the story in the *New York Times* (2003) about her debate with Princeton University philosophy professor, Peter Singer. Singer's ideas, which he published, included the ethical euthanasia of newborn babies with severe disabilities. Singer clearly stated that Johnson should have been euthanized at birth. Somewhat surprising was Dr. Singer's amazement that Ms. Johnson should feel personally insulted and demeaned.

6. IWDs Want Their Experiences, Perspectives, and History Incorporated Into Society or Is Disability Diversity or Deviance?

> **Results of failing to incorporate disability knowledge:**
> - IWODs forfeit valuable knowledge about the human experience.
> - Perpetuates the existential angst of acquiring a disability.
> - Because everyone has the potential to acquire a disability, disability knowledge should concern everyone.

Diversity is typically defined as variations that are desirable, and strengthen and improve the broader society. Deviance, on the other hand, is defined as undesirable variation that weakens the broader culture. Both are labels conferred upon individuals' dominant, powerful groups and, thus both are characterizations that are made possible only by social comparison. Neither diversity or deviance exists within individuals; it is the broader society who determines what constitutes diversity or deviance and then decides who is diverse and who is deviant. Both diversity and deviance is in the eye of the beholder.

When speaking of diversity, we often include such identities as race, ethnicity, culture, language use, gender, and sexual identity. In contrast, disability itself is considered deviance. Individuals who are labeled "diverse" are considered equal to the dominant group and thus, the label of diversity carries no hierarchical component. Diversity often translates into power and authority. The concept of deviance does have a hierarchal component, specifically deviance is variation that is thought to be pathology, inferiority, and threatening. Therefore, the label of "deviant" is *forced* upon the individual. Few people would choose to identify themselves as deviant. Further, most people prefer to align themselves with individuals who hold power and authority while few people want to align themselves with individuals who are considered inferior and powerless. Societies are motivated to learn about individuals considered to be diverse, but they want to ignore and segregate those thought to be deviant.

Technically, the concepts of diversity and deviance are neutral terms (without value judgments) and describe the same idea, specifically any deviation from the norm. Most of us would like to think that there is something extraordinary about ourselves when, in reality, most of us, including IWDs, are quite ordinary. To summarize, both deviance and diversity, in the most accurate terms,

- Are value-free terms.
- Are synonymous terms, simply meaning any aberration from the typical, average, ordinary, commonplace.
- When applied to individuals or groups, both deviance and diversity are the result of social comparison, meaning that the powerful, defining, dominant group determines who receives each label. Or, stated differently, neither diversity or deviance exists in individuals.

In common usage,

- Diversity is considered to be a positive trait and most societies value diversity.
- Deviance is thought to be pathology, weakness, threat, and inferiority and many societies ignore or segregate those labeled deviant.

IWDs do not self-identify as deviants and reject the Social Model of Disability with its emphasis upon inferiority and victimhood. Indeed, IWDs want their experiences, histories, and perspectives incorporated into the broader culture. John Hockenberry, a National Public Radio (NPR) newsperson and commentator, explained:

> Why is it that a person would not be considered educated or privileged if he went through school and never learned there was a France or a French language? But if a person went through school and knew nothing about disability, never met a disabled person, never heard of American Sign Language, he might be considered not only educated, but also lucky?
> (Fleischer & Zames, 2001, p. 205)

To answer Hockenberry's question, France and the French language are considered diversity whereas disability is considered deviance. Unquestionably, every educated person wants to learn about France, while few demonstrate any desire to learn about IWDs. Leonard Kriegel provided the explanation:

> The world of the crippled and disabled is strange and dark, and it is held up to judgment by those who live in fear of it. The cripple is the creature who has been deprived of his ability to create a self. . . . He is the other, if for no other reason than that by being the other will he be allowed to presume upon "normals." He must accept definition from outside the boundaries of his own existence.
> (1987, p. 66)

Notice the use of the word, "presume." Diversity is encouraged and invited whereas deviance must "presume" upon the majority group, in this case, "normals."

We have discussed that most IWODs, including professional service providers, tend to sensationalize and exaggerate the disability experience, sometimes finding IWDs inspiring or brave, all attempts at distancing themselves from IWDs. The concept of "normalcy" is enshrined, embedded, institutionalized, and legitimatized in most cultures. Societies tend to see normalcy as the ideal, rather than as a simple measurement tool. Most IWODs would not identify themselves as IWODs. Stated differently, most people who have disabilities do not think much about disability and, therefore, while IWODs would readily identify someone as having a disability, they would never think of themselves as *not* having a disability. Further, most IWODs do not identify with IWDs. Wendell (2006) explained: "Suffering caused by the body and the inability to control the body are despised, pitied, and above all, feared" (p. 267).

However, disability should be of interest to *everyone* since everyone has the potential to acquire a disability or to be diagnosed with a chronic illness. Learning about disability and IWDs will help to decrease the fear (or existential angst) that many IWODs experience. Joan Tollifson (1997) in a chapter entitled, "Imperfection Is a Beautiful Thing," explained:

> Imperfection is the essence of being organic and alive. Organic life is vulnerable; it inevitably ends in disintegration. This is the part of its beauty. True meditation delves into this mystery of life and death, discovering (not intellectually, but experientially) how porous and momentary everything is.
>
> (p. 106)

A university professor, who is blind, worries about the "Normals," feeling that they need a great deal of help. She also states that disability "forces people to question everything they take for granted as normal."

> There is more than one way to be a human being . . . On the surface, it seems a pretty innocuous statement, but in fact, it's quite revolutionary. It forces people to question everything they take for granted as normal. It's a message that needs to be spoken of still. . . . We say it by forcing our way into their notice, into their world.
>
> I worried about a lot of them so much, the Normals I know. If some of them ever become disabled, it will be a bad business. If they could just let

go of that fear, I think. I have the fear, too. I'm afraid of losing my hearing. But I know that if or when it happens, I'll make do somehow. Making do not such a foreign concept to me. For the Normals, making do is dreadful even to contemplate. What would life be without a leg, without eyesight, without hearing, they worry. Life would be life . . . I say. Flawed and limited in some ways, rich and varied in others.

I don't enjoy feeling like we [IWDs] exist to offer illuminating insights to the Normal. But in my more generous moments (few and far between as they are), I feel it's something worth doing. They (Normals) need a lot of help.

(Kleege, 2006, p. 182)

Notice that Kleege, in order to encourage IWODs to learn about disability, uses the word, "force," and Kriegel uses the words, "presume upon the normals." Both Kriegel and Kleege understand that knowledge of the disability experience is neither invited nor welcome.

Disability Language

Results of Inappropriate Disability Language

- Historically, IWDs have been forced to accept stigmatizing labels in order to receive services.
- Inappropriate disability language is a mirror society's prejudice and discrimination.
- Some words are inappropriate simply due to the *history* of their use and their *results*.
- Inappropriate disability language robs IWDs of their right to self-definition.
- Inappropriate disability language reflects IWODs' tendency to exaggerate and sensationalize disability.
- Euphemisms suggest that the word "disability" cannot be spoken and that disabilities cannot be addressed in an open manner.

The use of appropriate disability language is a critical concern of counselors because historically, especially in medical settings, IWDs have been forced to accept stigmatizing labels in order to receive services. If IWDs refused these paternalistic, devalued, and demeaning labels, often they were medically abandoned. Therefore, many IWDs are sensitive to the language used, especially by professional service providers, including counselors.

In this short section, we first discuss the power of language, then present some guidelines for using correct disability language (with the rationale for each of these guidelines). The third section discusses what has been termed "defiant self-naming." Finally, the debate over the use of person-first language, with both advantages and disadvantages, is presented.

The Power of Language

Language is a mirror of a society at a particular point in time. Thus, language is a cultural statement of beliefs and attitudes, but, more significant, language usage helps to construct laws and institutions. Positive, respectful words used to describe groups of people empower them, render them worthy of society's resources, such as respect, freedom, and justice, and provide access to any number of societal-provided opportunity structures, including education and employment. Disrespectful language used to describe individuals, taken to an extreme, can question the humanity and the perceived value of their lives. There is a long list of words that, in the past, were used to describe and define different groups of people which we would not use today. Some of the offensive and demeaning words were not deliberately coined to express less respect, less humanity, or of less value. However, language can be demeaning to entire groups of people. Disability language often reveals assumptions about society's perceived value of IWDs. Moreover, the language used to refer to IWDs may imply that their lives are not worth living (Smart, 2016). Often, it is not the word itself that is disrespectful, but the *history* of the use of the particular word. Nonetheless, language evolves and advances as societies gain a more accurate and realistic view of various groups of individuals. Learning and acquiring new vocabulary are often necessary when formerly disenfranchised groups gain political and economic power.

Counselors understand the importance of self-definition, understanding that many devalued groups have had negative definitions forced upon them by the dominant group. Individuals in these devalued groups do not accept these descriptions as self-definers and, furthermore, some individuals may question their membership in these categories. It's something like, "Do you think I am. . . ?" or "Do you think I belong with those people?"

Language can also separate groups of people. Separating groups of people from the broader society is termed "polarizing" or "distancing." Often, we are not fully aware of the distancing that results from what is seemingly innocuous language. Nonetheless, distancing language can result in segregation and isolation. Moreover, linguistically separating any group of people implies that everyone in any category is exactly alike, thus depriving individuals of their individuality and their right of self-definition. The phrase, "you people over there" communicates that the speaker does not identify with "those people."

Language can be reductionist, meaning that group identifiers describe only one aspect of the individual(s), failing to capture their entire identity. Reductionist labels can also focus on a single aspect of the individual which they do not consider relevant or important.

Disability Language Guidelines

Much of the language used to describe IWDs is derived from medicine, including the medical focus on dysfunction and impairment. Words with prefixes such as "dis/dys" or "in/im" denote absence or a lack of something. Some of these words are "disorder," "disease," "dyslexia," "dysfunction," "infirm," "invalid," and "impairment." These words are appropriate in medical settings, helping to diagnose, treat, and manage disabilities. In most other settings and usage, however, IWDs, however, often believe that these diagnostic terms convey social inferiority or weakness. In addition to reducing the IWD to their disability, medical diagnoses and labels fail to communicate the positive aspects of the disability. Many IWDs find their disabilities to have positive aspects and are proud of their mastery and management of the disability. Without doubt, disability is expensive, time-consuming, can be limiting, and IWDs require accommodations in order to meet widely held standards. IWDs typically do not reject these realities nor do they discount their medical diagnoses. They simply refuse the socially defined or socially ill-defined role of disability, wishing their disabilities to be socially acknowledged but also wanting equal social status. To many IWODs this last statement may appear irrational. After all, IWDs do have disabilities, how could they possibly think they're equal to IWODs? Nonetheless, there is nothing inherent in a disability that leads to the social devaluation of IWDs.

Medicine, especially psychiatry, has recognized the insulting and demeaning historical use of some diagnoses and, in the 5th edition of the DSM (American Psychiatric Association, 2013) changed the wording of several diagnoses. "Intellectual disability" has replaced "mental retardation," "illness anxiety" replaced "hypochondriasis," and "childhood onset dysfluency" has replaced "stuttering." Reaching further back in time, some medical diagnoses included words that no one would think to use today; yet the same diagnostic criteria describe both the outdated diagnosis and today's diagnosis. Jerome Groopman, physician/surgeon/author asserted that the words doctors employ to inform patients of their diagnoses are as powerful as surgical instruments.

> Language is as vital to the physician's art as the stethoscope or the scalpel. Of all the words the doctor uses, the name he gives the illness has the greatest weight. The name of the illness becomes part of the identity of the sufferer.
>
> (2000, p. 366)

A man (Mooney, 2017, October 12) described receiving his diagnoses when he was young in terms of the Jewish funeral and mourning practices.

> By third grade I had progressed from being one of "those kids" to being the "special ed." kid. I was found to have multiple language-based learning disabilities and attention deficit disorder. When the educational psychologist broke the news to my mom and me, it was if someone had died. Tissues on the table. Hushed tones. Mirrors covered. Sat shiva for the death of my normality. The tragedy of my problem wasn't lost on me, even at 8 years old. People thought something was wrong with me, and I knew it.

In Mooney's excerpt, he explained that even as a young child in school, he was aware of the ability ranking of the various reading groups. Perhaps the teachers really did believe by giving the reading group names of birds, they were succeeding in masking that the Sparrows were the reading group comprised of children with substandard reading skills while the Blackbirds and Bluebirds probably were average readers and the regal, majestic California Condors were the best readers.

> Sitting still was hard enough, but I also struggled with reading and was placed in the "dumb" group. Teachers didn't actually call us the "dumb" group, but let's be real: Everyone knew which group was the "smart" group and which wasn't—my school had the California Condors, the Blackbirds, the Bluebirds, and then over in the annex trailer building, the Sparrows. I spent the day reading "See Spot Run" while the Condors were probably finishing up "War and Peace."

We have learned that IWODs, including professional service providers, tend to sensationalize and exaggerate disabilities and their effects, often ascribing negative emotions to IWDs. Therefore, the use of emotional and sensational language to describe the onset, cause, or living with a disability is discouraged. Open-mindedness is difficult to maintain in societies which are saturated with these demeaning and insulting views of disabilities. Newspapers often use phrases such as "He was struck down," or "She is confined to a wheelchair," or "He is afflicted or he suffers from" "They were stricken with a debilitating disability" or "Their baby has a birth defect." The correct usage is: "He acquired a disability," "She uses a wheelchair," or "Their baby was born with a congenital disability." Films, and electronic media, also manipulate emotions (and often we're not aware of this manipulation). Robert David Hall, is a double amputee who plays Dr. Robbins on the American television program, *CSI*. Hall spoke about the more accurate portrayal of IWDs: "It used to be if you were disabled and on television they'd play soft piano music behind you. The thing I love about *CSI* is that I'm just Dr. Robbins" (Navarro, 2007, para. 8). In the same *New York Times* article, Navarro summarized:

> The heart-wrenching movie of the week and fund-raising telethons striving for cures have given way to amputee rock climbing on reality shows like the *Amazing Race* and doing the jive on *Dancing with the Stars*. Sitcoms and crime shows have jumped on the bandwagon, too. An actor who is paraplegic, for instance, depicts a member of the casino surveillance team on *Las Vegas*.
>
> (2007, para. 7)

Before the electronic media, disability (or rather, the sad, depressing, emotional portrayal of disability) sold books. The English author, Charles Dickens, wrote 16 major literary works, of which 14 had characters with disabilities (Byrd & Elliott, 1988; Smart, 2016). The portrayal of disability was a moneymaker! Who would pay to read/see a normal person, including a normal person with a disability?

Also, if the disability is not relevant in certain contexts, it should not be mentioned. For example, the sentence: "Dr. Stephen Hawking, who was quadriplegic, was the world's foremost astrophysicist," would be considered true, but reveals the speaker's fascination with the disability and therefore the phrase "who was quadriplegic" should be omitted. The following statement is correct: "Dr. Stephen Hawking, who was quadriplegic, required accommodations in order to give his lecture." In this second statement, Dr. Hawking's disability is relevant in order to provide appropriate accommodations.

Euphemisms

Euphemisms to describe disability are almost always kindly intentioned. Phrases such as "physically challenged," "special," "exceptional," and "different abilities" or "mentally different" are attempts to avoid the word "disability." Euphemisms are harmful (and inaccurate) because disability is neither a challenge or a small difference, both of which minimize the experience of living with a disability. IWDs often view such euphemisms as trivializing and condescending, suggesting that disability cannot be discussed in a candid manner. IWDs understand that their disability makes IWODs uncomfortable and the use of euphemisms shields the speaker from the reality of disability. Eric Weihenmayer (2001) is blind; he climbed Mount Everest and wrote a book describing his mountain climbing and the experience of blindness in general. In this excerpt, he understands the woman's need to shield *herself* from the word "blind."

> Once a lady wanted to ask me how long I had been blind, but she was too afraid to use the word *blind*. Maybe she thought that blindness was a kind of demon and just the mere mention of the word might give it the power to rise up and crush my spirit. So instead, she asked, "How long have you been a person of sightlessness?"
>
> (p. 85)

Defiant Self-Naming or "Gimp Pride"

"Gimp pride" seeks to imitate and ridicule the language usage of IWODs and is part of a disability pride movement. Linton (1998) described gimp pride:

> Cripple, gimp, and freak are used by the disability community. They are personally and politically useful as means to comment on oppression because they assert our right to name our experience.
>
> (Linton, 1998, p. 17)

Gimp pride is a way of ridiculing the prejudice and discrimination of the wider culture, including the use of euphemisms, exaggeration, and sensationalizing the disability experience. As with all in-group language, the use of gimp pride or gimp humor is not appropriate for IWODs to use. This defiant self-naming is meant to assert PWDs' right to self-label and thus maintain their pride and ownership of their disabilities. The message of gimp pride is, "I have a disability. Get used to it (and me)."

Gimp humor also communicates solidarity with the disability rights movement, in addition to rebelliously reclaiming the right of self-definition and ridiculing IWODs. Linton (1998) described gimp humor: Ridiculing the dominant group, IWODs, is part of gimp humor. Many IWDs refer to those without disabilities as "normies," "CRABs (Currently Regarded as Able-Bodied)," or "TABS

(Temporarily Able-Bodied)." Many ASD (Autism Spectrum Disorder) groups refer as non-autistics as "neurotypical." Also, many individuals with Asperger's syndrome refer to themselves as "Aspies."

The Controversy About the Use of Person-First Language to Describe IWDs

> **An Interesting Controversy**
> - The decision to use person-first language belongs to each IWD.
> - In the United States, person-first language is typically preferred. The federal civil rights law for IWDs is the Americans with Disabilities Act, not the Disabled Americans Act.
> - In the United Kingdom, Canada, New Zealand, and Australia, person-first language is typically not used.

The purpose of most disability language guidelines is to humanize disability and the people who experience disability. Examples of person-first language include, "a person with a disability," "a customer with a disability," "a student with a disability," "a client with a disability," or "a man with a disability." The purpose of person-first language is twofold. First, it communicates that the individual has many identities and, second, it refers to a more important status that is appropriate for particular situations. For example, "customers," "students," "technology users," and "clients" convey that the IWD does have a disability, but their needs often have little to do with the disability and also communicates that the IWD is a part of other groups, such as customers, students, and clients. Person-first language communicates that the IWD is a person first, and not a disability or, stated differently, the person is not the disability. We have learned that IWDs have often been categorized according to the type of their disability, such as "the blind," "the mentally ill," and "the intellectually disabled," suggesting that there is some sort of group identity and commonalities of individuals who have the same type of disability. No one likes to be categorized, especially categorization that is conferred by others. Categorization easily leads to stereotypes, such as "All blind people are musically gifted," or "Most of the mentally ill are dangerous people."

Language, of any type, reflects its culture and historical time. Certainly, people-first disability language is more commonly used in the United States. For instance, the title of the civil rights federal legislation for IWDs is not the Disabled Americans Act, but the Americans with Disabilities Act, emphasizing that basic civil rights are conferred on the basis of American citizenship.

There is some opposition to person-first language, both on an individual basis and on a group basis. On an individual level, the refusal to use person-first language to describe oneself may be considered a type of gimp pride. Sobsey (1994) described:

> One physically disabled person told [me] that she is not a woman with a disability, she is a disabled woman. She feels strongly that her life-long disability is an essential part of her as her gender or heritage, and she feels that the person-first rule fails to recognize this critical aspect of her identity. People should have the right to reject any labels that they do not like, and forcing an unwanted label on anyone is abusive.
>
> (p. 320)

Groups that do not advocate person-first language include the Deaf culture, preferring to be called a Deaf person. Also, the Deaf culture does use the term, "hearing impaired," considering it to be euphemistic. The Deaf culture is an unusual case due to the fact that it does not consider itself a disability group but rather as a culture, complete with its own language (American Sign Language), art, history, and literature. Advocate groups for individuals on the autism spectrum do not accept person-first language, arguing that they are not ashamed to be called "autistic people" (Silberman, 2015).

The United Kingdom, Canada, Australia, and New Zealand do not use person-first language. Disability: Ethics, Law, and Policy (Bickenbach, 2012), the author summarizes both the debate about first-person language and ends with stating his choice not to use person-first language.

> The symbols and language used to represent disability have sparked contentious debates over the year. In the *Handbook of Disability Studies* (Albrecht, Seelman, & Bury, 2001) and the *Encyclopedia of Disability* (Albrecht, 2006), authors from different countries were encouraged to use the terms and language of their cultures, but to explain them when necessary. . . . Scholars in the United States have preferred "people with disabilities" (people-first language), while those in the United Kingdom, Canada, and Australia generally use "disabled people." In languages other than English, scholars typically use some form of the "disabled people" idiom. . . . In my own writing, I have chosen "disabled people" because it stresses human diversity and variation.
>
> (p. 3)

From this short summary, we can see that language usage, of any type, reflects its culture and that nations that speak the same language, English, have different cultures and government systems. The argument that advocates the use of "disabled people," is based on the assumption that disability is widely considered to be diversity and variation, both positive terms. In contrast, many disability scholars think that disability is negatively viewed by the wider culture and is not considered diversity, but rather, as deviance and inferiority.

In the same excerpt, two disability scholars (DePoy & Gilson, 2010) argued against the use of person-first language on the basis of semantics, stating:

> [L]ocating disability "with a person" reifies its embodiment and flies in the very face of the social model that person-first language is purported to espouse. . . . We have not heard anyone suggest that beauty, kindness, or even unkindness be located after personhood.
> (cf. Bickenbach, 2012, p. 3)

On the one hand, these scholars are correct. No one would suggest saying "a person of beauty" or even the negative evaluation of "a person of unkindness." Overlooked in this argument is the *history* of the language used to describe IWDs, including the devaluation, categorization, stereotyping, inferiority, and paternalistic treatment, including the definition imposed upon IWDs by others.

Arguments against the use of these disability language guidelines include:

- Such use is cumbersome and awkward.
- It violates the sense of freedom of expression.
- Such guidelines are merely semantic contrivances which refer to the same individuals (IWDs) and the identical experience (disability).

The only valid argument against the use of person-first language is everyone's right to choose how they will be identified and referred to by others, including some disability groups, such as the Deaf culture and those with ASD. Occasionally, some IWDs refuse the use of person-first language, making the point that just as there is nothing negative about describing a person as a beautiful person, there is nothing wrong with the description of a disabled person.

There are terms used by IWDs to describe disability that are "in-group language" and are not appropriate for IWODs to use. Words such as "crip," "gimp," "cripple," "blinks," "freaks," or "crazies." This defiant self-naming serves two purposes: It gives the power of self-naming to a group that has been defined and labeled by others and it derides the euphemisms often used by outsiders. Often, disability rights activists emphasize a cross-disability social category, referring to individuals with physical, cognitive, intellectual, and psychiatric disabilities as the "Crip Culture" (Shaw, 1994).

Should counselors memorize a list of these disability language guidelines? Perhaps better, counselors should learn and understand the rationale behind each of these guidelines and *ask* each client about their language preferences.

Conclusion

Counselors consistently upgrade their skills and seek new understandings. Moreover, counselors do not avoid difficult and complex information and, in these ways, they are able to gain mastery and, in turn, allow CWDs to gain control, mobilize strengths and resources. However, in order to accomplish these goals, a therapeutic alliance must be formed.

Six basic, important beliefs about IWDs were discussed in this chapter, using many first person accounts to illustrate these concepts. The relationship formed between counselor and client is thought to be the most important aspect of the entire process and plays an important role in effectiveness and positive client outcomes. Moreover, empathy is the foundation of any counseling relationship.

Counselors without disabilities often are not aware that CWDs view them as IWODs. Counselors may not think of themselves as IWODs, but CWDs, do. For example, most counselors do not identify as a "sighted person," however, blind clients would think of their counselors in this way. Therefore, it is necessary for the counselor to effectively communicate empathy and understanding the disability experience. These six core beliefs may, at first glance, appear counterintuitive and, moreover, false, prejudicial, and discriminatory can persist (and thrive) for centuries.

Counselors focus on *client* change; however, the focus of this chapter has been *counselor* change and growth. Part of acquiring a more realistic, accurate worldview is discarding false, inaccurate ideas and replacing these with informed information, both of which are often uncomfortable.

The last topic discussed in this chapter was the use of language in referring to the disability and the people who experience disabilities. It was noted that language is power; language has a history; and the use of language results in the daily lived lives of individuals. Therefore, language is more than words or semantics. The use of many words and expressions is discouraged not because they are inaccurate, but because these words have a horrific history. The words "special," "exceptional," and "challenged" are used to describe IWDs; however, not only are these words meaningless euphemisms, but for IWDs these words evoke a history of segregation, marginalization, and institutionalization. Also, person-first language was discussed, including the criticisms that person-first language is cumbersome to use and is rarely used to describe other types of individuals. Both of these criticisms have some validity. However, the American civil right law for IWDs uses person-first language, titled the Americans with Disabilities Act (ADA) and not the Disabled Americans Act. For large groups of individuals who have not been allowed to define themselves, are often viewed as only their disability, or who have been categorized, person-first language is more humane, despite the cumbersomeness of its use.

References

Albrecht, G. L. (Ed.). (2006). *Encyclopedia of disability*. Thousand Oaks, CA: Sage.

Albrecht, G. L., Seelman, K. D., & Bury, M. (Eds.) (2001). *Handbook of disability studies*. Thousand Oaks, CA: Sage.

American Psychiatric Association. (2013). *The diagnostic and statistical manual of mental disorders-5*. Washington, DC: Author.

Bickenbach, J. E. (2012). *Ethics, law, and policy: Disability key issues and future directions*. Los Angeles, CA: Sage.

Byrd, E. K., & Elliott, T. R. (1988). Media and disability: A discussion of the research. In H. E. Yuker (Ed.), *Attitudes toward persons with disabilities* (pp. 82–95). New York, NY: Springer.

Cate, I. M. P., & Loots, G. M. P. (2000). Experiences of siblings of children with physical disabilities: An empirical investigation. *Disability and Rehabilitation, 22*, 399–408.

Corey, G. (1996). *Theory and practice of counseling and psychotherapy*. Pacific Grove, CA: Brooks and Cole.

DePoy, E., & Gilson, S. F. (2010). *Studying disability: Multiple theories and responses*. Thousand Oaks, CA: Sage.

Faull, K., Hill, M. D., Cochrane, G., Gray, J., Hunt, M., McKenzie, C., & Winter, L. (2004). Investigation of health perspectives of those with physical disabilities: The role of spirituality as a determinant of health. *Disability and Rehabilitation, 26*, 129–144.

Fleischer, D. Z., & Zames, F. (2001). *The disability rights movement: From charity to confrontation*. Philadelphia, PA: Temple University.

Garland-Thomson, R. (1997). *Extraordinary bodies: Figuring physical disability in American culture and literature*. New York, NY: Columbia University.

Garland-Thomson, R. (2016, August 19). Becoming disabled: Roughly one in five Americans lives with a disability. So where is our pride movement? *New York Times*. Retrieved from www.nytimes.com/2016/08/21/opinion/sunday/becoming-disabed.html Retrieved 02-26-2018

Groopman, J. (2000, November 13). Hurting all over. *New Yorker*. p. 78. Retrieved from www.newyorker.com/magazine/2000/11/13/hurting-all-over Retrieved 02–26–2018

Helwig, A. A., & Holicky, R. (1994). Substance abuse in persons with disabilities: Treatment considerations. *Journal of Counseling and Development, 72*, 227–233.

Hill, C. E., & O'Brien, K. M. (1999). *Helping skills: Facilitating exploration, insight, and action*. Washington, DC: American Psychological Association.

Johnson, H. M. (2003, February 16) Unspeakable conversations. *New York Times Magazine*. Retrieved from http://politicalinequality.blogspot.com/2005/12/harriet-mcbryde-johnson-unspeakable.html Retrieved 02-26-2018

Johnson, M. (2003). *Make them go away: Clint Eastwood, Christopher Reeve & the case against disability rights*. Louisville, KY: Avocado Press.

Johnson, M. (2012). *Politics of popcorn save me from Clint Eastwood*. Retrieved from www.ragged-edgemagazine.com/departments/closerlook/000947.html Retrieved 02–26–2018.

Kaier, A. (2016, August 24). Finding refuge in the skin I'm in. *New York Times*. Retrieved from www.nytimes.com/2016/08/24/opinion/finding-refige-with-the-skin-im-in.html Retrieved 02-26-2018

Karuth, D. (1998). If I were a car, I'd be a lemon. In N. Gould & A. Arkoff (Eds.), *Psychology and personal growth* (5th ed., pp. 46–52). Needham Heights, MA: Allyn & Bacon.

Kleege, G. (2006). *Blind rage: Letters to Helen Keller.* Washington, DC: Gallaudet University.

Kriegel, L. (1997). Falling down. In K. Fries (Ed.), *Staring back: The disability experience from the inside out* (pp. 41–49). New York, NY: Plume.

Linton, S. (1998). *Claiming disability: Knowledge and identity.* New York, NY: New York University.

Longmore, P. K. (2003). *Why I burned my book and other essays on disability.* Philadelphia, PA: Temple University.

Mackelprang, R., & Salsgiver, R. (1999). *Disability: A diversity model approach in human service practice.* Pacific Grove, CA: Brooks and Cole.

Marks, D. (1999). *Disability: Controversial debates and psychosocial perspectives.* London: Routledge.

Michalko, R. (2002). *The difference that disability makes.* Philadelphia, PA: Temple University.

Montgomery, C. (2006). "Little acts of degradation": Ragged Edge Online launches project Cleigh. Retrieved from www.raggededgemagazine.com/departments/closerlook/00713.html Retrieved 02-26-2018

Mooney, J. (2017, October 12). You are special! Now stop being different. *New York Times.* Retrieved 02-24-2018 www.nytimes.com/2017/10/12/opinion/learning-disabilities-attention-deficit.html?rref=collection%2Fcolumn%2Fdisability&action=click&content-Collection=opinion&region=stream&module=stream_unit&version=latest&content-Placement=10&pgtype=collection Retrieved 02-26-2018

Morris, J. (1991). *Pride against prejudice: Transforming attitudes towards disability.* London: The Women's Press.

National Public Radio. (1998, May). Inventing the poster child. In *The disability history project* [Radio documentary]. Retrieved from www.npr.org/programs/disability/ba_shows.dir/index_sh.html Retrieved 02-26-2018

Navarro, M. (2007, May 13). Clearly, frankly, unabashedly disabled. *New York Times.* Retrieved from www.nytimes.com/2007/05/13/fashion/13disabled.html?page Retrieved 02-26-2018

Oldenburg, A. (2014, March 16). Defined by determination. *USA Today,* B7-B8. Retrieved from http://usatoday30.usatoday.com/LIFE/usaedition/2014-03-17-Amy-Purdy-feature_ST_U.htm Retrieved 02-26-2018

Parritt, S. W., & O'Callaghan, J. (2000). Splitting the difference: An exploratory study of therapists' work with sexuality, relationships and disability. *Sexuality and Relationship Therapy, 15,* 151–169.

Pfeiffer, D. (2005). The conceptualization of disability. In G. E. May & M. B. Raske (Eds.), *Ending disability discrimination: Strategies for social workers* (pp. 25–44). Boston, MA: Pearson.

Putnam, M., Greenen, S., Powers, L., Saxton, M., Finney, S., & Dautel, P. (2003). People with disabilities discuss barriers and facilitators to well-being. *Journal of Rehabilitation, 69,* 37–45.

Shaw, B. (Ed.) (1994). *The ragged edge: The disability experience from the pages of the first fifteen years of the Disability Rag.* Louisville, KY: Avocado Press.

Silberman, S. (2015). *NeuroTribes: The legacy of autism and the future of neurodiversity.* New York, NY: Penguin Random House.

Smart, J. F. (2016). *Disability, society, and individual* (3rd ed.). Austin, TX: PRO-ED.

Sobsey, D. (1994). *Violence and abuse in the lives of people with disabilities: The end of silent acceptance.* Baltimore, MD: Paul H. Brookes.

Solomon, A. (2012). *Far from the tree: Parents, children, and the search for identity.* New York, NY: Scribner.

Thomson, R. G. (1997). *Extraordinary bodies: Figuring physical disability in American culture and literature.* New York, NY: Columbia University.

Tollifson, J. (1997). Imperfection is a beautiful thing, In K. Fries, (Ed.), *Staring back: The disability experience from the inside out* (pp. 104–112). New York, NY: Plume.

Toombs, S. K. (1995). Sufficient unto the day. In S. K. Toombs, D. Barnard, & R. A. Carson (Eds.), *Chronic illness from experience to policy* (pp. 2–23). Bloomington, IN: University of Indiana.

Uhlberg, M. (2008). *Hands of my father: A hearing boy, his deaf parents, and the language of love.* New York, NY: Bantam Books.

Weihenmayer, E. (2001). *Touch the top of the world: A blind man's journey to climb farther than the eye can see.* New York, NY: Dutton.

Wendell, S. (2006). Toward a feminist theory of disability. In L. J. Davis (Ed.), *The disability studies reader* (2nd ed., pp. 243–256). New York, NY: Routledge.

Wilson, D. J. (1990). *Living with polio: The epidemics and its survivors.* Chicago, IL: University of Chicago.

Young, S. (2014, July). Retrieved from www.ted.com/talks/stella_young_i_m_not_your_inspiration_thank_you_very_much Retrieved 02-26-2018

Five

ETHICAL CONSIDERATIONS AND GENERAL PRACTICE GUIDELINES

Broad, basic, and general guidelines for counseling clients with disabilities (CWDs) are presented in this chapter. However, before discussing practice guidelines, some basic assumptions are discussed, including four characteristics of clients with disabilities, five paradoxes in counseling CWDs, and ethical considerations in counseling CWDs. Much of these three introductory sections are repeated, summarizing from the preceding chapters or stating them in a slightly different manner. Nonetheless, these basic assumptions are necessary to consider before embarking upon general practice applications, because these will make these guidelines more easily understood.

Before discussing the first ten practice guidelines, this chapter discusses three introductory issues, including four characteristics of clients with disabilities, five paradoxes in providing services to clients with disabilities, and ethical considerations in counseling clients with disabilities. The second and final section presents practice applications.

Four Characteristics of Clients With Disabilities (CWDs)

1. CWDs have the same motivators as CWODs.
2. CWDs have multiple roles, identities, and functions.
3. CWDs are faced with the same life tasks as CWODs.
4. CWDs have the same range of emotions as CWODs.

There are difficulties and complexities in suggesting recommendations for working with clients with disabilities (CWDs). On the one hand, many of the skills necessary to work with CWDs are those used with clients without disabilities (CWODs) while on the other hand, there are counseling skills specific to CWDs. Frequently, the disability is not the presenting problem or the reason for which the CWD has sought counseling; but if the disability is ignored, a large and valued aspect of the individual's identity is discounted. Further, there are many commonalities in the perspectives and lived experiences of CWDs with all types of disabilities; but, the most significant meaning and definition of disability is the CWD's subjective, idiosyncratic response to the disability and their experiences. Paradoxically, most counselors in all specialty areas, have been trained to focus on individuals, helping clients to deal with their personal, unique concerns, and by implication, viewing the client as both the source and the solution to the problem. In counseling, this approach is often termed "intra-psychic" and also parallels the Biomedical Model of Disability. You will remember that in the Biomedical Model of Disability, the individual is considered the source of the disability and also is held responsible for any treatment or management. In contrast, many of the obstacles CWDs encounter have little to do with the individual or their disability, but are the result of a prejudiced, discriminating society that enforces unnecessary dependence, isolation, and loneliness. IWDs face social threats of which most counselors are unaware and, therefore, tend to disregard. Perhaps the greatest social threat to an individual is the idea that they must "earn" and "re-earn" the right to live. Carolyn Vash (1981), a disability scholar who contracted polio at age 16 and survived with a disability, explained:

> I felt that I had been slated to die but somehow tricked the great scythe wielder and lived . . . to be a damn drag on a number of people. A lot of my achievement trip was feeling I had to earn and re-earn my right to my place on the planet. What looked like ambition was actually paying penance for not having been gracious enough to just die.
>
> (p. 10)

Nevertheless, most helping professionals, including counselors, have wrongly conceptualized the obstacles encountered by CWDs to be their own responsibility.

The final paradox concerns the lack of the effective, accurate training and supervised experience in counseling CWDs and the compounding effects of a society whose media is saturated with prejudicial, condescending, limiting views of IWDs. These paradoxes are listed here.

Five Paradoxes in Providing Counseling Services to Clients With Disabilities

1. Counselors can build upon and expand basic counseling techniques, but at the same time, counselors will be required to understand, learn, and apply disability-specific skills. The acquisition of this awareness, knowledge, experiences, and skills requires effort, time, and practice.

2. Most often, the disability is not the presenting problem; but ignoring the disability discounts an important, valued aspect of the CWD's identity.
3. There are many commonalities in the disability experience among IWDs with all types of disability; but the most significant meaning of disability is the individual's subjective, idiosyncratic definition and experiences. The first type of information, the commonalities among all IWDs, is gained through education and training; the second type of information is achieved from the counseling relationship with an individual client with a disability.
4. Many of the obstacles in the lives of CWDs are *not* intra-psychic, having little to do with these clients nor their disabilities. Denied access to opportunities and presented with a narrow range of choices, both of which are mandated, maintained, and institutionalized by society, CWDs have not been able to achieve typical life tasks such as education, career, marriage, and parenthood. At first glance, this lack of achievement may appear to be related to the disability or to the individual with the disability. Nonetheless, in most cases, it is a prejudicial and ill-informed society that has limited opportunities for achievement.
5. Most counselors have little accurate and effective training or education in the disability experience, while simultaneously, counselors are the product of a culture and the media, which enshrines normalcy as the ideal way in which to be human.

Most CWDs have multiple roles and identities, are required to complete the same life tasks as anyone else, and have the same motivations and emotions as CWODs. All specialties of counseling have the philosophical assumption of understanding individual clients and promoting optimal human development across the lifespan, whether working with individuals, families, or groups. Access to all types of counseling, such as adolescent, marriage, career counseling, and many others, may be considered an opportunity structure that assists individual clients but also adds value to the broader society. Basic counseling skills provide a foundation on which to increase knowledge and skills. By strengthening individuals and assisting them to achieve their potential, society as a whole benefits. Counseling CWDs will require additional skills. At first, it may appear paradoxical to recommend viewing the CWD as an ordinary person while, at the same time, advocating learning about disability in general and understanding the client's disability and the meaning it has for the client. Nonetheless, CWDs are ordinary in terms of life tasks, motivations, and emotions, but they have the added responsibility of responding to a disability, both the medical management and treatment and responding to society's uninformed and negative reactions.

Carl Rogers (1951, 1961, 1980), a counseling theorist, considered clients to be the experts in their experiences and their capability to fulfill their potential. Rogers emphasized two points: First, the client (with or without a disability) is expert in their own needs and experiences, and, second, the client is capable of further self-discovery and growth assisted by counseling relationships in which the counselors relinquish their status and power of expertise. Thus, in Rogerian techniques, the balance of power is more symmetrical, with the counselor acting as a source of understanding and acceptance. In the Biomedical Model of Disability, the patient/client was often not considered an authority on their disability and, therefore, was required to submit control and decision-making to professionals. Many IWDs have been told by their doctors, "You wouldn't understand" or "I know what's best." However, the medical profession is changing, and physicians and other health care providers are trained and practiced in collaborative decision making with patients/clients. Most theories of counseling have actively encouraged client empowerment, achieved through a professional relationship in which the client feels safe, understood, and valued. Counselors are skilled in demonstrating respect for individual needs and differences, tolerating differences, and encouraging transformative learning.

In a chapter entitled, "Basic Counseling Skills," Goodman (2001) described two different ways in which counselors implement their counseling skills; one is "natural" and the other requires more consideration and attention:

> With experience, counselors integrate the component so that they become "natural," and counselors think about them only when confronted with clients who present difficulties to them.
>
> (p. 238)

Goodman does not define or describe "difficult clients" or why these clients may appear difficult to the counselor. Nor is Goodman specifically discussing CWDs, but CWDs are often considered as "clients who present difficulties." Most of the responsibility (and the source) for these difficulties is due to the counselor, rather than the client. Stated differently, counselors find some clients difficult because they have not been trained for or are not experienced with these types of clients. Therefore, it is the obligation of the counselor to gain skill and familiarity with these types of "difficult clients." When CWDs are thought to be "difficult," the counselor's first response should be an examination of their own reactions to the disability and the client. As we have learned, it is a human tendency, when feeling discomfort, to often blame others for own discomfort when, in reality, it is our own lack of knowledge and experience that makes many "difficult" clients difficult.

The following guidelines are broad and many overlap, yet each is addressed as a separate guideline, meriting discussion and explanation. These guidelines are basic and, because of this, may appear to be mechanistic and simplistic; however, they do serve as an introduction to understanding clients with disabilities. When counselors encounter individuals who appear ambiguous, there is a tendency for counselors to categorize people and simplify their motivations and emotions. Simplifying and categorizing CWDs are counterproductive on two counts. First, counselors may not be aware of their need for viewing the CWD in simplistic ways (or the reasons why). Second, most CWDS are highly aware of others' attempts to categorize them due to their past experiences with professional medical providers. Both clients and counselors bring their interactions with the wider world to the counseling session.

As we have learned in previous chapters, both counselors and CWDs are embedded in a world that has negative, degrading views of CWDs, and most CWDs will have had more contact with professional service providers than CWODs. Many of these previous interactions may have been demeaning and unpleasant for CWDs. It is possible for counselors to exert a negative influence on clients. Therefore, greater self-awareness on the part of the counselor is required. As with all clients, in order to establish trust and rapport with CWDs, the counselor must be willing to listen in order to understand the clients' self-identity and worldview. When counselors do not understand, it is better to ask the client, acknowledging a lack of information and experience, rather than making assumptions. Such an investment in time, purposeful listening, and the willingness to ask questions will be rewarded with greater client success. Optimal client motivation to engage in the counseling process requires counselors to invest effort, time, and self-examination, but these investments will produce successful engagement.

Ethical Considerations in Counseling Clients With Disabilities

Ethical Considerations

- Honesty about one's level of training, expertise, and skills
- Guarding against paternalism
- Providing informed choice and consent
- Not expecting CWDs to present "disability awareness seminars"

There are, however, safeguards in place to assist practicing counselors in gaining awareness of the areas in which more experience and skill-building are required, including supervised practice and in-service training. At minimum, counselors should be honest with both themselves and their clients about their qualifications, skill level, and professional experience. Counselors are taught the skills of self-monitoring and checking for understanding with clients, both of which facilitate understanding of the CWD's worldview, including their disability. Nonetheless, it is unethical to expect individual CWDs to present "disability awareness seminars to counselors during counseling sessions.

The principle of beneficence, especially concerning CWDs, can present difficulties. The American Counseling Association (ACA) Code of Ethics (2014) describes beneficence in this way: "Counselors encourage client growth and development in ways that foster the interest and welfare of clients and promote formation of healthy relationships." The ways in which the misguided kindness of others have resulted in unnecessary dependence, isolation, and reduced opportunity for IWDs were discussed in Chapter Four. Professional relationships, including counseling, guided by attempts at beneficence can result in paternalism in which the professional openly or subtly guides the client to outcomes. Examination of the counselor's motivation and, instead, consideration of the results for CWDs will reduce the tendency toward paternalism. Because of the desire to help, counselors may have a tendency toward paternalism rather than true beneficence. Especially, with CWDs, paternalism is often easier for the counselor. The principle and use of informed choice is one alternative to misguided use of beneficence:

> Informed choice sees the asymmetry of power and knowledge between patient and practitioner as a defect and regards the professional ethic of beneficence as paternalistic; as a corrective, it mandates disclosure of relevant risks and benefits.
>
> (Agich & Carson, 1995, p. 131)

If counselors are questioning if they are paternalistic with CWDs, the answers to three questions may help clarify: Is this in the best interests of my client, both long term and short-term? Is it possible that I don't know enough about disability that I am seeking the "easy, comfortable" solution? Have I informed the client of the alternatives, including advantages and disadvantages?

The risk of paternalistic attitudes and behaviors becomes greater when the counseling relationship is an asymmetrical power balance. Understanding that, in most counseling relationships, the counselor has greater power than the client, is a first step toward reducing the power differential. With CWDs, the power differential may be even greater simply because it is wrongly thought that IWODs are superior to IWDs. However, IWDs claim the right to self-determination which is in conflict with paternalism. In a study that interviewed IWDs, one participant did not speak about paternalistic behaviors of professionals, but rather spoke about paternalistic behavior in "the workplace and recreation."

> No matter how successful I may or may not have been thought, I think I will always feel that non-disabled peers in the workplace, recreation, or whatever, think they should take a greater role in helping me to decide what is and is not right or appropriate for me than they would take with their non-disabled peers. Civil rights means having the same powers of self-determination as everyone else has. Those of us with disabilities have a long way to go to achieve that.
> (Graf, Marini, & Blankenship, 2009, p. 27)

Much of the lapses into paternalism, especially in the medical professions, are based on the authority to confer resources and considerations such as financial benefits, entrance into treatment and/or management programs, educational programs, or opportunities for marriage and/or child rearing. Often, CWDs have felt that the unspoken assumption is "Accept our professional definition of you or you will not receive (financial benefits, civil rights, education, or be allowed to have adult sexual relationships)." Some IWDs have been faced with the threat of "medical abandonment" if they did not adhere to professional direction. In other words, if these IWDs did not comply with medical treatments (and the accompanying diagnosis) physicians would no longer treat them. Many CWDs have felt that these resources were not a regular part of treatment, but rather, these benefits and resources came with "strings attached," including accepting stigmatizing labels and diagnoses that are in conflict with their self-identification. Another unspoken assumption is the attitude, "The government gives you free money, so do not ask or expect anything else. Keep your aspirations modest."

Most counselors, with the exception of rehabilitation counselors, are not "gatekeepers" for societal resources and, more important, counselors learn, understand, and accept the client's self-identification. Moreover, counselors view each client as a unique individual, rather than a part of some diagnostic group such as "the blind," or "the mentally ill." For example, many IWDs do not use medical terminology to describe their disabilities because these labels are often negative and limiting.

General Practice Guidelines

The practice guidelines in this chapter are

1. Recognize that CWDs view their counselors as individuals without disabilities.
2. Provide accommodations in the counseling office.
3. Resist the urge to simplify the CWD's identity or to categorize the CWD.
4. Question your own biases.
5. Respect the client; respect the disability.
6. Establish rapport.
7. Do not confuse normalcy with the ideal.
8. Question if the environment is limiting the client's achievements.
9. Do not pathologize the disability.
10. Do not idealize the client's pre-disability life.

Recognize That CWDs View Counselors as Individuals Without Disabilities

> **Counselors Are Viewed as IWODS**
>
> - While most counselors without disabilities do not self-identify as individuals without disabilities, most CWDs will view counselors in this way.
> - CWDs may view their counselors as beneficiaries of able-bodied privilege.
> - CWDs often expect counselors to be uncomfortable with their disability.

Most counselors who do not have disabilities typically do not identify themselves as individuals without disabilities; but most CWDs *do* think of their counselors as IWODs. This dichotomy in thinking of people in two well-defined categories is often surprising to counselors, especially when most counselors have never thought of themselves as individuals without disabilities. Nonetheless, in spite of a counselor's lack of awareness in this regard, most CWDs think of their counselors as IWODs. Of course, occasionally, the counselor does have a visible disability or discloses an invisible disability to the CWD, thus avoiding this confusion.

Most counselors are aware of white privilege, straight privilege, male privilege, and other types of privilege, including the idea that those who belong to privileged categories often do not recognize that they are in a privileged category and, furthermore, are often oblivious to the fact that there are non-privileged groups. Abled-bodied privilege includes the elements of the other types of privilege, including the power, both individual and institutional, to enforce this privilege. However, able-bodied privilege adds another very powerful component, that of pathology and deviance as the basis of the disability, and therefore, of the privilege. On the other hand, everyone knows that there is nothing inherently pathological or deviant about non-whites, non-straights, or non-males. Additionally, no one lives in fear, to the point of denial, of becoming a member of one of these non-privileged groups. Why the difference between other non-privileged groups and IWDs? The short answer is the powerful influence of the combination of the Biomedical Model and the Moral/Religious Model of Disability. All Models of Disability are incomplete and most people, including counselors, are unaware that they apply these models inappropriately. Regardless of the way in which the counselors conceptualize themselves, CWDs are viewing counselors as IWODs.

Provide Accommodations in the Counseling Office

Accommodations in the Counseling Office

- The standard for the provision of accommodations is that accommodations must provide the same quality and degree of access that IWODs enjoy. Therefore, there should be no "back entrances," or "freight elevators."
- It should not be necessary to pre-schedule most accommodations. Accommodations should be readily available.
- Accommodations should be provided with dignity.
- It is illegal to ask the client with a disability to provide their own accommodations or to assume any of the costs.
- Counseling professional codes of ethics must expand to include both the provision and the quality of accommodations.
- Progress notes and other written summaries should include the description of the accommodations provided.

CWDs are aware that they are often viewed as "problems" or as being less worthy of investment, time, opportunities, or appropriate services. On the other hand, most IWODs, including professionals, are unaware of the lack of accommodations for IWDs. When doorways are not wide enough to accommodate wheelchairs, when braille signage is absent on elevators or door numbers, when there are no accessible bathrooms, or when Sign Language interpreters are not available, PWDs *do* notice. Each of these examples is a violation of federal law, the Americans with Disabilities Act (ADA). Furthermore, IWDs want accommodations with dignity. Businessowners, citing the expenses involved in providing "accommodations with dignity," have suggested that IWDs be carried up the stairs in a stranger's arms because there are so few customers with disabilities and the installation of an elevator would be cost prohibitive. The rationale for accommodations is to provide equitable access, equitable access defined equal to that of IWODs, both in quality and times of availability. Accommodations that are provided only during a few hours of each day or on specific days of the week are not considered equitable because PWODs have access all of the time and, therefore, are not required to schedule their lives around the availability of access.

Most people, with or without disabilities, would consider it undignified and dehumanizing to be carried in a stranger's arms. In addition to being quite unsafe, such a procedure would be a violation of personal space. Other examples of accommodations without dignity include remarks such as "Can't these deaf people lip read? Do you know how expensive it is to hire a Sign Language interpreter?" or "People in wheelchairs can use the freight entrance." The late Paul Longmore, a polio survivor and a disability activist often spoke at national and international conferences, necessitating a great deal of airline travel. Longmore used a wheelchair. Before the enactment of the Americans with Disabilities Act, conference planners would send an ambulance to pick up Longmore at the airport and Longmore would refuse to get in the ambulance, considering the ambulance to be both unnecessary and demeaning. He wanted to ride sitting up, rather than lying down. The conference planners justified the use of the ambulance, arguing that Longmore was provided with accessible transportation, but overlooking the need for respectful, dignified transportation.

It is illegal to expect clients with disabilities to provide their own accommodations or to pay any of the costs of these provisions. Both of these responsibilities rest with service providers. Counseling offices and agencies will find that, after physical and other accommodations are available, their number of CWDs will probably increase. A noticeable lack of accommodations is obvious to IWDs, at times, often causing them to feel uncomfortable and unwelcome.

Providing accommodations, supports, and modifications for CWDs is a necessary part of the process of developing trust and rapport in an agency. Support staff present the image of the agency because it is insurance clerks, administrative assistants, and intake counselors who first meet prospective clients and these professionals are part of the therapeutic milieu. Prospective clients may never return after an intake interview if they feel that they have been treated insensitively or rudely or are made to feel like that their needs are considered an imposition. As we learned in Chapter Four, many IWODs do not realize that their attitudes and assumptions, while not meant to be rude or demeaning, communicate that the IWD is an unwanted problem. It is true that CWDs do present additional demands on the agency, counselors, and support staff. However, without adequate training and orientation to the needs of CWDs, misunderstandings are likely to occur. Therefore, support staff and intake counselors will require training in three areas: disability etiquette, disability language, and necessary accommodations and modifications for CWDs. Some CWDs may require individualized supports or accommodations, but there are some general guidelines in the use of the appropriate language, orientation to the counseling process, including the accommodations provided.

Following are some examples of improper procedures reported by CWDs who use wheelchairs and bring a companion to the office, finding that the secretaries did not address them directly, but rather asked the companion what the CWD wanted. When a Sign Language interpreter was present, often the counselor directed all comments and questions to the interpreter rather than the client. Shouting at a deaf person is not helpful nor is shouting at a blind person. Some CWDs have reported that secretaries and other support staff interacted with them in patronizing and condescending ways, often using endearments, such "honey" or "dear." Adults with disabilities are adults and should be treated as such.

Of course, it is necessary for counselors to be trained and experienced in counseling CWDs, but if the agency itself or support staff are not also trained in basic disability issues, CWDs will not return for a second session. There are videos on disability etiquette, IWDs can give in-service training, and an introduction to disability law all will serve as starting points. The best source for learning about necessary supports, accommodations, and modifications is the client. Remember Brenda Premo, the high school and college student in Chapter Four? (Mackelprang & Salsgiver, 1999). Ms. Premo is blind and it was the teachers who asked her, "What will make this class better for you?" These teachers understood that it was the responsibility of the school and the teachers to provide accommodations, rather than the responsibility of the IWD. However, these teachers did first ask Ms. Premo which accommodations she needed. Counseling agencies are required, by law, to provide accommodations, but it will always help to ask the IWD which accommodations would work best.

Are disability accommodations expensive? The answer has two parts: First, many accommodations are not as expensive as is first thought. Physical accommodations, such as ramps and wide doorways, are convenient for many IWODs. Accommodations, such as written job descriptions, job promotion guidelines, and employment termination guidelines, benefit everyone, making job-related policies clear cut and standardized. The second part of the answer concerns the cost of under-educating and under-employing large segments of populations. In the United States, the Social Security Disability Insurance (SSDI) costs are easily determined and consume many tax dollars. Most disability economists believe that accommodations in education and employment would pay for themselves when greater numbers of IWDs are allowed to fulfill their potential, work in the open job market, and pay taxes.

Professional guidelines and codes of ethics for counseling must be expanded to include both the provision and quality of disability accommodations. For example, in most codes of ethics, typically found under the title Cultural Concerns, the qualifications, education, skill levels, and experience of foreign language interpreters are outlined. Using family members as foreign language interpreters is clearly a dual relationship and counselors understand this. On the other hand, the improper use of Sign Language interpreters, is not addressed in professional guidelines nor understood. (By the way, the first four words of the last sentence, "On the other hand," is a Deaf joke referring to signing with the hands.) In the same way that foreign language interpreters must be trained in the ethics of confidentiality and the Health Insurance and Portability and Accountability Act (HIPPA) compliance, Sign Language interpreters are also subject to these same professional/ethical expectations (Smart & Smart, 1995a, b, 1996, 1997a, b, c).

Progress notes for each session must also include a description of any accommodations. For example, if the services of a Sign Language interpreter are used, the level of certification of the interpreter must be included and perhaps an explanatory note on the type of introduction to the general terminology of counseling and of the agency should be provided. The ethics of counseling should also be addressed with the interpreter, although certified Sign Language interpreters adhere to a comprehensive code of professional ethics.

Resist the Urge to Simplify the Identity and Categorize Clients With Disabilities

The Automatic and Compelling Need to Simplify and Categorize Clients With Disabilities

- CWDs often appear ambiguous.
- Often IWODs are not aware that they are simplifying the identity of IWDs and placing them into categories.

A combination of factors makes IWDs appear ambiguous to IWODs, including counselors. The segregation of IWDs and the lack of both training and experience in disability issues combine to render IWDs, and their disabilities, ambiguous. The simplest way in which to view disability is binary or dichotomous; the individual has a disability or is "normal." The general training of counselors in which they learn to consider every client as an individual, with differing values, motivations, and feelings, allow counselors to view people and the world in much more complex terms than any binary system can. Every disability experience is unique to the individual; however, there are commonalities among IWDs. Most of these commonalities are related to the prejudice and discrimination in the larger society, rather than anything about the disability itself.

Having discussed the hierarchy of stigma toward various broad general categories of disabilities, which has been proven by empirical research, it therefore becomes necessary for counselors to ask themselves if they, in some way, conceptualize some disabilities as more stigmatizing than others.

Recognize That Working With CWDs Requires Counselors to Question Their Own Biases and Examine Their Misconceptions

> **Questioning Biases and Misconceptions**
> - Such self-examination is necessary for all clients; however, counselors may be required to engage in further self-examination with CWDs.
> - Counselors may not be aware of the extent of their misconceptions of CWDs.
> - "Counseling the counselor" may be necessary.

With all clients, counselors actively examine their own biases and feelings, openness to ideas, clients, and experiences which appear both ambiguous and complex. Didactic training and supervised practice techniques require counselors "to explore their own beliefs, motivations, emotions, and experiences" (Borders, 2001, p. 421). Counselors' unspoken assumptions, of which they may be unaware, convey powerful message to clients. Therefore, two important aspects of the working alliance must be remembered. First, counselors learn about themselves, and, second, counselors need to learn about IWDs. Two counselor educators explain the impact of the unique characteristics and responses of counselors.

> Helpers bring unique ways of viewing the world to the helping process. They contribute their personalities, beliefs, assumptions about the world, values, experiences, and cultural and demographic characteristics In addition, helpers bring their theoretical orientation (beliefs how to help) and their previous experiences in helping (both informal and formal).
>
> (Hill & O'Brien, 1991, p. 32)

Counselors are never completely objective, necessitating consistent self-examination and self-understanding. When counselors learn about different types of clients, whether the difference is gender, social class, ethnicity, sexual orientation, or disability, counselors are also learning about themselves. A counselor-educator/author (Gladding, 2000) labeled this tendency of counselors to distance themselves from clients as disidentification, "in which counselors becomes emotionally removed from clients. Disidentification may express itself in counselor behavior that is aloof, nonempathetic, hostile, cold, or antagonistic" (p. 158). However, learning about IWDs may be more stressful than learning about these other groups of people because most counselors experience existential angst with CWDs, fearing that they themselves may acquire a disability and counselors may wish to distance themselves both from the disability and the person who experiences a disability. As part of their training, some counselors have undergone personal counseling, both individual and group counseling, in order to become more aware of their own worldviews and difficulties and the effects these may exert on future clients. However, insightful and successful "counseling the counselor" rarely includes exploration of the counselor's emotional reactions to CWDs. A psychiatrist (Paris, 2015, p. 12) summarized: "Stigma is rooted in the fear of having a disability oneself. Rejecting the construct of disability protects us [professionals] from the possibility."

Over-identification with a CWD, although rare, can also occur. Susan Smith is a counselor who has a son with ASD. Her specialty is counseling parents of children with disabilities, describing her services as a combination of psychoeducation, referral services, and grief counseling.

> As a counselor, I envision myself gathering information and collaborating with specialists to uncover the facts so that I can assist families in restructuring their perspectives to start from a realistic framework.
>
> This does not mean glossing over the truly difficult and overwhelming feelings that accompany these families' situations. When I work

through my own circumstances, I find that I need to marry grief work and psychoeducation—honoring my feelings of loss while also gathering information about expectations and alternatives, some of which are positive in nature.

(Smith, 2010, p. 56)

Smith offers a variety of valuable services, including collaboration with other professionals. Importantly, she is aware that, because of her son's disability, she cannot be completely objective, feeling her own losses. The fact that she is aware of over-identification and expresses it so eloquently probably allows her to be more objective.

Counselors should ask themselves: How objective can I be with a CWD? How willing am I to listen to and understand the client's disability? Am I sensationalizing or exaggerating the client's disability? Do I automatically conclude that all of the client's motivations and behaviors are the result of their disability? Do I consider the possibility that many of the client's difficulties are the result of a prejudicial and discriminating environment? Do I automatically (and subconsciously) reject some possibilities because I am trying to protect my client from failure? Do I respect the CWD or, at some level, do I feel pity and sympathy? Am I trying to enforce my own idea of normalcy? Does hearing about the prejudice and discrimination encountered by my client threaten me? Am I willing to ask the client about the disability (and then listen and understand)? Do I feel frustrated that the client's disability, or the symptoms, cannot be entirely cured or eliminated?

In order to establish a working alliance, a warm, accepting, and safe counseling environment is necessary. In addition, a working alliance requires mutual understanding for counselor and client.

Respect the Client. Respect the Disability.

Respecting the Client and Their Disability

- Disability is not a minor inconvenience nor is disability a personal weakness, shortcoming, or disadvantage.
- Do not use euphemisms such as "differently abled," "physically challenged," "special," or "exceptional."
- Like birth and death, the onset of a disability or diagnosis of a chronic illness is an irreversible physical transition. Disability is chronic and lifelong.
- Disability is difficult, but not tragic.

> - IWDs do not want "honorary able-bodied status." Statements such as "I never think of you as disabled" are perceived as insulting.
> - "Disability-blind" counseling is not recommended, even when the client's issues have nothing to do with their disability. The disability is an important and valued part of the client's identity.

Disability is not a minor inconvenience nor is the IWD "differently abled." Disability is chronic, meaning that it will be never be cured or totally eliminated. Disabilities may require hours of care and maintenance each day and for some IWDs; life is not as spontaneous or unplanned as it is for most IWODs. IWDs must take their disability into consideration, including treatment and medication regimens and also the lack of physical access. While disability is not tragic, it is difficult, expensive, and requires management and continual monitoring to ensure that minor complications do not become secondary conditions. For example, a cold or sore throat for someone with a spinal cord injury may quickly progress to a life-threatening infection, requiring immediate hospitalization. For those with disabilities with a degenerating course, the future is less certain; planning for the future becomes difficult and may be frightening. At times, the disability is painful, and most IWODs, including counselors, try to distance themselves from physical pain.

Disability is one of three irreversible physical transitions. These irreversible physical transitions are birth, death, and the onset or diagnosis of a disability or chronic illness. Birth and death are the two *universal* irreversible physical transitions because everyone is born and everyone dies. Although disability is an irreversible physical transition, it is not universal because not everyone has or will have a disability. The only developmental stage at which the onset of a disability or diagnosis of a chronic illness is socially sanctioned and "expected," is old age. Disability is never sanctioned or expected in the other developmental stages. In contrast to physical transitions, the "accepted timing" of social transitions, such as education, career, marriage, and child rearing, has become much more flexible. Therefore, the socially endowed flexibility of the appropriate age at which to initiate and complete developmental tasks is viewed as a societal advance and even more important, as allowing greater individual freedom. The increased flexibility in the time of social transitions enlarges the individual's sense of autonomy and control. Further, many individuals may choose not to undertake formerly widely accepted developmental tasks, such as marriage and child rearing.

However, the possibility of acquiring a disability is almost never considered as an irreversible transition. Most IWODs assume they will never experience a disability or chronic illness, much in the same way that many people choose to ignore the eventuality of death (although most people have life insurance policies and prepare their wills). Further, most professional service providers, including counselors, want to be able to "help," and in the Biomedical Model of Disability, help means a total cure or, at minimum, a decrease in the symptoms. This is the "reductionist" tendency of the Biomedical Model because often neither cure nor reduction of symptoms is possible. This reality may be difficult for counselors to accept; nevertheless, the CWD understands the chronic nature of their disability. All Models of Disability are reductionist and no single model presents a complete picture of the disability experience. However, other models view "professional help" as increased functioning, more social integration, and basic human civil rights; all of these types of help are possible to achieve.

Many CWDs, especially those with congenital disabilities, have had atypical life experiences, such as extended hospitalizations, repeated surgeries and treatments, separation from parents and families, and perhaps residential schooling. In order to understand the CWD, it may be necessary to gain some awareness and understanding of these different types of life experiences.

In summary, while disability is not tragic, it is difficult, expensive, and requires management and continual monitoring to ensure that minor complications do not become secondary conditions. A broken leg which requires the individual to use a wheelchair until the leg heals is not considered a disability, nor is a bad case of the flu considered a chronic illness due to the fact that disabilities are lifelong experiences while a few months in a wheelchair or becoming sick with a time-limited illness are not lifelong experiences. This is especially true of those with congenital disabilities who have never experienced a time when they did not have a disability. In spite of this, many IWODs have told IWDs: "I know exactly how you feel. I spent three months in a wheelchair after a skiing accident."

Therefore, counselors should respect both the client and their disability, perhaps learning about the particular type of disability. While it is not possible for someone without the same type of disability to understand the daily lived experience of the disability, counselors should attempt to gain some insight into the demands and treatment of the disability. At the same time, the CWD should be accorded respect, viewing them as a capable and valid decision maker, as someone who is worthy of society's investment.

Respecting both the individual client and their disability requires a balance. On the one hand, a "disability blind" counseling relationship is not suggested.

Disability blindness implies that counselors totally ignore the disability. Most IWDs do not want honorary "able-bodied" status. Honorary "able-bodied" status is illustrated by the comment, "I don't think of you as having a disability." On the other hand, exaggerating and sensationalizing the client's disability are not recommended. The working alliance between client and counselor will be compromised if the counselor ignores the disability, or views the disability in an exaggerated way, or wants to "cure" the client.

Three-Step Process to Understand Client's Disability

1. Access large, standardized diagnostic systems to learn about the medical and physical aspects of the disability.
2. Read first-person accounts of individuals with the same type of disability in order to learn about the social and emotional aspects of the disability, including the hierarchy of stigma.
3. Most important, listen to the client, ask respectful, sensitive questions in order to demonstrate that the counselor is trying to understand the client, their experiences, and the disability.

Counselors can implement a three-step process in learning about a client's disability. The first step is accessing various large diagnostic systems, such as the ICD-10 (*International Classification of Disease*-10th edition) (WHO, 2001) and the DSM-5 (*Diagnostic and Statistical Manual of Mental Disorders*-5th edition) (American Psychiatric Association, 2013) and learning about the medical and biological aspects of clients' disabilities including type and time of onset, course of the disability, visibility, prognosis, and treatment. The second step is not always necessary, but reading first-person accounts of individuals with the same type of disability can assist the counselor in understanding the social and emotional impact, including the hierarchy of stigma. Finally, and most important and probably the step that requires the greatest amount of time, is simply listening to the client, asking respectful, sensitive questions, and demonstrating respect for both the client and their disability.

It may be helpful for counselors to conceptualize the disability and its management as analogous to Maslow's lowest stage in the hierarchy of needs. Abraham Maslow developed a stage theory of human development in which everyone has the potential to reach the highest stage, that of self-actualization or transcendence. Rather than using chronological age as stages, Maslow conceptualized human needs as motivating development, from lowest needs (which he termed "deficit" needs) to progressively higher needs.

Each ascending need, therefore, requires that the needs below it are satisfied. Maslow's hierarchy ranges from the lowest level needs of the biological person to the higher level of abstract, uniquely human needs. When one need is met, the individual will then become motivated to fulfill higher-level needs, Once a need has been met, it loses its motivational power. For example, after obtaining enough food and water, the individual will then begin to seek safety. The needs are universal, but they are culturally and socially shaped.

The lowest or first level of needs is the physiological needs of water, food, oxygen, sleep, and sex, which are deemed "deficit needs." If these basic needs are not met, the individual's life becomes dominated by fulfilling these needs.

The organism is dominated and its behavior organized by unsatisfied needs.

(Smart, 2012, p. 127)

Maslow's human developmental theory can be applied to IWDs, with medical stabilization immediately following the onset of the disability and care and treatment during relapses considered as physiological or "deficit" needs. During the time of acute care and treatment, the lives of IWDs are dominated by the disability, both its needs and limitations. During medical treatments and relapses, the Biomedical Model is both necessary and effective. However, after treatment is completed, most IWDs manage and monitor their disabilities, but their main life focus shifts to basic life tasks. Stated differently, IWDs adjust to a new "normal," and the disability is no longer the central organizer of their lives.

Maslow's theory is easily understood perhaps because it incorporates both physical needs and higher needs which are met in cultural, social, and also, in idiosyncratic ways. Including IWDs in Maslow's theory by adding the treatment and care of the disability into the lowest stage of physiological needs poses two challenges. First, the physiological, deficit needs of IWDs are not universal. Maslow understood that all humans, including IWDs, require oxygen, water, food, and sleep; thus these physical needs are universal. However, IWDs have additional needs such as the need for a ventilator to breathe or multiple surgeries or medications to treat emotional needs. Second, most IWODs (especially in developed nations) rarely worry about getting enough to eat and drink and according to Maslow, these needs are no longer needs because they have been met and they do not act as motivators. IWDs, on the other hand, must monitor and manage their disabilities on a daily basis. In spite of these two exceptions, Maslow's theory of a hierarchy of needs could be expanded to include IWDs because most IWDs are knowledgeable, skilled, and experienced in managing the physiological needs of their disabilities, the management becoming both routine and commonplace, or "normal."

There are two important differences in the physical needs of IWDs and IWODs. The lives of IWDs are usually more physically precarious. Complications and secondary conditions are common occurrences, even in disabilities with stable courses. Individuals with episodic or relapsing disabilities must continuously monitor their physical needs. In all disabilities, without continuous, careful management, death can occur. Meeting the physical needs of IWDs is typically more extensive and expensive. Second, IWDs are often defined, categorized, and stereotyped because of their physical needs while most IWODs are not defined by their physical needs, perhaps these needs are considered universal. Recognizing and addressing an individual's physical needs is different than defining the individual as their physical needs.

Establish Rapport With the Client Who Has a Disability

Establishing Rapport

- It is necessary to place the client's needs as the first priority.
- Clients should feel safe, empowered, and valued.
- Hearing the client's experiences of prejudice and discrimination may be unpleasant for the counselor.
- Counselors should not feel threatened by client resistance and testing. CWDs may be judging if counselors without disabilities can understand them and their disabilities.

The first step to creating a safe, non-threatening, and warm environment is the development of a helping relationship in which the client's needs are the first priority. Only in a mutually respectful, accepting environment can client needs be explored. Many theorists, such as Rogers, considered the counseling relationship to be the primary means to effect client change. "Rogers suggested that the client should be encouraged to fulfill his own potential: that the client is best authority on his own experience and thus is fully capable of achieving growth through self-discovery and self-directed growth" (Smithson & Kennedy, 2012, p. 129). Mutual rapport is necessary for the client to feel empowered, unthreatened, valued, and understood.

The rapport-building process is based upon a counselor's empathic understanding of the client and, while it is true that counselors never fully understand their clients and view the world exactly as they do, empathic understanding is a more natural, straightforward process with some clients than with others. Clients with disabilities present challenges to counselors because counselors frequently have misguided ideas about the disability experience. Counselors have developed counseling skills by professional practice and clinical supervision; but nonetheless, experiences outside the office play a role in determining the attitudes and behaviors of counselors. Typically more aware of their professional skills, counselors may still not recognize those behaviors and attitudes acquired by living in a society that often portrays CWDs in patronizing and demeaning ways. Society often promotes the false idea that the ideal way to be human does not include a disability. Furthermore, the media teaches that health, beauty, athleticism, and strength are necessary in order to achieve self-actualization. Both positive and negative unspoken assumptions and attitudes can be communicated to clients. The counselor may not aware of their lack of sensitivity and understanding, but CWDs understand patronizing and stigmatizing attitudes. Clients often want to know the counselor's beliefs and attitudes in order to determine if it safe to work with them. Only then, will clients feel comfortable in the counseling relationship.

The counselor's emotional reactions to clients may impede the relationship development. Counselors may wish to detach or distance themselves from CWDs in an attempt to protect themselves from the idea that they might someday have a disability. With all clients, counselors explore their own motivations, beliefs, emotions, and experiences, but with CWDs these needs are often greater.

CWDs may also engage in some mild "testing" behavior in an effort to determine the limits of the counselor's the counselor's trustworthiness, professional skills, and attitude and knowledge of IWDs. Although often not directed at the counselor personally, the counselor must be able to understand and tolerate this testing behavior without becoming defensive and, moreover, the counselor's openness to learn and understand will result in better client outcomes. It may take some time to determine the source or motivation of the CWD's resistance.

In short, the rapport-building phase of the counseling relationship, when working with CWDs, often requires greater counselor self-awareness, more openness to learning about the client's unique experience of disability, including prejudice and discrimination and, occasionally, willingness to tolerate client resistance. CWDs may engage in some mild oppositional behavior and/or may not initially provide full disclosure. Often, this type of client resistance is the client's attempt to determine if the counselor holds uninformed or prejudicial ideas about disability and, of course, the counselor should not feel threatened.

Do Not Confuse Normalcy (Absence of Disability) With the Ideal

> **Ways in Which Normalcy Is Thought of as the Ideal**
> - Disability is thought of as the absence of normalcy.
> - There is an evaluative component to normalcy. It is better to be "normal" than to have a disability.
> - The degree of normalcy is directly associated with the degree of humanity accorded to the individual.
> - Normalcy, although not clearly or universally defined, is better than having a disability.

Related to the idea of pathologizing IWDs are the definitions of disability and normalcy. In order to provide services, funding, and endowing citizens with civil rights, it is necessary to define disability; but in defining disabilities, many wrongly think that 1) disability is the absence of normalcy; 2) to be "normal," is better than to have a disability; 3) the degree of normalcy is associated with degree of humanity; and 4) normalcy is the ideal condition. The preceding sentences include many value-laden, but poorly defined, concepts such as "normalcy," "disability," "humanity," and "ideal." However, most IWODs are not required to consider these concepts and, not surprisingly, most IWODs do not find it necessary. In contrast, most IWD *do* contemplate these life-defining conceptions. Most IWODs would not describe themselves as individuals without disabilities, in large part due to the fact that IWODs belong to a valued category (those without disabilities). In contrast, IWDs understand that society places them in a devalued category; nonetheless IWDs do think of themselves as devalued or as belonging to the nebulous category of "the disabled." Only those IWDs who have remarkable accomplishments (for anyone with or without a disability) are considered individuals with other identities, rather than simply as an individual with a disability. Stephen Hawking, the British astrophysicist and Eric Weihenmayer, the American who climbed Mount Everest, are two examples. In contrast, those with severe and multiple disabilities, especially intellectual disabilities, understand that others often question their basic humanity.

Nonetheless, these four assumptions are human-made myths and are often not spoken or written in these clear terms and, worse, these assumptions are not recognized as patently false.

Counselors are more inclined to consider the underlying assumptions of "humanity" and "the ideal," especially counselors who consider themselves humanistic practitioners. However, in the general public, especially the media, normalcy is an enshrined ideal for which the individual is held responsible.

Basic training in disability issues often starts with these four myths. Counselors, through training and practice, are able to quickly identify the falsehoods of these statements because they understand that the definition of normalcy is based on the following:

- Value judgments that may mistakenly interfere;
- The environment in which the individual functions;
- Who is making the determination and what their motives are;
- The purpose of the assessment;
- The diagnostic tools, instruments, and classification system used (Smart, 2016, p. 15).

In the following excerpt, a disability scholar who is also a blind person, emphasizes that it is the academic discipline of statistics that has promulgated the idea of "normal."

> There is no flesh-and-bones human body that is normal, the only "normal body" is the one constructed from the "bare bones" of statistics. . . . This is the fiction that is presented to disabled person.
> (Michalko, 2002, p. 32)

The counseling and psychology professions have generally ignored IWDs and, because of this, there are no theories of development, including career development, or theories of counseling specialties, such as marriage and family, adolescent, racial and cultural, or LGBTQ. Without theories, testing instruments and assessment tools cannot be developed, tested, and validated for IWDs (D. W. Smart & J. F. Smart, 1997; J. F. Smart, 2012; J. F. Smart & D. W. Smart, 1995, a, b, c; 1997, a, b, c, d). Therefore, IWDs are often evaluated unfairly negatively because they have been judged in comparison with those without disabilities. The ACA *Encyclopedia of Counseling* (American Counseling Association, 2015) addressed the importance of testing assessments and presented cautions:

> Professional counselors must be cautious when selecting and using assessment methods that do not have norms appropriate to a particular client requiring a counselor's knowledge of how to adapt the methods used to the unique circumstances of that client without jeopardizing the validity of the results.
> (American Counseling Association, 2009, p. 33)

> **Counselors should:**
> - Understand that there are no counseling or developmental theories that have included IWDs.
> - Use standardized test results, especially results from personality tests, with caution.
> - Understand that results of standardized intellectual tests are often artificially lowered for IWDs.
> - Recognize that accommodations will be necessary.
> - Recognize that the description of these types of accommodations must be included in the written evaluation and description of results.

Therefore, standardized tests that are not normed on IWDs can yield spurious results. For example, the results of some psychological instruments may falsely indicate the presence of pathological hypochondriasis when the test-taker appears to be overly concerned with body functions. Nonetheless, most IWDs are *adaptively* concerned about body functions. Another example concerns the pathological diagnosis of dependence and, yet, IWDs who require the services of personal care attendants or who are respirator-dependent, these so-called symptoms of dependence are adaptive, to the point of being life-saving. Any type of paper-and-pencil or computerized test, including intelligence tests, classroom achievement tests, and licensing and certifying tests, for which accommodations are not provided, results in meaningless scores. Brenda Premo, who became progressively blind during her school years, reported that the only valid result of an intelligence test given to her was the fact that she was unable to read small print. Nonetheless, the low score falsely showed Brenda to have an intellectual disability and this IQ score may have remained in her records for years. The psychologist said he could not provide Brenda with the accommodations of large print or a magnifying glass because no one else used (or needed) these accommodations. If Brenda used them, the psychologist thought it would jeopardize the standardization of the intelligence test.

The use of accommodations will change the way in which the evaluation and results of testing are written. Disclosure of the test-taker's documented disability (and the source of the documentation) and a complete description of the accommodations will be included in the report.

Question if the Environment Is Limiting the Achievement of CWDs

> **History-Taking With CWDs**
> - One of the purposes of the history-taking process in counseling is to determine the level of past functioning and level of motivation and to predict these aspects in the client's future functioning.
> - These purposes often do not apply to CWDs because they assume that all clients have access to opportunity structures.
> - When interpreting a CWD's history as low-functioning, counselors may think this lack of achievement is entirely due to the individual himself or herself or to their disability.
> - Much of this lack of achievement is due to society's prejudice and discrimination which results in withholding access to opportunity structures such as education and the workplace.

Another counseling technique is the personal history in which the client's previous functioning in various areas is collected, described, and interpreted. Other purposes of the history taking include identifying the client's coping skills, level of motivation, strengths, and past goal-directed behaviors and the results of these behaviors. Particularly, in a strengths-based, wellness orientation of counseling, the client's personal history can reveal their successes, assets, and resources. For CWDs, counselors rarely consider that it is the environment which has limited their achievements.

> I couldn't remain at my job because the building wasn't accessible. I was an independent women making her own way who now must depend on others. Totally frustrating (Participant 61).
> (Graf, Marini, & Blankenship, 2009, p. 29)

Another participant stated,

> Presently, it's difficult to find some equilibrium with the anger I feel about being closed out of so many places because I use a wheelchair and the need to be "nice" in order to keep job, friends, et al.
> (Graf, Marini, & Blankenship, 2009, p. 30)

Two important points: The disability itself may be limiting, but more limiting are societal attitudes and laws. Eric Weihenmayer, who is blind and summited Mount Everest, used the fairy tale of "Goldilocks and the Three Bears" to illustrate his unsuccessful experiences in trying to get a dishwashing job in Cambridge, Massachusetts, while he was in college:

> Too big, too small, too fast, too hot, like a twisted version of the three bears—the story repeated itself again and again. I had thought somehow, that with my force of will, with my ingenuity, with my tenacity, I could eventually win people over and get what I wanted out of life. I hadn't realized that there were doors that would remain locked in front of me. I wanted so badly to break through, to take a battering ram to them, to bash them into a million splinters, but the doors were locked too securely and their surfaces were impenetrable. I never got a dishwasher job in Cambridge, but I did choke down an important lesson, that people's perceptions of our limitations are more damaging than the limitations themselves, and it was the hardest lesson I had ever had to swallow.
> (Weihenmayer, 2001, pp. 127–128)

What employer would not want an employee who was ingenuous and tenacious? Recognizing prejudice and discrimination was "the hardest lesson I ever had to swallow." Weihenmayer seems to have expected that his blindness would present difficulties in his job search because he states, "I could eventually win people over." But, counselors reviewing his job history, might jump to the conclusion that Weihenmayer was not tenacious nor ingenuous. Also, this is an example of pathologization of his disability, of which Weihenmayer is aware, when he stated "people perceptions of our limitations are more damaging than the limitations themselves."

In addition to employment opportunities, many IWDs have not attained typical societal-defined developmental tasks of adulthood such as marriage and parenthood. However, societal barriers are rarely considered when interpreting the history of IWDs. An important part of the history-taking process focuses on the client's relationships and social functioning. The excerpt explains these "significant barriers."

> For individuals with disabilities, expressions of sexuality have been both denied and heavily regulated and remain highly controversial. Although some disability-related government agencies have guidelines

and policies, such policies remain inconsistent, underutilized and predominantly focused on being "crisis reactive" rather than rights oriented.

(Harris, Heller, & Schindler, 2012)

The end goal of most theories of human development include autonomy, self-direction, planful agency, individuation but the major developmental theories have ignored the experience of disability and, moreover, assume that large scale, societal-provided opportunity structures are equally open to everyone. In the case of disability, the lack of achievement often has nothing to do with the individual's motivation or lack of planful effort.

Do Not Pathologize the Disability

Pathologization occurs when these 12 areas of wellness are ignored or minimalized:

1. Self-worth
2. Sense of control
3. Realistic beliefs
4. Emotional awareness and coping
5. Problem solving and creativity
6. Sense of humor
7. Physical fitness
8. Nutrition
9. Self-care
10. Stress management
11. Gender identity
12. Cultural identity

- Ironically, many IWDs have achieved, and actually work toward, these 12 aspects of wellness due to the demands of their disabilities.
- Many IWDs mistakenly believe that IWDs are continually depressed, bitter, and angry and, therefore, are of no use to themselves, their families, or society.
- IWDs are often thought of as "burdens" or "drains."
- Pathologization of disabilities often leads to fewer resources and less investment being accorded to IWDs.

The profession of counseling is moving toward a strengths and asset orientation and shifting from a focus on pathology and deficits. Myers and colleagues (2000) defined wellness as "a way of life oriented toward optimal health and well-being in which body, mind, and spirt are integrated by the individual" (p. 252). Wellness psychology and corresponding counseling practices focus on 12 areas, "self-of-worth, sense of control, realistic beliefs, emotional awareness and coping, problem solving and creativity, sense of humor, physical fitness, nutrition, self-care, stress management, gender identity and cultural identity" (Myers, Sweeney, & Whitmer, 2000, p. 643). Other definitions of wellness psychology and counseling include optimization of one's potential and individuals making choices for successful experiences. Hettler (1985), a public health physician, is considered the father of the modern wellness movement and physicians and other public health workers are considered the pioneers in wellness psychology. However, the wellness movement has not included IWDs, but does consider individuals of differing gender identities and cultural identities. On the one hand, most IWDs are wellness oriented, being pro-active in managing their disabilities, eliminating unnecessary obstacles and limitations, asserting their civil rights, and implementing idiosyncratic ways of directing their lives and claiming the right to make their own decisions. Ironically, due to the management of their disability, including emotional and physical demands, most IWDs are more skilled in all of these 12 areas of wellness than most IWODs. In many aspects, IWDs are expert practitioners of wellness psychology. A family member of an individual with a psychiatric disability described her adaptability: "I can now say that, like that old aluminum foil ad, I am 'oven-tempered for flexible strength'" (Marsh & Lefly, 1996, p. 7). A university professor who is blind compared her general adaptability to "Normals," the word she used to describe IWODs.

> There is more than one way to be a human being. . . . On the surface, it seems a pretty innocuous statement, but in fact, it's quite revolutionary. It forces people to question everything they take for granted as normal. It's a message that needs to be spoken of still. . . . We say it by forcing our way into their notice, into their world.
>
> I worried about a lot of them so much, the Normals I know. If some of them ever become disabled . . . it will be a bad business. If they could just let go of the fear, I think. I have the fear, too. I'm afraid of losing my hearing. But I know that if or when it happens, I'll make do somehow. Making do is not such a foreign concept to me. For the Normals, making do is dreadful even to contemplate. What would life be without a leg, without

eyesight, without hearing, they worry. Life would be life . . . I say. Flawed and limited in some ways, rich and various in others.

(Kleege, 2006, p. 182)

Many IWDs consider themselves physically healthy. One IWD described: "Even though I am in a wheelchair and can't walk, health and wellness means to me to do as much as you can for yourself" (Putnam et al., 2003, p. 2003). The point has been made that the experience of the disability includes functional limitations, perhaps pain, and most often, discriminating and prejudicial behavior of others. Acknowledging these realities does not mean that the CWDs view themselves as tragic victims. There are some IWDs who consider their lives after the onset/diagnosis of their disability to be more satisfying and fulfilling.

What is pathologization of disabilities? Following is a short list of descriptions of pathologizing behaviors:

- Underestimating the quality of life of IWDs
- Underestimating the future capabilities of children with disabilities
- Underestimating the positive effects of the disability
- Underestimating the happiness of IWDs
- Overestimating the effects of the disability

It may seem contradictory to state that according to the Biomedical Model, disability is pathology and, at the same time, recognize that it is possible to pathologize the disability experience. Pathologization exaggerates, sensationalizes, and overgeneralizes the existing limitations of the disability. Viewing disability as a tragic experience, in which the IWD is constantly depressed and demoralized is a type of pathologization.

In terms of disability, pathologization occurs when society (and helping professionals, such as counselors) view the self-actualized life is impossible for IWDs. Pathologization occurs when counselors fail to see the strengths, abilities, skills, and characteristics of IWDs and, indeed, many of these positive assets are a *result* of the disability. Many professional service providers, including counselors, express more negative views of the client's disability than the client does. In the past, medical professionals tended to overestimate the negative effects of the disability, underestimated the well-being and life satisfaction of ventilator-assisted polio survivors, and much of the scholarly/research literature on disability referred to IWDs as "burdens" and "drains." Another type of pathologization involves withholding preventive care or the widely practiced resistance to investing societal resources in IWDs. Notably, he academic and medical literature has consistently hypothesized emotional pathology and failed to examine health and wellness issues (Charmaz & Paterniti, 1998).

Often physicians and other service providers have confused healthy adaptation to the disability as pathological denial. Solomon (2012) discussed family adaptation to a child with a disability, summarizing, "A doctor's or social worker's refusal to believe parents' reality because it is happier than anticipated is a kind of betrayal" (p. 25). According to this family, their healthy adaptation to the disability was thought by the doctor to be a type of betrayal perhaps because the doctor wanted the family to accept their judgment of the disability. Continuing, Solomon stated, "Although most families find meaning in their predicament, fewer than one in ten [service providers] believed it." One mother of a child with a disability stated that the family's social and professional circle became constricted. "I was determined not to be around folks who saw us a tragic. Unfortunately, that included my family, most professionals, and just about everyone else I knew" (Solomon, 2012, p. 25).

Pathologization is reductionistic because it fails to consider the positive aspects of disability and, as we have learned, IWODs tend to sensationalize the effects of the disability. One woman tried to explain the mundane, ordinary nature of her disability as follows: "Putting on my artificial leg is no more distressing to me than you putting on your socks and shoes" (DeLoach & Greer, 1981). If this woman were born with a congenital limb deficiency, putting on her artificial leg would *never be* emotionally distressing, but if the loss of her leg occurred later in life, immediately after the amputation it probably was an emotionally demanding experience, but eventually putting on her artificial leg became a normal, routine part of her day. Some disability authors have considered the need of IWODs to pathologize disability as a way for IWODs to maintain their sense of superiority (Wright, 1983). Morris (1991) explained, "Not all of us view our disability as the unmitigated disaster and diminishment that seems expected of us" (p. 97). Morris also reported that when IWDs refuse unwanted help, IWDs are accused of "having a chip on our shoulder" (p. 97). Another author concluded: "The combination of the false perceptions of disability as tragedy and constant grieving serves to make the lack of disability (or normality) appear valuable, desirable, and superior" (Smart, 2016, p. 246).

Not only do most IWODs often have an emotional reaction to disability, but most IWODs do not understand disability behavior. It is a human tendency to "fill in the blanks," often without realizing it. Therefore, it is easier to jump to the conclusion that the man in a wheelchair who falls asleep in meetings is bored and uninterested. The truth, however, is that this colleague takes large doses of antispasmodic medications that make him sleepy. If counselors do not understand certain behaviors, they are not able to correctly interpret the behaviors or the motivations for the behavior. Clients who cancel counseling sessions at the last minute may be thought of as uncooperative when, in reality, CWDs often are required to rely on public transportation which is not always predictable and punctual. (This is another example of a narrower range of choices available to CWDs. Most CWODs have a car or other private transportation available 24 hours a day, seven days a week.) A final example of normalizing disability behavior concerns American President Franklin D. Roosevelt. Roosevelt was a flamboyant, outgoing American president. He used a wheelchair because he was a polio survivor. Everyone thought that the commonly seen navy-blue cape he wore was part of his showy costume, much like his cigarette holder. However, the wool cape was actually a disability accommodation because a cape is easier to manage (than a coat) when sitting in the wheelchair. Most people knew that President Roosevelt could not walk. Winston Churchill stated, "His legs refused their office." However, Roosevelt did not want to remind people of his wheelchair or disability and became quite adept at presenting himself as an IWOD.

More than 50 years after Roosevelt's death a $48 million monument was erected in Washington, DC, sculpted from South Dakota granite, with many of Roosevelt's famous statements carved into the base encouraging Americans through the Great Depression and World War II. However, the monument did not show Roosevelt's disability or his wheelchair, demonstrating the need to hide or minimize Roosevelt's paralysis. A small contingent of IWDs protested at the monument site, with wheelchair user Mike Deland, chairman of the National Organization on Disability (NOD) stating, "You have missed the essence of the man." Others, including past Presidents Bush, Ford, Carter, and Clinton stated that the monument was a misreading of Roosevelt and "a grave misstatement of history for generations to come" (*Time*, April 28, 1997).

Ways in which counselors can guard against pathologization include:

- Actively look for ways in which the client has achieved mastery of the disability.
- Actively look for the sources of the CWD's problems in their sociopolitical environment, rather than automatically assuming that the disability or the client is to blame.
- Do not sensationalize or impose your own emotional reactions to the client and the disability.

- Understand that you do not understand. Make an effort to understand "disability behavior." This might involve directly asking the client.
- Inform CWDs of the opportunities, resources, and options that are available to everyone.
- Use the same language and terminology as the client to describe the disability (unless, of course, it's insider humor).

Do Not Idealize the Pre-Disability Period of the IWD's Life

Idealization of the Pre-Disability Period Often Occurs

- Only possible in acquired disabilities, especially those acquired in adolescence or in midlife.
- Most acquired disabilities are not anticipated and cause great losses.
- Family members who idealize the individual's pre-disability past communicate that they like the IWD better without a disability.
- Counselors can (unthinkingly) idealize the client's pre-disability past.

For individuals with congenital disabilities or disabilities acquired very early in life, they have no pre-disability identity. They do not remember life without their disability. For those with acquired disabilities, especially disabilities acquired in adolescence or middle age, there *is* a pre-disability identity, with memories of relationships, skills, possible financial security, status, and accomplishments. The acquisition of the disability often results in losing friends, families, partners, occupational skills, and position in the community. Coupled with most people's refusal to contemplate the acquisition of a disability and the great losses that accompany most disabilities, IWODs, including counselors, often unthinkingly idealize the client's pre-disability life. Many individuals with acquired disabilities conceptualize their lives in two distinct periods, pre-disability and post-disability. In the collection of first-person accounts of the survivors of the polio epidemics, a common expression was used: BP and AP, Before Polio and After Polio.

These losses, with the accompanying shock of acquiring a disability, can be overwhelming. Nonetheless, most IWDs move beyond the stages of shock and depression. Many IWDs have developed compensating techniques, formed deep and satisfying relationships, and developed alternative "work-arounds." Many individuals with acquired physical disabilities state, "I escaped into my mind," often meaning that they returned to school and entered into professions which did not require physical skills. Many IWDs are also proud of their mastery of their disability. Amy Purdy, the woman who appeared on the television program, *Dancing With the Stars*, had both her legs amputated due to a fast-moving bacterial infection. Purdy explained that she was initially shocked and depressed, but also described her acceptance: "it was extremely traumatic at the time, but I'm so beyond that. I've done so much with my life" (Oldenburg, 2014).

It is perhaps a common human tendency to idealize the past; but IWDs, after accepting the disability, are proud of the mastery of the disability and feel that the disability is a valuable part of their self-identity. The idea of the disability as an important part of identity is often expressed by, "I wouldn't be me without my disability." Idealizing the individual's pre-disability past may be a type of pathologization, but it communicates the message: "I liked you better when you didn't have the disability." Charles Mee contracted polio as a teenager in the 1950s, resulting in a disability which required him to walk with crutches. By Mee's account, his father never got over his pre-disability memories of his son.

> For the rest of his life after I had polio, my father carried a picture of me in his wallet that he had taken at the halftime of a football game. I was sitting on the grass with my teammates while the coach talked to us. My father had come around to the side of the group, and as I turned to look at him, he took the picture: an adolescent boy in the vigor of youth, a strong jaw and neck, a crewcut, massive shoulders with the football pads. . . . I always took the fact that he carried that picture with him as a sign of disappointment in me, and it filled me with rage. . . . The photograph was still on a table not far from his bed when he died at the age of ninety-four.
> (Mee, 1999, p. 170)

Conclusion

The practice guidelines presented in this chapter are based on the preceding four chapters, including the medical aspects of disability, the differing models of disability, and the importance of considering possible long-standing attitudes and beliefs, while not intentionally meant to be harmful, do result in limiting the life choices of IWDs and often communicate the counselor's lack of knowledge and awareness of the CWD's identity and experience. The six core beliefs also pointed out that not all kindness and beneficence result in positive counseling outcomes. Nonetheless, one of the core beliefs of all type of counseling advocates placing the client's needs first. Counselors can guard against paternalism, masquerading as beneficence and kindness by asking four questions: "Is this in the best interests of my client?" "Am I seeing, as much as possible, my client's perceptions of reality?" "Do I consider my client to be a valid decision-maker and expert on their life?" and "Are any of my counseling relationships based on a lack of knowledge or experience with IWDs?" Simply asking these questions will lead to answers that, in turn, will result in positive client outcomes.

The practice guidelines provided in this chapter also illustrate the need for wider professional collaboration, including consultation with clinical psychologists, ADA compliance officers, and Sign Language interpreters.

References

Agich, G. J., & Carson, R. A. (1995). Chronic illness and freedom. In S. K. Toombs, D. Barnard, & Carson, R. A. (Eds.), *Chronic illness: From experience to policy* (pp. 129–153). Bloomington, IN: University of Indiana.

American Counseling Association. (2014). *ACA code of ethics*. Alexandria, VA: Author. https://www.counseling.org/resources/aca-code-of-ethics.pdf

American Counseling Association. (2015). *ACA encyclopedia of counseling*. Hoboken, NJ: Wiley.

American Psychiatric Association. (2013). *The diagnostic and statistical manual of mental disorders-5*. Washington, DC: Author.

Americans with Disabilities Act Amendments of 2008, 42 U.S.C. 12101 *et seq.* Retrieved from www.usdoj.gov/crt/adaaa.cfm

Americans with Disabilities Act of 1990, 42 U.S.C. 12101 *et seq.* Retrieved from www.usdoj.gov/crt/ada.homal.htm

Borders, L. D. (2001). Counseling supervision: A deliberate educational process. In D. C. Locke, J. E. Myers, & E. L. Herr (Eds.), *The Handbook of Counseling* (pp. 417–432). Thousand Oaks, CA: Sage.

Charmaz, K., & Paterniti, D. A. (Eds.) (1998). *Health, illness, and healing: Society, social construction and self*. Los Angeles: Roxbury.

DeLoach, C., & Greer, B. G. (1981). *Adjustment to severe disability: A metamorphosis*. New York, NY: McGraw-Hill.

Gladding, S. T. (2000). *Counseling: A comprehensive profession* (4th ed.). Columbus, OH: Merrill.

Goodman, J. (2001). Basic counseling skills. In D. C. Locke, J. E. Myers, & E. L. Herr (Eds.), *The handbook of counseling* (pp. 237–256). Thousand Oaks, CA: Sage.

Graf, N. M., Marini, I., & Blankenship, C. J. (2009). One hundred words about disability. *Journal of Rehabilitation, 75*, 25–34.

Harris, S. P., Heller, T., & Schindler, A. (2012). Introduction, background, and history. In R. Heller & S. P. Harris (Eds.), *Disability through the life course* (pp. 1–37). Thousand Oaks, CA: Sage.

Hettler, W. (1985). Wellness: Encouraging a lifetime pursuit of excellence. *Health Values: Achieving High Level Wellness, 8*, 13–17.

Hill, C. E., & O'Brien, K. M. (1991). *Helping skills: Facilitating exploration, insight, and action.* Washington, DC: American Psychological Association.

Kleege, G. (2006). *Blind rage: Letters to Helen Keller.* Washington, DC: Gallaudet University.

Mackelprang, R., & Salsgiver, R. (1999). *Disability: A diversity model approach in human service practice.* Pacific Grove, CA: Brooks and Cole.

Marsh, D. T., & Lefly, H. P. (1996). The family experience of mental illness: Evidence for resilience. *Psychiatric Rehabilitation Journal, 20*(2), 3–13.

Mee, C. (1999). *A nearly normal life: A memoir.* Boston, MA: Little, Brown.

Michalko, R. (2002). *The difference that disability makes.* Philadelphia, PA: Temple University.

Morris, J. (1991). *Pride against prejudice: Transforming attitudes towards disability.* London: The Women's Press.

Myers, J. E., Sweeney, T. J., & Whitmer, J. M. (2000). *American counseling association encyclopedia of counseling.* Alexandria, VA: American Counseling Association.

Oldenburg, A. (2014, March 16). Defined by determination. *USA Today,* B7–B8. Retrieved from http://usatoday30.usatoday.com/LIFE/usaedition/2014-03-17-Amy-Purdy-feature_ST_U.htm

Paris, J. (2015). *A concise guide to personality disorders.* Washington, DC: American Psychological Association.

Putnam, M., Greenen, S., Powers, L., Saxton, M., Finney, S., & Dautel, P. (2003). People with disabilities discuss barriers and facilitators to well-being. *Journal of Rehabilitation, 69,* 37–45.

Rogers, C. R. (1951). *Client-centered therapy: Its current practices, implications and theory.* Boston, MA: Houghton Mifflin.

Rogers, C. R. (1961). *On becoming a person.* Boston, MA: Houghton Mifflin.

Rogers, C. R. (1980). *A way of being.* Boston, MA: Houghton Mifflin.

Smart, D. W., & Smart, J. F. (1997). DSM-IV and culturally sensitive diagnosis: Some observations for counselors. *Journal of Counseling and Development, 75,* 392–398.

Smart, J. F. (1998). Multicultural rehabilitation education: Issues of implementation. *Rehabilitation Education, 12,* 167–173.

Smart, J. F. (2012). *Disability across the developmental lifespan.* New York, NY: Springer.

Smart, J. F. (2016). *Disability, society, and individual* (3rd ed.). Austin, TX: PRO-ED.

Smart, J. F., & Smart, D. W. (1995a). Issues in vocational evaluation of Hispanics with disabilities. In D. Crawford, F. Curnutt, D. I. Eargle, P. Leung, K. Robinson, & S. Sabelli (Eds.), *Directions in rehabilitation counseling.* New York, NY: Harleigh.

Smart, J. F., & Smart, D. W. (1995b). The use of translators/interpreters in rehabilitation. *Journal of Rehabilitation, 61,* 14–20.

Smart, J. F., & Smart, D. W. (1995c). Acculturative stress: The experience of the Hispanic immigrant. *The Counseling Psychologist, 23,* 25–42. I.F. 1.878.

Smart, J. F., & Smart, D. W. (1997a). Disability issues in translation/interpretation. In M. B. Labrum (Ed.), *American translators association scholarly monograph series* (p. IX). Amsterdam: John Benjamin.

Smart, J. F., & Smart, D. W. (1997b). Culturally sensitive informed choice in rehabilitation counseling. *Journal of Applied Rehabilitation Counseling, 28,* 32–37.

Smart, J. F., & Smart, D. W. (1997c). Vocational evaluation of Hispanic clients. Chapter 10 in F. Chan & D. Wong (Eds.), *Vocational assessment: Evaluation for people with disabilities.* Chicago: Vocational Psychology Press.

Smart, J. F., & Smart, D. W. (1997d). The racial/ethnic demography of disability. *Journal of Rehabilitation, 63,* 9–15.

Smith, S. (2010, July). Distress and hope in families raising children with special needs. *Counseling Today, 52,* 54–56.

Smithson, E. F., & Kennedy, P. (2012). Organization and planning in person-centered and hospital-based rehabilitation services. In P. Kennedy (Ed.), *The Oxford handbook of rehabilitation psychology* (pp. 128–142). New York, NY: Oxford University.

Solomon, A. (2012). *Far from the tree: Parents, children, and the search for identity.* New York, NY: Scribner.

Vash, C. L. (1981). *The psychology of disability.* New York, NY: Springer.

Weihenmayer, E. (2001). *Touch the top of the world: A blind man's journey to climb farther than the eye can see.* New York, NY: Dutton.

World Health Organization. (2001). *International classification of functioning, disability and health.* Geneva: Author.

Wright, B. A. (1983). *Physical disability—A psychosocial approach.* New York, NY: Harper & Row.

Six

UNDERSTANDING THE EXPERIENCE OF DISABILITY

Counseling Practice Guidelines

In this chapter, more practice applications are provided. Keep in mind that many of these practice guidelines overlap with one another. While some of the experiences and perceptions do not directly concern the counseling relationship, they are often a pervasive part of the lives of IWDs and, therefore, CWDs may wish to discuss them. For counselors, it is often challenging to completely understand the experiences of their clients and, with CWDs, it may be even more difficult. Furthermore, many IWODs often attribute the causes and antecedents of IWDs' difficult daily lives to the disability or to the individuals with the disabilities when, in fact, most of the difficulties are socially and politically constructed (ADA, 1990; ADAAA, 2008).

Practice guidelines outlined in this chapter are

1. Recognize the cost-benefit analysis of disclosure/nondisclosure.
2. Recognize the burden of bureaucracy.
3. Do not confuse sympathy with empathy.
4. Do not confuse denial of the disability role with denial of the disability.
5. Respect the client's assistive technology.
6. Understand the importance of contributing to others.
7. Recognize that IWDs often redefine autonomy and independence.
8. Encourage mutual support groups.
9. Recognize that sexuality is an important part of the IWD's identity and life.
10. Recognize the infantilization that IWDs often experience.

Recognize the Psychological and Emotional Cost-Benefit Analysis of Disclosing an Invisible Disability

Characteristics of an Invisible Disability
- There is no correlation between degree of visibility of the disability and degree of severity. An invisible disability can be very impairing.

> - There *is* a correlation between degree of visibility of disability and societal prejudicial attitudes and behaviors. Generally speaking, there is more discomfort, prejudice, and discrimination directed toward individuals with invisible disabilities.

Some disabilities are visible, such as amputations, blindness, and deafness. Other disabilities become visible due to the assistive devices used, such as wheelchairs, insulin pumps, and hearing aids. In the era of telecommunications and globalization, such dichotomies between visible and invisible disabilities are less clear. For example, it is becoming commonplace to hire job applications after telephone interviews. Therefore, in these circumstances, the IWD could choose to hide a visible disability. Also, remember that IWDs are often encouraged to hide or minimize their disability in order to make IWODs comfortable. President Franklin Roosevelt of the United States, after the onset of polio at age 39, never walked again, which most Americans knew. However, Roosevelt did not want to *remind* the public of his disability. There are very few photographs of Roosevelt in a wheelchair and only one of his bare legs. He was never photographed being carried by one of his sons or by Secret Service agents. Roosevelt, therefore, is an example of someone with a visible disability who chose to minimize it; but at the same time, Roosevelt was a polio survivor with extraordinary resources. However, most individuals with visible disabilities do not have the choice of disclosure.

Invisible disabilities include various psychiatric disabilities, borderline intellectual disabilities, learning disabilities, and many chronic illnesses. There is no correlation between degree of severity and degree of visibility. Many invisible disabilities have multiple functional limitations, disrupt relationships and jobs, and often include pain. Furthermore, there tends to be more prejudice and discrimination for individuals with invisible disabilities. With visible disabilities, IWODs feel, right or wrong, that they understand the disability because there is less ambiguity. For individuals with invisible disabilities, there is greater ambiguity, IWODs feel less in control and more discomfort. Adding to the ambiguity of invisible disabilities is the relapsing or episodic course of many invisible disabilities. At times, the individual seems well or "their own self," and at other times, the individual "cannot get out of bed or has to go to the hospital." IWODs may ask, "do they have a disability or don't they?" The combination of the invisibility of the disability and the relapsing course often results in marginality.

Some research has shown that those with invisible disabilities have a more difficult response simply because these IWDs ask the same questions. In a study of children with seizure disorders, the researchers found "heightened marginality" among the children.

> Some studies ... report that children with diseases which produce little significant disability (e.g. epilepsy) may have more psycho-social problems than their physically disabled peers. Barker, Wright, Meyerson, and Gonick's (1953) concept of "marginality" acknowledged the heightened ambiguity experienced by children with minimal disabilities. These youngsters neither enjoy the benefit of being "normal" nor evoke the environment support and allowances accorded more clearly handicapped children.
>
> (Whitt, 1984, p. 83)

It is unclear how Whitt defines "little significant disability," but seizure disorders can be fatal.

Cost-Benefit Analysis of Disclosing an Invisible Disability

Benefits of Nondisclosure

- Allows the individual to choose the point of disclosure, in timing and to whom.
- Allows the individual to show their positive characteristics, talents, and skills before disclosing.
- May be considered a defense against unwarranted prejudice and discrimination.

Costs of Nondisclosure

- No accommodations are provided.
- Negative characteristics are attributed to the IWD.
- Others with the same disability who have disclosed consider the person who "passes" as disloyal.
- The individual has lost an opportunity to advocate and educate others about the disability.
- There might be more problems if the disability is discovered.

> - The individual sacrifices the solidarity, support, and understanding of associating with others IWDs.
> - Most important, the individual pays an emotional cost for hiding the disability which is a central and valued part of their identity.
>
> Benefits of Disclosure
>
> - Accommodations are provided.
> - The truth is often better than negative (and false) assumptions (Smart, 2016, p. 351).

The Americans with Disabilities Act (ADA) mandates that an individual's disability must be disclosed before accommodations can be provided or protection under the law afforded. In the case of employers, if the individual does reveal their disability, the employer is required to keep this information confidential.

Without disclosing their disabilities, IWDs place themselves in a position of listening to "spastic," "fruitcake," and other derisive jokes. Also, when an IWD does not reveal his or his disability, others with the same disability (who are aware of the disability) consider the lack of disclosure to be disloyalty. For example, many in the disability rights community consider Roosevelt to be a "closet crip." As recently as ten years ago, Roosevelt's lack of disclosure (or hiding and minimizing his paralysis) once again became controversial. Planning a monument in Washington, DC, to Roosevelt and his presidential achievements during the Great Depression and World War II, the disability rights movement loudly protested when the statue of Roosevelt did not include his wheelchair. The disability rights movement prevailed and the Roosevelt statue shows him sitting in a wheelchair.

We have learned that the ADA and the identity politics of IWDs have resulted in a type of pride movement, such as "I'm disabled; Get used to it!" Taking an identity that has been discredited and deemed inferior and deviant and creating a proud, social identity is a recent development. Of course, there have always been IWDs who were open about their hidden disabilities. Nonetheless, with the prejudice and discrimination toward IWDs, those IWDs who were able to "pass" as non-disabled, often did. "Passing" as non-disabled was considered to be a "work-around." Disability is a multifaceted experience, both for the individual and for society as a whole. Weisskopf, who has a hand amputation, has made a conscious choice to *refuse* to hide his prosthesis or to wear an artificial hand, which would everyone would immediately recognize as a prosthesis. The artificial hand did not have the functional capability of a rubber hand, but it would help others to be more comfortable and less stressed in Weisskopf's presence than the steel prosthesis. Weisskopf decided that increased functioning for himself overruled the reactions of others.

> Function was only part of the problem. The idea of trying to pass had begun to trouble me. It made me feel as if I had something to hide or to be ashamed of. When I started to go bald, I shaved my head. No comb-overs, transplants, or toupees for me. So why try to conceal a handicap? I was proud of how I had lost my hand. The stump had a story to tell.
>
> (Weisskopf, 2006, p. 37)

However, Weisskopf's disability was a visible physical disability, acquired in a heroic manner, by saving lives in combat. All three of these aspects, the visibility, the type of disability, and the manner of acquisition, typically result in less prejudice and discrimination against them. Moreover, Weisskopf's acquired his disability after the passage of the Americans with Disabilities Act which rendered disabilities more socially acceptable.

An account which showed a different approach to disclosure concerns Richard Cohen (2004) who was 25 years old when he was diagnosed with multiple sclerosis. He was a television news broadcaster and journalist. Today, he is a writer and journalist, both jobs that have the flexibility necessary for someone with an episodic course disabiity. Multiple sclerosis is an invisible disability with an episodic course, as symptoms come and go, which makes planning and organizing one's life difficult. Cohen wrote his own "private rulebook" concerning the limits of his disclosure/nondisclosure when applying for work as a journalist.

> I learned a valuable lesson then and there. Honestly is not the best policy. Candor about health problem works in the confines of academia and maybe in the movies. Full disclosure does not work so well in the real world. Hard times in a competitive industry at a tough moment in history leave little room for dealing fairly with a serious illness. People with serious problems can be perceived as weak candidates for employment in the dollars-and-cents world. The right to do has currency when nothing is at stake. . . . Don't tell nobody nuthin. . . . My stealth approach bothered me enough to write my private rulebooks outlining when dishonestly went too far and when it was permissible.
>
> (pp. 54–55)

Cohen's excerpt shows that he understands that he is being treated unfairly, but not illegally. (The Americans with Disabilities Act was passed before this experience took place.) With the social environment and his type of disability, he consciously took the decision to not disclose, although he did feel guilty.

Obviously, passing as non-disabled may extract a large emotional price. Choosing to conceal a part of one's identity which is a central, valued, and important part of one's self creates constant dissonance. Adding to this sense of dissonance is the awareness that society's prejudice is not ethical or warranted. As Cohen's excerpt shows, passing also conflicts with one's moral code of honesty and integrity. Finally, the passing individual might be anxious that others will divulge their disability at an inopportune time or circumstance.

Counselors can assist CWDs in deciding whether to disclose. Often, this decision is made on a case-by-case basis, choosing to disclose in one circumstance and not to disclose in other circumstances. Disclosure is a personal decision, partially based on past experiences. In Cohen's excerpt, his decision was made after he had disclosed his disability to a prospective employer and had been refused the job. He determined, "Honesty is not the best policy." For adults with congenital disabilities or disabilities acquired early in life and had parents who hid their children's disabilities and told the children, "Let's not tell anybody about your little problem," the debate about nondisclosure/disclosure may be very difficult. Disclosure in such cases may mean going against the parents' wishes and disrupting family dynamics. Counselors with some understanding of disability and the disability experience and who are willing to listen and interpret the client's life story and perceptions, can guide the individual to make their own decisions, including the circumstances and timing of disclosure.

Recognize the Burden of Bureaucracy—"The Warrior in Me Gets Tired"

The Lives of IWDs Are Circumscribed by Bureaucracies

- Waiting lists for services can take years.
- In order to establish eligibility for services, documentation of the disability is often required.
- Many IWDs feel that they must accept demeaning and stigmatizing diagnoses in order to receive services.
- Bureaucratic policies determine medical services, employment opportunities, access to transportation, and housing options.
- Many IWDs feel that they must "choose their battles," weighing choices carefully.

- Battling bureaucracies for resources, services, and benefits is burdensome and "batters the IWD's sense of justice."
- American Social Security Disability Insurance (SSDI) acts as a financial disincentive for obtaining employment.

When IWDs telephone or email to schedule a counseling appointment and then arrive for their first appointment, much of the intake procedure may appear to be another frustrating, burdensome, and often incomprehensible bureaucratic hurdle. Certainly, like the other helping professions, counseling services are increasingly assuming administrative tasks, turning to third party payment systems, such as insurance companies or government agencies and complying with government regulations, such as HIPPA. Often, the client must be "tracked" and occasionally the number of visits allowed is predetermined. Everyone, with or without a disability, must deal with different types of bureaucracies and very few of us have much tolerance for many of the aspects of bureaucracy, such as waiting lists which can result in months of waiting. In addition, producing eligibility documents, waiting for documentation of insurance coverage, completing proof of income statements, and signing client agreements may take time and patience. Many IWODs, including counselors, are not aware of the way in which bureaucracy circumscribes the daily lives of IWDs and, indeed, many of the choices available to IWDs are determined by bureaucratic regulations. Not only are medical services and financial benefits determined by administrative guidelines, but also the living arrangements, opportunities for work and education and social integration can only be obtained through negotiating bureaucracies. Furthermore, counselors may not be aware of the limited range of choices, imposed by government regulations or other administrative procedures and may attribute behaviors and choices of IWDs to personal failings of the client.

Disability policies and payment systems are often illogical. One IWD described the illogic: "Medicare will pay for a (wheel)chair but doesn't require proper fit. Then you are stuck with an improper chair for the life of the chair (5–10 years), a long sentence when you are stuck in a bad chair 16 hrs/day" (Participant 11) (Graf, Marini, & Blankenship, 2009, p. 31).

Seventy-eight individuals with spinal cord injuries were asked to respond to open-ended questions about their experience of living with a disability. The researchers (Graf, Marini, & Blankenship, 2009) summarized: "By far, most participants chose to write about Environmental access issues; all of which were negative" (p. 28). Not one of the 78 participants considered their environment to be helpful and accommodating. One woman described her financial difficulties:

> Since becoming disabled I have found it hard to do normal daily activities and pay all the bills that come along with my disabilities.... Unfortunately I have found it hard to get a home loan due to the doctor bill I have been unable to pay. Unfortunately I had to choose whether to feed my children or pay a doctor. There are a lot of bills that come along with being disabled but very little assistance. I have been told I make too much for help through Social Services.... Where is the help financially for the disabled?
> (Participant 88; Graf, Marini, & Blankenship, 2009, p. 31)

In a study which interviewed 99 adults with long term disabilities including people with conditions such as cerebral palsy, polio, multiple sclerosis, amputations, and spinal cord injuries in Portland, Oregon, the San Francisco Bay area, and Houston, Texas, one participant explained the relentless demands of trying to gain access and to receive services:

> Many participants drew a strong connection between feeling depressed or de-moralized and facing the many barriers associated with living with a disability. "There is a warrior in me, and that warrior gets tired. And the frustration of having every part of your life affected again and again by thoughtless people, by crooked bureaucrats.... It's constant.... It takes so much out of you."
> (Putnam et al., 2003, pp. 39–40)

This excerpt is not a quote from the participants themselves, but rather the study authors' summary of some main themes that emerged. Notice that the problem (which was associated with depression) was not the disability, but the barriers imposed by "thoughtless people" and "bureaucrats."

One woman considered obtaining resources, services, and funding required careful planning, balancing the need for these resources against the need for (almost) "friends" and "allies." Another IWD explained:

> We've only got so much in the way of resources, and we've got to pick our battles if we want to have a life. The closer to home that we muddy the waters, the narrower the world in which we can relax. We learn that certain battles will not be supported by others, and choosing not to fight at least lets us retain the illusion that we have more friends and allies than we really do.

> Constant battering against my sense that I deserve justice, and the way other people (often unconsciously) remind me that just isn't even something that can be contemplated when it comes to people like me.
> www.raggededgemagazine.com/departments/closerlook/000713.html

In a qualitative study of 40 parents with children with disabilities Resch et al. (2010) found four themes. According to the authors, the most important theme was dealing with bureaucracies.

> Access, or more pointedly lack of access, to important information and needed services was the most salient and overarching area of concern for the participants in our study. Parents indicated that they often encountered many challenges related to access. As one parent noted: "*I mean it's been a fight for anything, it's unbelievable.*" Another parent shared the sense of rejection she often felt as she attempted to obtain services: "*You have to understand where we are coming from first. We get so many no, no, no, no, no.*"
>
> (p. 142)

In the United States, an example of a federal bureaucracy narrowing the life choices of IWDs is the financial incentives of the Social Security Administration (SSA). The SSA provides financial disability benefits and pays for the costs incurred by the disability, such as prescription medication, some assistive technology, and medical care. For those with severe and multiple disabilities, the costs of the medical benefits exceeds the amount of the monthly disability check. If the IWD earns more than a certain predetermined amount of money, they lose the SSA benefits. Therefore, many IWDs cannot earn enough money to cover the costs of the disability, many health insurers do not give benefits for preexisting conditions (the disability is considered a "preexisting condition") and because of these disincentives, the IWD has no choice but to remain on SSA. The disability scholar, Longmore (2003), concluded:

> We, like all Americans, have talents to use, work to do, our contributions to make to our communities and country. We want the chance the work and marry without jeopardizing our lives. We want access to opportunity. We want access to work. We want access to the American Dream.
>
> (p. 258)

Jason was born with Down syndrome. His mother describes her experience with bureaucracies, using words such as "killed me," "battle," and "painful irony."

Jason was there to put his arms around me when the bureaucracies had nearly killed me. Services are seldom available to anyone who does not have the wherewithal to battle agencies. Doing so, often requires education, time, and money—which is a painful irony given that these services are intended to benefit people who may be short on all three.

(Solomon, 2012, p. 177)

For IWDs, the need to negotiate bureaucracies permeates and circumscribes their lives, far more than IWODs. Furthermore, dealing with bureaucracies is not simply frustrating. In many cases, IWDs feel that their sense of self and of justice has been questioned or violated.

Most counselors are not in an evaluative role as gatekeepers to disability resources and benefits; but there are some instances in which IWDs may not understand this. Intake procedures which clearly delineate the roles of the agency and counselor will help CWDs understand the nature of the counseling relationship. In addition, support staff should explain the rationale for the paperwork and other agency administrative requirements.

Do Not Confuse Sympathy With Empathy

The pitfalls of counselors feeling pity and sympathy toward their clients have been discussed. Self-examination of the counselor's reactions and responses to CWDs is a first step toward eliminating sympathy, especially when it is understood that there are very important differences between sympathy and empathy.

Differences Between Sympathy and Empathy

- If counselors view the client's disability as a "burden," then it is an easy step to think of the client with a disability as a "victim."
- Sympathy for a client with a disability often allows professionals to feel better.
- Empathy between counselor and client is based on mutual respect; sympathy is not positive regard but a downward comparison, communicating to the client that they are somehow perceived as inferior or incapable.
- Empathy is understanding; sympathy is judgment.
- Empathy is based on an equal division of power; sympathy increases the power differential in favor of the counselor.

- Empathy empowers the client, both in the short term and the long term. Sympathy disempowers the client because it leads to lowered expectations and lack of adherence to standards, all of which are harmful. Sympathy often results in counselors "enabling" clients.
- Empathy is strengths-based and asset-oriented; sympathy is deficit oriented.
- Empathy promotes client independence. Sympathy often leads to client dependence and, at times, overprotection and the counselor's efforts to shield the CWD from stress and the possibility of failure (Cimarolli, 2006).
- Empathy leads to a greater range of choices and options for the client. Counselors who feel sympathy for the clients may, unwittingly, narrow the range of client choices.
- Empathy, and the accompanying respect, allows for greater communication between counselor and client. Sympathy is perceived by the client as patronizing and condescending.
- Empathy leads to client choice; sympathy leads to paternalism.
- Empathy is non-possessive; sympathy can lead to possessive behaviors and attitudes on the part of counselors.
- Empathy enlarges the scope of the counseling relationship because empathy allows the counselor to confront irrational, irresponsible, dysfunctional, or destructive client behaviors. Sympathy often discourages counselors from challenging the clients.

After twenty years as director of the Office for Resources for Students with Disabilities at a university, Harris (1992) explained that "often high school and university transcripts were splashed with the milk of human mercy." He further explained:

> Misguided acts of perceived kindness are a much harder construct to deal with than even overt negative discrimination. One of the reasons for this is that generally neither party understands the pernicious nature of this behavior. It may be years before the person with the disability realizes that he/she has been victimized by inadequate preparation and a lack of necessary preparation.
>
> (Harris, 1992, p. 208)

Enabling destructive behaviors or "looking the other way" with CWDs often begins with counselors and other service providers thinking something like this: "He got me to do things for him that I would never do for anyone else" or "I thought she deserved something" (because of the disability). Such attitudes can lead to reducing or altogether waiving standards.

Why would counselors feel sympathy for their CWDs? First, counselors are embedded in a general culture that views disability as tragic inferiority and tends to sensationalize and exaggerate the effects of a disability. Second, counselors, at some level of awareness, may feel frustrated by their inability to reduce the symptoms and impact of the disability because counseling itself is a "helping profession." Nonetheless, in most counseling relationships with CWDs, the disability is not the "problem." Third, it often "feels good" to service providers when they are sympathetic toward CWDs. Finally, counselors often confuse beneficence with client autonomy and confuse sympathy with empathy (as the previous bullet list shows). However, in discussing the ethical principle of beneficence, the ACA Handbook (2009) quoted from Section A of the American Counseling Association 2005 Code of Ethics: "Counseling encourages client growth and development in ways that foster the interest and welfare of clients and promote formation of healthy relationships" (American Counseling Association, 2014, p. 179).

IWDs have been ambivalent in their responses to competent, caring, and hardworking professionals who have assisted them, sometimes to the point of saving their lives or changing their lives in a positive direction. On the one hand, IWDs might feel grateful to these professionals and, on the other hand, IWDs feel an underlying sense of discomfort and resentment. The explanation for this ambivalence, or part of it, may be found in the difference between sympathy and empathy. Paternalism, sympathy, and control are a powerful combination and, without question, these attitudes and the resulting services have, at times, led to positive outcomes, especially in medical settings. Nonetheless, the primary quality of the counseling relationship is the focus on client needs and this is a difficult focus to maintain when counselors are ill-informed about disability and are responding to their own needs to "rescue" the client and to deny their own existent angst. In counseling, any definition or description of "helping," must be led by the client. Thinking about professional services, and the professionals who provide these services, IWDs' ambivalence often is gratitude and, at the same time, resentment because IWDs feel that they have paid too great a price, in terms of self-respect. At times, IWDs may question if the means (paternalism, sympathy, and pity) is worth the ends (highly skilled services). Counselors must guard against the tendency to, unwittingly, attach conditions upon which understanding is based.

Do Not Confuse Denial of the Disability Role With Denial of the Disability Itself

---

Denial of the Social Role of Disability

- Does not mean the individual denies the presence of their disability.
- It is "society" that has determined the social role of disability. Most of "society" has not experienced a disability and yet they create the social role of disability.
- This social role of disability is unwritten, but nonetheless, exerts a powerful influence.
- The advances in medicine, civil rights, and assistive technology challenge the social role of disability and, therefore, result in social structural lags.

Roles typically include a set of behaviors that members of a society acquire and often becomes the individual's self-identity. For example, outdated social roles for women which were popular decades ago, included the expectation that women would marry, stay at home, raise children, and not enter the workforce. Roles include social, educational, and occupational expectations and often place incessant demands on individuals. Demographic changes and medical advances have outpaced social role expectations. This gap between reality and the available role expectations is termed "structural lags." Science and population changes have moved faster than our societal institutions and create perplexing questions about roles. For example, what are the role expectations of 100-year-old people?—a group that previously was so small but now is becoming larger. What are the role expectations of men?—when the majority of women are in the work force, and with the demographic and socioeconomic shifts that have recently emerged. One of these demographic/medical advances is the large increase in the number of IWDs. The question arises: What should IWDs be expected to do?

Counselors should:

1. Become aware of these demeaning and unrealistic social role expectations.
2. Distinguish between denial of disability (which is typically pathological) and denial of the social role expectations (which is highly adaptive).
3. Self-monitor to assess if counselors are, unknowingly, subscribing to the social role expectations of disability.

Who is society and why does society have the privilege of deciding who and what everybody will be? Social values are often driven by those in power and, in the case of IWDs, those in power have been those who do not have disabilities. In the case of IWDs, society is confused about which roles to "assign" to IWDs, and compounding the issue, most social roles in force are outdated and inaccurate. The role of counselors in addressing social expectations is threefold. First counselors need to be aware of these demeaning and unrealistic role expectations; second, counselors need to clarify the difference between refusal to accept the stigmatizing, deviant role expectations and the unwillingness to accept the disability; and third, counselors need to self-monitor to ensure that they are not imposing aspects of these role expectations on their CWDs.

Expectations of the Social Role of Disability

- Accept your social inferiority because of your (so-called) biological inferiority, pathology, and deviance.
- Keep your aspirations modest because, after all, our tax dollars are spent on you. Resources are scarce.
- Try to be as "normal" as possible. In fact, your degree of humanity is directly correlated with your degree of perceived normalcy.
- Accept your social and occupational role entrapment.
- Never show negative emotions, such as hostility, anger, or frustration. If IWDs show negative emotions, they are the result of having an "attitude" or a "chip on their shoulder."
- Be brave, cheerful, and inspirational. IWDs are not allowed to have a bad day or a bad mood.
- Be prepared to offer "disability awareness seminars" to strangers, regardless of how inconvenient or intrusive.

When these role expectations are clearly stated, it becomes apparent why no IWD would accept these expectations or definitions of their position in society. However, when IWODs, including service providers, are confronted with IWDs who are assertive, expect basic civil rights as citizens, and can become frustrated and angry when they are denied access, accommodations, or respect, there is a tendency to say, "These IWDs have not accepted their disability." Or "They're just angry because they're disabled." Or "They're hypersensitive and just not good sports." Or "They're having a bad day." All of these responses place blame on the IWD and, therefore, IWODs are not required to examine their attitudes.

The pressure for IWDs to express only positive emotions is explained by an anthropology professor at Columbia University. He became paralyzed and eventually died due to a tumor in his spine.

> [A]s the price for normal relations, PWDs must comfort others about their condition. They cannot show fear, sorrow, depression, sexuality, or anger, for this disturbs the able-bodied. The unsound of limb are permitted only to laugh. The rest of the emotions, including anger and the expression of hostility, must be bottled up, repressed, and allowed to simmer or be released in the backstage of the home. . . . As for the rest of the world, I must sustain their faith in their immunity by looking resolutely cheery. Have a nice day!
>
> (Murphy, 1990, p. 108)

In the film, *Murderball*, the intense rivalry between the Canadian and American wheelchair rugby teams was apparent. In a pregame interview, an athlete stated, "I'm not here for a hug. I'm here for a medal." This comment illustrates that IWDs can be competitive and tough and, furthermore, they are not afraid to openly acknowledge these typical feelings of athletes. It is noteworthy that most athletes (without disabilities) would not compare hugs with medals and perhaps this is due to the common stereotype that all IWDs are "sweet."

The Most Demanding (and Unrealistic) Aspects of the Social Role of Disability

- Try to be as "normal" as possible.
- Minimize or "hide" your disability (if possible).
- At minimum, do not remind others of your disability.
- The question arises; what emotional price does the IWD pay in order to make others "comfortable" with their disability?

Another IWD described social acceptance of IWODs as an "ever-elusive carrot," considering the carrot to be unobtainable.

They (IWDs) must display a continuous cheerful striving toward some semblance of normality. The evidence of their moral and emotional health, of their quasi-validity as persons and citizens, has been their exhibition of the desire to become like non-disabled people. This, of course, by definition, is the very thing that people with disabilities cannot become. Thus, they have been required to pursue a "normality" that must forever elude them. They have been enticed into a futile quest by having dangled before them the ever-elusive carrot of social acceptance.

(Longmore, 2003, p. 221)

This IWD mentions the role expectation of trying to appear "normal," either by minimizing or hiding the disability. Families often impose expectations of normality upon their members with disabilities. Linton (1998) described the way in which families imposed the appearance of normalcy upon their children (who used wheelchairs).

Many people have been told that when family pictures were taken as they were growing up, they were removed from their wheelchairs, or they were shown only from the waist up, of they were excluded from pictures altogether. The message is that part this part of you, your disability, or a symbol of your disability, your wheelchair, is unacceptable, or in the last case, you are not an acceptable member of the family. . . . The message (is) "you are like everyone else, but only as long as you hide or minimize your disability."

(pp. 20–21)

This IWD mentions the role expectation of trying to appear "normal," either by minimizing or hiding the disability. This role expectation imposed upon IWDs is motivated by the need of IWODs to feel comfortable when interacting with IWDs. In contrast, IWDs' effort to restore functioning or to reduce symptoms are highly adaptive behaviors, which are self-determined because, after all, IWDs understand their disability and their life needs and wishes. Many times, in an effort to gain social acceptance, IWDs have sacrificed functioning. The "hearing aid effect" is one example, referring to individuals who will not wear their hearing aids except at home. These individuals sacrifice hearing for social acceptance, feeling that here is some sort of stigma against hearing aids and those who use them.

The question becomes: When considering the social role expectations of IWDs, who is responsible for changing? IWDs agree that it is IWODs who should alter their expectations. Today, there is a growing awareness of the damaging effects of the urge to "appear more normal" simply to gain social acceptance. Facial cosmetic surgery for children with Down syndrome provides an example of an IWD (in this case, the parents of the IWD) undertaking procedures which do not increase functioning but rather allow the child to appear more normal. Down syndrome involves intellectual disability and related social and behavioral social characteristics. The cosmetic surgery involves tongue reduction and implants in the nose, chin, cheeks and jaw and reduction of the epicanthal fold in the eyelids. Cosmetic surgery would not improve the child's intellectual functioning. Parents who advocate the surgery claim that, with a more "normal" appearance, their children would have more social integration, including increasing their opportunities for marriage. Nonetheless, according to Goeke (2003) 88% of parents refuse the surgery, because the consensus was, "society does not have the right to decide what is 'normal' or 'beautiful,' and by extension, to determine who is a candidate for physical alteration" (p. 327). Other parents termed the cosmetic surgery to be "barbaric," "revolting," and "child abuse." These parents felt that their children were beautiful as they were born and the responsibility for alteration should be placed on society, to accept their children as they are. Note: Some surgeries for children with disabilities are not undertaken for cosmetic purposes or to increase the children's attractiveness and social integration, but rather to increase the child's functioning. Cochlear implants, for example, are performed on small children (and others) in order to increase their hearing.

> Counselors should understand that, without knowledge of the individual and their disability, they cannot interpret the IWD's behavior.

There is a difference between the "disabled role" and the disability itself. Not surprisingly, most IWDs accept their disability, are experts in its management and treatment; however, most IWDs refuse the "disabled role" and, frequently these IWDs are punished by IWODs. In Goffman's classic book, *Stigma: Notes on a Spoiled Identity* (1948) a man with a newly acquired disability (blindness) was shocked at the disabled role that he was expected to assume:

> I was expected to join this world (the blind world). To give up my profession and to earn my living making mops. I was to spend the rest of my life making mops with other blind people, eating with other blind people, dancing with other people. I became nauseated with fear, as the picture grew in mind.
>
> (p. 37)

The man is not fearful of his blindness, but rather the social role of blindness. He expresses the wide-reaching definition of these role expectations by referring it as another world, "the blind world." This example happened more than 75 years ago and, today, this person would not be expected to give up his profession. Rather, accommodations and assistive technology would be provided so that he could continue working at his previous job. However, in this example, the social and occupation role entrapment are evident. The occupational role entrapment is mop making and the social role entrapment is dancing and eating with other blind people, regardless of their ages, interests, or previous experience. Society has assigned his occupational and social roles based on his master status, that of having a disability. This example also illustrates the fact that different types of disabilities had specific occupational roles. Deaf men often worked in printing factories because they would not hear the loud machinery and deaf women were placed in clerical and secretarial training, all at a very early age. Children without disabilities were given academic training to prepare for university and children with disabilities were given vocational training in the trades. Today, those with intellectual disabilities continue to experience occupational role entrapment and this role entrapment has acquired a derisive title, the Five Fs, food, filth, flowers, filing, and folding. Food referred to work in fast-food restaurants; filth was janitorial work; flowers referred to landscaping and gardening work; filing was simple clerical, office work; and folding was work in laundries.

Respect the Client's Assistive Technology—The Kindness of Machines

Counselors

- May not understand the importance and emotional attachments that many clients with disabilities feel toward their assistive technology (AT).
- Should remember that rapport-building cannot be complete until counselors understand the AT and the client's idiosyncratic perception and meaning.
- Should understand that many AT devices are not useful if the counseling office is not accessible.
- Should collaborate with AT engineers to assist IWDs in choosing AT.

Many CWDs will arrive at the counseling office with assistive devices and technology (AT) with which the counselor is unfamiliar. Counselors are not only ill-informed about the operation of the various types of AT, but they may not understand the importance and emotional attachment that many CWDs feel toward their AT. Asking questions and using other clarifying techniques will allow the counselor to understand: 1) the functioning and uses of the AT and 2) the way in which the CWD views their own AT. Rapport building cannot proceed until the counselor understands the idiosyncratic meaning of the client's AT. For example, many IWDs do not like others touching their wheelchairs. Indeed, there have been cases in which IWDs have had their wheelchairs "hi-jacked," when others have moved the chair (and the IWD in the chair) without permission. Done with the best of intentions of "helping," IWDs consider such "help" to be intrusive, unwanted, and disrespectful. Some IWDs have reported that these attempts at assistance have damaged the wheelchair. Therefore, it is imperative to ask before touching the client's AT.

The use of AT may require changes in physical accessibility, such as the widening of doorways to allow large, power wheelchairs to pass through. Other AT devices may not be immediately apparent, such as cochlear implants or prostheses that are covered by clothing. However, other IWDs who use similar AT devices are aware of AT use in others. In the same way that those wearers of contact lenses recognize others who use contact lens, AT users have the expectation of the use of these devices, allowing them to notice when others use AT. This might be a case of, "It takes one to know one." Counselors typically do not expect clients to use concealed or semi-visible AT and, therefore, often do not recognize AT use in their clients.

Occasionally, CWDs find it necessary to adjust their AT during the session or re-position themselves in their wheelchairs, which counselors may initially find disconcerting and unexpected. The use of audio recordings by blind clients might make counselors uncomfortable or uneasy. Communication, and the entire counseling session, when the client uses a communication board will require greater patience of the counselor. The use of Sign Language interpreters is not technology, but rather involves the presence of another individual in the session, and requires counselor training and education in the proper use of these interpreters. Typically, codes of ethics for counseling professional organizations are silent on the use of interpreters.

It is difficult to overstate the importance to IWDs of assistive technology, sometimes referred to as assistive techniques. Assistive technology includes devices such as wheelchairs, hearing aids, communication boards, walking canes, cochlear implants, public transportation equipped with lifts for wheelchairs, and prosthetic limbs. Assistive technology has become increasingly sophisticated, computerized, individualized, and expensive. For centuries, assistive technology was mechanical devices usually built at home by a family member. President Roosevelt's favorite "wheelchair" was a small kitchen chair to which wheels had been added. He liked the wheelchair because, only in this wheelchair, could he pass through the doorways of the White House; other commercially manufactured wheelchairs were too wide for doorways. Obviously, Roosevelt could have afforded to pay for the most advanced power wheelchair, but these power chairs require accessible environments, such as ramps and wide doorways, and wheelchair lifts into vans. Roosevelt did not live long enough to see the advent of power wheelchairs and lifts into cars. Instead, one of his sons and the Secret Service men, who accompanied him, lifted the President in and out of cars, placed him at speaking podiums, and literally put him to bed. Thinking of the example of the President of the United States in the 1930s and 1940s helps in understanding that few people who used wheelchairs (at that historical period) enjoyed the privileges that Roosevelt did and, therefore, their lives would have been quite limited and narrow. These constricted lives are unthinkable today, at least in developed nations, because of advances in power wheelchairs and lifts. Wheelchair sports are another example of the way in which progress in assistive technology has improved the lives of IWDs. There were no wheelchair sports until the 1980s, when the sports wheelchair was invented. Today, there are customized wheelchairs for different types of sports.

The wars in Iraq and Afghanistan have greatly spurred improvements in prostheses—artificial arms and legs. Many of the wounded veterans in these wars have experienced traumatic amputations rather than torso wounds or death, due to body armor. (Their survival rates have also greatly improved due to emergency medicine techniques.) Governments have applied pressure to manufacturers of prostheses to improve their products, thus benefitting both military veterans and civilians. Remember Amy Purdy who competed on the American television program, *Dancing With the Stars*? She uses prostheses and she could not have competed if she had used old-fashioned wooden legs. The *USA Today* reporter explained Purdy's artificial legs: At the time of the *Dancing With the Stars* producers telephoned and asked Purdy to audition, she was in Sochi Russia, participating in the Paralympics. In this way, a disability advance, in this case, highly technical and functional prostheses, evolved from exclusive military use to civilian use, including competing in dance contests.

> During her first day of rehearsal, she realized her walking legs wouldn't work for dancing. "My calf muscles were wanting to expand, but they

couldn't because they're in carbon fiber. So it was painful." Luckily there was a prosthetic shop at the Sochi Paralympics. "They rounded the outsides of my legs for my calves to expand." And now, she says, she's not in any pain. "At this point, my legs fit well enough to do what I'm going to be doing. I'm snowboarding and dancing, and in between, I'm walking really far."

(Oldenburg, 2014, para. 13)

Purdy's example illustrates two points. First, assistive technology is highly specialized and individualized, most of us are not aware that different activities require different types of prostheses. Second, Ms. Purdy's prostheses illustrates the Functional Model of Disability in which nothing changes in the individual or in the disability itself. Rather, in this model, lack of functioning is defined as the disability and restoring functioning is the "cure" for disability. It is the prostheses that changes the definition of disability. Purdy's example also illustrates the Environmental Model of Disability because, fortunately, there was a prosthesis workshop in Sochi, Russia. The *Dancing With the Stars* producers telephoned her while she was in Sochi, Russia, and, because time was short, she needed to begin rehearsing her dance routine while still in Russia. But, at the time, she did not own dancing prostheses. Luckily, there was a specialized prosthesis workshop at the Olympics.

Military veterans with visible disabilities also illustrate an aspect of the hierarchy of stigma. In Chapter Two, we learned that the perceived cause of disabilities decreases or increases the degree of stigma society accords. There are other perceived aspects of disabilities that influence societal stigma, but here we are only considering perceived cause. Briefly, the hierarchy of stigma in ascending order, from least stigma to most stigma is: disabilities thought to be caused by "noble" endeavors, such as wartime service, congenital disabilities, acquired physical disabilities, and the disability with the greatest stigma, according to perceived cause, psychiatric disabilities. Most often, military veterans with spinal cord injuries value function as more important than appearing "normal." In the following excerpt, from an article entitled, *Going Back to Civvy Street*, World War II Canadian veterans adamantly refused to use the crutches that the doctors and nurses advocated:

It didn't make much sense spending all that energy covering a short distance (on crutches) . . . when you could do it quickly and easily with a wheelchair . . . it didn't take long for people to get over the idea that walking was that essential.

(Tremblay, 1996, p. 153)

An American war correspondent, Michael Weisskopf, lost his arm and hand when he was riding in a Humvee (a military vehicle) with three soldiers in Iraq. A grenade was thrown into Weisskopf's vehicle. He caught it, and, in catching the grenade saved four lives, his own and those of three soldiers. In the following excerpt, he relates his decision to give up a plastic hand (which probably would have made others more comfortable with his disability) and use an electronic prosthesis:

> Before Iraq, the technology of arm prostheses hadn't changed much since World War II. The tiny population of amputees created little market incentives. Miguelez [the prosthetist] used the burst in demand from Walter Reed (Hospital) to lean on manufacturers for progress. Before long, he was outfitting Iraqi war amputees with an electronic hand that opened and closed 2½ times faster and could be programmed to function at different speeds and grip strength.
>
> The cosmetic arts had also improved. I received a silicone hand that was so lifelike it passed for real in social settings. But, Pretty Boy, as I called it, kept tearing and afforded the precision of a boxing glove. It was too spongy to grasp anything small and too slippery to hold most object for long.
>
> (Weisskopf, 2006)

Almost everyone, with or without a disability, uses technology and would not consider living without computers, mobile phones, the internet, and navigational devices. It is difficult to imagine an educational or work setting that does not require the skilled use of technology. Also, technology has rendered the world safer for everyone. In the same way as IWDs, IWODs consider the availability of technology to be an important part of quality of life, including education, work, and recreation. Nonetheless, IWDs enjoy additional benefits including: more privacy, greater independence, and increased functioning. Assistive technology such as TDD telephones and flashing alarms have saved the lives of Deaf people. Most IWDs enjoy less privacy than IWODs. Deaf people often use Sign Language interpreters; blind people have used human scribes and readers; and many with severe and multiple disabilities hire personal care attendants (PCAs) to dress them and help them in using the bathroom, including assisting in evacuating the bowels. Everyone enjoys privacy; but IWODs often experience less privacy, due to their disability (and the prejudice and discrimination of society). Remarkably, the very dehumanization of technology is appealing to IWDs. Machines do not get sick; they maintain confidentiality, and they do not refuse to assist when irritated or in a bad mood. Machines and technology require maintenance and, at times, they crash and break down (or become "disabled"). Nonetheless, technology is more reliable than most personal care attendants.

The following excerpt illustrates the lack of privacy for middle-aged adults in a nursing home and the life-changing quality of AT, in this case, a communication board. Ann (age 42) can walk, but her speech is difficult to understand. Linda (age 52) uses a wheelchair and speaks very slowly.

> The attendants didn't speak English and our speech is not so good so there was no communication. Also, we had no privacy. Men, women, anyone would just walk in at any time. They treated us as non-persons and I guess they felt that you can't intrude on a non-person. We were going crazy just trying to be sane. Now I just use it [communication board] when people don't understand me. Places like the doctor's office where it's important for people to understand me. It's really a last resort. I know myself and when I get anxious, I can't talk.
>
> (cited in Scherer, 2005, p. 96)

Environmental controls were first developed for IWDs, allowing them to "operate" thermostats, air conditioners, and locks on doors. It has been posited that many IWDs will be able, in the future, to live at home rather than in hospitals and long-term care centers because medical electronic monitoring will provide the same level of care provided by institutions, which are not private spaces.

The experience of IWDs using assistive technology has five additional aspects for IWDs.

Five Additional Aspects of AT for IWDs

- AT is very humanizing because it is reliable and affords greater privacy and safety.
- Many IWDs consider AT to be an extension of their bodies.
- Many IWDs have an emotional attachment to their AT.
- Individualized and customized AT is expensive. IWDs cannot go to the internet or a store to buy AT "off the shelf."
- AT was initially developed to assist IWDs to function more "normally." Today, AT often allows IWDs to have "better-than-normal" functioning than IWODs. For example, prosthetic legs can "telescope" to be shorter or longer and can perform many more functions than the human leg. This may appear to be an interesting side note, but the possibility (and probability) of AT making IWDs "hyper-normal" will become increasingly significant.

People with congenital disabilities do not have memories of living without a disability; however, many remember the day they received their AT. Two IWDs explained:

> "When I got my electric cart, my life started all over again." Another said, "I've always had cerebral palsy. But I have before the chair and after the chair. I got this chair and I thought 'Whoa. I can hit the road whenever I want to.' And I have more energy and a lot more fun."
> (Putnam et al., 2003, p. 43)

Those with acquired disabilities or chronic illnesses diagnosed later in life also remember the acquisition of AT devices as life-changing and life-enhancing.

Some IWDs speak of their AT in terms of a relationship (Smart, 2016, p. 363). The following examples show these types of emotional attachments: One man said, "I loved my first wheelchair with a passion that embarrasses me, now" (Kriegel, 1964, p. 52). A polio survivor who lived in an iron lung for more than 40 years (a metal tube that acts as a ventilator) who referred to his iron lung as his "second skin," and the war correspondent, Weisskopf, who named his plastic arm Pretty Boy. Many IWDs give names to their AT. The woman with the congenital disability of cerebral palsy (cited earlier) clearly remembers the day she received her first wheelchair. The *New York Times*, in an article entitled, "My Supercharged, Tricked Out, Bluetooth Wheelchair Life Force" (Savin, 2017, December 15), eloquently described the emotional attachment she and her friend Olantis felt toward their wheelchairs. Oltanis named his wheelchair "Roscoe," while Savin's wheelchair is named "Anita." Note the somewhat derisive term of "walkie."

> My friend Olantis and his chair, Roscoe, emit more life than I've seen from any walkie. He tricked out Roscoe with some seriously powerful Bluetooth speakers through which he blasts music which matches his mood. . . . I wasn't just envious that Roscoe had the horsepower to go so much faster [than her own wheelchair].
>
> I make the two mile commute most weekdays to fulfill my duties as a doctoral student at the University of California, Berkeley—to attend class, work as a teaching assistant, research or go to meetings. Anita [her power wheelchair] helps me from home to school and in and out of the buildings on campus as I deal with my collection of conditions—asthma, Type I diabetes, Ehler-Danlos syndrome and dysautonomia among them. Anita allows me to stay in the game and remain competitive as a student

and teacher, despite the daily exclusions and presumptions of incompetence I face.

Disability scholars (Scherer et al., 2005) advocate the inclusion of counselors on the AT team, the team of assistive technologists. The AT team is comprised of professionals such as prosthetists, physical therapists, and medical providers, who determine the unique combination of the disability, needs, desired functioning in designing and fitting AT. There are some IWDs who receive individualized and customized AT, use the AT a few times, and then throw the AT in the closet, never to be used again. This inability or refusal to use AT is termed "technology abandonment." Scherer and her colleagues consider including counselors on the AT team to be cost effective, because there would be fewer cases of technology abandonment:

> Counselors study perceptions and attitudes of users and others toward particular technologies, and determine how technologies fit within their activities and contribute to their abilities in daily life. Individuals are more likely to use AT when the device meets their personal preferences and expectations, when they were involved in the selection, have realistic expectations, and the device provides perceived value and support and there is informed caregiver support. Given the uniqueness of the disability experience for any individual, it is crucial that counselors be included in the AT team.
>
> (Scherer et al., 2005, p. 1330)

Finally, an IWD acknowledged the expense of AT, stressing that without well-paying employment, IWDs may be unable to purchase the AT:

> I think we would all agree that the cost for health and maintaining health for Americans with disabilities is a lot more. It costs a lot more . . . in terms of motorized wheelchairs. . . "accessible technology" or devices to help with the activities of daily living unless we can get hired at jobs that pay enough money for us to be able to afford these particular items.
>
> (Putnam et al., 2003, p. 42)

Technology is a fast changing world; individualized and complex technology is expensive; the IWD has to negotiate changing roles and lifestyles, all of which require counselors to become informed about their clients' use of AT and the meaning of the AT for them.

Understand the Importance of Contributing to Others—
Doing Our Fair Share

> **The Human Need to Contribute to Others**
>
> - Historically, IWDs have been labeled as "burdens" and "drains" who have only been consumers of resources and services.
> - Like IWODs, IWDs want to be equal partners and contributors.
> - Equal social status relationships, including intimate and romantic relationships, are difficult when IWDs are not viewed as contributors.
> - Disability laws and policies, such as Social Security, act as financial disincentives. IWDs often cannot "afford" to work (and use their talents and skills). If IWDs work, they forfeit their Social Security.

Contributing to one's family, social groups, and community in general is a basic human need and may be even more important for IWDs because they have often been thought of as "burdens" and "drains" who consume the scarce resources produced by "contributors." Putnam et al.'s (2003) survey study of individuals with a wide range of disabilities found those interviewees who were in a committed relationships expressed their need to contribute to the relationship: One participant explained:

> And those of us in relationships . . . struggle with that sense of real strong responsibility. Not just to earn the money, But, also to contribute to household duties . . . feel like we're doing our fair share.
>
> (p. 41)

In this same study, a woman polio survivor felt that giving of herself was more important than donating money. She considers these opportunities to be personally rewarding, a "Godsend."

> I went to work for the Texas Polio Survivors Association. And that has been a Godsend to me. It has been so wonderful working with all these people and feeling like I'm contributing that didn't have to do with a dollar sign. Contributing something of myself, compassion, sympathy, just listening if they want to talk or socializing with them, if that's what it takes.
>
> (Putnam et al., 2003, p. 40)

Not only is the IWD expressing the need to contribute, but they are also expressing the difficulties when the word "struggle" is used. Eric Weihenmayer (2001) is blind and successfully climbed Mount Everest. In the following excerpt, he emphasizes the importance of being a full and equal partner (in contrast to being an inanimate object, a football), stressing the importance of his contribution, "I wanted them to put their lives in my hands."

> I refused to be the weak link of the team. I wanted them to put their lives in my hands, as I would put mine in theirs. I would carry my share. I could contribute as any other team member. I would not be carried up the mountain and spiked on top like a football. If I were to reach the summit, I would reach it with dignity.
>
> (p. 5)

Re-read Paul Longmore's excerpt in this chapter in which he stated that access to the workplace helps fulfill the "dream" of using their talents and making contribution to their community (see p. 258). For Longmore, the opportunity for employment not only provides financial security but fulfills deeper needs, echoing Maslow's hierarchy of needs. The late Paul Longmore was a polio survivor who used a wheelchair and earned a PhD in American history, having spent ten years writing a scholarly book on George Washington, *The Invention of George Washington*, published by the University of California. Longmore was offered a research fellowship at the prestigious Huntington Library. However, a letter from the Social Security Administration (SSA) informed Longmore that if he received one dollar in book royalties or accepted the paid research fellowship, he would lose his Social Security Disability Income (SSDI). SSDI provides a small living stipend, but more important, SSDI pays for disability-related expenses, such as medications, wheelchairs, medical treatment, and hospitalizations. Longmore responded by staging a carefully planned book-burning which received both newspaper and television coverage. He wanted to expose the irrationality of SSDI: Before the actual demonstrations, which was filmed for television, Longmore rehearsed the burning: "I didn't want to set *myself* on fire." In the following excerpt, Longmore described his feelings:

> I somberly watched the fire consume my book. I had planned the protest. I had rehearsed how to burn the book. I had even thought about what sort of expression I should have on my face. But I could never have prepared for the emotional effect on me of the act itself. I was burning my own book, a book I had spent ten years of life laboring over, a book that earned my Ph.D. in history, a book I felt proud of and, in fact, loved. It was a moment of agony.
>
> (Longmore, 2003, p. 253)

Longmore was an experienced, effective national disability rights activist and he planned and practiced a public act of protest, burning his book. However, he had not anticipated his "agony" on burning a labor of love because of irrational and outdated federal laws.

For a group of individuals who have been thought of as "burdens" or "drains" on society, the self-identity as contributors to the broader community is extremely important for IWDs. Furthermore, society, including institutions such as governments, impede IWDs in their efforts to contribute.

Encourage Mutual Social Support Groups

> **Social Support Groups for IWDs and Their Families**
> - The internet has greatly expanded the possibilities and potential for social support groups.
> - These types of social support groups are especially helpful for those with low-incidence disabilities, making those with these types of disabilities feel less isolated.
> - Most disability support groups are composed of individuals with the same type of disability.

Throughout this book, a cross-disability perspective, which includes all three broad categories of disabilities—physical disabilities, cognitive disabilities, and psychiatric disabilities—has been implemented. However, a cross-disability viewpoint is central in the Civil Rights Model of Disability. In the Civil Rights Model, the "problem" of disability is the lack of civil rights for all IWDs with all types of disabilities. Civil rights, including social integration, access to large opportunity structures such as education and the workplace, and government-mandated accommodations are important to every IWD. Civil rights for IWDs is an issue for everyone, including IWODs.

In contrast to the cross-disability perspective, social support groups for IWDs are typically composed of individuals with the same type (and severity) of disability. There are also social support groups for parents, spouses and partners, and family members of IWDs. Most often, mutual social support groups do not have a professional service provider as a leader, but the group organization, administration, and methods are determined by the group as a whole. Some groups have articulated goals and others simply offer socialization. As technology advances, the internet becomes a means of social support, especially for those with low-incidence disabilities. As discussed in Chapter Two, the number of individuals with low incidence disabilities is increasing as the rate of infant mortality decreases. For example, infants with congenital disabilities often have disabilities that physicians have rarely treated. Indeed, at times, both the diagnosis and prognosis of low-incidence disabilities are vague and open to change. Social support groups of low-incidence disabilities are more likely to use the internet and other electronic means of communication.

Skilled and experienced counselors who specialize in group work could be of great help with disability support groups, after training and clinical practice and supervision in disability issues. As discussed in the previous chapters, IWDs do not consider themselves to belong to a social category, because society assigns them to a devalued and pathological category. Most often, IWDs are not invited to join other mutual social support groups based on their other (and often more important) self-identities. If a man with a disability wanted to join a male support group, he might be invited to join a disability support group because his disability is, in the eyes of most IWODs, his master status. If a woman of African descent who also has a disability wished to join a support group for women, or a group for sexual minorities, or a group for ethnic minorities, or a group of aging individuals, she would be invited to find a disability social support group because her most salient attribute is thought to be her disability.

Functions of Mutual Social Support Groups for IWDs

- Reduces isolation and loneliness.
- Normalizes the experience of disability.
- Eliminates the stress of dealing with insensitive IWODs.
- Provides validity to the experience of disability.
- Improves the quality of life of IWDs.
- Allows IWDs to contribute to others.
- Provides role models.
- Answers questions concerning the management of the disability.

American federal surveys of IWDs have sought to determine the type and number of social and entertainment events IWDs attend and, without exception, these surveys have shown that IWDs experience far fewer social experiences than IWODs. IWDs do not attend concerts or theater performances, see films, or eat in restaurants as often as IWODs do (Brault, 2012, Final Report). Disability mutual social support groups provide opportunities for socialization, normalize the experience of disability due to the numbers of individuals in a room with the same type of disability, and clearly show that when a large of number of people share the same experiences, it is social history rather than being personal, individualized shortcomings. In the following excerpt each of these functions is illustrated by Joan Tollifson (1997) who was born with a congenital limb deficiency. She joined a support group of women with disabilities.

> After a lifetime of isolating myself from other disabled people, it was an awakening to be surrounded by them. For the first time in my life, I felt like a real adult member of the human community. Finally, identifying myself as a disabled person was an enormous healing. It was about recognizing, allowing, and acknowledging something that I had been trying to deny, and finding that disability does not equal ugliness, incompetence, and misery.
>
> (p. 107)

Before Tollifson joined this group, she described her life as "a private hell" (p. 107). Reviewing this excerpt, she gains membership in the adult human community, felt healed (not that her disability was cured); she learned, for the first time, that disability was not ugliness, incompetence, and misery, thus invalidating many of her perceived negative self-descriptors. Tollifson also learned that the prejudice and discrimination directed toward her and her disability were experienced by every group member and, in this way, she escaped from her "private hell."

If everyone in a disability mutual social support group experiences the same type of disability, then the disability "disappears," allowing these IWDs to feel "normal." The way in which the word "normal" is used here simply means that the disability is considered ordinary and natural and the group member is not viewed exclusively as their disability. It would be impossible in a group comprised of individuals with the same disability to be identified as an individual *solely* on the disability! Group members do not feel the stress of responding to insensitive IWODs who ask intrusive questions; but, at the same time, felt that they could openly speak about their disability to individuals who really understood. In these ways, the "social construction" of disability is eliminated and group members shed the pathological and deviant identity imposed upon them by society.

Two researchers (Crawford & Ostrove, 2003) interviewed members of a social support group of women with disabilities. These researchers asked Carol if anyone understood her experiences as a deaf woman. The researchers described her reaction to the question as bewilderment. Carol replied, "Who really understands my disability? My mother was determined to make me talk and she succeeded. But to understand deafness? I don't know. I don't know anyone who understands" (p. 190). Reading this excerpt, we see that either Carol has never been asked this question or that the question seems absurd to her, or both. Carol's mother is an important person in her life, but in this case, not even a mother could fully understand Carol.

Almost everyone receives a great deal of social support from two sources: families and workplaces. However, most IWDs live in families whose members do not have disabilities. Jobs, and their social associations are often meaningful and fulfilling; but a great number of IWDs are not employed. One woman with an acquired disability told interviewers that she felt more comfortable at the hospital than at home.

> Then you go home and you're not amongst people going through similar experiences. You know, for me, even my own family didn't realize as much as the people here (Queen Elizabeth Hospital in New Zealand) did. What I was going through y'know. They can't go through it for you.
> (Faull et al., 2004, p. 137)

In this excerpt the value of social support for parents of children of disabilities is shown:

> Initially, I realize we are checking each other out, wondering about the children's problems, curious about adaptation others have found, and amazed there could be so many of us. We are like wounded geese, still flying on an altered course to assist our children. While our lives have never been the same since our children arrived, we have all survived. That in itself is a miracle. I am humbled by the commitment of these other parents and immensely relieved that I am not alone. I am also aware that my troubles sometimes pale in comparison to what other parents are managing. Somehow knowing their problems, makes my problems seem less overwhelming than scenarios I never imagined. It is our commonality of experience, however, which leads to new understanding.
> (Toombs et al., 1995, pp. 29–30)

This mother eloquently expressed several points. First, she is amazed that there are so many other parents who have children with disabilities. Second, she described the birth of children with disabilities to be "like wounded geese still flying on an altered course." Third, she employs social (downward) comparison, viewing the disabilities of other children to be more "overwhelming." It would be difficult to make social comparisons in any other group, other than this support group of parents. It is interesting that investigations that evaluate self-esteem in the context of disability suggest that it is not disability per se but the contextual, physical, social, and emotional dimensions that affects the sense of self. The Biomedical Model cannot completely explain the causes of self-esteem in IWDs. Opportunities for social comparison and support with other IWDs can build self-esteem, a strength of the Social Model not addressed by the Biomedical Model.

Disability mutual support groups fulfill many important functions, in both emotional ways and in providing practical suggestions. A woman with multiple sclerosis offered these insights: "Those who share their journey offer the richest resource" (Toombs et al., 1995, p. 25). And "Celia laughs with relief, partly because I have suggested a hopeful solution, but also because we have been afraid together (Toombs et al., 1995, p. 25).

The following story concerns a woman with a newly acquired spinal cord injury (SCI). She explained that she became less frightened as she received answers to her questions from another woman with a SCI, whom she refers to as her mentor.

> [H]ow the mentor got around and what had happened to her, how she dealt with cooking and how she dealt with her kids, how she had sex and what kind of bed she had. Lots of different questions [about] life and living.... Spasticity and, oh God, just everything.... And the more I learned, the less scared I got.
>
> (Veith et al., 2006, p. 291)

Disability social support groups also provide role models. The former Assistant Secretary of the US Department of Education and a disability activist, Judith Huemann, contracted polio as a child. She was in her twenties when she met her first role model, in spite of her activism in other "established" groups. Today, Huemann is a positive role model for many young girls, with or without disabilities. In the following excerpt, she recounted that she never met a role model until she was more than 20 years old.

> When we go into most "establishment" organizations, we hardly meet any disabled individuals, there are not peers that we can look up to, I never met a disabled professional until I was in my twenties. I had only non-disabled

role models—who were not role models to me because I am disabled. Some mutual social support groups are national in scope and, in addition to social support, provide opportunities for socialization and recreation.

The *Disability Rag*, an online blog for IWDs, may be considered another type of mutual social support group. At times, the language is angry and frustrated, but the emotions are authentic and the experiences, information, and opinions are always offered as helpful recommendations. The *Disability Rag* is available to everyone, but IWDs probably understand the contributions in ways that IWODs cannot.

Recognize That Sexuality Is an Important Aspect of the CWD's Self-Identity and Self-Esteem

Cultural and societal assumptions view sexuality in IWDs to be different than that of IWODs, and most of these well-entrenched stereotypes and assumptions are false. Sexuality is defined idiosyncratically; however, at the same time, most adults consider the expressions of their sexuality to be a quality of life issue, including self-acceptance of the various aspects of sexuality. These aspects include, "gender, physical appearance, capabilities, body adornment, behavior, and lifestyle" (Brodwin & Frederick, 2010, p. 37). Body image is another important aspect of the individual's sexuality. Body image has been defined as "The unconscious representation of one's own body . . . believed to be at the root of the individual's self-concept and personal identity" (Livneh & Cook, 2005, p. 190). Another important part of body image is the individual's perception of how others view their body. "Most people are not entirely satisfied with their appearance and everyone, with or without disabilities, lives in a society obsessed with beauty, athletic abilities, and sexual allure" (Smart, 2016). Therefore, many people invest time, effort, and money into trying to enhance their body image, both to themselves and to others.

An aspect of a positive body image is the ability to control one's body, and individuals with seizure disorders, or tremors, or spasticity, or neurocognitive disabilities do not have the degree of control that others take for granted. In addition, many visible disabilities are considered to be unattractive, including adaptive technology, such as hearing aids, wheelchairs, and prostheses. Comments such as "You're beautiful for a girl in a wheelchair" are both incomprehensible and insulting to IWDs. Do these type of comments communicate that the girl would be *even more* beautiful if she didn't use a wheelchair? Comments such as these, in which the "compliment" is given with misguided kindness, clearly communicate negative stereotypes. Why not say, "You're beautiful?"

Neither researchers nor practicing professionals address the sexuality of IWDs, simply assuming that IWDs are not sexual beings. The little training and professional practice on sexuality in IWDs is based on two different assumptions. The first component is directed toward the mechanics of sex and is often provided to men with spinal cord injuries with little or no discussion of affection or love. For women with disabilities there is no mention or discussion. The second component is the (unconscious) dissemination of myths, including the following.

Myths About IWDs and Their Sexuality

- IWDs are asexual, completely uninterested in sex or sexuality.
- IWDs are oversexed and have uncontrollable urges. Therefore, IWDs are to be feared.
- IWDs are dependent and childlike and thus need to be protected.
- IWDs should marry other IWDs.
- Disability breeds disability and, therefore, it is best if IWDs are *not* allowed to bear children.
- All sexual problems of IWDs are due to their disabilities.
- If an IWD marries an IWOD, it is because the IWOD cannot attract another IWOD (the "loser" syndrome) or the IWOD is a "saint" for taking an inferior partner when they "could have done better" (Brodwin & Frederick, 2010).

Some researchers have shown that in school during sex education classes, the children with disabilities were excused, sent to recess or the library. The assumption was that these children would never need sex education. IWDs have been considered sexually deviant, either asexual or oversexed. Disability developmental counselors present a broad, general summary of the way in which the sexuality of IWDs is addressed.

> For individuals with disabilities, expressions of sexuality have been both denied and heavily regulated and remain highly controversial. Although some disability-related government programs have guidelines and policies, such policies remain inconsistent, underutilized and predominantly focused on being "crisis reactive" rather than rights oriented.
> (Harris et al., 2012)

Adults with disabilities are frustrated when their physicians do not address their sexual needs. Crawford and Ostrove (2003) completed a qualitative study entitled, "Representations of Disability and the Interpersonal Relationships of Women with Disabilities." In the two excerpts that follow, women with disabilities focused on their sexuality.

> Eleven of the 13 interviewed highlighted the images of the disabled as asexual. Thirteen participants (all of them) also noted the ways in which negative assumptions regarding their sexuality resulted in dismissive treatment.

In the next excerpt, it appears that a 51-year-old woman has received the identical response to her expressions of sexuality throughout her life.

> A women age 51, who is blind and has spina bifida said, "It seems as though most people thought of us as asexual. I don't know if other people have run into that, but I have. No matter what age group we are in they seemed surprised when I talk about boys and being attracted."

A man with a disability described his perceptions of the role of men:

> Man's evaluation of himself is basically in two areas: His employment and his sex life. . . . These two things are so important . . . and absolutely down to the base of what every man I know feels.
> (Putnam et al., 2003, p. 39)

In the *New York Times*, a woman with cerebral palsy described the way in which her sexuality, interacted with her disability, focusing first on her own sexual development. Cerebral palsy is a congenital disability with a degenerating course.

> (When I was very young) I wore a leg brace to bed in those days, a metal rod that buckled with a leather strap below my knee and attached to an ankle-high shoe. Though I felt the weight of this contraption . . . and I knew I limped because the meanest girl on our block had told me, it went without saying that in the beautiful future would I walk, and even run, with grace.
> My cerebral palsy is relatively mild. I have clear speech, and though I walk slowly and awkwardly, I get around fine. In my 20s, if I considered my C.P. at all, it was through the lens of vanity. How noticeable was my limp? Was I beautiful in spite of it? The answer, I assumed, was in the response I got from men. It was hard to decode. Apparently I was appealing enough to sleep with but not to be picked as a girlfriend.
> (Grtiz, 2017, Feb. 8)

The next excerpt could be entitled, "You're Broken; Therefore You Will Never Be Pretty." The writer tells that she is subject to society's pressure on girls without disabilities to be slim and have straight hair. As a young child, she accepted this responsibility and tried to straighten her hair. Eventually, she becomes aware that even if she were to measure up to society's demands for attractiveness, it would not matter because she is a girl in a wheelchair.

> [Y]ou're hearing from every well-intentioned stranger that you're broken and you need to be healed. There is something wrong with you and you need to be fixed. But you know you won't ever be "fixed." You're walking like this (and eventually rolling like this) for life. You were okay with this until the world started telling you that on top of being completely imperfect like every other girl, you're also broken—thus making you completely undesirable.
>
> You, my dear crippled girl, will never be pretty. You'll be cute. You'll be cute to adults who like to patronize you and squeeze your cheeks and treat you like a child for the rest of your life. Adults will automatically think that because you're in a wheelchair, you're broken. You will never be cute to the boy in your 8th grade class who has the perfect hair and great smile. He'll never think you're pretty because, quite frankly, you're a broken girl. All those unsolicited prayers from creepy mall strangers never kicked in.
>
> [Y]our entire life you have received "compliments" from strangers that were really just slaps in the face—constant reminders that you are just a crippled girl. . . . Wheelchairs and scars are not sexy.
>
> You'll be a virgin forever. People who are not sexually desirable don't have sex. They don't get married. They don't have kids. They probably don't even get kissed. People with disabilities are basically asexual, right?

Counselors should:

- Review the list of myths about sexuality and IWDs and determine if they might have, unknowingly, internalized some of these myths.
- Be prepared to discuss the CWD's sexuality in an open and direct manner. While in most counseling specialties, the topic of sexuality is often peripheral to the presenting problem, the CWD should feel empowered to candidly discuss this.
- Refer to counselors with more training, skill, and experience in dealing with sexual issues, if considered necessary.

Recognize the Infantilization Experienced by PWDs

More than 45 years ago, Wolfensberger (1972) used the term, "eternal children" to describe the infantilization, especially on an institutional level, of IWDs:

> Adults [with disabilities] may be cast into the roles of eternal children by being encouraged to play children's game and to follow children's school schedules rather than adult work schedules; by children's decoration and children's clothing; by funding of services for adults coming from departments charged with serving children; and by such names as "day care center" for day programs for adults.
>
> (p. 205)

An architect described the infantilization of IWDs on an institutional level, referring to physical environments that do not provide accommodations, thus making it necessary for adults with disabilities to become childlike.

> [the built environment] is designed [for] adults, literate, numerate, physically fit specimens, with good hearing and 20:20 vision.... As an architect, I am often struck how little people register about the spaces they are in and why they feel uncomfortable or otherwise. In a way, this lack of awareness places the individual in a child-like reliance on the spaces to contain them, as an infant does of its mother.
>
> (Van Royan, 1997, p. 5; cf. Marks, 1999, p. 83)

Adults with disabilities often experience difficulties when crossing the border between childhood to adulthood. In the following excerpt, a woman described leaving the "protective custody of family life," trying to enter the adult world of employment "like standing before a firing squad."

> With one extremely painful exception, as long as I was in the protective custody of family life or college, scheduled and lived without exercising my rights as an adult citizen, the forces of society were kindly and unruffling. It was after college, business schools, and innumerable stretches as a volunteer worker on community projects that I was often bogged down by the medieval prejudices and superstitions of the business world. Looking for a job was like standing before a firing squad. Employers were shocked that I had the gall to apply for a job.
>
> (Goffman, 1963, p. 34)

The woman is qualified for the jobs, having attended college, business schools, and successfully working in volunteer positions. She mentions her "rights as an adult citizen" and, in the next sentence, describes job interviewers as "bogged down by medieval superstitions."

Considering IWDs as children is related to paternalism, unnecessary dependence, and charity. Rarely, is it considered that it is society, including the built environment, which withholds adult status from IWDs. Unable to work, or marry, have children, or to have financial independence and security, IWDs are not allowed to achieve adult status.

When only children are portrayed as IWDs, the charitable giving is increased. Poster children are now considered "forced representatives" of an entire group, all IWDs. However, the use of poster children began during the polio epidemics, and proved highly effective. Advertisers understood that the combination of innocence and tragedy was a moneymaker, something like "The larger lump in the throat, the larger the check." Poster children were not viewed as responsible for their disability and the randomness of polio elicited pity. There were no poster adults, adults who had disabilities as a result of polio. Adults just did not pull in the money.

Occasionally, the disability itself makes the IWD feel childlike and dependent. Margaret Robinson described her experience of apraxia following a stoke, which evoked the helpless feelings of a crying, unattended baby. (Apraxia is the inability to move, a common result of strokes.)

> To lose the ability to walk was to lose all sense of safety. Who would come when I needed to be propped up in bed so I wouldn't choke on a sip of water or when I needed a bedpan or a blanket? To lose my ability to walk was to be thrown back to memories of being an infant left in a closed room for hours, screaming.
>
> (Robinson, 1997, p. 88)

While some of the childlike qualities of IWDs are a result of the disability, it is society who is responsible for most of the infantilization of adults with disabilities.

Conclusion

At this point, many guidelines for practices have been outlined, including their rationale. These guidelines and practice applications are not difficult to understand; however, actually implementing them in ethical and effective ways is more difficult. Nonetheless, the first step in understanding new procedures is to become aware of the need for these procedures and some of the possible problems, and even harm, that can result if these are not integrated into counseling practice.

More than most professions (that serve IWDs) counselors are in a unique position to understand the needs of IWDs. Counselors understand the uniqueness and individuality of each client, which includes their past experiences and family and partner histories. Counselors also understand that clients cannot progress and achieve if they are not supported by their environments. Another important counseling basic orientation is that of meeting the needs of the clients first and viewing the client as an independent decision maker. These understandings provide a firm foundation on which to add awareness, knowledge, and skills to work with clients with disabilities and their families.

Counselors also know that skilled practice must be preceded by awareness and knowledge. Practice, including supervised practice, will allow counselors to integrate these skills into their repertoire of professional capabilities.

References

Agich, G. J., & Carson, R. A. (1995). Chronic illness and freedom. In S. K. Toombs, D. Barnard, & R. A. Carson (Eds.), *Chronic illness: From experience to policy* (pp. 129–153). Bloomington, IN: University of Indiana.

American Counseling Association. (2009). *Handbook of counseling*. Alexandria, VA: Author.

American Counseling Association. (2014). *ACA code of ethics*. Alexandria, VA: Author.

Americans with Disabilities Act Amendments of 2008, 42 U.S.C. 12101 *et seq*. Retrieved from www.adaaa.gov/ Retrieved 02-26-2018

Americans with Disabilities Act of 1990, 42 U.S.C. 12101 *et seq*. Retrieved from www.ada.gov/ada_archive.htm www.justice.gov/crt/disability-rights-section Retrieved 02-26-2018

Barker, R. G., Wright, B. A., Meyerson, L., & Gonick, M. R. (1953). *Adjustment to physical handicap and illness: A survey of the social psychology of physique and disability*. New York: Social Science Research Council.

Brault, M. W. (2012). *Americans with disabilities: 2010*. Retrieved from www.census.gov/prod/2012pubs/p70-131.pdf Retrieved 02-26-2018

Brodwin, M. G., & Frederick, P. C. (2010). Sexuality and societal beliefs regarding persons living with disabilities. *Journal of Rehabilitation*, 76, https://www.questia.com/library/journal/1G1-240913502/sexuality-and-societal-beliefs-regarding-persons-living

Cimarolli, V. R. (2006). Perceived overprotection and distress in adults with visual impairment. *Rehabilitation Psychology*, 51, 338–345.

Cohen, R. M. (2004). *Blindsided: Living a life above illness: A reluctant memoir*. New York, NY: Harper Collins.

Crawford, D., & Ostrove, J. M. (2003). Representations of disability and the interpersonal relations of women with disabilities. *Women and Therapy*, 26, 171–191.

Goeke, J. (2003). Parents speak out: Facial plastic surgery for children with Down syndrome. *Education and Training in Developmental Disabilities*, 38, 323–333.

Goffman, E. (1963). *Stigma: Notes on the management of spoiled identity*. Englewood Cliffs, NJ: Prentice Hall.

Graf, N. M., Marini, I., & Blankenship, C. J. (2009). One hundred words about disability. *Journal of Rehabilitation*, 75, 25–34.

Grtiz, O. (2017, February 8). Love, eventually. *New York Times*.

Harris, R. W. (1992). Musings from 20 years of hard-earned experience. *Rehabilitation Education, 6*, 207–211.

Harris, S. P., Heller, T., Schindler, A., & van Heumen, L. (2012). Current issues, controversies, and solutions. In T. Heller & S. Harris (Eds.), *Disability through the life course* (pp. 39–102). Thousand Oaks, CA: Sage.

Kriegel, L. (1964). *The long walk home*. New York, NY: Appleton-Croft.

Linton, S. (1998). *Claiming disability: Knowledge and identity*. New York, NY: New York University.

Livneh, H., & Cook, D. (2005). Psychosocial impact of disability. In R. M. Parker, E. M. Szymanski, & J. B. Patterson (Eds.), *Rehabilitation counseling: Basics and beyond* (4th ed., pp. 187–224). Austin, TX: PRO-ED.

Longmore, P. K. (2003). *Why I burned my book and other essays on disability*. Philadelphia, PA: Temple University.

Marks, D. (1999). *Disability: Controversial debates and psychosocial perspectives*. London: Routledge.

Murphy, R. (1990). *The body silent in America*. New York, NY: Norton.

Oldenburg, A. (2014, March 16). Defined by determination. *USA Today*, B7–B8. Retrieved from http://usatoday30.usatoday.com/LIFE/usaedition/2014-03-17-Amy-Purdy-feature_ST_U.htm Retrieved 02–26–2018

Putnam, M., Greenen, S., Powers, L., Saxton, M., Finney, S., & Dautel, P. (2003). People with disabilities discuss barriers and facilitators to well-being. *Journal of Rehabilitation, 69*, 37–45.

Resch, J. A., Mireles, G., Benz, M. R., Grenwelge, C., Peterson, R., & Zhang, D. (2010). Giving parents a voice: A qualitative study of the challenges experienced by parents of children with disabilities. *Rehabilitation Psychology, 55*, 139–150.

Robinson, M. (1997). Renascence. In K. Fries (Ed.), *Staring back: The disability experience from the inside out* (pp. 87–92). New York, NY: Plume.

Savin, K. (2017, December 15). My supercharged, tricked out, Bluetooth wheelchair life force. *New York Times*.

Scherer, M. J. (Ed.) (2005). *Living in the state of stuck: How technology impacts the lives of people with disabilities*. Cambridge, MA: Brookline.

Scherer, M., Sax, C., Vanbiervliet, A., Cushman, L., & Scherer, J. (2005). Predictors of assistive technology use: The importance of personal and psychosocial factors. *Disability and Rehabilitation, 27*(21), 1321–1331.

Smart, J. F. (2016). *Disability, society, and individual* (3rd ed.). Austin, TX: PRO-ED.

Solomon, A. (2012). *Far from the tree: Parents, children, and the search for identity*. New York, NY: Scribner.

Tollifson, J. (1997). Imperfection is a beautiful thing. In K. Fries (Ed.), *Staring back: The disability experience from the inside out* (pp. 104–112). New York, NY: Plume.

Toombs, S. K., Barnard, D., & Carson, R. A. (Eds.). (1995). *Chronic illness: From experience to policy*. Bloomington: University of Indiana.

Tremblay, M. (1996). Going back to civvy street: A historical account of the Everest and Jennings wheelchairs for Canadian World War II veterans with spinal cord injuries. *Disability and Society, 11*, 146–169.

Van Rooyan, J. (1997). 'There's no such thing as a building.' *NewSquiggle: The Nesletter of the Squiggle Foundation. Autumn:* 5-6

Veith, E. M., Sherman, J. E., Pellino, T. A., & Yasui, N. Y. (2006). Qualitative analysis of the peer-mentoring relationship among individuals with spinal cord injuries. *Rehabilitation Psychology, 51*, 289–298.

Weihenmayer, E. (2001). *Touch the top of the world: A blind man's journey to climb farther than the eye can see*. New York, NY: Dutton.

Weisskopf, M. (2006, October 2). "How I lost my hand, but found myself." *Time*, 28–37.

Whitt, J. K. (1984). Children's adaptation to chronic illness and handicapping conditions. In M. G. Eisenberg, L. C. Sutkin, & M. A. Jansen (Eds.), *Chronic illness and disability throughout the life span: Effects on self and family* (pp. 69–102). New York, NY: Springer.

Wolfensberger, W. (1972). *The principle of normalization in human services.* Toronto, ON: National Institute on Intellectual disability.

World Health Organization. (2001). *International classification of functioning, disability and health.* Geneva: Author.

Seven

INTEGRATING COUNSELING PRACTICES WITH SOCIETAL ISSUES

At this point, readers are aware of the pervasive prejudice directed toward IWDs and the limited range of choices they often experience. At the end of this chapter, and the end of the book, the concept of disability transcendence is described and it is also recommended that counselors look for and facilitate transcendence. The prejudice of society juxtaposed with disability transcendence may appear mutually exclusive or, more simply stated, it may be thought that it is not possible for someone to transcend a disability in a prejudicial society. However, that is the point of transcendence, that it is under the personal control of the individual and that part of disability transcendence often includes advocacy and activist efforts to dismantle prejudicial systems and societies and to support individual CWDs in reaching that goal.

The first part of this chapter discusses the images and practices of society in which IWODs, including counselors, may not be aware. Nonetheless, IWDs are very aware of these issues and, moreover, counselors can be equipped to become aware of the prejudicial and limiting images and behaviors. Simply becoming cognizant of the reality of these images, attitudes, and behaviors will allow counselors to first look, and perhaps, find them. If IWODs are not aware of the prejudice and discrimination, they cannot challenge them. Jokes about IWDs are often tolerated; but jokes about other disenfranchised groups are not tolerated. Counselors skilled in disability issues may be required to challenge colleagues who, unknowingly, express inaccurate and prejudicial views of disability.

In this chapter, seven practice guidelines are suggested:

1. Recognize the demeaning images of IWDs in the general culture.
2. Recognize that IWDs may be members of other disenfranchised groups.
3. Support and acknowledge the caregiver.
4. Screen for abuse and neglect.
5. Recognize activism and advocacy as adaptive behaviors.
6. Look for and foster transcendence.
7. Collaborate with medical providers.

Recognize the Demeaning Images of IWDs in the General Culture

> **Demeaning Images of IWDs**
> - Demeaning images of any group lead to social threats.
> - Social threats lead to prejudice and discrimination and, for IWDs who acquire a disability later in life or who are diagnosed with a chronic illness, their prejudice and discrimination becomes self-identifiers.
> - The Biomedical Model definition of disability as pathology and deviance reinforces these demeaning images.
> - Due to the segregation of IWDs, many IWODs have not had close relationships with IWDs and, therefore, cannot question or challenge these demeaning images.
> - Advocating abortion, infanticide, or assisted suicide for any subclass leads to these individuals feeling the need to justify or defend their existence.

Every client faces social threats because everyone lives in a family, culture, community, and society. Social threats include attitudes, beliefs, and behaviors that often lead to individuals questioning their self-worth and the value of their group to the greater society. A strong self-identification and deeply rooted ego strength are necessary to deflect social threats; otherwise, individuals internalize these demeaning societal images. In this way, social threats (and their meanings) become self-identifiers. One woman who acquired a disability later in her life summarized the way in which she had internalized these demeaning images when she stated, "I had always thought that people with disabilities were weirdos and creeps. Now I am a person with a disability!" Another individual with a psychiatric disability related that some of the difficulty in accepting his disability was the "conditioning" he had received since he was young.

> I cannot tell you how difficult it is for a person to accept the fact that he or she is schizophrenic. Since the time we were very young we have all been conditioned to accept that if something is crazy or insane, its worth is automatically dismissed. . . . The nature of this disorder is that it affects the chemistry that controls your cognitive processes.
>
> (Frese, 1997, pp. 145–146)

Demeaning images of IWDs have a long history, for example, as medieval morality plays or "freak shows," and permeate literature. The mass media has only recently changed its image of IWDs. Print media, especially literature, portrayed IWDs in simplistic and negative ways. For example, Charles Dickens, the great British author, wrote 16 major literary works of which 14 had a character with a disability (Byrd & Elliott, 1988). Dickens, and other authors, often used IWDs as allegories or metaphors for weak, pathetic, or criminal individuals. These characters with disabilities were not given personalities, social roles, and did not live with families. They were often embittered and angry about their disability and which was only relieved by a character without a disability who helped the disabled character to accept their devalued status. In the *Christmas Carol*, Dickens inverts the character with a disability into a sweet, kind boy who wishes everyone well in order to act as a foil to the miserly and unfeeling Mr. Scrooge. Tiny Tim was described as "lame," and is carried on his father's shoulders. Marks (1999) summarized other characters from literature who had disabilities: "Captain Hook and Richard III plot and scheme in order to gain vengeance on a world each sees as responsible for his wounds" (pp. 167–168). J. Morris (1991), the English disability scholar, wrote about the way in which disability is utilized in literature:

> Disability is used as a metaphor, as a code for the message the non-disabled writer wishes to convey. In doing this, the writer draws on the prejudice, ignorance, and fear that generally exist toward disabled people, knowing that to portray a character with a humped back, with a missing leg, with facial scars will evoke certain feelings in the reader or the audience. The disability is used to induce a sense of unease, the more the cultural stereotype is reinforced.
>
> (p. 93)

Due to continual, pervasive social threats to IWDs, they face greater social threats than IWODs. In contrast to other disenfranchised groups, such as ethnic/racial groups, or women, or LGBTQ people, progress has lagged in the portrayals of IWDs, and thus remained unchallenged. The Biomedical Model with its definition of disability as pathology and deviance may play a role in maintaining centuries of demeaning images of IWDs in the media. A disability scholar from the United Kingdom (Shakespeare, 1999) summarized: "The use of disability as a character trait, plot device, or as atmosphere is a lazy short-cut. . . . Above all, the dominant images [of disabled people] are crude, one-dimensional and simplistic." Another disability scholar (Zola, 1992), in a chapter entitled, "Any Distinguishing Features?: The Portrayal of Disability in the Crime Mystery

Genre," discovered that most of the criminals portrayed had a visible physical disability. Perhaps because Zola had a visible disability, he became aware that most criminals in the media had a distinguishing, visible disability. As a result, viewers associated visible physical disabilities with crime and villainy. At the same time, the majority of the consumers of crime mysteries were not aware of the implied prejudice against IWDs. Other disenfranchised groups are typically not viewed as deviance, but as diversity.

A mother of a newborn with achondroplasia (dwarfism) told of her first reaction to the diagnosis:

> The physical therapist said, "Oh well, it's dwarfism": and she went on about his (her baby son) being a dwarf. She didn't see my reaction was to just fall backwards because to me dwarfism or being a dwarf, was the troll under the bridge in Three Billy Goats Gruff.
>
> (Ablon, 1989, p. 351)

Rod Michalko (2002) became progressively blind throughout his adolescence. He wrote about his experiences of watching television and films when he was a teenager. When young, he felt fearful watching the portrayal of blind people and, only when he was older, he realized that it was "the fear of seeing myself."

> In my teens, I saw blind people on television and in the movies and sometimes came across a blind character in a book. They were all portrayed as victims of misfortune. . . . When I saw blind people in the movies or on television and even when I saw the "real" blind ones, I saw incompetence, sadness, and poverty. And I saw misfortune. Whether my perception was accurate or not is irrelevant; that's just what I saw. What I did not see when I saw these blind people is just as significant as what I did see: I did not see me. Still, when I saw them, I experienced a nebulous fear that I later understood was the fear of seeing myself.
>
> (p. 24)

Referring to the media in the United Kingdom, Barnes (2012) noted the myths surrounding disability and the people who experience them, commenting, "one of the persistent stereotypes and a major obstacle to disabled people's successful integration into society" (p. 11). "[the media] dilutes the humanity of disabled people by reducing them to objects of curiosity" (p. 12).

Barnes (2012) also included the print media, stating that both "quality" newspapers and the "tabloid" press exaggerated and sensationalized individuals with intellectual disabilities. "Newspaper articles sensationalizing the connection between intellectual impairments and criminality are common in both the tabloids and the 'quality' papers" (p. 19).

Another social threat that IWDs experience includes the public debate of such issues as assisted suicide for IWDs, abortion of fetuses with disabilities, and infanticide of newborns with severe and multiple disabilities. Needless to say, these are complicated issues and it is not the answers to these moral and ethical dilemmas which are of concern here. What is of concern here are the social threats these ethical concerns present to individuals who are currently living with these particular types of disabilities. The social message is: "The fewer people like you, the better." Further, IWDs may feel required to justify and defend their lives.

A mother of a son with a disability, Robbie, was asked if Robbie could be a poster child for the charity, the March of Dimes. Robbie's mother was told that poster children raise a great deal of money for charity. Still, the mother refused.

> "I'm sorry," I explain, "but I don't feel comfortable telling my son that he is doing this to prevent other children like him. We're trying to help him understand where he fits into a world that is often more confused than he is about his problem. I can't put him out there as something to 'prevent.' This poster thing also seems to use these kids to collect money, yet you tell me none of its goes toward addressing their problems now. That sort feels dishonest."
>
> I realize that I have given away potential "celebrity" status for Robbie by declining their invitation. I have also risked being labeled an ungrateful parent. But I think I have been true to what I really want for him. Free lunches and pictures in the newspaper are not going to help push his wheelchair into a community that sees him as something that should not have happened.
>
> (Toombs, Barnard, & Carson, 1995, pp. 32–33)

Fortunately, the media are changing their portrayal of IWDs; one indicator is the number of actors with disabilities who portray characters with disabilities. Also, characters with disabilities are increasingly portrayed as ordinary people, with social roles, families, and careers. In these types of portrayals, the disability is not hidden and, yet, it is not relevant to the plot. An article in the *New York Times* by Mireya Navarro (2007) noted these changes, quoting Robert David

Hall, who is a double amputee and played a coroner on the popular US television series, *CSI*.

> It used to be that if you were disabled and on television, they'd play soft piano behind you. The thing I love about *CSI* is that I'm just Dr. Robbins.
>
> (para. 8)

> The heart-wrenching movie of the week and fund-raising telethons striving for cures have given way to amputees rock climbing on reality shows like the *Amazing Race* and doing the jive on *Dancing With the Stars*. Sitcoms and crime shows have jumped on the bandwagon, too. An actor who is paraplegic, for instance, depicts a member of the casino surveillance team on *Las Vegas*.
>
> (para. 7)

The media are changing, perhaps due to the combination of rising numbers of IWDs, the identity politics of IWDs, and the introduction of federal civil rights laws, such as the Americans with Disabilities Act (ADA). Presently, there are television programs that portray the lives and families of people with disabilities in a more realistic way. "The mass media have potential to teach and shape public attitudes about disability and the people who experience them" (Smart, 2016b, p. 147).

Recognize That IWDs May Be Members of Other Disenfranchised Groups

IWDs as Members of Other Disenfranchised Groups

- Typically, disability is the "master status" even for those who belong to other disenfranchised groups. "Disability is the ultimate 'other'" (Ferguson & Nusbaum, 2012, p. 73).
- Most IWODs do not view IWDs as a disenfranchised group.
- It is erroneously thought that other disenfranchised groups do not deserve their disenfranchisement whereas IWDs do deserve to be disenfranchised.
- Intersectionality is described as the combination of two or more disenfranchised statuses in one individual.
- Scholars and activists have not included IWDs in their definitions of intersectionality.
- Laws typically do not redress grievances against people who are subject to multiple, intersecting forms of discrimination.

- Intersectionality is experienced by some IWDs.
- Intersectionality can be found in the higher rates of disability for racial/ethnic individuals due to sociopolitical factors.
- Historically, IWDs who belonged to other disenfranchised groups received inferior services.
- LGBTQ individuals with disabilities are disadvantaged by institutional prejudice and discrimination, such as insurance policies, marriage laws, and health care systems.

The theory of intersectionality holds that one individual can be identified as belonging to several disenfranchised statuses and, IWDs have multiple self-identities and society often considers IWDs to be members of other minority groups. Succinctly stated, intersectionality describes multiple minority statuses in a single individual. The concept of intersectionality was introduced by an American civil rights advocate and professor at the University of California, Los Angeles law school, Kimberle Williams Crenshaw, www.law.columbia.edu/news/2017/06/kimberle-crenshaw-intersectionality.

IWDs are rarely discussed in the counseling or social justice literature (Kelsey & Smart, 2012) perhaps because 1) disability is considered the "master status" or the most important (or only) identification of the IWD, eclipsing other types of identity, such as gender, racial/ethnic identity, or sexual orientation; 2) disability is considered to be deviance, rather than diversity; and 3) individuals in other minority groups do not elicit existential angst from others while IWDs are fearful reminders of everyone's potential to acquire a disability. Therefore, the academic and professional literature in counseling is silent on the ways in which membership in other disenfranchised groups intersects with the disability experience. The intersectionality of disability with other types of disenfranchisement is rarely discussed in the rehabilitation literature. Nor is disability addressed in the cultural/ethnic/sexual minority literature.

The intersectionality of race and disability is felt in this young American male.

> I've gotten used to the stares . . . it's like—and especially if it's a young African American male in a wheelchair. I can almost read their minds. Gang member. Drug dealer. It's always negative.
>
> (Putnam et al., 2003, p. 43)

> **Three Reasons Why Disability Is Rarely Considered as Part of Intersectionality**
>
> 1. Disability is considered the master status and, therefore, no other identity is important.
> 2. Other minority statuses are labeled "diversity," whereas disability is labeled "deviance."
> 3. Individuals of other minority statuses do not elicit existential angst, but IWDs become fearful reminders of everyone's potential to acquire a disability.

More than 30 years ago, two feminist disability scholars, Fine and Asch (1988), summarized:

> To date, almost all research on disabled men and women seems simply to assume the irrelevance of gender, race, ethnicity, sexual orientation, or social status. Having a disability presumably eclipses these dimensions of social experience. Even sensitive students of disability . . . have focused on disability as a unitary concept and have taken it to be the "master status" but apparently the exclusive status for disabled people.
>
> (p. 3)

Advocacy efforts for women, racial and ethnic groups, and LBGTQ individuals have succeeded in achieving national awareness while IWDs are not part of the national consciousness. Those who are not women, racial or ethnic minorities, or LBGTQ individuals have some awareness and understanding of their long history of prejudice and discrimination. Most everyone understands that members of these disenfranchised groups have formed a political identity and actively advocate for their rights as citizens. In contrast, most IWODs are unaware that IWDs have recently established a political identity.

> A person without a disability may recognize someone using a wheelchair, a guide dog or a prosthetic limb, or someone with Down syndrome, but most don't conceptualize these people as having a shared social identity and a political status. "They" merely seem to be people to whom something unfortunate has happened, for whom something has gone terribly wrong. The one thing most people do about being disabled is that they don't want to be that.
>
> (Garland-Thomson, 2017)

Garland-Thomson (2017) succinctly captured the difference in the way society views members of other disenfranchised groups and how IWDs are thought of. Members of these other identity groups are often asked, "Who are you?" while IWDs are asked, "What's wrong with you?" The first question is related to the concept of diversity while the second question is related to deviance.

One woman with diabetes described four sources of prejudice and discrimination. First, she has an invisible disability (diabetes) and this invisibility masks the discipline and dedication of managing what could be a life-threatening disability, explaining "when I do manage to control my diabetes, it's at a cost of almost every other element of your life." Second, she thinks that others blame for her having developed diabetes because she is overweight. Third, because she is a woman, she feels the responsibility to be slim, and, fourth, because she is black, she thinks that others hold an "unconscious bias" in which black people are thought to be "inherently lazy, deviant, sick, unclean."

> I've always known my body needed transforming—or that other people thought it did. . . . (As a child) I saw the attention my grandmother lavished on my skinny cousin contrasted against the frustration she expressed shopping for clothes that fit me. . . . I've found my fatness compounds (the blame). My body is visibly off kilter, a symbol for lethargy, lack of self-regulation, ill health, indolence. Combine this with the misbelief that there is a cure for diabetes—that cure being willpower—and everybody is suddenly an expert on how to fix me. It'd be impossible not to internalize that I am to blame. There is the issue of my blackness, too which, many, because of unconscious bias, interpret as inherently lazy, deviant, sick, unclean.
> (R. Solomon, 2016)

Note that IWODs (mistakenly) believe that they know the cause of this woman's disability and, further, they also think they know the treatment. Both of these false beliefs place the responsibility on the individual.

"The disabled" are the only "open" minority group, meaning that anyone, at any time, can acquire a disability or be diagnosed with a disability. The potential for anyone to acquire a minority status (the disability) at any time renders the experience of intersectionality different from other types of intersectionality. When women, LGBTQ individuals, or anyone in a disenfranchised group acquires a disability, they often express surprise at the added source of discrimination and prejudice. This may be compounded because the civil rights laws protecting IWDs are often weak, frequently misinterpreted, and unenforced. In the past, before the passage of the Americans with Disabilities Act, the burden of proof rested with the IWD. This is changing.

The concept of intersectionality has identified the reality of experience for different minority groups, but intersectionality has rarely, if ever, been applied to IWDs. Typically, a combination of racial or ethnic groups, women, LBGTQ groups, and those of lower socioeconomic classes is considered when describing intersectionality. It seems clear that for most civil rights activists IWDs are excluded.

Nonetheless, two important points merit discussion. First, IWDs do experience intersectionality, and, second, when seeking redress for denial of civil rights, laws recognize only one minority status per court case. Therefore, intersectionality is a somewhat nebulous and difficult concept to legally describe and enforce. An American legal scholar Stefan (2001) described the results of the case of *Johnson v. Thompson* (1992), as "one of the most crushing examples of the way in which the law's obsession with neat categories results in the denial of relief [for those] who are subject to multiple, intersecting forms of discrimination" (Stefan, 2001, p. 155). Stefan described the case:

> Researchers at the University of Oklahoma decided to investigate the effects of treatment on the survival rates of infants born with spina bifida. To further their research, they divided infants born at the hospital with spina bifida into two categories, those who would receive treatment and those would not—obviously without the knowledge or consent of the parents of the children who did not receive treatment. The way the children were divided was based on the researchers' perceptions of the parents' ability to take care of their children, so the children of poor, minority parents did not receive treatment, and the children of more economically stable parents did. Virtually every one of the children who did not receive treatment died. Virtually every one of the children who did receive treatment lived.

When the parents of the babies who died discovered that treatment had been deliberately withheld based on the researchers' perceptions, they sued. The court ruled that the parents did not have a case based on race because babies from poor families who were white died. In addition, according to the court, the families did not have a case based on disability because some of the infants with spina bifida survived.

The concept of intersectionality may be applied to racial and ethnic individuals with disabilities. In addition to the personal experience of added prejudice and discrimination, racial and ethnic minority groups experience higher rates of disability due to entrenched sociopolitical causes. Lack of insurance, lack of education, and employment in physically dangerous and demanding jobs result in more disabilities. These three factors are interrelated and cannot be termed "causes"; nonetheless, racial and ethnic groups experience more disabilities than whites and more important, these rates could be decreased if these sociopolitical factors were reduced. Also, counselors understand that racial and ethnic individuals are often misdiagnosed as having a psychiatric disability or an intellectual disability due to faulty testing procedures. Lack of English language abilities and use of tests which are not culture-free or standardized on racial/ethnic groups produce questionable results. Additionally, counselors understand that minority individuals are more often diagnosed with stigmatizing psychiatric disabilities than whites (D. W. Smart & J. F. Smart, 1997; J. F. Smart & D. W. Smart, 1997a, b, c, 2006).

Furthermore, IWDs of racial/ethnic minorities have typically received fewer services at inferior facilities than whites. These facts are clear-cut examples of the intersectionality of disability and racial/ethnic minority status. Here are two examples: During the American polio epidemics in the Jim Crow South, African Americans who contracted polio were not allowed to be treated by white doctors or nurses or to be treated in the better equipped "white hospitals" or "white rehabilitation centers." Concerning the disability of deafness, the residential schools for Deaf African American children were inferior to the white deaf schools. Better trained teachers and administrators contributed to the higher quality of the white schools. Nonetheless, white deaf schools were not academically rigorous and, therefore, did not prepare their graduates for college or university. Most of the "curriculum" consisted of vocational training. Many of these schools forced the children to abandon Sign Language and learn speech. However, residential schools for deaf African American children had even lower standards in all three of these aspects, when compared to residential schools for deaf white children.

The only African Americans at Roosevelt's Warm Springs Resort were servants. Using their own money, the Roosevelts founded Warm Springs, a resort/treatment facility at a natural source of hot springs in the state of Georgia. At Warm Springs, Roosevelt recuperated and frequently visited for rest and treatment. He also felt more comfortable about his paralysis and did not try to hide or minimize it. Roosevelt expanded Warm Springs and opened it to other polio survivors. Here white polio survivors would come, without cost, for treatment and recreation. Roosevelt felt that IWDs typically did not receive the luxuries and dignities that others did and, therefore, he determined that meals would be served on linen tablecloths, with silver, china, and crystal. Moreover, there would be servants to serve the meals and act as "runners" and assistants to the polio survivors. Eleanor and Franklin Roosevelt wanted to invite African American polio survivors, but political pressure from the Southern Democrats would not allow this. In response, Mrs. Roosevelt built a resort/ treatment center at Tuskegee, Alabama for African Americans. Nonetheless, African Americans were not allowed at Warm Springs, except as able-bodied servants. This is another experience of the intersectionality of two disenfranchised categories. President Roosevelt died at Warm Springs where he went to rest.

IWDs who are LBGTQ may be considered to be subject to intersectionality because they experience prejudice and discrimination from two sources. In spite of the fact that several professional organizations have provided guidelines for counseling lesbian couples, to date, such as the American Psychological Association, there are no guidelines for counseling gay and lesbian couples with disabilities. Insurance policies and law have been slow to recognize gay and lesbian marriage as do laws concerning power of attorney and wills. In many states, gay partnerships and marriages were not legally recognized, nor protected by law until recently. Many gay and lesbian individuals with disabilities have reported that medical personnel often did not recognize their partners as spouses. Standardized forms that elicit personal information often do not include check boxes for non-heterosexual partnerships. One IWD summarized, "If there were a form I could check off, I wouldn't have to go into this big song and dance right there. I could just check a box." Three disability scholars (Hunt et al., 2006; Hunt, Milsom & Matthews, 2009) conducted interviews with 25 lesbians with physical disabilities in an effort to determine how the disability affected the partnership and the way in which they were treated by rehabilitation professionals. As they analyzed the responses to the interviews, two themes concerning institutional practices emerged: 1) navigating legal and financial concerns, including insurance and power of attorney, exacerbated the weak disability and medical laws; and 2) coping with the responses of professionals. One woman summarized, "A lot of times when my partner's role was discounted, then particularly hospital social workers would start making plans as if I had no support system, which wasn't accurate" (p. 174).

To summarize, IWDs who belong to one or more disenfranchised groups (in addition to having a disability) do experience prejudice and discrimination from multiple sources and it is often difficult to determine the exact source. IWDs may wonder, am I being discriminated against because I'm Hispanic, gay, poor, aging, or is it because of my disability? Or is the prejudice and discrimination some sort of blurry, vague combination? Further, intersectionality applies to IWDs who belong to two, three, or four other disenfranchised groups. The

IWD may experience more than one disability, making it difficult to determine if one disability elicits more prejudice than the other.

On a legal and institutionalized basis, intersectionality experienced by IWDs is compounded by the weak laws that protect IWDs and the laws that protect other disenfranchised groups. IWDs, historically, have not been considered diversity, enriching and strengthening the broader culture; rather, IWDs have been seen as deviance, something to be prevented, cured, or otherwise eliminated. The power and longevity of the Biomedical Model of Disability, in which most of the general public conceptualized disability as pathology and inferiority, contributed to the idea that disability is not diversity, but deviance and, furthermore, the disability was the fault of the individual or their family.

Support and Acknowledge the Caregiver

Caregivers of IWDs

- There is little support, training, or preparation for family caregivers.
- Caregiving covers a broad range of duties.
- Due to the twin realities of the greater numbers of IWDs and the deinstitutionalization movement, many IWDs are cared for by their families. Families are now facing challenges that they never anticipated.
- Society's lack of preparation for these medical and demographic changes is considered a "structural lag."
- The longer lifespans of IWDs results in many elderly parent caregivers and raises the question of who will care for family members with disabilities following the death of their parents.
- Caregiving of family members with disabilities has been "gender structured," meaning that most of this caregiving is provided by women.
- Counselors will be asked to provide family and marriage counseling.

Families and spouses/partners are assuming more responsibility for the care of IWDs. A combination of several factors have led to this change in family life, including the increasing number of IWDs, the deinstitutionalization movement, and the aging of IWDs. In spite of the extent of these caregiving needs, there is little preparation or support for families. Two disability scholars (Elliott & Shewchuk, 2003) explained:

> Family caregivers often receive very little formal preparation or support. Typically, caregivers are not compensated for their services, and yet they are expected to operate competently as extensions of health care services, helping a loved one perform self-care tasks, adhere to behavioural regimens, and execute therapeutic directives in the home environment. Changes in formal health care provision have compelled people with severe physical disability to assume ultimate responsibility for their ongoing health and when they are unable to assume manage this responsibility, their family caregivers then may have more influence on health outcomes than any single health provider.
>
> (Elliott & Shewchuk, 2003, p. 149)

Elliott and Shewchuk clarified the numerous tasks and responsibilities of family caregivers and pointed out that they are often unacknowledged and unsupported. Marriage and family counselors could assist in providing therapeutic support.

Medical advances, including the development of antipsychotic medications and antidepressants, led to the deinstitutionalization movement (Grob, 1992; Torrey, 1992). Many of those released from institutions simply went home to live with their families or spouses. However, the assumption that *all* of these former residential patients had a combination of resources, including somewhere to live, someone who would take responsibility for their care, and access to community outpatient psychological care was, seemingly, not considered or questioned (Accordino, Porter, & Moore, 2001). With deinstitutionalization, the task of medicine and science was to develop the medications that would allow individuals to live at home or in other livings arrangements of their own choice, resulting in more humane treatment for individuals with psychiatric disabilities and saving money for governments and insurance companies. However, it was "society's" responsibility to ensure that social conditions were in place to assist and support formerly institutionalized patients. These medical advances outpaced social changes. This gap is termed a "structural lag."

The deinstitutionalization movement has also affected infants with severe disabilities, allowing them to live at home with parents and siblings. In addition to medical advances and demographic changes, federal laws and insurance policies have been enacted that allow many individuals who previously lived in institutions to have more control over their disability benefits and are given the option to choose to live outside of institutions. The introduction of special education for children with disabilities in the 1960s as an entitlement, provided in community neighborhoods, also spurred the deinstitutionalization movement.

Without the availability of community education, many parents placed their newborn infants in institutions. Therefore, a combination of medical advances, demographic changes, and federal law and entitlements, all coalesced in a short time period. This combination resulted in a much higher quality of living for IWDs. In spite of this, most IWODs who do not have friends or family members with disabilities probably have not noticed this extensive change.

Many IWDs report a preference for living at home and it is their parents who act as caregivers (Braddock, & Hemp, 2006). It is hardly surprising that, with the longer life spans of IWDs, many of these parent/caregivers are elderly.

> In the United States, the majority of adults with intellectual and developmental disabilities live at home with family caregivers, and 25% of these caregivers are over 60 years of age. In addition, a National Alliance on Mental Illness (NAMI) survey found that over 40% of persons with mental illness lived with parents, many of whom were elderly. The number of aging caregivers providing care to relatives with disabilities will continue to increase in the coming decades.
> (Harris, Heller, & Schindler, 2012, p. 70)

The question arises: Who will care for these IWDs when their parents are too elderly or pass away? Many times, the answer is siblings. The longer life spans of IWDs also means that they will experience many of the common degenerating effects of aging, but IWDs also tend to experience age-related deterioration earlier than IWODs and many experience secondary conditions and complications. The aging process of IWDs is complicated by several chronic conditions that are more prevalent than in the general population.

> Several chronic conditions seem to be more prevalent among individuals with disabilities than in the general population, including non-atherosclerotic heart disease, hypertension, hypocholesteremia obesity, heart disease, diabetes, respiratory illness, osteoporosis, and pressure sores. Mobility impairments, thyroid disease, psychotropic drug polypharmacy. . . .
>
> People with developmental disabilities have some age-related concerns similar to those of people without disabilities, but they also have unique health concerns (Lightfoot, 2007). They have, on average, twice as many health problems as the general public. Syndrome-specific effects link to special risk factors. People with Down syndrome, for example, have an earlier onset of Alzheimer's disease. Persons aging with cerebral palsy may experience earlier onset arthritis related to excessive joint wear and tear,

chronic pain, gastroesophageal reflux, contractures, and bowel and bladder disorders.

(Harris, Heller, & Schindler, 2012, p. 72)

Widespread use of families as caregivers of individuals with severe disabilities is a relatively recent phenomenon. However, demographic and social changes have transformed the definition of family and the familiar concept of a family as a mother and father and children, with extended family nearby is becoming less common. The conceptualization of a family has often been termed the "nuclear family." However, greater responsibility is often placed upon an individual caregiver, especially in the light of the recent increases in single parenthood coupled with the geographic mobility for employment. Increasing numbers of babies with congenital disabilities are born to single mothers who have no extended nearby to assist in childcare. In spite of this, most research and scholarship about "caretaker" families are based on the outmoded nuclear family. Much of this literature focuses on caregiving for an elderly spouse, perhaps due to the fact that this type of caregiving is considered to be normative, or widely accepted.

In the past, most caregiving of IWDs of any age, was performed by females, mothers, wives, and oldest daughters. As sex roles become flexible, female-dominated caregiving will be less prevalent. A recent exception to the common arrangement of females providing care for IWDs, is adults in the severe range of Autism Spectrum Disorders (ASD) who are, more typically cared for by a brother after the parents of have died. Perhaps this reliance on a brother may be due to the fact that there are more males with ASD than females (Silberman, 2015). For hundreds of years, in the case of hearing children of adults who are deaf (CODAs), the oldest daughter acted as the interpreter between the signing world of her parents and the speaking world, even when there were older sons in the family.

Jane Hawking, former wife of Stephen Hawking, the British astrophysicist with a degenerating neuromuscular disability, linked her experience of providing care with the passage and enforcement of laws (Hawking, 2007). Note that Hawking's first sentence begins with a description of British disability law.

1970. . . saw the passing of the Chronically Sick and Disabled Persons' Act. Though it was hailed across the world as a historic breakthrough in asserting the rights of the disabled, the government refused to implement it fully for many years, leaving already hard-pressed individuals to conduct their own campaigns for its enforcement locally.

> Our letters of protest to the City Surveyor were met with a superior disdain. The City Surveyor had never before heard of disabled people wanting to cross the city as far as Marks and Spencer (a large department store) to buy their own underwear, so he failed to see the need for such an expedition—as if disabled people and their families had no right to venture that far. Injustice spurred us into action. Why should Stephen have to suffer restraints on his lifestyle other than those inflicted by an unkind Nature? Why should short-sighted bureaucrats be allowed to make life doubly difficult for him?
>
> (pp. 159–160)

Perhaps one of the most eloquent passages in Jane Hawking's book described the gap between the "artificial glamour" of the public award ceremonies and the very private reality of caring for a man with a severe disability. Ms. Hawking, in the first line of the following excerpt, illustrates the wide array of services expected of her, 24 hours a day, seven days a week. Throughout the same time period, she was raising two small children.

> I was chauffeur, nurse, valet, cup-bearer and interpreter, as well as companion-wife, all at once. When finally all the intervening hurdles between the customary tenor of life in Cambridge and the glitzy London social scene had been surmounted, we would appear, always late, decked out in evening dress—complete with the hand-tied bow tie on which Stephen insisted—in a sparkling ballroom or dining room to be greeted by the assembled ranks of the scientific intelligentsia, peers of the realm, and assorted dignitaries.
>
> The artificial glamour of these occasions was simultaneously entertaining and irritating. While I enjoyed myself, I was inevitably aware of the hours ahead. There would be no coachman to drive us home from London after midnight or to help get Stephen ready for bed, and the next morning we would be back in our routine. I would be dressing Stephen, feeding him his breakfast, his pills, and his tea, then I would clean the house and put two or three loads of washing into the machine before peeling the onions and potatoes for the next meal. . . . There would be no glass slipper either, even though there might be a glistening gold medal, set on a bed of satin and velvet, to remind us that the previous evening had not been just a passing dream. Even the medals disappeared from view after a day or two. Since the house was subject to occasional, opportunistic petty theft, the medals had to be consigned to the bank vault, rarely to be seen again.
>
> (p. 242)

Most remarkable about Ms. Hawking's experiences is the absence of anyone or any agency who was aware of or expressed interest in the Hawkings' daily lives.

The onset or diagnosis of a disability or chronic illness within a family is typically an unanticipated event, bringing stresses and losses. Further, the onset or diagnosis of a disability is considered to be a "silent transition," a transition which can be viewed as a turning point, necessitating a change in self-identity and in the way in which others view the IWD. Indeed, each member of the family must redefine himself or herself. The deepest meaning of life, humanity, and family are questioned. In spite of the enormity of this transition, society does not support, aid, or guide IWDs through this period. There are greeting cards that express sympathy for other typically difficult transitions, such as the death of a partner, an individual's hospitalization, and retirement; but, there are no greeting cards for acknowledgment of the acquisition of a disability, making this a "silent transition."

A newly acquired or recently diagnosed disability presents stresses, ambiguities, and losses. The typical question is: "Why us?" Family and marriage partners understand that all families and partnerships involve typical patterns of communication and behaviors, some of which may assist in successful responses to a disability and others that may heighten the stresses of disability. Family members are often at different levels of acceptance and adaptation. Financial losses when one partner must relinquish their job to provide caregiving, coupled with expensive treatments and extensive remodeling of the family home, place extensive demands upon the most resilient and resourceful families.

As would be expected, those families who adapt best to a disability and the accompanying caregiving responsibilities are those with a great number of tangible and intangible resources, such as money, excellent insurance, and support from extended family and friends. Families who demonstrate role flexibility and encourages interdependence, individuation of each member and provide resources for family members to develop their potential typically respond to disability in more adaptive ways. A challenge orientation, rather than a focus on deficit, is also correlated with family adjustment. Of course, families are not able to maintain these positive responses all the time and, like most relapses, counseling may be required to assist the family in regaining their equilibrium. A research study summarized:

> Rigid families tend to be more rigid in their family role responsibilities, more individualistic, and have difficulty in exchanging opinions or sharing emotions openly. Families that can adapt their boundaries and transactional pattern and can explore alternatives are better able to manage and survive the effects of stress.
>
> (Kosciulek & Lustig, 1998, p. 12)

Family goal setting, especially establishing goals that are within the family's control, allow every member of the family to grow and develop. Family and marriage counselors can assist families in dealing with a disability, helping members to openly express their emotions, proactively select personally relevant goals, and deal with societal prejudice and discrimination. Separating the individual from the disability, especially psychiatric disabilities has allowed families to remain close. Counseling provided with a focus on resilience and stress reduction, not concentrating only on negative emotions and burden, helps families to view the disability as an opportunity for growth.

Other researchers have questioned the assumption that all family caregiving is burdensome, stating "Some people find personal meaning and thrive in the caregiving role. Our results caution against a view of caregiving as a uniformly stressful experience" (Elliott, Kurylo, & Rivera, 2002, p. 698). Twenty years ago, a research study on 103 caregivers of a family member with a psychiatric disabilities found many positives, including, pride in doing their best, making a difference in other's lives, contributions to the mental health system, enhanced coping effective, personal growth and development, better perspectives and priorities, and improved personal qualities (Mannion, 1996).

Screen for Abuse and Neglect

Abuse and Neglect of Individuals With Disabilities

- Defining duty to warn.
- The ethical principle of duty to warn is considered more important than maintaining confidentiality.
- IWDs experience twice the rate of sexual, physical, economic abuse, and crime than IWODs.
- IWDs experience longer periods of abuse, by many perpetrators, and for longer periods of time.
- In addition to physical and sexual abuse, IWODs are at risk for disability-specific abuse.
- Disability-specific abuse includes
  1. Medication manipulation;
  2. Withholding medications;
  3. Destruction or withholding of assistive technology (such as wheelchairs);
  4. Neglecting to provide necessary services, such as feeding and toileting;

> 5. Personal care attendants working while intoxicated or high;
> 6. Stealing disability benefits checks.
> - In many institutions and residential schools, staff members choose to ignore or overlook the abuse.

Recognizing abuse, and the legal and ethical responsibility to report the abuse, are essential components in counselors' training and practice. Abuse is typically defined as unwanted "physical, sexual, emotional, economic or psychological abuse that is designed to exert power and control" (Lee, 2009, p. 162). Professional codes of ethics mandate, and all states and territories of the United States now have legal statutes that require, counselors to report abuse. In codes of ethics, reporting abuse is a higher duty than protecting the confidentiality of the client. Remley and Herlihy (2001) clearly described duty to warn:

> A duty to protect from harm arises when someone is especially dependent on others or is some way vulnerable to the choices and actions of others. Persons in a vulnerable position are unable to avoid risk of harm on their own and are dependent on others to intervene on their behalf. When counselors, through their confidential relationship with clients, learn that a vulnerable person is at risk of harm, they have a duty to act to prevent the harm. This is a higher duty than the duty to maintain confidentiality.
> (p. 95)

Before contacting legal authorities or protective services and developing interventions, counselors (with their supervisors) must first recognize that abuse is taking place. Further, counselors can act as advocates for awareness and prevention of abuse. Typically, training programs in all counseling specialties provide training on screening techniques, including the types of abuse, the prevalence of abuse, and risk factors. Training on reporting abuse typically includes the use of policy manuals, consultation with supervisors, accurate record-keeping and documentation, and the need for professional liability insurance.

In spite of the fact that IWDs experience more abuse than IWODs, counselors are not trained to screen or recognize abuse experienced by IWDs. National surveys have found physical and sexual abuse of IWDs to be double the national rate for those without disabilities (National Council on Disability, 2004; Saxton et al., 2006). Another survey found that noninstitutionalized women with disabilities were twice as likely to experience physical violence than nondisabled women

(Albrecht, Seelman, & Bury, 2001). The statistics of prevalence of abuse for IWDs do not reveal the full extent of the harm and exploitation. Many questionnaires ask the simple question, "Have you ever experienced abuse?" and provide a simple choice, yes or no. Therefore, these questionnaire only provide estimates of prevalence. However, IWDs, when compared to IWODs, not only experience higher rates of abuse, but IWDs also experience abuse of increased severity, multiple forms of abuse, longer durations of abuse, and abuse by a greater number of perpetrators. IWDs are at risk for the types of abuse experienced by IWODs; but IWDs are also at risk for experiencing disability-related abuse. More than 25 years ago, Sobsey's study (1994) revealed that individuals with severe intellectual abilities were raped far more often than persons with mild intellectual disabilities. In addition to sexual, physical, economic, and emotional abuse, IWDs are at risk for having necessary services, medications, and equipment withheld.

In institutions for IWDs, such as nursing homes and residential schools for blind and deaf children, there are many adult care providers who prey on the power differential. Abusers choose victims who cannot defend themselves, cannot escape, and who will not be believed if they report the abuse (Sobsey & Doe, 1991, Sobsey & Mansell, 1993). Hospitals, residential schools, and other institutions can be closed environments with little supervision, oversight, or staff accountability. Without locks on bedroom doors, privacy is compromised. It is often easy to isolate a victim. Children with disabilities are especially vulnerable. On the Public Television Service (PBS) program *Paralyzing Fear* (Public Broadcasting Service, 1998), a documentary on the American polio epidemics, an adult woman, who contracted polio as a child, was interviewed. As a small child, she had experienced a long hospitalization, quarantined from everyone, including her parents. One night she was homesick and crying. The nurse came in and said, "If you don't stop crying, I'm going to unplug your ventilator." As the adult woman related this incident for the television program, she cried. In all probability, the nurse would not have unhooked the ventilator, but as a child, the little girl believed that the nurse would. The power differential is often great between children, or anyone with disabilities, and professionals. Many care providers were not subjected to background criminal checks, had committed abuse at one institution, were caught and fired, and simply found another job and continued their abuse. Some children were young enough and their disability so severe that they weren't aware that they were being abused. Many children could not distinguish between the abuse and an examination at the physician's office.

In the oral history of Canadian World War II veterans with spinal cord injuries, they described their experiences in a rehabilitation hospital. One participant noticed the staff's method of controlling "a few cerebral palsy chaps."

There were a few cerebral palsy chaps there. . . . If they transgressed any rule . . . they'd take their wheelchairs away from them and leave them in bed for two weeks.

(Tremblay, 1996, p. 153)

We can assume that the military veterans with spinal cord injuries were not "punished" in the same way. This short excerpt illustrates the greater power differential between men with cerebral palsy (CP) and the hospital staff. CP, in addition to affecting mobility and motor control, can affect communication abilities and can involve intellectual disability. Although, in this excerpt, we know only that these men with CP experienced mobility impairments, it can be seen that the power differential between men with CP and hospital staff was greater than with military veterans. Also, this excerpt is an example of the hierarchy of stigma, both in the difference between physical disabilities and intellectual disabilities and in the difference between two different types of onset. (CP is a congenital disability.) Finally, these veterans probably understood the importance of self-assertion and refused to be punished.

Abuse and Neglect of Individuals With Disabilities

- Before the Americans with Disabilities Act, deaf people did not have access to emergency help.
- IWDs, especially those with severe disabilities are not accorded respect, credibility, or prestige, and, therefore, the legal system is not always quick to believe allegations of abuse. For IWDs, the threshold of belief is much higher.
- Abusers use these excuses:

  1. IWDs, especially those with multiple, severe disabilities, are not quite human and, therefore, abusers do not feel empathy or guilt;
  2. IWDs are thought to be insensitive to pain;
  3. Many personal care attendants feel overworked and underpaid and feel like "I deserve something more";
  4. Abusers are encouraged by the vulnerability of their victims;
  5. Some abusers have claimed that their victims enjoyed their sexual abuse.

A personal care attendant (PCA) has a great deal of power over their employer, the IWD. While most IWDs would prefer living at home and employing a PCA, rather than living in an institution, the PCA does have access to the IWD's body, checkbook, and credit cards. Researchers interviewed men with disabilities about their experiences of abuse. The title of the article is: "We're All Little John Waynes: A Study of Disabled Men's Experiences of Abuse by Personal Care Attendants" (Saxton et al., 2006). One of the men interviewed described his experience of abuse.

> He and I got into the verbal altercation . . . so he thought he would put me in my place by throwing me upon the back of the (wheel)chair, then letting me hang there. I'm on a ventilator. . . . I had already been off for an hour and a half, and I was getting winded. . . . He just kept screaming at me, (forced me) to apologize to him . . . hardly able to breathe, and I'm supposed to apologize to some guy. He really scared the hell out of me.
>
> (p. 4)

Ms. Wheelchair Florida (2014) told of her abuse:

> You stay. You stay and you don't say a word to anyone else. Who would believe you anyway? If you left, no one else will ever love you. You're lucky your broken, imperfect self even found one person to love you. So what if he beats you, refuses to let you have your wheelchair, forces himself on you, and tells you you're worthless. At least he loves you, right?
>
> I stayed for two years. I stayed while he hit me. I stayed while he spit in my face. I stayed while my friends told me I was so lucky to have him in my life. I stayed while other kids at school said he was stupid for dating me because I was just the girl in the wheelchair. I stayed while he screamed at me and pulled my hair. I stayed while my family told me he was such a nice guy. I stayed.

Earlier in the article, she explained why she endured the abuse: "People who are not sexually desirable don't have sex." "You can either be desirable or you can be disabled and since you've already got that wheelchair, I guess we know which path you'll be taking." "Your dad told you that you could be anything you want—you could change the world. But the rest of the world told you that you'll be nothing. You will simply be a drain on society. You can't contribute." Abusers often undermine the self-image of their victims and this is facilitated by a society that demeans IWDs.

The Deaf culture lobbied for the end of "communication violence." Communication violence is the lack of emergency services for deaf people, including visual flashing alarms for warning. Deaf people have been victimized or died when these were not available. Without the availability of qualified Sign Language interpreters, Deaf people were required to write everything about their abuse. Today, laws mandate the availability of these emergency communications. Emergency shelters for those leaving abusive situations must be wheelchair accessible with nurses (typically on call) available to assist with personal needs.

There is a "structural normality of abuse against IWDs" (Smart, 2016a, p. 149), meaning that the abuse is often ignored or not believed. Caregivers often ignore or "turn a blind eye" to the behavior of abusers/colleagues. Saxton and his colleagues asked the men with disabilities why they did not report their abuse. The answer was the same: "The cops won't do anything." Often, IWDs, when they attempted to report their abuse, were told that they needed more medication or that they were lying. Also, due to the fact that IWDs often do not have a great deal of status, prestige, or credibility, the justice system gives lighter and shorter sentences to aperpetrators of crimes against IWDs (Zavirsek, 2002).

Counselors trained in recognizing abuse and neglect of IWDs will be prepared to fulfill the legal and ethical obligations of "duty to report." Understanding the powerful combination of four aspects of crime, neglect, and abuse of IWDs provides a starting point. These four aspects are 1) abuse that is specific to the disability, 2) the lowered thresholds of credibility accorded to IWDs, 3) the pervasive devalued identity of IWDs which allow abusers to excuse themselves, and 4) the living arrangements of IWDs, often in institutions, which do not protect the safety and privacy of IWDs.

Recognize Activism and Advocacy as Adaptive Behaviors

Activism and Advocacy Are Adaptive Behaviors for Many IWDs

- Typically, activism goes beyond personal needs, promoting civil rights for all IWDs.
- IWDs are protected by fragile laws that often are not enforced.
- Many IWDs feel that their advocacy and activism has made them better people.
- Many disability advocacy groups train IWDs in activism.
- According to a large, national survey, two-thirds of IWDs believe that the Americans with Disabilities Act has improved their lives.

Self-advocacy is a part of the lives of most IWDs, simply because they must respond to pervasive and generalized prejudice and discrimination, which often goes unnoticed by the general culture. For some IWDs, advocacy and activism goes beyond personal, individualized needs, promoting providing civil rights, access to opportunities, and the deconstruction of unnecessary barriers for all IWDs. As noted previously, IWDs are protected by laws that are fragile, vague, and often poorly enforced. Disability advocacy on an individual level requires tenacity and ego strength to push for accommodations and civil rights. Eric Weihenmayer (2001) told of his mother's advocacy and persistence, and expressed his gratitude to her. As a child, Weihenmayer was gradually losing his vision and school administrators tried to refuse him admittance.

> I don't know how my mother found the strength to oppose the world. Maybe it's simply a mother's primal instinct to nurture and defend her child. She was as unprepared as the administrators sitting across from us. Somehow, though, she believed in me. I was just a little boy with my ink-smudged nose pressed against the page. I had nothing yet to prove myself, so how she saw strength, opportunity, and promise, while other people saw problems, obstacles, and limits, I'll never know for sure.
>
> (p. 14)

The first and last sentence express the same idea—"I don't know how my mother found the strength." Many adults with congenital disabilities look back on their childhoods and express both amazement and gratitude for parents who demanded (and received) services. Weihenmayer's short paragraph showed that his mother "opposed the world" when she was "unprepared." The expression "opposed the world" gives an indication of the widespread lack of opportunity for IWDs. Children with congenital disabilities have "nothing to prove" to themselves and these children must rely on parents to act as their advocates. Until recently, there has been little training in advocacy for parents of children with disabilities or adults with disabilities

Judith Huemann contracted polio when she was 18 months old and grew up in Brooklyn, New York. Due to the effects of the polio, Huemann uses a wheelchair. She is one of the most active and successful disability advocates, both on the national and international level. In 1993, Huemann was named assistant secretary for the Office of Special Education and Rehabilitation Services (OSERS) for the US government. Huemann tells of her childhood filled with her mother's advocacy efforts on her behalf, including fighting to have her daughter admitted to mainstream public elementary school. After graduation from Long Island University in 1969 and obtaining a teaching license, New York school districts would not hire Huemann because of her wheelchair. Before the enactment of the Americans with Disabilities Act, public buildings were not accessible. "Because Heumann took her oral, written, and medical examinations in buildings that were physically inaccessible, she had to be carried up and down the stairs" (Fleischer & Zames, 2001, p. 72). One of Huemann's first acts of self-advocacy was publishing a newspaper article entitled; "You Can Be President of the United States with Polio, but You Can't Teach School." Referring to President Franklin Roosevelt, in a very public way to a wide audience, she showed the irrationality of the New York school system for refusing her a teaching position Huemann was eventually hired as a teacher.

Today, the advocacy efforts of Eric Weihenmayer's mother and Judith Huemann's parents would probably not be necessary because they won their battles and, in winning these battles, educational and employment opportunities are becoming increasingly available to IWDs. These parents, and others like them, are considered "pioneers" in the disability rights community.

Others relate the way in which their disability advocacy efforts have made them better people. In the book, *Far From the Tree*, the author (Solomon, 2012) related the experience of parents Sara and David whose son was born with a severe congenital disability. The diagnostic process was long, requiring many different types of tests, including an EEG. An EEG measures and records electric activity in the brain.

> Sara and David took Jamie for an EEG. The EEG technician was digging into Jamie's skull as she applied the electrodes. "That's when we became advocates," David explained. "That's when we said, 'No goddammit! You are not going to do that with our child.' That was a first; I had always been a well-behaved person who followed the rules. Jamie has made me a far better lawyer. He has forced me to develop advocacy skills that have sprung from passion as opposed to intellectual argument."
>
> (p. 640)

The father, David, can pinpoint the exact point at which he became a disability advocate, not only for his child, but for others and David considers his disability advocacy to have made him "a far better lawyer."

Self-descriptions of advocates often illustrate their depth of conviction: Nancy is a mother of two children with autism, she described herself and 19 years of advocacy.

> Having advocated and fought for these kids now for 19 years, my entire personality has changed. I'm quick to pick a fight; I'm argumentative. You don't cross me. I have to do what I have to do, and I'm going to get what I want. I was never like that before.
>
> (Solomon, 2012, p. 238)

Advocacy can be an individual response to a disability which, in addition to gaining rights, services, and opportunities for IWDs, acts as a positive adaption to the disability. Disability rights movements are composed of many individuals, most with disabilities, who publicly and unitedly promote the rights of IWDs. Some of these large groups are based on a single type of disability, such as ASD (Autism Spectrum Disorder) while other advocacy groups have a cross-disability focus, meaning that rights and opportunities for individuals with all types of disabilities are promoted. The electronic media have empowered these rights movements.

Social support groups often act as catalysts for self-advocacy. Learning advocacy skills, through participation in support groups, occurs in two steps: first, the IWD, or their family, becomes aware, for the first time, that there are many others with the same type of disability; and second, the advocacy and self-efficacy skills of other IWDs are modeled and taught. In the following excerpt, a mother of a young children with a disability followed this two-step process. Note that depth of amazement ("stunned wonder") at learning that other people live successfully with this type of disability, and then note the specific advocacy skills the mother learns.

> A mother of a 2-year-old boy with dwarfism who has begun attending the Little People of America event summed this up when she said to with stunned wonder, "There are a lot of them!" Until this beloved child unexpectedly entered her family, she had no idea that achondroplasia is the most common form of short stature or that most people with the condition have average-size parents. More important, she did not know how to request the accommodations, access the service, enter the communities, or use the laws that he needs to make his way through life. But because he is hers and she loves him, she will learn a lot about disability.
>
> (Garland-Thomson, 2016)

Due to the fact that achondroplasia is a relatively low-incidence disability (meaning that not many people have this type of disability) it is necessary to attend national social support groups, such as The Little People of America.

At national or regional meetings, groups of large numbers, all with the same disability, meet face-to-face.

Max Cleland is a US senator who has served on the Senate Armed Services Committee. As a member of the Georgia State Senate, he wrote the state law for accessibility to public buildings. A Vietnam veteran who is a triple amputee, he has advocated for IWDs and military veterans at a high level of government with a great deal of visibility. Cleland wrote a book, *Strong at Broken Places* (1980), in which he described the way in he which he acquired his disability, in 1968 in Vietnam: "Then I saw the grenade. It was where the chopper had lifted off. It must be mine, I bent down to pick up the grenade. A blinding explosion threw me backwards."

The American with Disabilities Act (1990) and the Amendments (2008) have changed the lives of IWDs, resulting in a cohort group of IWDs who were born after 1990 and, therefore, have no memory or experience with widespread prejudice, discrimination, or institutionalization. Frieden (2010) surveyed leaders in the disability community from all 50 states and concluded that most IWDs believed that the ADA improved their lives.

> Overall, 90 percent of survey respondents believe that the quality of life for people with disabilities in communities across the United States has improved greatly since the passage of the ADA. Two thirds of survey respondents with disabilities believe the ADA legislation has had more influence on their lives than any other social, cultural, or legislative change in the last 20 years.

Look for Transcendence

Maslow's Theory of Transcendence

- Maslow believed in the vast potential of human capacity.
- Transcendence is sometimes referred to as "self-actualization."
- To achieve transcendence, Maslow believed that individuals must be in a supportive environment.

As a humanist psychologist, Abraham Maslow did not conceptualize human development in biological, chronological terms, or as a series of developmental tasks to be accomplished. Because Maslow was a humanist, he believed in the vast potential of humans and their capacity, indeed, their innate need to reach their full potential (Smart, 2012). Reaching one's full potential is termed "self-actualization" and "given a supportive environment, humans naturally mature into trouble-free, effective adults. Humanists substitute the word 'striving' for 'development,' which indicates that self-actualization is the end goal" (Smart, 2012, p. 125). Self-actualization, therefore, is the end goal, rather than the reduction of pain or tension, or seeking the greatest degree of pleasure. Maslow believed in the innate goodness of humans.

Maslow's Hierarchy of Needs

- Physical needs, such as oxygen, water, food, sleep, and sex.
- Safety needs such as stability, safety, and security.
- Affiliation needs, including a sense of being loved and accepted and a sense of belonging.
- Esteem needs: the individual bases their self-identity on competencies.
- Transcendence or self-actualization in which the individual reaches the pinnacle of their potential.

Maslow developed a "hierarchy of needs," in which there are five levels (Maslow, 1968). The lowest level is *physiological needs*, including water, food, oxygen, sleep, and sex. (Note: There is some debate if sex if an actual physiological need.) The second level is termed *safety needs* and includes security, protection, stability, and freedom from fear and chaos. The third level is *affiliation and acceptance*, meaning the individual feels loved and accepted and feels a sense of belonging. The fourth level is *esteem needs* in which the individual bases their self-identity on competencies. The fifth level is *self-actualization* in which the individual reaches the pinnacle of his abilities. The first two levels, are termed deficit needs because if these needs are not met, the individual's life is dominated with fulfilling these needs. The last three levels are considered to be growth needs because meeting these needs leads to satisfaction and individual improvement and expansion. The needs of one level must be met before the individual can progress to filling the needs of the next level. After these lower level needs are met, the needs of the next higher level become motivating. As with the onset or diagnosis of a disability, no one can totally predict that they will never be faced with meeting deficit needs (Maslow, 1970, 1971).

Reed (1991) summarized Maslow's concept of transcendence:

There is a universal human desire for transcendence and connectedness. Transcendence is defined as a level of awareness that exceeds ordinary, physical boundaries and limitations, yet allows the individual to achieve new perspectives and experiences. Awareness of self-transcendence refers to the developmental maturity whereby there is an expansion of self-boundaries and an orientation toward broadened life perspectives and purposes.

(p. 64)

Maslow's theory of development can be applied to other cultures because he acknowledged the basic humanity of everyone by recognizing basic biological needs. Of course, societies and cultures have different *methods* of fulfilling these needs, but all of humanity have biological and security needs. The higher levels of needs in Maslow's theory are both defined and met in individual ways, some of which are culturally influenced.

As with the other notable developmental theorists, Maslow never considered IWDs in his theory (Smart, 2012). However, Maslow's theory of human development has the capability, depth, and breadth to include IWDs (Smart, 2012). Maslow did not think that biological needs, after they have been met, act as motivators to reach higher levels of development. Freud, in contrast, thought biological urges and instincts influenced behavior throughout the lifespan. Also, Maslow acknowledged the importance of societal and social support, but he defined the highest levels of development as self-determined and self-evaluated. In contrast, Erik Erikson, another notable developmental theorist, considered higher levels of development to be motivated by the individual's need and desire to meet socially mandated expectations.

Maslow's Concept of Self-Actualization or Transcendence

The final level of needs (and development) is more difficult to describe because each individual determines both what they want and how they will reach these goals. In his later writing, Maslow used the terms "self-actualization" and "transcendence" interchangeably. Self-actualization is a combination of maturity, creativity, happiness, wisdom, autonomy, independence, and a concern for others. Concern for others includes a sense of justice, morality, and ethics, all of which they apply to others and themselves. Therefore, self-actualized individuals hold themselves accountable for their behavior. Due to the fact that they are highly independent, individuated, and autonomous, they are not threatened by the achievement of others. Transcendence includes a positive outlook, with active perseverance, initiation of goal-directed activities, and a challenge orientation. Typically, self-actualized individuals have some all-consuming passion in life, such as human rights or some creative or artistic endeavor (Maslow, 1971). Maslow is famous for this statement: "A first rate soup is better than second-rate poetry," expressing the idea that there is creativity, productivity, and contribution in all human endeavors. Self-actualizers enjoy doing something for its own sake, rather than as a means to an end and this trait frees the individual from dependence on external judgments, whether positive or negative.

Self-actualization includes the ability to feel the full range of emotions, including pain, fear, and the stress of ambiguity. They focus on goals, taking concrete steps. Believing in continual learning, being open to inspiration and new ideas are part of self-actualization or transcendence.

Self-actualized individuals are able to forge and maintain deeply intimate and loving relationships with others, all without being possessive of others. Empathy and the ability to share the experiences of others are characteristics of self-actualized people. They are able to repair damaged relationships, building stronger bonds. These individuals demonstrate skill in mobilizing social support systems and reciprocating when others require assistance. Self-actualizers tend to be more democratic, meaning that they can associate with all types of individuals (Maslow, 1968, 1970, 1971).

Those who are self-actualized do have weaknesses; but a combination of traits and abilities allow them to change or simply accept these weaknesses. This combination of traits and abilities includes their greater self-knowledge and self-awareness of their motives, needs, and perceptions and their ability to take responsibility for their behavior. Self-actualized individuals also are less prone to impose their own standards and perceptions upon others. Finally, self-actualizers are skilled at conceptualizing and implementing "work-arounds," or alternatives or compensations to their shortcomings. If circumstances cannot be changed, self-actualizers are able to accept this.

A disability scholar, Carolyn Vash (Vash, 1981; Vash & Crewe, 2004), applied Maslow's concept of transcendence to IWDs, including all of the traits and capacities of Maslow's description of self-actualization, but adding several disability-specific characteristics.

Transcendence in Individuals With Disabilities

Transcendence

- Goes beyond acceptance of disability.
- The IWD feels that their life is better with the disability.
- Incorporates all of the aspects of Maslow's definition of transcendence and includes other disability-specific elements.
- The IWD often feels that the disability is a gift.

- At times, transcendence is associated with religious and spiritual ideals, but not always.
- The IWD typically:

Takes pride in the mastery of the disability;
Finds meaning and purpose in the disability;
Discovers personal strengths;
Seeks out new experiences;
Reevaluates goals and identities;
Assists other IWDs.

Not all IWDs reach the stage of transcendence; nonetheless, some do. Re-reading the paragraphs describing the various attributes of self-actualized individuals or individuals who have reached transcendence we can easily see that these individuals have reached a highly developed stage. It may follow that most IWODs cannot conceptualize IWDs as having these traits, perhaps because IWDs are thought to be somehow emotionally damaged due to their disabilities, continuously depressed, bitter, and angry. There is a time-worn expression, "Twisted body, twisted mind." This prejudicial (and false) overgeneralization is presently being discounted and discarded.

Re-reading Reed's (1991) description of transcendence, it is apparent that IWDs may have *more* opportunities for transcendence due to their disabilities. Following are a few first-person accounts of reaching transcendence. Note that in all these accounts, achieving transcendence was neither easy nor quick. For a woman with an amputated arm, it took 25 years to look closely at her arm, and a man with a spinal cord injury described an eight-year journey. Nonetheless, with the exception of Joan Tollifson, who has a congenital disability, it can be seen that all of these disabilities had an acute, traumatic onset, necessitating a sudden change in just about everything in these individuals' lives.

Joan Tollifson, born with a congenital limb deficiency accepted society's prejudice and discrimination as self-identifiers and abused alcohol. ("I drank to die.") Tollifson avoided looking at her amputated arm, stating, "I remember the first time I actually looked closely at my arm without looking away. I was twenty-five years old at the time" (1997, p. 106). She described her transcendence as first refusing to accept society's prejudice and discrimination and second as seeing her disability as a gift and a possibility for freedom and possibility.

> Being disabled is a deep wound, a source of pain. But like all wounds, it is also a gift. As Eastern wisdom has always known, it is hard to tell good luck from bad luck. . . . Having one arm is an endless koan. It is what it is, which is unknowable, and it attracts a lot of ideas, stories, and images. Caught up in the negative story, I felt ashamed, incomplete, and not okay. I drank to die. Later on, caught up in a more positive story, I felt pride and a sense of identity. . . . In a way, I have gone back to the innocence of a baby. When little babies encounter my arm—the arm that ends just below the elbow—it is seen as just another interesting shape to explore and put into their mouths. There is nothing scary or taboo about it. . . . Not labeling what appears as either a deficit or an asset, perfect or imperfect, beautiful or ugly, but wondering openly without conclusion, without trying to get somewhere else. In such open being there is freedom and possibility for the new, even in the mist of what we call imperfection or limitation. I don't mean that the injustices or pain circumstances disappear, but they no longer bind us in the way they did.
>
> (1997, p. 111)

A koan in Zen Buddhism is a paradox that is used to meditate on to gain enlightenment.

At another point in her story, Tollifson recognizes that ideal of physical perfection is counterfeit, calling perfection "cardboard." "Imperfection is the essence of being organic and alive. Organic life is vulnerable. . . . Cardboard ideals of perfection are flat and pale by comparison (1997, p. 112).

In Stockbridge, England, Alex Lewis became a triple amputee in less than a month and yet he remarked that the "year of illness was the most brilliant of his life" (de Freytas-Tamura, 2017). In a *New York Times* article, Lewis' experience is recounted:

> Alex Lewis had been enjoying pints of Guinness with friends one cold evening when his throat started feeling scratchy and he came down with the flu. Or so he thought.
>
> Days later, he was fighting for his life.
>
> A mysterious bacterium wormed its way into his body, tearing away at his flesh and turning his skin purplish-black. His lips disintegrated, leaving a gaping hole where his mouth had been.
>
> In less than a month, he lost his feet, then his legs and his left arm, physically becoming half the man he used to be. He was unrecognizable to many around him, including his 2-year-old son, who was too scared to hug him.

When Lewis left the hospital, he realized that he needed to change his "laid-back" attitude and started to take on the responsibility of the paperwork for the two pubs, the catering service, and the bakery that he and his wife owned. She switched roles with her husband and while he managed the paperwork, she managed other aspects of their businesses. One of the idiosyncratic losses Lewis felt deeply was his inability to drink a great deal of alcohol.

> Now that his body weight—around 84 pounds—is less than half than it used to be, he can't have more than a few pints. I know people will say, "If you're a big drinker, you've got hollow legs," and I think there's a bit of truth to that.

Staying sober has other benefits:

> A drunk in a wheelchair is not a good thing, not very clever, especially if you've got no arms. It's one thing to fall out of a wheelchair when you have arms, but it's another thing when you've got no arms and, you know, just face plant.

The British National Health Service (NHS) has paid some of his medical expenses, including costs of making his home accessible, prostheses, and rehabilitation costs. In addition, Lewis has calculated the costs that he and his wife will pay for disability costs that are not covered by NHS and, therefore, set up a trust to help cover these costs. Lewis has gone to Greenland on a kayaking trip with British military veterans who are amputees. His conclusion and description of transcendence was succinct: "I try to get on with it."

A sense of humor is often part of transcendence. An Australian motivational speaker, Nick Vujicic, was born without arms and legs. In a speech presented in Laguna Beach, California, in 2006 (Basheda, 2006) Nick's sense of humor was evident. Nonetheless, he prefaced his speech with this statement "I'm not here to say I understand your pain" (p. 1). His parents had formed a small church in Australia and the members of the congregation mourned when he was born. But Vujicic does not mourn or grieve about his disability; part of his response is due to his sense of humor. During his international speaking tours, people ask what happened to him. Nick has a one-word reply: "CIGARETTES!!!" At the end of his speeches, Vijicic threatens his audience, "If you run fast, I'm going to get someone to throw me at you" (p. 7). He drives a car with computerized controls and Nick likes to drive up to a stoplight, catch the eye of another driver stopped at the light, and then turn completely around in the driver's seat. The look of amazement on the other driver's face is amusing to Vijicic. The title of the newspaper article describing his speech was, "No Arms, No Legs—No Worries."

In a research study, short statements illustrate differing aspects of transcendence of a disability. Participant 59 felt that he has had more experiences since the acquisition of his spinal cord injury (SCI):

> My spinal cord injury has allowed me to participate in activities that I feel I never would have had if it had not happened. I have completed 11 marathons, travel nationally playing wheelchair rugby and earned a master's degree since my injury 13 years ago. I feel that I never would have done these things had my SCI never happened.
> (Graf, Marini, & Blankenship, 2009, p. 30)

The researchers summarized some of the data, stating:

> Life learning was discussed by 16 participants. Many of them described a shifting of values and greater appreciation for the "simpler things in life" (Participant 6). They discussed the reevaluation of their lives which moved them to become more observant, more grateful, and better people. "I've learned the value of simple, everyday things like being able to get dressed and go shopping, and I've been blessed with the ability to see many hidden beauties that most people would overlook in their busy lives!" (Participant 27). Participant 14 wrote, "living with disability causes a person to reevaluate their priorities in life. Much of what was important before acquiring a disability becomes trivial afterward." Finally, Participant 72 wrote, "By acquiring a disability I began a tough journey for eight years. The journey itself, however, has made me a better person and allowed me to see life more clearly."
> (Graf, Marini, & Blankenship, 2009, p. 33)

Individuals with psychiatric disabilities also experience transcendence. A woman of an adult son told of their experience of transcendence, both for her son and for herself, as a caregiver.

> My son has great willpower. He has graduated from college, also got his master's degree and has been working as a chemist for the past two years. My son has been hospitalized six times (four of which were court commitments) and he has been homeless. Through my stubbornness we rescued him from the streets. He is now so well and enjoying life. It gives me gratification that I never gave up hope.
> (Marsh & Lefly, 1996, p. 10)

A woman with a psychiatric disability describes far-reaching effects of her self-actualization. Note the number of times she refers to her self-image in this short excerpt. Also note the way in which she separates the disability from the process of becoming well.

> The illness itself has not had any good effects, but the process of getting healthier has, especially on my spirituality, my self-image, my character, and personal qualities. Now I have a greater sense of serenity, self-liking, wonder at the world, and caring for myself and others.
>
> (Marsh & Lefly, 1996, p. 10)

This woman's description of the results of "becoming healthier" could be a textbook definition of transcendence and self-actualization.

Collaboration With Medical Providers

The Importance of Counseling-Medical Collaboration

- There are emotional and social aspects to all disabilities.
- No one profession can serve all the needs of individuals with disabilities.
- Counseling-medical collaboration is humane, ethical, and cost-saving.
- Counselors will be required to learn about the medical aspects of disability and physicians will be required to learn about the various specialty areas and theoretical orientations of counseling.

There are social and emotional aspects to all disabilities and all disabilities have physical qualities. IWDs have multiple roles, identities, and functions and, therefore, they want access to counseling services, in the same way as IWODs seek counseling. Concerns with career development, relationships, sexuality and gender identity, and spirituality, to name a few, are issues for IWDs. Due to the twin realities of the greater number of IWDs and their rising expectations for services from counselors, the training, education, and clinical practice of counseling will evolve to address the needs of IWDs. The counseling professions have a collective responsibility to serve IWDs, and it follows that counselors will develop collaborative relationships with medical care providers.

In Chapter Three, the various Models of Disability were described and one of the conclusions drawn was the need for many types of professionals to serve

IWDs. Each Model of Disability has a different definition of disability, requiring varying types of treatments. Two Models of Disability, the Moral/Religious and the Biomedical did not, in the past, require professional collaboration since only one type of profession was tasked with responding to all the needs of IWDs. In the Moral/Religious Model, it was spiritual advisors such as priests, ministers, and pastors, and in the Biomedical Model physicians were tasked with providing all services for IWDs. It is the greater society that places certain responsibilities upon professions and, today, it is obvious that no single profession, regardless of how specialized and skilled, can serve all the needs of IWDs. In the following excerpts, two men with disabilities received excellent medical care, but also would have benefitted from counseling. The first man, Jack Hofsiss, experienced a diving accident in a swimming pool which resulted in his paralysis.

> The one thing that surprised me through all of this was the real lack of either interest or concern about depression after an accident. There is much more concern about your physical therapy, making sure your lungs are clear, all the things that might have physically happened to you. "Can you move this? Can you feel that?" But the emotional things, no . . . help was offered.
>
> (Hofsiss & Laffey, 1993, p. 86)

In a chapter entitled, "Never Enough Time: How Medical Residents Manage a Scarce Resource," the authors (Yoels & Clair, 1998) observed the frustration of a patient who is "cut short" and ignored by a resident physician and, as noted in the chapter title, the physician does not have the time (or training) to address the patient's "personal, emotional responses." In the following excerpt, the first visit of a medical resident to a Vietnam combat veteran is recorded.

> The patient has suffered war wounds including major facial disfigurement. Early in the exam the doctor comments on the patient's war wound and says he must have taken quite a while to get over that. The patient takes an audible breath, hesitates, and then states that he had to come to terms with it as part of life, reflecting his personal, emotional responses to the event, in short, the meaning of the wounds for him. The resident immediately cuts him short by saying, "I meant physically." The examination then proceeded along the rather narrow tracks "constructed by the biomedical diagnostic model."
>
> (p. 136)

Both of these individuals with acute, traumatic onset disabilities would have benefitted from counseling. Counselors who are trained in disability issues and who are skilled in collaboration with physicians could have provided flexible care packages, benefitting both the patients and the physicians. Such counseling would have been ethical and humane, but also probably would have resulted in cost-saving. The fact that the events described in these short excerpts occurred years previously is an indicator that the lack of attention to their emotional needs during the period of the medical stabilization was deeply felt for a long period of time.

Typically, counselors have not engaged in professional collaboration with physicians, and training, supervised practice, and experience may be necessary to help counselors bridge the world of counseling to the world of medicine. On the other hand, the successful therapeutic combination of talk therapy and medication has been a step toward physician-counselor collaboration. Physician-counselor collaboration will require physicians to understand some basic knowledge with counseling practices and counselors will need to learn some medical aspects of disabilities and their treatment. For example, for many types of disabilities, daily treatment compliance is essential, but many disability management techniques are difficult, at times painful, and require detailed and complicated doses or procedures. Strict diets, physical activity, and physical therapy are often daily requirements for many types of disabilities. Nonetheless, small complications can lead to hospitalization and complications are the rule rather than the exception (Harris, Heller, & Schindler, 2012). In a book entitled *Disability Through the Life Course*, specific suggestions for counselors facilitating disability management compliance using cognitive behavioral therapy were provided.

> Non-compliance may be due to impaired perceived treatment efficacy. From the patient's perspective, he or she is making sacrifices now to protect against something bad happening in the future. From this point of view, there may be little tangible sense of how his efforts are making a positive difference from one day to the next. It is understandable that some people may then choose to ignore the demands of their treatment regime now and take a gamble on the future. If patients do not believe that a recommended action, such as taking medications, is contributing an observable, positive, short term impact, they will do not do it. If they believe the prescribed treatments are making it worse, they will be reluctant to cooperate (Baird & Clarke, 2012, p. 396). This is especially important to mental illness, such as depression, when the client stops taking meds when feeling better or any other relapsing disability.
>
> (Harris, Heller, & Schindler, 2012)

To summarize, emotional reactions often influence an IWD's compliance. The degree of adherence is also related to perceived self-efficacy. Regardless of physicians' medical skills, the patient may not comply with treatment. The skills that counselors bring to these types of collaboration include eliciting the IWD's perception of the disability, understanding the perception of the medical treatment, and focusing on identifying markers of treatment outcomes. Reading the preceding excerpt, it can be seen that different types of disability courses often act as predictors of medical/treatment compliance. Individuals with relapsing or episodic course disabilities are more prone to noncompliance because unpredictability results in stress, which often results in denial. Relapsing or episodic disabilities are a source of unpredictability and the stress of worrying about the onset of an episode of symptom exacerbation is, itself, a stressor. While not exactly full-blown symptoms, fluctuating energy levels and fatigue are part of episodic disabilities. Counselors understand that individuals with relapsing or episodic course disabilities often do not receive a great deal of support from family and colleagues, often hearing remarks such as "But you've been so well for so long." Even individuals with these types of disabilities experience surprise and disbelief when a relapse occurs. Finally, counselors are trained to assist clients with dealing with relapses, learning from each episode, securing the necessary assistance and supports, and reducing both the frequency and duration of the episodes.

This rather lengthy explanation of disabilities with one type of course, relapsing or episodic, aids in understanding 1) the necessity of strict adherence to disability treatment regimens and the serious nature of noncompliance; 2) the emotional response of the individual to these treatment regimens; and 3) the successful outcomes, and their predictors, of counseling techniques in aiding clients with treatment compliance. Each type of disability, with differing courses and varying treatment regimens, can be integrated into both medical and counseling services. When both physicians and counselors understand the same case conceptualization, collaboration can be strengthened by consistent treatment goals.

Successful case management will require professionals on teams to forge working relationships with other professionals and, further, many of these professionals may never have worked together. For example, engineers, technologists, and architects often do not understand the emotional needs of IWDs, but these professionals greatly increase the quality of life for many IWDs. In terms of individual IWDs, the expertise and skill (not to mention the cost) of these professionals might be wasted if a counselor does not address the emotional needs and desires of the IWD. In addition to providing a more complete treatment package for clients, incorporating counselors on treatment teams will result in lowered health care costs.

A cover article in an American weekly newsmagazine, *Time* (2006, October 2), demonstrated the effectiveness of using both medical and counseling services, in this case, a psychologist. Michael Weisskopf, a senior reporter for *Time* magazine, was reporting on the Iraq war in Bagdad. One night while riding in a Humvee with three soldiers, a grenade was thrown into the Humvee, and, unthinkingly, Weisskopf picked it up. Consequently, he saved four lives (including his own) and lost most of his right hand. Weisskopf's article was entitled, "How I Lost My Hand and Found My Life." Obviously, he came to view his gains greater than the loss of his hand. The following excerpt describes Weisskopf's hospitalization at a Veterans Affairs Hospital and shows the way in which case collaboration between physicians, a psychologist, and a prosthetist helped Weisskopf find his life. Counseling by the psychologist provided the key to Weisskopf's acceptance of his disability.

> As I tossed and turned in the early hours of Independence Day (July 4), the simple truth of the psychologist's words hit me. It was true: I was mad at myself . . . and it was that anger that was preventing me from savoring the achievement of a lifetime: saving my own skin and that of three others. My failure to get rid of the grenade before it exploded was only the first in a long list of wrongs I would have to pardon before I could finally put the ordeal behind me.
>
> I had gone to Iraq for adventure and glory, discounting the interests of family and friends.
>
> I had blithely ridden into danger with little to gain journalistically.
>
> I had focused more on the loss of my hand than on the higher importance of preserving life.
>
> (p. 37)

The three soldiers were probably happy that Weisskopf was on the Humvee, whatever the reason. Later, Weisskopf describes the way in which assistive technology (AT), a prosthetic hand, contributed to his recovery.

> Before Iraq, the technology of arm prostheses hadn't changed much since World War II. The tiny population of amputees created little market incentive. Miquelez [the prosthetist] used the burst in demand from Walter Reed [Hospital] to lean on manufacturers for progress. Before long, he was outfitting Iraq war amputees with an electronic hand that opened and closed 2½ times faster and could be programmed to function at different speeds and grip strengths.

The cosmetic arts also had improved. I received a silicone hand that was so lifelike it passed for real in social settings. But Pretty Boy, as I called it, kept tearing and afforded the precision of a boxing glove. It was too spongy to grasp anything small and too slippery to hold most objects for long.

Function was only part of the problem. The idea of trying to pass had begun to trouble me. It made me feel as if I had something to hide or to be ashamed of. When I started to go bald, I shaved my head. No comb-overs, transplants or toupees for me. So why try to conceal a handicap? I was proud of how I had lost my hand. The stump had a story to tell.

(p. 37)

Conclusion

In the past, the counseling professions have shown limited collective commitment to providing services to clients with disabilities (CWDs), and, because of this, there are few practice guidelines available. This lack of commitment is shown by the scant mention of CWDs in codes of ethics, academic accreditation guidelines, and the absence of disability education. The counseling profession, with the exception of the specialty of rehabilitation counseling, simply assumes that there are no clients with disabilities or that general counseling techniques and skills are sufficient for working with CWDs. In contrast, most counseling educational/training programs provide training for working with clients of differing cultural, ethnic, and linguistic groups, supported and reinforced by accreditation guidelines, graduation requirements, codes of ethics, and eligibility requirements for licensure and certification. In the future, it is hoped, that counseling CWDs will not be peripheral to the counseling professions, but rather, achieve parity with multicultural counseling.

References

Ablon, J. (1989). Families with dwarf children. In S. C. Hey, G. Kiger, & D. Evans (Eds.), *The changing world of impaired and disabled people in society* (pp. 350–358). Salem, OR: Society for Disability Studies and Willamette University.

Accordino, M. P., Porter, D. F., & Moore, T. (2001). Deinstitutionalization of persons with severe mental illness: Context and consequences. *Journal of Rehabilitation, 67,* 16–21.

Albrecht, G. L., Seelman, K. D., & Bury, M. (Eds.) (2001). *Handbook of disability studies.* Thousand Oaks, CA: Sage.

Americans with Disabilities Act Amendments of 2008, 42 U.S.C. 12101 *et seq.* Retrieved from www.usdoj.gov/crt/adaaa.cfm Retrieved 02-26-2018.

Americans with Disabilities Act of 1990, 42 U.S.C. 12101 *et seq.* Retrieved from www.usdoj.gov/crt/ada.homal.htm

Baird, D. E., & Clarke, D. M. (2012). Diabetes mellitus. In P. Kennedy (Ed.), *The Oxford handbook of rehabilitation psychology* (pp. 387–413). New York, NY: Oxford University.

Barnes, C. (2012). The social model of disability: Valuable or irrelevant? In N. Watson, A. Roulstone, & C. Thomas (Eds.), *The Routledge handbook of disability studies* (pp. 12–29). London: Routledge.

Basheda, L. (2006, July). No arms, no legs—no worries. *Orange County Register*, 1, 7.

Braddock, D., & Hemp, R. (2006). Growth of US public spending for intellectual/developmental disabilities slowed down 2002–04. *Mental Retardation, 44*(1), 77–80.

Byrd, E. K., & Elliott, T. R. (1988). Media and disability: A discussion of the research. In H. E. Yuker (Ed.), *Attitudes toward persons with disabilities* (pp. 82–95). New York, NY: Springer.

Cleland, M. (1980). *Strong at broken places*. New York, NY: Berkeley.

Crenshaw, K. (2017). Retrieved from www.law.columbia.edu/news/2017/06/kimberle-crenshaw-intersectionality Retrieved 02–26–2018

deFreytas-Tamura, K. (2017, February 3). For quadruple amputee, years of illness "was the most brilliant." *New York Times*.

Elliott, T. R., Kurylo, M., & Rivera, P. (2002). Positive growth following acquired physical disability. In C. R. Synder & S. Lopez (Eds.), *Handbook of positive psychology* (pp. 678–699). New York, NY: Oxford University Press.

Elliott, T. R., & Shewchuk, R. M. (2003). Social problem-solving abilities and distress among family members assuming a caregiving role. *British Journal of Health Psychology, 8*, 159–163.

Ferguson, P. M., & Nusbaum, E. (2012). Disability studies: What is it and what difference does it make? *Research & Practice for Persons with Severe Disabilities, 37*, 70–80.

Fine, M., & Asch, A. (1988). *Women and disabilities: Essays in psychology, culture, and politics*. Philadelphia, PA: Temple University.

Fleischer, D. Z., & Zames, F. (2001). *The disability rights movement: From charity to confrontation*. Philadelphia, PA: Temple University.

Frese, F. (1997). Twelve aspects of coping for persons with serious and persistent mental illness. In F. Spaniol, C. Gange, & M. Hoehler (Eds.), *Psychological and social aspects of psychiatric disability*. Boston, MA: Center for Psychiatric Rehabilitation, Boston University.

Frieden, L. (2010, July 26). Impact of the ADA: Results from the 20th anniversary survey. Retrieved from www.southwestada.org/html/whatsnew/whats_new.html

Garland-Thomson, R. (2017, August 19). Becoming disabled: Roughly one in five Americans lives with a disability. So where is our pride movement? *New York Times*.

Graf, N. M., Marini, I., & Blankenship, C. J. (2009). One hundred words about disability. *Journal of Rehabilitation, 75*, 25–34.

Grob, G. N. (1992). Mental health policies in the America: Myths and realities. *Health Affairs, 11*(3), 7–22.

Harris, S. P., Heller, T., & Schindler, A. (2012). Introduction, background, and history. In R. Heller & S. P. Harris (Eds.), *Disability through the life course* (pp. 1–37). Thousand Oaks, CA: Sage.

Hawking, J. (2007). *Travelling to infinity: My life with Stephen*. Richmond: Alma.

Hofsiss, J., & Laffey M. (1993). Jack Hofsiss and Maureen Laffey. In J. K. Smith & G. Plimpton (Eds.), *Chronicles of courage: Very special artists* (pp. 78–87). New York, NY: Penguin Random House.

Hunt, B., Matthews, C., Milson, A., & Lemmel, J. (2006). Lesbians with physical disabilities: A qualitative study of their experiences with counseling. *Journal of Counseling and Development, 84*, 163–173.

Hunt, B., Milsom, A., & Matthew, C. R. (2009). Partner-related rehabilitation experiences of lesbians with physical disabilities: A qualitative study. *Rehabilitation Counseling Bulletin, 52*, 167–178.

Kelsey, D. J., & Smart, J. F. (2012). Social justice, disability, and rehabilitation education. *Rehabilitation Research, Policy, and Education, 26*, 231–240.

Kosciulek, J. F., & Lustig, D. C. (1998). Predicting family adaptation from brain-injured family stress. *Journal of Applied Rehabilitation, 29,* 8–12.

Lee, R. W. (2009). Domestic violence. In *The American counseling association encyclopedia of counseling* (pp. 160–162). Alexandra, VA: American Counseling Association.

Lightfoot, E. (2007). Disability. In J. A. Blackburn & C. D. Dulmus (Eds.), *Handbook of gerontology: Evidence-based approaches to theory, practice, and policy* (pp. 201–229). Hoboken, NJ: John Wiley.

Mannion, E. (1996). Resilience and burden in spouses with mental illness. *Psychiatric Rehabilitation Journal, 20,* 13–24.

Marks, D. (1999). *Disability: Controversial debates and psychosocial perspectives.* London: Routledge.

Marsh, D. T., & Lefly, H. P. (1996). The family experience of mental illness: Evidence for resilience. *Psychiatric Rehabilitation Journal, 20*(2), 3–13.

Maslow, A. H. (1968). *Toward a psychology of being* (2nd ed.). Princeton, NJ: Van Nostrand.

Maslow, A. H. (1970). *Motivation and personality* (2nd ed.). New York, NY: Harper.

Maslow, A. H. (1971). *The further reaches of human nature.* New York, NY: Viking.

Michalko, R. (2002). *The difference that disability makes.* Philadelphia, PA: Temple University.

Morris, J. (1991). *Pride against prejudice: Transforming attitudes towards disability.* London: The Women's Press.

Ms. Wheelchair Florida 2014: Stop telling me that I'm pretty for a girl in a wheelchair: How your words contribute to violence against women with disabilities. Retrieved from http://mwfl2014.blogspot.com/2014/06.stop-telling-me-that-im-pretty-for-girl.html?spref=fb&m=1

National Organization on Disability. (2004, June 24). Landmark survey finds pervasive disadvantages. [Press Release]. Washington, DC: NOD. Retrieved from http://nod.org/research_publications/surveys_research/harris Retrieved 02–26–2018

Navarro, M. (2007, May 13). Clearly, frankly, unabashedly disabled. *New York Times.* Retrieved from www.nytimes.com/2007/05/13/fashion/13disabled.html?page Retrieved 02–26–2018

Public Broadcasting Service. (1998). *Paralyzing fear: The story of polio in America.* (Item no. PFPA 401). [Television documentary]. Arlington, VA: Author.

Putnam, M., Greenen, S., Powers, L., Saxton, M., Finney, S., & Dautel, P. (2003). People with disabilities discuss barriers and facilitators to well-being. *Journal of Rehabilitation, 69,* 37–45.

Reed, P. G. (1991). Toward a nursing theory of self-transcendence: Deductive reformulation using developmental theories. *Advances in Nursing Sciences, 13*(4), 64–77.

Remley, T. P., Jr., & Herlihy, B. (2001). *Ethical, legal, and professional issues in counseling.* Upper Saddle River, NJ: Prentice Hall.

Saxton, M., Curry, M. A., McNeff, E., Limont, M., Powers, L., & Benson, J. (2006). We're all little John Waynes: A study of disabled men's experience of abuse by personal assistants. *Journal of Rehabilitation, 72,* 2–13.

Shakespeare, T. (1999). The sexual politics of disabled masculinity. *Sexuality and Disability, 18,* 53–64.

Silberman, S. (2015). *NeuroTribes: The legacy of autism and the future of neurodiversity.* New York, NY: Penguin Random House.

Smart, D. W., & Smart, J. F. (1997). DSM-IV and culturally sensitive diagnosis: Some observations for counselors. *Journal of Counseling and Development, 75,* 392–398.

Smart, D. W., & Smart, J. F. (2006). Models of disabilities: Implications for the counseling profession. *Journal of Counseling and Development, 84,* 29–40.

Smart, J. F. (2012). *Disability across the developmental lifespan.* New York, NY: Springer.

Smart, J. F. (2016a). *Disability, society, and individual* (3rd ed.). Austin, TX: PRO-ED.

Smart, J. F. (2016b). Counseling individuals with disabilities. In I. Marini & M. S. Stebnicki (Eds.), *Professional counselors desk reference* (2nd ed., pp. 417–421). New York, NY: Springer.

Smart, J. F., & Smart, D. W. (1997a). Disability issues in translation/interpretation. In M. B. Labrum (Ed.), *American translators association scholarly monograph series* (p. IX). Amsterdam: John Benjamin.

Smart, J. F., & Smart, D. W. (1997b). Vocational evaluation of Hispanic clients with disabilities. In *The Hatherleigh guide to vocational and career counseling* (pp. 209–231). New York, NY: Hatherleigh.

Smart, J. F., & Smart, D. W. (1997c). Vocational evaluation of Hispanic clients. Chapter 10 in F. Chan & D. Wong (Eds.), *Vocational assessment: Evaluation for people with disabilities.* Chicago: Vocational Psychology Press, Amsterdam: John Benjamin.

Sobsey, D. (1994). *Violence and abuse in the lives of people with disabilities: The end of silent acceptance.* Baltimore, MD: Paul H. Brookes.

Sobsey, D., & Doe, T. (1991). Patterns of sexual abuse and assault. *Sexuality and Disability, 9,* 29–40.

Sobsey, D., & Mansell, S. (1993). The prevention of sexual abuse of people with developmental disabilities. In M. Nagler (Ed.), *Perspectives on disability* (2nd ed., pp. 283–292). Palo Alto, CA: Health Markets Research.

Solomon, A. (2012). *Far from the tree: Parents, children, and the search for identity.* New York, NY: Scribner.

Solomon, R. (2016, October 12). I have diabetes: Am I to blame? *New York Times.*

Stefan, S. (2001). *Unequal rights: Discrimination against people with mental disabilities and the Americans with disabilities act.* Washington, DC: American Psychological Association.

Tollifson, J. (1997). Imperfection is a beautiful thing. In K. Fries (Ed.), *Staring back: The disability experience from the inside out* (pp. 104–112). New York, NY: Plume.

Toombs, S. K., Barnard, D., & Carson, R. A. (Eds.) (1995). *Chronic illness: From experience to policy.* Bloomington, IN: University of Indiana.

Torrey, E. F. (1992). *Nowhere to go: The tragic odyssey of the homeless mentally ill.* New York, NY: Harper & Row.

Tremblay, M. (1996). Going back to civvy street: A historical account of the Everest and Jennings wheelchairs for Canadian World War II veterans with spinal cord injuries. *Disability and Society, 11,* 146–169.

Vash, C. L. (1981). *The psychology of disability.* New York, NY: Springer.

Vash, C. L., & Crewe, N. M. (2004). *Psychology of disability* (2nd ed.). New York, NY: Springer.

Weihenmayer, E. (2001). *Touch the top of the world: A blind man's journey to climb farther than the eye can see.* New York, NY: Dutton.

Weisskopf, M. (2006, October 2). "How I lost my hand, but found myself." *Time,* 28–37.

Yoels, W. C., & Clair, J. M. (1998). Never enough time: How medical residents manage a scarce resource. In K. Charmaz & D. A. Paterniti (Eds.), *Health, illness, and healing: Society, social construction and self* (pp. 131–164). Los Angeles: Roxbury.

Zavirsek, D. (2002). Pictures and silences: Memories of sexual abuse of disabled people. *Journal of Social Welfare, 11,* 270–285.

Zola, I. K. (1992). "Any distinguishing features?" The portrayal of disability in the crime-mystery genre. In P. M. Ferguson, D. L. Ferguson, & S. J. Taylor (Eds.), *Interpreting disability: A qualitative reader* (pp. 223–250). New York, NY: Columbia University.

Eight

UNDERSTANDING THE INDIVIDUAL'S RESPONSE TO DISABILITY

Counseling Practice Guidelines

The focus of this book changes in the concluding four chapters. The focus now shifts to the individual, whereas Chapters Four through Seven emphasized the effects of the environment, both social and governmental, upon IWDs. There are two reasons for learning about the environmental effect of disability upon the individual. First, most IWDs consider the prejudice, discrimination, and misguided attempts at charity to be greater diftxficulties than the medical management of the disability. Second, everyone is a product of their environment and, in the case of IWDs, the acquisition or diagnosis of a disability occurs in an environment which (almost always) views disability as negative, pathological, and tragic. Cohen (2004) explained, in a single sentence, the effect of his diagnosis: "The label of winner had been replaced with label of damaged goods" (p. 27). Any type of self-esteem, goal attainment, or decision making for IWDs transpires in a society that is highly ill-informed and prejudicial against disabilities and, thus, society often includes IWDs themselves. Cohen's sudden and dramatic change in self-identity illustrates the relationship between societal prejudice and self-identity of an individual who has received a diagnosis of disability. Counselors are not only professional service providers but they are also part of general society and, therefore, they may hold the same prejudicial and simplistic views of IWDs.

This chapter discusses 1) the relationship between the counseling professions and the Biomedical Model of Disability; 2) the important difference between the words "acceptance" and "response"; and 3) two paradoxes that individuals with acquired disabilities encounter. The second part of the chapter outlines various types of theories of response to disabilities, including 1) Wright's Theory of Cognitive Restructuring (1960, 1983); 2) the stage theory; and 3) a consideration of the ways in which acquisition of a disability can be considered a developmental task.

In Chapter Three, Models of Disability were described and discussed, recognizing that these models provide the basis for counseling case conceptualization and treatment plans. Consideration of all these models will help counselors to view the CWD as more than their disability. In this chapter, however, only one model is discussed, the model which is non-interactional, the Biomedical Model. Stated in basic terms, the Biomedical Model considers the IWD to experience some sort of pathology or loss and the IWD requires the services of highly qualified, skilled, and specialized experts who diagnose and determine treatments. This simplistic, one-sentence description of the Biomedical Model is also a historical definition of the treatment of IWDs, because with the exception of the Moral/Religious Model, the Biomedical Model has the longest history. Certainly, for the general public, the Biomedical Model is the most straightforward and clear cut; but this ease in understanding does not mean that there are not other valid models.

Thinking of the historical treatment of IWDs (which was often horrific) and openly discussing the limitations of the Biomedical Model, does not imply any criticism of physicians and other medical providers nor suggest that IWDs condemn or refuse medical treatment.

Counseling's Relationship to the Biomedical Model of Disability

- Counselors, like physicians, provide highly skilled and specialized services, having earned graduate degrees and becoming licensed.
- Case conceptualization includes the counselor's definition of the "problem" and the appropriate counseling techniques to "solve" the problem. Many counselors must render diagnoses in order to receive payment.

There are nine functions of Models of Disability. In the Biomedical Model, physicians fulfill two of these functions, tasked with the diagnosing the "problem" and determining the "solution" to the "problem" of disability. However, it is society that has relinquished the "problem" of disability to the medical professions. Science, technology, and medicine serve society and consider themselves value-free, understanding that it is the broader society that holds the responsibility to determine values. To cite a single example, there are increasing numbers of infants who survive pregnancy, birth, and the neonatal period, but survive with a congenital disability. As a society, we have decided that a congenital disability is preferable to death, but it is the medical professions who have made it possible for society to consider these value-laden decisions, by developing medical procedures to permit greater numbers of newborns to survive. Discussion of the limitations of the Biomedical Model does not suggest that medical professional services should be abandoned. The limitations of the Biomedical Model may also be applied to the counseling professions because much of the education and training have been based on the Biomedical Model, with counselors being trained and skilled in highly specialized expertise. The counseling professions have parallels with the medical professionals in that it is the larger society who has endowed the counseling professions with the authority to provide counseling services. Furthermore, no one advocates discarding counseling practices, skills, techniques, and best practices when counseling CWDs. Both medical and counseling interventions are evolving to include patients/clients in the decision making process. Another way in which medical and counseling professions have evolved is the recognition that physicians and counselors should collaborate in case management.

There are limitations to all models and no one model completely describes the disability experience. Full social integration and conferring civil rights are part of the "solution" to disability, but if these two conditions were fully met, there would still be the medical aspects of the disability. To say that disability is *entirely* a social construct is wrong. To say that disability is *mainly* a social construct would be more accurate and realistic. To say that disability is *entirely* a medical construct would also be inaccurate and unrealistic because there are significant social, environmental, and civil rights issues to all disabilities.

Consideration of all the Models of Disability shows us that disability is a complex, multifactorial experience and that thinking a single model has the explanatory power to completely describe disability and to suggest all possible "solutions" is both simplistic and unrealistic. There are two fundamental requirements placed upon counselors; first, to gain training and experience in serving IWDs (which would *add* to their expertise). Counselors can be ineffective and, perhaps, even harmful if they base their techniques and practices on inaccurate information, false stereotypes, paternalism, or sympathy. Therefore, counselors are required to learn new information and *actively unlearn* stereotypes and prejudices. The second fundamental requirement is collaboration in case management with other professionals, including physicians. The words "complex" and "multifactorial" used to describe disability suggest that a team of experts is necessary with the clear understanding that it is IWDs themselves who are equal partners in decision making. Taking the single example of the disability of learning disabilities, three experts described case management, implementing the expertise of various professionals:

> The study of LDs [learning disabilities] can be traced to several diverse disciplines including psychology, medicine (i.e., ophthalmology, otology, neurology, pharmacology) linguistics, and education. . . . Each of these professionals will evaluate, describe, and treat LDs in term of his or her own professional point of view.
>
> (Henley, Algozzine & Ramsey, 1996, p. 2017)

While Henley et al. do not specifically mention counseling services, there are many services that counselors can provide to individuals with learning disabilities and, further, counseling services can be as valuable and effective as the other professional specialties these authors discussed.

Responding to Disability

Many disability scholars advocate the use of the word "responding" or "response" rather than "adaptation," "adjustment," or "acceptance of disability," feeling that these last three words and phrases *unnecessarily* pathologize the experience of disability. Many IWDs believe that there are many positive aspects of their disabilities while, simultaneously acknowledging negative elements. Also, the use of these words imply that disability is always unpleasant, deviant, and pathological. Therefore, for our purposes, the words "response" or "reaction" will be used, although occasionally when quoting first-person accounts or referring to research studies, "adaptation" and "acceptance" will be used. Indeed, most theories that discuss the individual's reaction to their disability are labeled "acceptance of disability." Reynolds Price, an author, playwright, professor, and poet, wrote about his paralysis he acquired at the age of 51. Price explained the onset of his disability and his eventual response as if he were a great war novelist and his cancer and disability were the enemies.

> Then, I got into a war that in many ways was even more challenging than Hemingway, Willian Styron, and James Jones go to. I was a whole army that the war was declared against. The cancer was out to get me and nobody else.
>
> (Price, 1994, p. 127)

> Initially, I didn't want to go out at all. I got very agoraphobic. If you're in this condition, there are all kinds of problems. I mean going to the bathroom, you've got to learn a whole new way of doing that—just everything, your clothing your dress, the way you eat a meal; it's like having to learn Chinese at the age of fifty-one. But damn it, you either learn it, or you die.

Or you become someone who is so wretched and miserable mean that no one can stand to be around you. I call it my after-life, this new life I have.
(Price, 1994, p. 126)

Responding to a disability is not a one-time event, but rather a lifelong process. Nonetheless, for the most part, the individual's response following medical stabilization will be discussed here. The individual's response is considered; but, with the acknowledgment that there are strong environmental forces which interact with individual responses.

Two Paradoxes in the Individual's Response to an Acquired Disability

Paradoxes
1. The individual (with an acquired disability) has the same self-identity and public identity as before the disability. On the other hand, the individual who has acquired a disability is a different person, both to himself and to others.
2. The individual's (with an acquired disabilities) pre-disability coping and problem-solving skills will assist them to deal with the disability. On the other hand, the individual has never encountered the "problem" of disability (nor ever considered the possibility).

Most IWDs feel that they are the same individual they were before the acquisition or onset of their disability, with the exception of some psychiatric disabilities and traumatic brain injury in which personality changes are one of the symptoms. However, many first person accounts of an acquisition of a disability describe the way in which many colleagues, family members, and friends considered the disability to have completely changed the individual, someone they no longer know.

Second, many of the coping skills they have used and developed in responding to problems and stressors can be used in responding to the disability. Many adults have transcended financial difficulties, family break-ups, and many other types of unexpected difficulties and, therefore, these individuals have self-identities as skilled problem solvers with many adaptive skills. Nonetheless, regardless of the successful outcomes of previous problem solving and decision making, many individuals with acquired disabilities feel unprepared to respond to a disability and, furthermore, some of these well-developed coping and adaptation skills may not apply to a disability. Nonetheless, most adults have never been required to respond to a disability nor have they considered the possibility. A 24-year-old individual who acquired an orthopedic disability during the American polio epidemics felt like a "young child who had been dropped into a big black hole" all because of a "simple" case of polio. Polio might have been simple, but responding to polio was overwhelming.

> But, suddenly I woke up one morning and found that I could not stand. I had had polio and it was as simple as that. I was like a very young child who had been dropped into a big, black hole. . . . The education, the lectures, and the parental training which I had received for twenty-four years didn't seem to make me the person who could do anything for me now.
>
> (Goffman, 1963, p. 35)

> Something happened and I became a stranger. I was a greater stranger to myself than anyone. Even my dreams did not know me. They did not know what they ought to let me do—and when I went to dances or parties (in my dreams) there was always an odd provision or limitation—not spoken of or mentioned, but there just the same. I suddenly had the very confusing mental and emotional conflict of a lady leading a double life. It was unreal and it puzzled me, and I could not help dwelling on it.
>
> (Goffman, 1963, p. 35)

Several first-person accounts of adults who acquired disabilities spoke of the experience as, "I lived in a different country." Robert Murphy, a professor of anthropology at Columbia University, was middle-aged when he became paralyzed from a tumor of the spinal cord. Eventually Murphy died. He used his academic discipline to understand and describe his disability, detailing his response process as a "sojourn," (a long journey) into a "radically different" culture.

> Just as an anthropologist gets a better perspective on his culture through long and deep study of a radically different one, my extended sojourn in disability has given me, like it or not, a measure of my estrangement far beyond the field of my trip. I now stand somewhat apart from American culture, making me in many ways a stranger. And with this estrangement has come a greater urge to penetrate the veneer of cultural differences and reach an understanding of the underlying unity of all human experience.
>
> (Murphy, 1990, pp. 102–103)

For some IWDs, in addition to the onset of the disability, there are other times when they are required to respond to and adjust to their disability, most of which are idiosyncratically defined and described. Two men described their hospital stays during the medical stabilization of their disabilities as calm and unfrightening. For Hofsiss, the full impact came when he returned home. Jack Hofsiss was paralyzed from a diving accident in a swimming pool:

> Still, in no way was I prepared for returning home. The hardest part is those first two or three months after you get back home. When you're in the hospital, the anonymity of the space allows you to keep at a distance that your life has been unalterably changed and played around with. But when you get home, you're surrounded by all the things of daily life before the accident: Then you walk into the kitchen to get yourself a cup of coffee or a glass of milk. No longer. That's where the serious adjusting takes place.
>
> (Hofsiss & Laffey, 1993, p. 81)

The New York artist, Chuck Close, understood the full extent of his paralysis only after 12 days of medical stabilization:

> But my recollection was that it [medical stabilization] was quite calm and not as scary as when the deadening reality of the kind of day-in and day-out existence of not being able to move really set in. On the tenth, eleventh, twelfth day you haven't moved a muscle from the shoulders on down, and people are rolling you over and back, attaching tubes and things, *that's* when you think, "Oh, it's never going to get any better this." That's when it gets really scary.
>
> (Close, 1993, p. 17)

For another woman, the most difficult experience was when she had to relinquish her job:

> I felt dreadful when I had to give up work. It was the most shattering experience I had had because going out to work you felt a part of society, you were contributing, you were earning your own money. You also had your friends that you went to work with, and then suddenly you were cut off. You were in the house alone. Also, of course, financially you are worse off. You were lonely, you felt useless, on the scrap heap, finished, and it really was a bad time.
>
> (Campling, 1981, p. 115)

Individual Factors That Facilitate a Positive Response to Disability

Factors in the Individual

Tangible Factors

1. Financial resources
2. Comprehensive insurance coverage
3. High levels of education
4. A long and successful work history
5. Remarkable achievements before the onset/diagnosis of the disability

Intangible Factors

1. A challenge orientation
2. Supportive family
3. The ability to establish a social support group

There are individual assets and circumstances which typically help the individual respond to a disability. Some of these are tangible, such as financial resources, good insurance, a high level of education, and a varied work history. Just as important are intangible resources such as family support, including marriage or partnership, and a strong social network. In the National Public Radio (NPR) *Disability History Project* (1988a) a lawyer who survived childhood polio with lower limb paralysis, understood that his family's financial resources provided him with increased choices and advantages:

> One of the first people I saw working with a disability was the crippled newsie on the corner—the guy who couldn't use his legs who had a little knuckle board who dragged himself around to sell newspapers. I knew that except for the money my family had, that could very easily be me and it scared me to death.

Helen Keller, the American disability advocate, was both deaf and blind, resulting from a childhood infection. Helen's family had the resources to contact Samuel Gridley Howe at the Perkins School for the Deaf in Boston, Massachusetts. The Kellers had read a newspaper article about Howe's success in teaching a deaf and blind woman using new methods. Howe also trained a few teachers in these methods, one of whom was Annie Sullivan. The Kellers employed Annie Sullivan who taught the child, Helen, to speak, read, and write. The popular film and stage play, *The Miracle Worker*, portrayed Annie Sullivan teaching the young Helen. Helen Keller's greatest resource was Annie Sullivan who stayed with her for 49 years, teaching, assisting, and traveling with Helen on her lecture circuit. At that historical time period, there were many deaf and blind children and adults who lived and died at home or in institutions; both their existence and histories remain hidden. Helen Keller was able to fulfill her considerable potential because of Annie Sullivan. Helen Keller was Annie Sullivan's sole focus in life. As a side note: Assistive technology, today, often replaces the functions of paid companions or attendants.

Those with resources such as education and a varied work history have more options. For those with physical disabilities, a high level of intelligence is a valuable resource which is not affected by the disability. Many theories of response posit that transferable and alternative paths are essential "work-arounds" and the greater the number of resources available to the IWD, the more work-arounds the IWDs can marshal. Achievements and public recognition attained before the onset/diagnosis of the disability contribute to greater acceptance of disability. Stephen Hawking, Christopher Reeve, and American President Franklin Roosevelt achieved both success and public recognition before their disabilities. Stephen Hawking, the late British physicist, was a graduate student at Cambridge University before his diagnosis of amyotrophic lateral sclerosis (ASL); the late American actor, Christopher Reeve, had a successful film career before his spinal cord injury (SCI) and President Roosevelt had achieved a measure of success in politics before he contracted polio. Without these previous achievements, their adjustment to their disabilities probably would not have been so positive and, moreover, these successes often contributed to greater financial resources, which helped to offset the costs of their disabilities. Also, all three of these men were very intelligent and experienced physical disabilities that did not impair their intellectual and cognitive abilities.

A Positive Response to a Disability

Many IWODs falsely think that IWDs obsess about their disabilities and that disabilities are always a negative and unhappy experience. These misperceptions lead to the conceptualization of a disability as a 24/7 experience of sadness and passivity. Of course, it is difficult to accurately imagine the lives of others, but IWODs tend to sensationalize and exaggerate the disability, most often in negative terms. Moreover, IWODs often do not question their assumptions, especially with a pervasive media that constantly reinforces these falsehoods. Further compounding these misjudgments is the lack of relationships with IWDs, which could facilitate a more accurate portrayal of disability. Counselors, trained in active listening, relationship building, and empathy will be more open to learning exactly what the experience of disability is, especially the client's idiosyncratic perception of their disability.

In spite of the great variability in the types of disabilities, many varying environments, and differing levels of stigma directed toward different types of disabilities, it is possible to list some general positive attributes, emotional responses, and behaviors. Positive cognitive and emotional responses require flexibility, tolerance for ambiguity, and strength to redefine the self and the disability. The IWD constructs an idiosyncratic idea of "normality," which includes family, marriage and partnerships, social relations, work, and leisure. This new normality also includes medical treatment. Acquisition of a disability or the diagnosis of a chronic disease results in "emotional disequilibrium," in which the individual is confused, frustrated, and often overwhelmed. The way in which many IWDs, and their families express the process of regaining emotional equilibrium is "I returned to a new normal."

Behavioral responses are easier to operationalize and include active mastery of the disability including medical compliance and careful monitoring to reduce the number of complications and secondary conditions. Medical compliance does not automatically translate to passivity; rather, the IWD understands the importance of the medical and physical aspects of their disability, but without exaggerating the limitations or losses.

The simultaneous management of many types of disabilities is difficult, time consuming, expensive and, occasionally painful. However, difficult does not mean tragic. For example, young children have learned to execute some of the management of their disabilities such as the mother telling her daughter, "Don't forget to take off your leg when you go into the swimming pool." Most children do not have prostheses and, therefore, do not need reminding to remove them. Certainly, the responsibility for a prosthesis is an added life task, but most children do not think that prostheses are tragic.

Life with a disability is often a life well-lived, that is, idiosyncratically defined as meaningful, purposeful, and rewarding. The IWD remains engaged with life and, in some cases, becomes more self-actualized after the onset of the disability. Included in such self-actualization is a high level of social interest and goal-directed behavior.

A positive response to a disability necessitates a great deal of ego strength to recognize and resist prejudicial attitudes of others. For example, the clinical picture of a psychiatric disability is incomplete without considering the considerable level of stigma directed toward people with psychiatric disabilities.

In first-person accounts, many IWDs recall that it took a great deal of time before they realized that some of their encounters with others were prejudicial and undeserved. For this reason, social support groups of IWDs can be very helpful. Many IWDs feel that they deserve prejudicial treatment. Joan Tollifson has a congenital limb deficiency, missing an arm and hand. In this excerpt, she describes the healing provided by a mutual support group of IWDs:

> After a lifetime of isolating myself from other disabled people, it was an awakening to be surrounded by them. For the first time in my life, I felt like a real adult member of the human community. Finally, identifying myself as a disabled person was an enormous healing. It was about recognizing, allowing, and acknowledging something that I had been trying to deny, and finding that disability does not equal ugliness, incompetence, and misery.
> (Tollifson, 1997, p. 107)

It may appear remarkable that Tollifson had a "lifetime" of thinking of herself as ugly, incompetent, and miserable. She described her change in self-identity as "an awakening" and "enormous healing." Tollifson also regarded her life before she joined the support group of women with disabilities as "a private hell."

A sense of humor, including "in-group" humor with other IWDs, often acts as a coping strategy. Remember the Australian, Nick Vujicic, born without arms or legs who told audience members that if they left early before his speech had concluded, "If you run fast, I'm going to get someone to throw me at you." A study conducted in New Zealand investigated the role of spirituality as a healthy response to physical disabilities. In one of the concluding paragraphs, the authors summarized the value of a sense of humor.

> Notably the ability to laugh at oneself and with others about experiences and situations [was important]. A dominant characteristic of humor described that it was "in-house" or "black," and in some way at the expense of the teller. Stories often told of catastrophic experiences [in] which humor was used to make more bearable and acceptable an aspect of normal life. Humor such as this was seen to indicate an ability to view oneself from the outside and to see oneself in the context of a wider picture. Moreover, it [humor] was considered to reflect the New Zealand cultural norm of understatement, together with an awareness of life which is precious and enjoyable.
> (Faull et al., 2004, p. 137)

A Poor Response to Disability

A Poor Response to Disability Includes:
- Unnecessary dependence upon others
- Social isolation
- Feelings of inferiority
- Loss of self-esteem
- Refusal to engage in treatment and therapy
- Internalized anger and depression
- The need to hold someone, including oneself, responsible for the disability
- Feeling a total lack of control

There are negative responses to disability such as unnecessary dependence upon others, social isolation, feelings of inferiority, refusing to engage in treatment and therapy, loss of self-esteem, and internalized anger and depression. Empirical research has shown that failure to forgive others or oneself for the cause of the disability results in a negative response to the disability. Carolyn Vash (1981) discussed the negative power of blame:

> Accidents, in which an official designation of responsibility is made, are simply the most obvious case. To believe that a permanent disability resulted from a momentary, foolish act of one's own may strongly affect reaction to the disability itself—at least until the feelings of self-blame are resolved. Blaming someone else may have an even stronger impact. Keith, who lost a leg when the motorcycle he was riding collided with a truck, become consumed with hatred toward the truck driver, especially after the courts found him at fault. Fred, shot in the spine accidentally by his young brother, believes both of their lives would have been better if their parents had permitted him to express the anger he felt.
>
> (p. 11)

Michalko (2002) who became progressively blind during his adolescence, described the freedom from self-blame as a "charm" and "comforting."

> Medicine does have its charm. Its explanation of phenomena such as cancer are far more attractive than those to be found in religious ideas involving the omission or commission of acts, which lead to guilt and self-blame.

> Medicine's neutral physiological depiction of cancer leads us away from such self-blame to the more comforting, "it just happened." There is nothing that we did or did not do that causes cancer, it "just happens."
>
> (p. 35)

> I have nothing to do with the onset of my blindness since I have no role to play in the configuration of my genetic makeup. My blindness is caused by flawed genes and not by a flawed self or any other kind of self for that matter.
>
> (p. 33)

In the following excerpt, a man is shown to feel that he has never had any control or independence in his life, both before the acquisition of the disability and after. Note that he recognizes that other IWDs have worked and had families, but these opportunities were not available to him.

> I was born, educated, broke my neck, and I'll die and be buried just down the road here about half a mile, so my life hasn't been that much. . . . My life had no value. [The interviewer than asks, "Not even to you?"] No, because I didn't get a chance to do anything with it. It was not mine when I was a kid; it belonged to the parents. By the time I got to be 16, getting ready to go out and do something for myself, you break your neck, and that's it. I mean, a lot of people do work that are handicapped; they earn money and have families—stuff like that. But once I was hurt, none of that applied to me any longer. I didn't care about it or think about it or nothing. I just kind of hunkered down for the long pull, I guess. You make the best of what you've got. There's nothing going to happen to me in life after that—not to me there wasn't. I knew that.
>
> (Crewe, 1997, p. 38)

In the following excerpt, a man with a spinal cord injury describes the need for counseling (terming it "mental rehabilitation") and gives one negative result of not receiving counseling, i.e., drinking. He stresses the importance of counseling by claiming that emotional adaptation is "90 percent of physical rehabilitation."

> People in this condition need mental rehabilitation more than anything else. Because that is 90 percent of physical rehabilitation. (Rehabilitation doesn't) want to face that because it's too expensive. So you adapt. You

develop coping mechanisms and some of them, like drinking are not good ones. If way back they had given us good coping mechanisms, a lot of problems could have been prevented.

(Scherer, 1993, pp. 159–160)

In the same book, *Living in a State of Stuck*, another man with a spinal cord disability spoke of "anger that just sits there and grows."

I wish I'd had counseling regularly . . . on a fairly regular basis. I'm not sure what would've come out of it, but if you see someone enough, eventually you're going to say something. Try to bring things out, some of the anger, and things like that. That was something that was never done, and that anger just sits in there and grows.

(ibid., p. 160)

Two Theories of Acceptance of Disability
- Cognitive restructuring
- Stage theory

One of these theories, cognitive restructuring, was developed specifically as a response to disability whereas the stage theory was originally advanced to describe the process of dying and has been used with other types of losses, such as divorce. By far, the theory that is most accepted by disability scholars is the stage theory, but there are cautions and limitations to both of these theories. Neither of these theories can be considered complete because 1) neither of these theories acknowledges the IWD's environment; 2) neither of these theories discusses the intersectionality of multiple identities and roles; and 3) the entire responsibility for responding to a disability is assumed to lie with the individual.

Commonalities Between Cognitive Restructuring and the Stage Theory
- None of these theories suggests that the disability should be ignored, hidden, or minimized.
- Counselors are trained and experienced in the technique of active listening and, with CWDs, active listening is paramount in learning about the disability experience.

- All of these theories of acceptance suggest many practice applications in which counselors have training and skills, such as cognitive restructuring, cognitive behavioral theory (CBT), values clarification, assertive training, self-efficacy, substance abuse seeking out social support, and sexual counseling.
- Nonetheless, in order to practice effectively and ethically, it will be necessary to learn the ways in which disability issues apply to these theories. Therefore, counselors will require additional training and experience, some of which was to include *unlearning* narrow, prejudicial, and stereotyped attitudes.

Cognitive Restructuring

Cognitive restructuring or reframing has been found to be effective in counseling individuals with various problems such as depression, substance abuse, and eating disorders. At its most basic, cognitive restructuring holds that when individuals change their thinking, they can reduce their stress, anxiety, and other negative emotions. The problem itself is not changed, or even reduced, but the individual's appraisal, attribution, or interpretation of events changes or improves. Finding positive alternatives changes the *perception* of the disability. Wright's acceptance of disability theory is the only theory that was specifically developed for use with IWDs. The use of cognitive restructuring with disability originated with Beatrice Wright and, indeed, Wright's theory is considered the first theory of acceptance of disability. She interviewed World War II veterans who returned to veterans' hospitals in the United States with physical disabilities such as paralysis, amputations, hearing loss, blindness, and disfigurements, spending years interviewing these veterans, developing the first theory of "acceptance of disability," entitled "cognitive restructuring." She published her book, *Physical Disability: A Psychosocial Approach*, in 1960. Therefore, Wright's theory, at its narrowest interpretation, would apply only to those with acquired, physical disabilities. However, cognitive restructuring has been used with individuals with cognitive and psychiatric disabilities and with parents of babies with congenital disabilities. Wright was clear in stating that her cognitive restructuring included active medical management of the disability.

Wright found four basic aspects of adaptation to disabilities and recognized that all of these aspects were based on the veterans' rethinking, re-evaluating, and reinterpreting their disability. She labeled these four points 1) enlargement of the scope of values which are not in conflict with the disability; 2) subordination of the physique; 3) containment of disability effects; and 4) transformation from comparative to asset values.

> **Wright's Theory of Acceptance of Disability: Cognitive Restructuring**
> - Enlargement of the scope of values
> - Subordination of the physique
> - Containment of disability effects
> - Transformation from comparable to asset values

When individuals, with or without disabilities, enlarge the scope of their values they find strengths, skills, and talents within themselves of which they were previously unaware. When IWDs enlarge their scope of values, they find values that do not conflict with the disability. First-person accounts of acquiring a physical disability often include this summary, "I escaped into my mind." Note the action verb, "escaped." Often, individuals with physical disabilities discovered their intellectual abilities and capitalized on these. In a collection of first-person accounts of surviving polio, Robert Owen described the way in which he enlarged his scope of values:

> Robert Owen recalls that before polio struck when he was twelve, he was constantly in trouble, and fought to and from school. In addition to fighting, he also "loved to play football and things like that." He remembers that prior to polio, he "had only read about three books in my whole life." After he returned to school, following a year of rehabilitation, he focused on his studies. Owen is convinced that if he hadn't had polio, he probably would not have become a physician.
>
> (Wilson, 1990, p. 202)

The second point of Wright's theory is subordination of the physique, meaning that one's body, personal appearance, and attractiveness begin to fade in importance. Rather than thinking that one's body is the only, or the most important part of self-identity, the IWD begins to reconsider their self-identity, reconceptualizing self-identity as one's personality, characteristics, talents, skills, spirituality, relationships, and past experiences. This is not easy because IWDs live in a society that considers the human body to be a symbol of competence, morality, value, and desirability. In the same way elderly individuals also experience a shift in subordinating the importance of their physiques. Two disability scholars describe the effects of physiognomy. The false science of physiognomy posited that it is possible to determine personal characteristics by looking at an individual's outward appearance.

> Physiognomy became a paradigm of access to the ephemeral and intangible workings of the internal body. Speculative qualities such as moral integrity, honesty, trustworthiness, criminality, fortitude, cynicism, sanity, and so forth, suddenly became available for scrutiny by virtue or the "irregularities" of the body that enveloped them. For the physiognomist, the body allowed meaning to be inferred from the outside in; such speculative practice resulted in the ability to anticipate intangible qualities of one's personhood without having to await the "proof" of actions or the intimacy of a relationship developed over time. By "reasoning from the exterior to the interior," the trained physiognomist extracted the meaning of the soul without the permission or participation of the interpreted.
> (Mitchell & Synder, 2010, p. 282)

The science of physiognomy has long been discarded, but many vestiges of physiognomy remain in our culture, such as associating happy, fulfilling lives with physical attractiveness, thinking that beautiful people are happy and the not-so-beautiful live tortured, miserable existences. Perhaps some of the ideas of the false science of physiognomy has contributed to the idea of "twisted body, twisted mind," and contributed to a genre of literature and film, "horror," in which the villain displays a visible physical disability. Nonetheless, these myths make the individual's response to a visible disability difficult. Other authors explain that IWDs often incorporate these stigmatizing attitudes toward visible disabilities into their self-identity.

> It is therefore conceivable that the social appraisals of a person's differences, vis-à-vis stigma and causal attributes, could impact the adjustment process of an individual with a visible disability.... Yet what seems pivotal is the extent to which the inducement of OSA [objective self-awareness] may lead the individual to interpret the negative appraisals as being *realistically* based. In other words, can one's personal beliefs about oneself stand up against the perception that others believe differently—and for how long?
> (Phemister & Crewe, 2004, p. 150)

The third point is "containment of disability effects," which means neither denying nor minimizing the effects of the disability. In Cohen's initial response to his diagnosis of multiple sclerosis, he does not contain the effects of MS. He stated, "The label of 'winner' was replaced with 'damaged goods.'" His initial and, perhaps emotional, response was global and all-encompassing. Most IWDs, after varying lengths of time, return to "normality," meaning a new, redefined normality that includes the disability. This new normality includes return to the family, social life, and vocational development, all "normal" undertakings, but which now include a disability. Containment of negative aspects is the antithesis to a global negative judgment, such as "My life is ruined" or "There's nothing left to live for" or "I'd rather be dead." A woman with a disability described containment by comparing her disability identity to her ethnic and gender identities, making the point that she was proud of all three identities, in spite of the fact that each had negative aspects.

> I'm proud of being Italian. There are things I am ashamed of, like the existence of the Mafia—but these things do not stop me from embracing my Italian-ness. I love being a woman, but I hate going through menopause. But I wouldn't want a sex change operation just because of menopause. Certainly the pain and physical limitations of disability are not wonderful, yet that identity is who I am. And I am proud of it.
>
> (Fleischer & Zames, 2001, p. 202)

The fourth point, "transformation from comparative to asset values" simply means that rather than focusing on the losses of the disability, the IWD focuses on their assets. This does not mean that the IWD denies or does not acknowledge the losses, but that they make a cognitive effort to look for their intact assets. Comparative values that make adaptation more difficult include IWDs comparing themselves to IWODs or comparing their disabled selves to their non-disabled selves. Randy Souders felt that his disability (paralysis) saved him from a mediocre life in "a mediocre little ad agency."

> It's odd. If I had a crystal ball to see what would have happened had I had not had the injury I don't see myself having done what I've done at all. I would probably have a mediocre position in a mediocre little ad agency and be like the rest of society—up to my ears in debt, just trying to get by—and frustrated that I didn't go for something that would have truly inspired me all along. . . . I don't know that I would have dedicated myself to art. Art was a vital part of my recovery from my injury. I found myself in a situation of being the same person in a new body, one that didn't work, along with the loss of self-esteem and self-confidence and all the things that come along with a traumatic injury. One I realized that I still had a

chance at being creative and of value through my artwork, I just really focused in on that. It was a real part of my recovery.

(1993, p. 153)

Stephen Hawking, the British theoretical physicist, was diagnosed with amyotrophic lateral sclerosis (ALS) at age 21 when he was a graduate student at Cambridge. ALS is a deteriorating disability which typically results in death. Some of Hawking's response began in his dreams. Take notice of his understatement, such as "a bit of a shock" and "I was at loose ends." He considers his diagnosis "a cloud hanging over me."

> The realization that I had an incurable disease, that was likely to kill me in a few years was a bit of a shock. How could something like that happen to me? Why should I be cut off like this? . . . Not knowing what was going to happen to me, or how rapidly the disease would progress, I was at loose ends.
>
> My dreams at that time were rather disturbed. Before my condition had been diagnosed, I had been very bored with life. There had not seemed to be anything worth doing. But shortly after I came out of the hospital, I dreamt that I was going to be executed. I suddenly realize that there were a lot of worthwhile things I could do if I were reprieved. Another dream, that I had several times, was that I would sacrifice my life to save others. After all, if I were going to die anyway, it might as well do some good. But I didn't die. In fact, although there was a cloud hanging over my future, I found to my surprise, that I was enjoying life in the present more than before. I began to make progress with my research.

(White & Gribbin, 1993, p. viii)

One IWD realized that his newborn son was his motivator. In spite of his disability, he had someone to live for, his newborn son.

> Another severely burned interviewee (now a grandfather) . . . had been given the last rites and was expected to die. Against hospital rules, his wife brought their infant son into his room to say good-bye. It was at that moment the new father decided that he would fight to live despite his injuries because he wanted to watch his son grow up. "My family became my motivation to survive."

(Holaday & McPhearson, 1997, p. 348)

Changing one's thinking is not easy or straightforward. It requires sustained and consistent motivation. Nonetheless, cognitive restructuring includes a *proactive* element and allows the IWD and their family and friends to respond to the disability with intentionality, rather than simply *reacting* to events. Cognitive restructuring includes an element of openness and clarity, rather than refusing to think or speak about a disability. Thinking in terms of family and friends, cognitive restructuring allows, even requires, speaking about the disability. Taking time to think about thinking often results in clear and direct responses and has the potential to reduce automatic, emotional responses based on preconceived false stereotypes and prejudices. Families, friends, and IWDs themselves are often confused, frightened, and their thinking is disorganized. Applying cognitive restructuring to the experience of disability is often especially effective because most IWDs have never entertained the idea that they might acquire a disability and there is a tendency to convert prejudice and discrimination into self-identifiers.

The Stage Theory of Responding to Disability

Stages
1. Shock
2. Denial (defensive retreat)
3. Depression
4. Anger and personal questioning
5. Adaptation and integration
6. Transcendence

The stage theory is the most widely recognized and used theory of responding to a disability. There are six stages in this theory and these typically appear in the following sequence: shock, defensive retreat (denial), depression or mourning, anger or personal questioning, and adaptation and integration. In an earlier chapter, Vash's concept of transcendence was added as a sixth stage, although Vash thought that not all IWDs reached transcendence. The stage theory presents broad, general guidelines to the process of responding to a disability, at the acquisition or onset and throughout the IWD's life as they negotiate various developmental milestones and life tasks. Arnold Beisser (1987) contracted polio on a train trip to report for military duty during World War II. He became paralyzed from the neck down and required the use of a ventilator (an iron lung) to breathe. He described his response to the paralysis as a marriage, a lifetime relationship, with some bad times, but mostly good. Beisser had recently graduated from medical school and became a psychiatrist, a medical specialty he could practice while lying in an iron lung.

In the first stage, shock, the IWD is overwhelmed, confused, and their thinking is disorganized. The enormity of the disability, including the treatments, makes the individual feel out of control of their life. As discussed earlier, no one ever considers the possibility that they may acquire a disability or be diagnosed with a chronic illness. Much like the adage, "Thee, but not me," we often think that disabilities happen to other people, but not to us. Indeed, the first question often is, "Why me?" On further contemplation, many IWDs conclude, "Why not me?" The IWD in the following excerpt describes the shock as being "in the midst of a hurricane."

> When everything is over, I think I will be able to really sum up a lot of the feelings that I have inside that I find hard to express or I don't have the words for. When everything is over, I think I'll probably find a lot of things inside of me. Isn't that what happens? Like when you are in the midst of a hurricane it's real hard to kind of . . . figure out everything. But once you are out of it, you can kind of go, "hey, yeah, I was in the middle of that hurricane and this is what happened."
>
> (Buki et al., 2007, p. 339)

The artist, Chuck Close (1993) described the sudden onset of his paralysis.

> I was at Gracie Mansion in New York giving an award to someone. I suddenly had a tremendous pain in my chest that went through my back and my arms. I thought it was a heart attack. I went across the street to Doctors Hospital where, within a very short time, I was totally paralyzed from the neck down. It was several days before they figured what had happened, which was that an occluded or collapsed spinal artery had cut off the flow of blood to my spine and knocked out nerves all over my body. Virtually everything from the shoulders down was affected.
>
> (p. 17)

Roberts Perkins wrote about his psychiatric disability in a book titled, *A Life Spent in the High Latitudes* (1996). In this excerpt, he talks about the shock of his diagnosis, using *physical* sensations ("being hit on the side of the head with a flat board") to illustrate the *emotional* shock.

> In the spring of 1968, I was nineteen and a freshman at Harvard College. I was soon to leave school, without even passing "GO" or finishing the year to start a journey. A journey I have yet to complete. . . . To have the wind knocked out of you, hard, at nineteen. To give you the feeling of it, I'd hit you on the side of the head, when you were least expecting it, with a flat board or a piece of rubber tubing. The shock of the thing!
>
> (pp. 5, 15)

The second stage, denial or defensive retreat, is often considered to be adaptive and therapeutic, allowing the IWD, and their family, to prevent emotional flooding and allow the IWD to gradually assimilate information about the disability, allowing the individual to maintain their self-identity (Langer, 1994; Smart & Smart, 1997; Stewart, 1994). There are three types of denial: 1) denial of the disability; 2) denial about the permanence of the disability; and 3) denial about the implications of the disability. Completely denying the presence of a disability is rather rare, but occasionally individuals may assert that their diagnoses are wrong. Much more common is denial of the permanence of the disability, expressed in statements such as "I'll soon be myself again" or "I'm sure the doctors can cure me." Denial of the implications of the disability is expressed as "I'll soon walk out of here." Or "When will he be better?" or "I'll soon be my old self." Families also engage in denial when they ask physicians when will he be able to return to his pre-disability life. The American President, Franklin Roosevelt, denied the implications of his paralysis. Roosevelt always stated that "I will walk someday." This was impossible since his hip muscles had been destroyed by polio. Perhaps this form of denial helped Roosevelt respond to his disability. Nonetheless, Roosevelt maintained this belief for the rest of his life after he became paralyzed.

Richard Cohen is a journalist who was diagnosed with multiple sclerosis at age 25. Cohen's writing skills allowed him to describe his denial, explaining that he "lived in the house of denial," comparing his denial to a type of shelter. Also note that Cohen considered "ignorance" as an ally.

> My radar screen was blank, not even plugged in and turned on.
>
> (2004, p. 13)

> For months, I had lived in the house of denial, Now, in one moment, it had given way. It had been a flimsy structure, built on wishful thinking, but it had sheltered me from the weight of a reality that I could not bear to confront. Ignorance had been my ally; I had not even asked many questions

of the doctors. Silence was an odd tactic for a journalist who, by trade, is all questions all the time. But I did not want to know too many facts. Facts would lead to truth and truth had been unacceptable. I was facing facts now. I had to admit to myself that I had MS.

Years would pass, however, before I easily and openly acknowledged my illness. Knowledge came slowly, too.

(Cohen, 2004, p. 22)

As a teenager, Louis Sternberg contracted polio and lived in an iron lung because all of the muscles from his neck down were paralyzed, including those necessary for breathing. In the following excerpt, Sternberg's denial included both walking and breathing, neither of which he was able to do.

Louis Sternberg asked his physician when he was going to walk out of the respiratory center. After a long, painful pause, the doctor told him that not only would he never walk again, he would also probably never breathe again without assistance. Sternberg heard himself scream, "You sonofabitch, you're lying!"

(Wilson, 1990, p. 94)

Deegan (1991) described her denial (and anger), which helped her to survive "those first awful months." Deegan was perceptive enough to understand that her denial was normal.

Needless to say, we didn't believe our doctors and social workers. In fact, we adamantly denied and raged against these bleak prophesies for our lives. We felt it was just a mistake, a bad dream, a temporary set-back in our lives. We just knew that in a week or two, things would get back to normal again.

We felt our teenage world was still there, just waiting for us to return to it. Our denial was an important stage in our recovery. It was a normal reaction to an overwhelming situation. . . . It was our way of surviving those first awful months.

(p. 48)

A woman who experienced a stroke and the resulting apraxia clearly described the way in which she refused (or denied) information about her disability. Apraxia is a common result of strokes, and other types of brain damage, in which a person is unable to move. Note that she hides the booklet from herself.

> A booklet explaining apraxia lay under a pile of books where I'd hidden it. As long as I didn't read it, as long as I didn't put words to what had happened . . . my own acknowledgment of it didn't have to cut so deeply. I could postpone the pain of acceptance.
>
> (Robinson, 1997, p. 89)

Phantom limb sensation, in which the individual feels the false presence of an amputated limb, may be another type of denial. Miles O'Brien described his phantom limb sensation and pain. He is a freelance journalist who was on assignment in the Philippines when a heavy case of photographic equipment fell on his left forearm. He described the way in which this injury progressed to an amputation, and the subsequent feeling that his arm was still there. O'Brien also hid his amputation from his family in the United States.

> What began as a fairly bad bruise evolved into something life-threatening: active compartment syndrome, which blocks blood flow. When I got to a doctor in Manila, he recognized the problem and sent me in for emergency surgery. He tried to save the arm, but it was too late. It was a life-or-limb decision. But, when the anesthesia receded and I rejoined the world of the living, I was convinced that the doctor had saved it.
> . . . while my arm may be missing physically, it is there, just as it always has been, in my mind's eye. I can feel every digit. I can even feel the watch that was always strapped to my left wrist. . . . Doctors don't really know how to treat pain in a part of the body that is no longer there.
> . . . I hadn't let anyone know what had happened to me for more than a week. Maybe I could just heal a little, then sneak back home. You know, denial. . . . But, there was also a practical problem: As a freelancer, I eat what I kill. I had spent a lot of money on travel and on hiring local help. I had to deliver the work or take a huge loss. So I wrote my scripts, and when friends and family checked in, I acted as if all was well.
>
> (O'Brien, 2014, p. 36)

Refusing to accept information or to insist that a mistake has been made or to seek out other doctors are all examples of denial. Denial is considered adaptive and therapeutic, if it does not continue for too long. Long-term denial will prevent the IWD from fully engaging in medical stabilization and rehabilitation. Denial, if continued for too long, reduces or eliminates the IWD's motivation to respond to the disability. A disability scholar (Naugle, 1991) offered a practice recommendation, when dealing with the denial of the IWD, terming it "dosage of information," carefully estimating the amount and type of information the IWD can tolerate. Timing of the information is also important. Naugle summarized:

> Equally important is the concept of dosage. If the individual is overwhelmed with information that material is less likely to be accepted. Failure to recognize and accommodate an individual's tolerance level for distressing information may have the effect of interfering with participation in any treatment regimen. Small "doses of information allow the individual to assimilate that information at a more controlled, self-determined rate."
>
> (p. 147)

Denial can be intergenerational, persisting for decades, although this is rather rare. A young French girl, Emmanuelle Laborit, was born deaf. As a young child, Emmanuelle did not speak words, but rather "shrieked."

> Uncle Fifou, my father's older brother, was the first to say, "Emmanuelle makes shrieking sounds because she can't hear herself." My father claims it was my uncle who "was the first to arouse our suspicions." "The scene is frozen in my mind," says my mother.
>
> My parents didn't want to believe it. To such an extent, in fact, that it was only much later that I found out my paternal grandparents had been married in the chapel of the National Institute for the Deaf in Bordeaux. What's more, the institute's director was my grandmother's stepfather. In an attempt to hide their concern, perhaps, or to avoid facing the truth, my parents had forgotten all about that!
>
> (Laborit, 2010, pp. 599–600)

Another type of denial is often used by families of IWDs and service providers. Families and service providers often encouraged IWDs to not discuss their disability and, after medical stabilization, IWDs were told to "get on with their lives." Marc Shell (2005) contracted polio as a child and stated, "My own father did not speak with me directly about me having had polio" (p. 84). This type of denial required IWDs to repress or deny their feelings about the disability. American veterans of World War II and the Korean War who returned home with disabilities were given medical care and physical rehabilitation but not psychological rehabilitation. These veterans were told to forget about their disabilities (and their war experiences). Perhaps these families and service providers thought that by denying their disabilities (or minimizing them) would prevent

IWDs from becoming depressed. Asking or encouraging them to deny their disabilities has now been recognized as counterproductive.

A pediatrician (Batshaw, 2001) described the use of denial by professionals, asserting that physicians often avoid a "reality which may be painful for the parent and the professional." In order to do this, Batshaw made clear distinctions between the diagnoses of "developmental delay," "developmental disability," and "mental retardation" or "intellectual disability."

> Physicians used the term *developmental delay* to describe a young child who is slow in developing but has the potential to catch up. This contrasts with the term *mental retardation* [*intellectual disability*,] which implies a permanent and significant slowness in development. The term *developmental delay* is often used in describing a premature infant; it is rarely appropriate to be used for a child older than 2–3 years of age. Unfortunately, professionals often used the term *developmental delay* long after it has become clear that the child has mental retardation [intellectual disability]. It then becomes a way of avoiding the reality that may be painful to the parents and to the professional.
>
> (p. 54)

Denial is most common in episodic (or relapsing) disabilities, especially when the episodes or relapses are infrequent. With infrequent relapses, individuals are fully functioning the majority of the time and often "forget" they have the disability. This type of denial often leads to medical noncompliance since individuals "feel fine" for long periods of time. Many types of psychiatric disabilities and autoimmune diseases are episodic and, often, the required medications produce unpleasant and debilitating side effects, both of which lead to discontinuing medications. This type of denial is nonadaptive and can be harmful.

The third stage is termed depression or mourning and while denial is past-oriented, in which the IWD tries to retain their pre-disability identity, depression is future-oriented in which the IWD sees an uncertain future. Apathy, withdrawal from others, lack of energy and motivation, and loss of hope are the emotional symptoms of this stage and lack of appetite and sleeping problems are the physical symptoms. At times, IWDs may feel, "My family would be better off without me" or "I have nothing to live for" and, in some cases, IWDs may be put on suicide watch. In the following excerpt, a man with a spinal cord injury (SCI) speculated that the depression following the acquisition of disability may be greater than the grief following the death of a loved one. Note also the way in which he combines depression with denial.

> If someone is stuck in the grieving process . . . it's like an adjustment to death. The only thing is, for an injury or disability, it's not as easy to adjust as with a death because with a death, the person's no longer there. With a disability, you have a constant reminder. So, sometimes it takes even longer to grieve and adjust. A lot of people turn to alcohol and drugs, which is a way of going through denial. As long as you're smashed, you can forget about your disability.
>
> (Scherer, 1993, p. 115)

Also comparing her depression with mourning the death of her daughter, a mother recounted her reaction to her daughter's diagnosis of a mental illness:

> The problems with my daughter were like a black hole inside of me into which everything else had been drawn. My grief and pain were so intense sometimes that I barely got through the day. It felt like a mourning process as if I were dealing with the loss of the daughter I had loved for 18 years and for whom there was so much potential.
>
> (Marsh, 1992, p. 10)

Personal questioning and/or anger are the predominant emotions in the fourth stage. The onset or diagnosis of a disability often contradicts very deeply held beliefs about the fairness of the world. This false belief holds that good things happen to good people and bad things happen to bad people. This is a comforting belief, albeit a false one. The onset of a disability is often random and, therefore, challenges another false, but deeply held, idea: specifically the idea that individuals completely control their lives. While it is true that individuals exert control over most of their lives, no one has total control. The idea that disabilities happen to others and while not to ourselves is another incorrect idea.

The out-of-control feelings of randomness can lead to personal questioning at the deepest level, such as "Why did God let this happen to me?" or "Why me and not that jerk over there?" "Why did the drunk driver escape without any injuries and I am now quadriplegic?" IWDs lose their trust in the world. One way to reduce the impact of the seemingly randomness of the disability is to look for someone to blame, either others or, sometimes, themselves. Finding someone to blame makes the world seem less unpredictable and random. Even self-blame can restore a feeling of control. (However, assigning blame has been found to impede a positive response to a disability.)

Charles Mee contracted polio as a teenager when he and his family drove to visit his older sister at college, a trip from Chicago to Colorado. Lying in the hospital after the diagnosis, Mee spent hours trying to remember every restroom he had used in several states, wanting to discover exactly where contracted polio. Compulsive, prolonged, obsessive questioning and searching for a well-defined cause often hinders physical rehabilitation and emotional responses. It is often more helpful to understand the difference between the cause of the disability and the meaning and purpose of the disability. The cause of the disability often is unknown, or is considered a type of responsibility that can then devolve into blame. In contrast, the meaning and purpose of the disability are not medical questions, but can be considered therapeutic responses that often include the individual's religious, spiritual, and philosophical belief systems. Thus, questioning the cause is a medical question and questioning the meaning and purpose of the disability are personal and emotional questions.

Mee begins to question his lifelong religious faith and, in his quest for answers, he visits a Jesuit priest.

> [Mee said:] "I've lost my faith. I no longer believe in God."
> "I see," the priest said. And then he made a mistake. Instead of honoring my thoughts and feelings—instead of gently exploring the anger that had taken me to this place I was in—he decided to bully me, to intimidate me back into the church with his superior reasoning.
>
> (Mee, 1999, p. 202)

A man with a spinal cord injury (SCI) thought that his anger could have been reduced if he had received counseling. He did not see a counselor and "that anger just sits in there and grows."

> I wish I'd had counseling regularly . . . on a fairly regular basis. I'm not sure what would've come out of it, but if you see someone enough, eventually you're going to say something. Try to bring things out, some of the anger, and things like that. This was something that was never done, and that anger just sits in there and grows.
>
> (Scherer, 1993, p. 160)

Note the use of the words "regularly" and "fairly regular." This IWD understands that a single counseling session would not have been enough to uncover the source of his anger. He understood that he was angry, but he also knew that without counseling the anger would not abate, but rather increase. He also understood that the timing of the counseling was important; he needed counseling immediately after his injury.

Anger is a negative emotion, for the IWD who is angry and for family members and professional service providers who experience the IWD's anger. Often, individuals who have survived traumatic injuries have been told, "At least you survived" or "There are other people a lot worse off than you." Both of these statements are true, but, at the same time, these facile statements deny or minimize the IWD's feelings. Obviously, the IWD cannot "hear" or believe these statements. Erik Weihenmayer (2001) described his anger at his orientation and mobility instructor, Mrs. Mundy, and his assistive technology, a cane, both of which would give him the skills to expand his world. Weihenmayer became progressively blind as a teenager.

> Until this point, my anger flowed at the world like water from a sprinkler, spraying in too many directions to be dangerous, but in my brief meeting with Mrs. Mundy, I had found a target, a perfect candidate on whom to focus the force of my rage. I hated my cane almost as much as I was learning to hate Mrs. Mundy. In my mind they both represented the vast gulf that existed between me and everyone else. No matter how hard I tried, I'd never be able to bridge that insurmountable expanse.
>
> (p. 49)

Weihenmayer's anger is pervasive ("flowed at the world"), diffuse ("spraying in all directions"), deep ("my rage"), and illogical ("both the cane and Mrs. Mandy represented "the vast gulf"). He also understood that his anger was futile.

Re-read Michael Weisskopf's account of his anger "that was preventing me from savoring the achievement of lifetime." The psychologist at the Veterans Affairs Hospital helped Weisskopf to understand the irrational basis of his anger. Before counseling, he had considered his traumatic injury to be "only the first in a long list of wrongs I would have to pardon before I could finally put the ordeal behind me" (Weisskopf, 2006, p. 37).

The fifth stage is integration and acceptance and is reached when the individual 1) understands and accepts the reality of the disability; 2) establishes goals and chooses values that do not conflict with the disability; 3) uses personal strengths and abilities; 4) engages in medical stabilization and rehabilitation; and 5) marshals and maintains a social support system. Patricia Deegan (1991), who was diagnosed with a psychiatric disability explained the concept of acceptance.

> In fact, our recovery is marked by an ever-deepening acceptance of our limitations. But rather than being an occasion for despair, we find that our

personal limitations are the ground from which spring our own unique possibilities. This is the paradox of recovery, that is, in accepting what we cannot do or be, we begin to discover who we can be and what we can do.

(p. 50)

In Deegan's short excerpt, it can be seen that acceptance is an individual experience ("our own unique possibilities") and it seems paradoxical that acceptance of limitations leads to possibilities and self-discovery. In the next excerpt, Weihenmayer uses the word, "ironically," rather than the word, "paradoxically," conveying the same concept that acceptance of disability leads to self-discovery and "bitter relief."

Ironically, as I relinquished my grip on sight, I sank into bitter relief. I had not a clue how I would survive as a blind person, how I would cook a meal, walk around, read a book, but trying to live as a sighted person was becoming more painful than blindness could ever be, and the uncertainty of what each tomorrow would bring was almost more terrifying. I knew nothing about blindness. I had no action plan. While I couldn't see well enough to . . . see an equation on the blackboard, I also couldn't accept myself as being blind. But one thing I knew: compared to this in-between world, total blindness couldn't be any worse or any more terrifying.

(p. 47)

The last stage of acceptance of disability is a concept borrowed from Abraham Maslow, the noted humanist/psychologist/theorist. Carolyn Vash felt that it is possible for some IWDs to achieve transcendence, a step beyond acceptance and integration; indeed, considering the disability to be a gift that has opened new possibilities and experiences and feeling that life, for them, is enhanced by living with a disability.

Transcendence

- Goes beyond acceptance of disability.
- The IWD feels that their life is better with the disability.
- Incorporates all of the aspects of Maslow's definition of transcendence and includes other disability-specific elements.
- The IWD often feels that the disability is a gift.
- At times, transcendence is associated with religious and spiritual ideals, but not always.

> - Incorporates forgiveness—both for self and others.
> - The IWD typically
>
> Takes pride in the mastery of the disability;
> Finds meaning and purpose in the disability;
> Discovers personal strengths;
> Seeks out new experiences;
> Re-evaluates goals and identities;
> Assists other IWDs.

It may follow that most IWODs cannot conceptualize IWDs as having these traits, perhaps because IWDs are thought to be somehow emotionally damaged due to their disabilities, continuously depressed, bitter, and angry. There is a time-worn expression: "Twisted body, twisted mind." This prejudicial (and false) overgeneralization is presently being discounted and discarded.

A summarization of a series of interviews of IWDs (Boswell, Knight, & Hamer, 2001), stated that these individuals had "a conception of self not based on the traditional medical view, but upon a broader, more holistic view that encompasses self, spirit, and society" (p. 20).

Re-reading Reed's (1991) description of transcendence, it is apparent that IWDs may have *more* opportunities for transcendence because of their disabilities. Below, are a few first-person accounts of reaching transcendence. Note that in all these accounts, achieving transcendence was neither easy or quick. For a woman with an amputated arm, it took her 25 years to look closely at her arm, and a man with a spinal cord injury, described an eight-year journey. Nonetheless, with the exception of Joan Tollifson, these stories of the lengthy time needed to achieve self-actualization, it can be seen all these disabilities had an acute, traumatic onset, necessitating a sudden change in just about everything in the individuals' lives.

Joan Tollifson, born with a congenital limb deficiency, accepted society's prejudice and discrimination as self-identifiers and, consequently, abused alcohol. ("I drank to die.") Tollifson avoided looking at her amputated arm, stating, "I remember the first time I actually looked closely at my arm without looking away. I was twenty-five years old at the time" (1997, p. 106). She described her transcendence as first, refusing to accept society's prejudice and discrimination and second, as seeing her disability as a gift and an opportunity for freedom and growth.

> Being disabled is a deep wound, a source of pain. But like all wounds, it is also a gift. As Eastern wisdom has always known, it is hard to tell good luck from bad luck. . . . Having one arm is an endless koan. It is what it is, which is unknowable, and it attracts a lot of ideas, stories, and images. Caught up in the negative story, I felt ashamed, incomplete, and not okay. I drank to die. Later on, caught up in a more positive story, I felt pride and a sense of identity. . . . In a way, I have gone back to the innocence of a baby. When little babies encounter my arm—the arm that ends just below the elbow—it is seen as just another interesting shape to explore and put into their mouths. There is nothing scary or taboo about it. . . . Not labeling what appears as either a deficit or an asset, perfect or imperfect, beautiful or ugly, but wondering openly without conclusion, without trying to get somewhere else. In such open being there is freedom and possibility for the new, even in the midst of what we call imperfection or limitation. I don't mean that the injustices or pain circumstances disappear, but they no longer bind us in the way they did.
>
> (1997, p. 111)

A koan in Zen Buddhism is a paradox that is used to meditate on to gain enlightenment.

At another point in her story, Tollifson recognizes that ideal of physical perfection are counterfeit, calling perfection "cardboard."

> Imperfection is the essence of being organic and alive. Organic life is vulnerable. . . . Cardboard ideals of perfection are flat and pale by comparison.
>
> (1997, p. 112)

In Stockbridge, England, Alex Lewis became a triple amputee in less than a month and yet he remarked that the "year of illness was the most brilliant of his life" (de Freytas-Tamura, 2017). In a *New York Times* article, Lewis' experience is recounted:

> Alex Lewis had been enjoying pints of Guinness with friends one cold evening when his throat started feeling scratchy and he came down with the flu. Or so he thought.

> Days later, he was fighting for his life.

> A mysterious bacterium wormed its way into his body, tearing away at his flesh and turning his skin purplish-black. His lips disintegrated, leaving a gaping hole where his mouth had been.

In less than a month, he lost his feet, then his legs and his left arm, physically becoming half the man he used to be. He was unrecognizable to many around him, including his 2-year-old son, who was too scared to hug him.

When Lewis left the hospital, he realized that he needed to change his "laid-back" attitude and started to take on the responsibility of the paperwork for the two pubs, the catering service, and the bakery that he and his wife owned. She switched roles with her husband and while he did the paperwork, she managed other aspects of their businesses. One of the losses Lewis felt deeply was his inability to drink a great deal of alcohol.

Not that his body weight—around 84 pounds—is less than half than it used to be, he can't have more than a few pints. "I know people will say, 'If you're a big drinker, you've got hollow legs,' and I think there's a bit of truth to that."

Staying sober has other benefits, saying:

A drunk in a wheelchair is not a good thing, not very clever, especially if you've got no arms. It's one thing to fall out of a wheelchair when you have arms, but it's another thing when you've got arms and, you know, just face plant.

The British National Health Service (NHS) has paid some of his medical expenses, costs of making his home accessible, prostheses, and rehabilitation costs. In addition, Lewis has calculated the costs that he and his wife will pay for disability costs not covered by NHS and set up a trust to help cover these costs. Lewis has gone to Greenland on a kayaking trip with British military veterans who are amputees. His conclusion and description of transcendence was succinct: "I try to get on with it."

A sense of humor is often part of transcendence. An Australian motivational speaker, Nick Vujicic, was born without arms and legs. In a speech presented in Laguna Beach, California in 2006 (Basheba, 2006) Nick's sense of humor was evident. Nonetheless, he prefaced his speech with this statement "I'm not here to say I understand your pain" (p. 1). His parents formed a small church in Australia and the members of the congregation mourned when he was born. During his international speaking tours, people asked what happened to him. Nick has a one-word reply: "CIGARETTES!!!" At the end of his speeches, Vujicic threatened his audience, "If you run fast, I'm going to get someone to throw me at you" (p. 7). He drives a car with computerized controls and Nick likes to drive up to a stoplight, catch the eye of another driver stopped at the light, and turn completely around in the driver's seat. The look of amazement on the other driver's face was funny to Vujicic. The title of the newspaper article describing his speech was, "No Arms, No Legs—No Worries."

In a research study, short statements illustrate differing aspects of transcendence of a disability. Participant 59 felt that he has had more experiences since the acquisition of his spinal cord injury (SCI):

> My spinal cord injury has allowed me to participate in activities that I feel I never would have had it had not happened. I have completed 11 marathons, travel nationally playing wheelchair rugby and earned a master's degree since my injury 13 years ago. I feel that I never would have done these things had my SCI never happened.
> (Graf, Marini, & Blankenship, 2009, p. 30)

The researchers summarized some of the data, stating:

> Life learning was discussed by 16 participants. Many of them described a shifting of values and greater appreciation for the "simpler things in life" (Participant 6). They discussed the reevaluation of their lives which moved them to become more observant, more grateful, and better people. "I've learned the value of simple, everyday things like being able to get dressed and go shopping, and I've been blessed with the ability to see many hidden beauties that most people would overlook in their busy lives!" (Participant 27). Participant 14 wrote, "living with disability causes a person to reevaluate their priorities in life. Much of what was important before acquiring a disability becomes trivial afterward." Finally, Participant 72 wrote, "By acquiring a disability I began a tough journey for eight years. The journey itself, however, has made me a better person and allowed me to see life more clearly."
> (Graf, Marini, & Blankenship, 2009, p. 33)

Individuals with psychiatric disabilities also experience transcendence. A woman of an adult son told of their experience of transcendence, both for her son and for herself, as a caregiver.

> My son has great willpower. He has graduated from college, also got his master's degree and has been working as a chemist for the past two years. My son has been hospitalized six times (four of which were court commitments) and he has been homeless. Through my stubbornness we rescued him from the streets. He is now so well and enjoying life. It gives me gratification that I never gave up hope.
> (Marsh & Lefly, 1996)

A woman with a psychiatric disability describes far-reaching effects of her self-actualization. Note the number of times she refers to her self-image in this short excerpt. Also note the way in which she separates the disability from the process of becoming well.

> The illness itself has not had any good effects, but the process of getting healthier has, especially on my spirituality, my self-image, my character, and personal qualities. Now I have a greater sense of serenity, self-liking, wonder at the world, and caring for myself and others.
> (March & Lefly, 1996, p. 10)

This woman's description of the results of "becoming healthier" could be a textbook definition of transcendence and self-actualization.

Assisting other IWDs is often a component of transcendence and can be helping individual IWDs or helping all IWDs. Mentorship and role modeling are examples of one-on-one assistance and advocacy work and obtaining civil rights for all IWDs are intended to help IWDs as a group. A man with a traumatic brain injury (TBI) described the way in which he helped "newbies," especially those who were "lifers." He feels he has two contributions to those with recently acquired disabilities: he has one and a half years of experience and he is not a professional service provider, but instead, "just another client." He understands that he possesses hard-earned credibility.

> I help anyone who walks through that door. I try to make them feel at home, you know, and I know what it's like, and I went through it when I first got here. I'm a peer to them, I'm just another client—so they'll listen to me. I can calm them down. I can sit down, I can talk to them, I can help them out—I've had a year and a half to practice, you know—so everyone who comes, I'll help them in any way I can.
> (Nichols & Kosciulek, 2014, p. 26)

One of the most remarkable stories of transcending a disability is that of Jack Hofsiss. Hofsiss, many years before he became quadriplegic as a result of a diving accident in a swimming pool, was the director of the film, *The Elephant Man*. *The Elephant Man* told the true story of Joseph Carey Merrick, an Englishman with a genetic condition, neurofibromatosis, which presents as overgrowths of flesh on the face and body. He first appeared in London "freak shows" and then lived in a hospital until his death. Hofsiss considered making *The Elephant Man* to be the best experience of his life.

It's odd, but I'm beginning to see a greater unity in my life. I came to terms with the worst experience of my life, which was this accident, and the best experience of my life, which was the pure, sweet sense of satisfaction that *The Elephant Man* gave me—the sweetness of working on that piece of material and being responsible for a large number of people knowing about the man and what he was like and how much we had to learn from him.

(Hofsiss & Laffey, 1993, pp. 86–87)

Two IWDs have found answers and meaning in their religious/spiritual views, but ascribe different motivations to God. The first individual does not want to think that God would deliberately cause her disability, stating that "God allows things to happen." The second individual thinks that God had some purpose in the acquisition of her disability, stating, "because there's some reason, or purpose that God intended to fulfill through a disability."

My disability has brought me from the mentality that God makes things happen to the mentality that God allows things to happen. Because if I think of it as He made it [disability] happen, it does nothing but make me angry. But, if I think of it as if He allowed it to happen as a natural course of the world, then I can think, "Okay, what kind of positive things can I do with this?"

(Boswell, Knight, & Hamer, 2001, p. 23)

My reactions [to disability] came as a result of believing that this is probably not just a freak accident that I became quadriplegic. But, has some purpose of the world I live in, and that I am not just here . . . but because there's some reason, or purpose, that God intended to fulfill through a disability.

(Boswell, Knight, & Hamer, 2001, p. 23)

Advantages of the Stage Theory

1. Allows the IWD to understand their own feelings and reactions, allowing a type of "psychoeducation."
2. Helps to validate and "normalize" emotional recovery.
3. Facilitates the most suitable types of counseling.
4. Recognizes that the adjustment or response is a process and not a one-time event.

5. Supports both short-term and long-term goals.
6. Facilitates (requires) case management.

Two disability scholars who have written extensively about the stage theory succinctly summarize:

> The process of adaptation is not irreversible. Individuals who experience a chronic illness or sustain a permanent disability may regress to an earlier phase or skip one or more of the phases of psychosocial adaptation. Phases of adaptation comprise nondiscrete and categorically overlapping reactions that may fluctuate and blend with one another, providing for the experience of more than one reaction at a time. Attempts to specify the duration of each phase, or of the entire adaptation process, are futile at best.
> (Livneh & Antonak, 1997, p. 19)

These authors are clear in stating that 1) these stages are not completely separate (rather, these stages are nondiscrete); 2) it is possible to experience more than one stage simultaneously; 3) individuals can "recycle" back to previous stages; and 4) response is not a one-time event. Therefore, the stage theory of response to disability, in contrast to many developmental theories, is not linear, always in the direction of improvement. Also, it has never been stated that these stages always appear in this particular sequence or that specific time guidelines can be applied to each stage. Also, the stage theory acknowledges that events in the individual's life can inaugurate the need to repeat these stages of response. Changes in medication, acquisition of assistive technology, the onset of secondary conditions and complications, and the deterioration of the disability are disability-related changes. Typical life events, such as gaining employment, entering school or university, marriage, and parenthood are positive life events that may require IWDs to respond to their disability, using the stage theory. Life events, which are typically considered negative, such as job loss, failing school, divorce, or death of a loved one, occur to everyone, and IWDs may find their responses to these exacerbated by their disability, or society's prejudice and discrimination against IWDs. Therefore, reactions to these negative events can often be described by the stage theory.

There are criticisms and shortcomings of the stage theory, but the theory has been found to be enduring because it describes many people's reactions. The strongest criticism has been termed "social oppression" (Kendall & Buys, 1998, p. 17) suggesting an oversimplification, something like, "This is Tuesday, so you must be in denial." This is an overstatement, of course, but the idea that *every* IWD with every type of disability, varying resources, and differing personalities, *invariably* experiences these stages in this *exact sequence* on a schedule. Of course, counselors must guard against telling the client what they are feeling; as that might be oppressive. In the following excerpt, a mother of a baby with a congenital disability recounts that she moves through all the stages of response in a single day, or even a single hour.

> I had read many times about the grief surrounding the birth of a child with defects, but the literature had not seemed to apply to me. My life certainly included denial, anger, bargaining, depression, and acceptance. But these were not milestones on a timeline, but were aspects of every day, sometimes every hour. Furthermore, there was little grief attached to the "expected baby." The grief was tied up with the whole mental picture I had for myself, my family, and our future. Feeling that I had failed myself, Kurt [her husband], Beth [the baby], the family, and even society itself, what I really had lost was whole sense of self-esteem.
>
> (Miller, 1988, p. 145)

Kendall and Buys added "Stage models of adjustment also normalize responses such as denial and distress following acquired disability, which may lead rehabilitation workers to expect, or even encourage, such responses" (p. 17). However, helping individuals to understand their own feelings, many of which are negative and unpleasant, is therapeutic and informing them that many others have experienced, and do experience, these unpleasant emotions is even more therapeutic. This process is termed "normalization" and "universalization." Perhaps simply psychoeducation, describing negative feelings of IWDs to themselves, their families, and professional service providers often provides understanding and, with understanding, relief is possible. Counselors understand that some clients, with or without disabilities, feel worse before they feel better and being warned of this possibility can prevent the client's early termination. In the stage theory of response to disability, many IWDs do experience typical, common "normal" depression, anger, and questioning and they do feel worse before they feel better. All of these emotions are unpleasant to experience, both for the IWD and others, but they are normal, meaning commonplace, to be expected, and typical. Social and professional abandonment can occur if others do not understand these typical, but very unpleasant, reactions.

Assisting and supporting IWDs and their families throughout the response process can avoid problems such as family disintegration and even suicide.

Utilizing the stage theory helps many professionals and family members to examine their own responses to the IWD. For example, it has been suggested that some professionals are uncomfortable with angry patients, avoiding these patients and giving only minimal care (Clanton, Rude, & Taylor, 1992). At times, these negative emotions can lead to isolation of IWDs, which creates further problems. Smart (2016) summarized:

> [F]amily members can be educated about the importance of noncritical acceptance of the IWD's denial. Family members learn that confronting or arguing with the IWD is counterproductive. Another example concerns the individual who is in the anger stage. Often, this anger is expressed toward the accessible people—family members or care providers. Helping family and caregivers to understand that the anger of the IWD is an attempt to regain balance and control will reduce their stress and help to eliminate compassion fatigue and burnout. Therefore, if caregivers and family members understand the stages of adaptation, it is less likely that the IWD will become socially isolated. The stage theory promotes hope and optimism and provides a starting point for assisting the IWD. Deegan (1997) stated, "Hope is contagious."
>
> (p. 53)

When service providers consult and assess the stage of response the IWD is experiencing, complementary treatment plans and goals can be implemented. While it is true that some individuals present differently to various caregivers, case conferencing in order to access of stage of response has the potential to utilize the skills and insights of different types of professionals. Additionally, when family members are included, a more complete picture of the IWD's pre-disability emotional functioning can be obtained.

The stage theory is applicable to stable course disabilities and acquired disabilities. Therefore, individuals with episodic or relapsing disabilities generally do not experience these stages. Further, individuals who acquire disabilities later in life often do not progress through these stages because, on both an individual level and on a societal level, the acquisition of a disability is considered to be a part of old age. In congenital disabilities it is the parents who experience these stages.

Intentionality

The social learning theorist Albert Bandura can also be considered to be a humanist. The social learning aspect of his theories includes the ideas that people have the ability to learn, to self-monitor, and self-correct. The humanist aspect includes the optimistic ideas that people are resilient, flexible, and continue to learn and grow throughout their lifespan. He (1986) believed that individuals "must master new competencies to fulfill changing demands throughout their life span" (p. 20). Bandura labeled the first step to self-efficacy, "intentionality." Intentionality is defined as confronting and defining needs and difficulties and determining the necessary responses. Rather than reacting to a situation, individuals purposefully respond. The concepts and methods of intentionality can be applied to the disability experience.

Three Types of Intentionality
1. Cognitive intentionality
2. Affective intentionality
3. Behavioral intentionality

Strictly speaking, cognitive restructuring refers only to thinking, but it has expanded to include emotional reactions and behavioral responses. Thus, behavioral responses can be considered as techniques of cognitive behavioral therapy. *Cognitive intentionality* includes conceptualizing the disability as a challenge which can be met and, moreover, there might be positive aspects to the disability. *Affective intentionality* includes emotional regulation, allowing time and space to react and grieve and afterwards, expecting a return to emotional equilibrium. *Behavioral intentionality* leads to clear, unambiguous statements of the way in which the disability will be managed, including obtaining the best medical care, seeking out appropriate role models, and structuring other types of social support. For episodic or relapsing disabilities, some families engage in "relapse drills" in which the family practices responding to the relapse. Such drills include recognizing the prodromal (warning) signs of a relapse, responding to the relapse, returning to former levels of functioning (or the "new" normal) and learning from each episode or relapse. While the physical aspects of the relapses may not be predictable, the cognitive, emotional, and behavioral responses can be predictable and manageable. These types of relapse drills often involve including professionals, asking for guidance and support *before* the relapse.

Cognitive, emotional, and behavioral intentionality appear straightforward, both in the processes and the benefits. Nonetheless, restructuring the way in which IWDs, and their families, think and respond to disability is an ongoing effort, often requiring readjustments. Two authors (Harper & Peterson, 2000) comprehensively explained the way in which parents can teach children with disabilities how to discuss their disabilities, clearly describing cognitive and affective intentionality.

> The issue of what to tell others should be discussed with all children who have a chronic illness [and disability], explanations and understandings should be reviewed periodically, and each individual should be given a specific set of explanatory strategies to offer to peers and friends. These explanations obviously require some individualized tailoring for the child . . . related to his or her conceptual level, current and ongoing medical condition, prior experiences and understanding of the disorder, and social and emotional status. They should be rehearsed to ensure that the dialogue is used and easy to deliver. The "tone" of these dialogues has a major impact on these social interactions with peers; how one says something may be more crucial than what one says.
>
> (p. 129)

In the following excerpt, all three types of intentionality are implemented. In addition, the importance of normalizing negative feelings of siblings is advocated.

> Even more important, however, is your ability to convey to your other children that their feelings are *normal*—whether these feelings consist of irrational self-blame or resentment because of the extra attention you may need to give your child with a disability. "It's okay to feel angry. Mommy and Daddy sometimes feel like that ourselves," is often the best response, even as you remind your older children that it is *not* okay to act out these feelings of resentment in ways that can hurt other people. Saying this may be difficult for you, but it is preferable to responses such as, "How can you say that about your brother? Don't you know that he has a problem?" The ability to listen sympathetically to your other children in this fashion is directly linked to how well you have been able to deal with such feelings yourself.
>
> (Coplan & Trachtenberg, 2001, p. 7)

Clearly pointed out in this excerpt is that, in order to implement proactive and emotionally satisfying intentionality strategies with their children, parents must first resolve and understand their own feelings about their child with a disability.

Deficit Breeds Growth

Three developmental psychologists (Baltes, Staudiner, & Lindenberger, 1999) wrote about a radical idea, an idea that was in opposition to most, if not all, developmental theories. They labeled their ideas and theory as "deficit breeds growth," and expanded on Gehlen's (1956) ideas in which Gehlen posited that all humans were "beings of deficits." Baltes et al. wrote first about "successful aging," but later expanded their model to include IWDs, essentially advocating for a balance of potential for growth, reduction and management of biological loss, and redefining success and self-actualization. They explained, "Such a metamodel should be able to harbor a great diversity of outcomes and goals, accommodate different success criteria" (p. 87). Biological decline, aging, and the acquisition of a disability, in their view, can lead to growth and greater development, which would not be possible without these so-called losses. Therefore, much of the deficit breeds growth philosophy parallels Vash's concept of transcendence.

Traditionally, many developmental theorists believed that human development waned and eventually stopped when individuals reached middle-age and progressed into old age. Linking development to biological age made it seemingly apparent that when individuals started to experience biological declines, all types of developmental progress were ended.

Opposing views of other great developmental theorists considered human development to be an upward trajectory that results in greater autonomy, freedom, and control. The individual may attain many achievements, some societal expectations and others idiosyncratically meaningful. Developmental progress also includes the idea of individuation, meaning that individuals have the power of self-definition, and that as individuals become older, they increasingly become different from others, sometimes referred to as "differentiation." As a group, adults are more heterogenous whereas infants and children tend to be more homogenous groups. Adults tend to have more ego strength, a combination of self-knowledge, self-direction, and autonomy. These developmental goals are common in Western, developed nations and, therefore, may not apply to other types of societies.

Consideration of the Acquisition of a Disability as a Developmental Task

The acquisition of a disability can be considered a developmental task that requires individuals to change their identities and assume new roles and responsibilities and the initiation and completion of many developmental tasks often celebrated by rites of passage. Both the initiation of developmental tasks and their successful completion represent significant events in individuals' lives. For some developmental tasks, individuals may want to revert to an earlier developmental stage, and this may be termed a "transition." Adolescence is a good example of the idea of wanting to stay in an earlier period of development, childhood, while expecting the privileges and opportunities of adulthood. Everyone understands that transitions require time and the support of others. Transitions also require adjustment periods and for others to accommodate the individual's need for time. Rites of passage communicate to the individual that necessary growth is required of them and, also, promise the support of friends, family, and general society. The provision of societal resources accompany developmental tasks including public school, driver's licenses, entrance into the military, higher education, and career options. Developmental tasks are often difficult, demanding, and often appear as "a jump into the unknown." Therefore, the support of family, friends, and society is necessary. Many developmental tasks and rites of passage are defined by biology (such as chronological age) and/or by religion (such as first communion, baptism, marriage, or death). The developmental theorist, Erik Erikson, termed transition points as "crises," or decision points, stating that these transitions were times of great vulnerability, but also enlarged potential.

Birthday parties, the Tooth Fairy, graduation ceremonies, weddings, and funerals are all socially sanctioned, meaning that these rites of passages and the associated development tasks are recognized, celebrated, or honored by others and that resources are provided. These resources can include money under a child's pillow for a baby tooth, piñatas at birthday parties, cakes, gifts, casseroles, teddy bears, flowers, and greeting cards. Few people would consider ignoring the landmark events of their friends or family members, such as having a new baby, or graduating from university, or entering the military. People travel long distances to attend parties, receptions, ceremonies, and funerals, all with the intent of showing encouragement and honoring the individual as they progress to the next development. Often, the individual wears different types of clothing and assumes a new name or title, signifying that the individual has changed. Graduation robes, wedding dresses, and military uniforms communicate that new responsibilities and privileges await.

Social moratoriums are becoming more accepted as mortality rates drop and as lives become longer and choices proliferate. Social moratoriums are defined as societally endowed resources of time, money, and, sometimes services for a period of time in which the individual is released from the responsibilities of life. A social moratorium is a clearly defined time period, allowing individuals to redefine themselves and defer important life decisions, such as marriage, area of university study, and future occupational pursuits. The most common type of social moratorium is the "gap year" between high school graduation and entrance into university. The societal resources that allow these social moratoriums are considered wise investments, both on an individual and societal level, because it is thought that entering into lifelong relationships and occupations before adequate contemplation and planning may result in expensive failures. Social moratoriums also allow individuals to separate from past disadvantages, such as economic poverty, poor school performance, difficulties with the legal system, and substance abuse (Smart, 2012, p. 16). Entering the military, performing international service volunteer work, and travel are examples of social moratoriums.

Socially supported developmental tasks are not always positive. Seemingly negative changes such as divorce and job loss are increasingly being recognized as developmental tasks while death and dying has always been recognized and honored as rites of passage.

However, the acquisition of a disability is rarely considered to be a developmental task with the corresponding rites of passage in spite of the fact that individuals are required to change their identities and new roles and responsibilities are required of them. In the same way that successfully completing traditional development tasks require social acknowledgement and support, these types of resources are necessary at the time of the acquisition of a disability or the birth of a baby with a disability. Instead, becoming an IWD is termed "a silent transition." Friends and families do not understand what they're supposed to say or do nor will they be able to buy a greeting card which would help to convey their feelings.

The extended period of time required for medical stabilization and physical rehabilitation can act as a "social moratorium." Marsh and Lefly (1996) explained the value of social moratoriums when applied to acquired disabilities: "A catastrophic event [such as a disability] generally results in disintegration of existing patterns, which in turn offers the opportunity for constructive integration" (p. 3). Hospital treatment and rehabilitation in large centers can be time-consuming and many IWDs feel that they have used the time wisely to redefine themselves, consider alternative possibilities, and pursue alternative paths. One man explained:

> I look at it like this, I was a 25-year-old hellion with a shaved head before my accident. I think I'm a better person than what I was then. I took life for granted, and boom, I got a big awakening.
> (Boswell, Dawson, & Heininger, 1998, p. 30)

> **Difficulties in Conceptualizing the Acquisition of a Disability as a Developmental Tasks**
> - Disabilities are almost universally thought to be a loss and decline of development.
> - Most developmental tasks are considered to be the result of epigenetic growth.
> - The acquisition of a disability is a silent transition, without societal sanctions.

We have discussed in the previous chapters the way in which society, as a whole, denies the possibility and reality of disabilities and the people who experience them. Further, disability is almost universally thought to be loss and decline. In contrast, most developmental theories are considered epigenetic. Epigenetic, once only used in biological terms, means that humans progress to higher levels of development in a linear trajectory. The prefix "epi" means "upon" and "genesis" means beginning or emergence. Indeed, our physical growth and development is epigenetic because we become larger, stronger, and more coordinated (until middle age or old age). The first developmental theories closely followed biological growth, using chronological age as a basis. Progress through both biological and social stages are cumulative and hierarchical. Emotionally and socially, development is also thought to be epigenetic and hierarchal because individuals develop strengths, skills, and accumulating advantages. The individual, according to most developmental theories retains the skills and strengths from previous developmental stages and incorporates these into higher stages while, at the same time, acquiring new and better skills and strengths. Another source of development is the capability to choose one's environment, typically favoring environments which allow the individual success. While everybody understands that no one has unlimited choices, most people expect a wide range of choices.

In the past, disability has not been thought of as epigenetic growth, of hierarchical progression, or as an opportunity to accumulate advantages. Epigenetic growth means "upward and onward" and disability seemed to automatically exclude such ideas. Autonomy, control, independence are not often thought to include the disability experience and the capability to choose one's best environment is often not available to IWDs. Rather than a life of planful competence, in which advantages and rewards accumulate, IWDs have been to live lives of accumulating disadvantages. Many large societal and governmental opportunity structures have been inaccessible to IWDs, making it difficult, if not impossible to accrue lifelong advantages such as education, work, and equal social status.

Conclusion

In this chapter, the individual's response was considered, including the contradictory feelings of the individual after the acquisition of their disability or diagnosis of chronic illness. Specifically, the individual knows that they are basically the same person, but also understands that they have never considered or prepared for a disability.

Factors, both tangible and intangible, that contribute to a healthy response to a disability were presented. Both positive responses and negative responses were defined. Two theories of response were described, cognitive restructuring and the stage theory. Finally, a new approach to conceptualizing the onset of a disability was presented. This new approach suggested viewing the onset of a disability as a developmental life task.

References

Baltes, P. B., Staudiner, U. M., & Lindenberger, U. (1999). Lifespan psychology: Theory and application to intellectual functioning. *Annual Review of Psychology, 50*, 471–507.

Bandura, A. (1986). *Social foundations of thought and action: A social cognitive theory.* Englewood Cliffs, NJ: Prentice-Hall.

Basheba, L. (2006, July). No arms, no legs—no worries. *Orange County Register*, 1, 7.

Batshaw, M. L. (Ed.) (2001). *Children with disabilities* (4th ed.). Baltimore, MD: Paul H. Brookes.

Boswell, B., Knight, S., & Hamer, M. (2001). Disability and spirituality: A reciprocal relationship with implications for the rehabilitation process. *Journal of Rehabilitation, 67*(4), 20–25.

Boswell, B. B., Dawson, M., & Hamer, M. (1998). Quality of life as defined with adults with spinal cord injuries. *Journal of Rehabilitation, 64*, 27–32.

Buki, L. P., Kogan, L., Keen, B., & Uman, P. (2007). In the midst of a hurricane: A case study of a couple living with AIDS. In A. Dell Porto & P. Powers (Eds.), *The psychological and social impact of illness and disability* (6th ed., pp. 329–350). New York, NY: Springer.

Campling, J. (1981). *Images of ourselves: Women with disabilities talking.* London: Routledge Kegan Paul.

Clanton, I. D., Rude, S. S., & Taylor, C. (1992). Learned resourcefulness as a moderator of burnout in a sample of rehabilitation providers. *Rehabilitation Psychology, 37*, 131–140.

Close, C. (1993). Chuck Close. In J. K. Smith & G. Plimpton (Eds.), *Chronicles of courage: Very special artists* (pp. 14–28). New York, NY: Penguin Random House.

Cohen, R. M. (2004). *Blindsided: Living a life above illness: A reluctant memoir.* New York, NY: Harper Collins.

Coplan, J., & Trachtenberg, S. W. (2001). Finding out your child has a disability. In M. L. Batshaw (Ed.), *When your child has a disability* (pp. 3–10). Baltimore, MD: Paul H. Brookes.

Crewe, N. M. (1997). Life stories of people with long-term spinal cord injury. *Rehabilitation Counseling Bulletin, 41*, 26–42.

Deegan, P. E. (1991). Recovery: The lived experience of rehabilitation. In R. P. Martinelli & A. E. Dell Porto (Eds.), *The psychological and social impact of psychiatric disability* (3rd ed.) (pp. 47–54). New York, NY: Springer.

deFreytas-Tamura, K. (2017, February 3). For quadruple amputee, years of illness "was the most brilliant." *New York Times.*

Faull, K., Hill, M. D., Cochrane, G., Gray, J., Hunt, M., McKenzie, C., & Winter, L. (2004). Investigation of health perspectives of those with physical disabilities: The role of spirituality as a determinant of health. *Disability and Rehabilitation, 26,* 129–144.

Fleischer, D. Z., & Zames, F. (2001). *The disability rights movement: From charity to confrontation.* Philadelphia, PA: Temple University.

Gehlen, A. (1956). *Urmensch und Spätkultur: Philosophische Ergebnisse und Aussagen.* Bonn, Germany: Athenäum.

Goffman, E. (1963). *Stigma: Notes on the management of spoiled identity.* Englewood Cliffs, NJ: Prentice Hall.

Graf, N. M., Marini, I., & Blankenship, C. J. (2009). One hundred words about disability. *Journal of Rehabilitation, 75,* 25–34.

Harper, D. C., & Peterson, D. B. (2000). Neuromuscular and musculoskeletal disorders in children. In R. G. Frank & T. R. Elliot (Eds.), *Handbook of rehabilitation psychology* (pp. 123–144). Washington, DC: American Psychological Association.

Henley, M., Algozzine, R. F., & Ramsey, R. (1996). *Characteristics of and strategies for teaching students with mild disabilities* (6th ed.). Upper Saddle River, NJ: Pearson.

Hofsiss, J., & Laffey M. (1993). Jack Hofsiss and Maureen Laffey. In J. K. Smith & G. Plimpton (Eds.), *Chronicles of courage: Very special artists* (pp. 78–87). New York, NY: Penguin Random House.

Holaday, M., & McPhearson, R. W. (1997). Resilience and severe burns. *Journal of Counseling and Development, 75,* 346–356.

Kendall, E., & Buys, N. (1998). An integrated model of psychosocial adjustment following acquired disability. *Journal of Rehabilitation, 64*(3), 16–20.

Laborit, E. (2010). Selections from the *Cry of the Gull.* In L. J. Lennard (Ed.), *The disability studies readers* (3rd ed., pp. 599–618). New York, NY: Routledge.

Langer, K. G. (1994). Depression and denial in psychotherapy of persons with disabilities. *American Journal of Psychotherapy, 49,* 113–120.

Livneh, H., & Antonak, R. F. (1997). *Psychosocial adaptation to chronic illness and disability.* Gaithersburg, MD: Aspen.

Marsh, D. T. (1992). *Families and mental illness: New directions in professional practice.* New York, NY: Praeger.

Marsh, D. T., & Lefly, H. P. (1996). The family experience of mental illness: Evidence for resilience. *Psychiatric Rehabilitation Journal, 20*(2), 3–13.

Mee, C. (1999). *A nearly normal life: A memoir.* Boston, MA: Little, Brown.

Michalko, R. (2002). *The difference that disability makes.* Philadelphia, PA: Temple University.

Miller, J. (1988). Personal statement: Mechanisms for coping with the disability of a child—A mother's perspective. In P. W. Power, A. E. Dell Orto, & M. B. Gibbons (Eds.), *Family interventions throughout chronic illness and disability* (pp. 136–147). New York, NY: Springer.

Mitchell, D., & Synder, S. (2010). Narrative prosthesis. In L. J. Davis (Ed.), *The disability studies reader* (3rd ed., pp. 274–287). New York, NY: Routledge.

Murphy, R. (1990). *The body silent in America.* New York, NY: Norton.

National Public Radio. (1998, May). Inventing the poster child. In *The disability history project* [Radio documentary]. Retrieved from www.npr.org/programs/disability/ba_shows.dir/index_sh.html Retrieved 02–26–2018

Naugle, R. I. (1991). Denial in rehabilitation: Its genesis, consequences, and clinical management. In R. P. Marinelli & A. E. Dell Otto (Eds.), *The psychological and social impact of disability* (3rd ed., pp. 139–151). New York, NY: Springer.

Nichols, J. L., & Kosciuleck, J. (2014). Social interactions of individuals with traumatic brain injury. *Journal of Rehabilitation, 80,* 21–29.

O'Brien, M. (2014, July 18). My new life with one arm. *This Week*, 36–37.
Perkins, R. (1996). *Talking to angels: A life spent in high latitudes.* Boston, MA: Beacon.
Phemister, A., & Crewe, N. (2004). Objective self-awareness and stigma: Implications for persons with visible disabilities. *Journal of Rehabilitation, 70,* 33–37.
Price, R. (1994). *A whole new life: An illness and a healing.* New York, NY: Atheneum.
Reed, P. G. (1991). Toward a nursing theory of self-transcendence: Deductive reformulation using developmental theories. *Advances in Nursing Sciences, 13*(4), 64–77.
Robinson, M. (1997). Renascence. In K. Fries (Ed.), *Staring back: The disability experience from the inside out* (pp. 87–92). New York, NY: Plume.
Scherer, M. J. (1993). *Living in the state of stuck: How technology impacts the lives of people with disabilities.* Cambridge, MA: Brookline.
Shell, M. (2005). *Polio and its aftermath: The paralysis of culture.* Cambridge, MA: Harvard University.
Smart, J. F. (2012). *Disability across the developmental lifespan.* New York, NY: Springer.
Smart, J. F. (2016). *Disability, society, and individual* (3rd ed.). Austin, TX: PRO-ED.
Stewart, J. R. (1994). Denial of disabling conditions and specific interventions in the rehabilitation counseling setting. *Journal of Applied Rehabilitation Counseling, 25*(3), 7–15.
Smart, J. F., & Smart, D. W. (1997). Culturally sensitive informed choice in rehabilitation counseling. *Journal of Applied Rehabilitation Counseling, 28,* 32–37.
Tollifson, J. (1997). Imperfection is a beautiful thing. In K. Fries (Ed.), *Staring back: The disability experience from the inside out* (pp. 104–112). New York, NY: Plume.
Vash, C. L. (1981). *The psychology of disability.* New York, NY: Springer.
Weihenmayer, E. (2001). *Touch the top of the world: A blind man's journey to climb farther than the eye can see.* New York, NY: Dutton.
Weisskopf, M. (2006, October 2). How I lost my hand, but found myself. *Time,* 28–37.
White, M. & Gribbin, J. (1993). *Stephen Hawking: A life in science.* New York: NY: Penguin.
Wilson, D. J. (1990). *Living with polio: The epidemics and its survivors.* Chicago, IL: University of Chicago.
Wright, B. A. (1960). *Physical disability—A psychosocial approach.* New York, NY: Harper & Row.
Wright, B. A. (1983). *Physical disability—A psychosocial approach* (2nd ed.). New York, NY: Harper & Row.

Nine

UNDERSTANDING SOCIAL ROLE DEMANDS OF INDIVIDUALS WITH DISABILITIES

Counseling Practice Guidelines

Factors in the disability and social role expectations are considered in this chapter. Disabilities, in general, have been discussed in previous chapters, including the measurement, diagnosis, and definition of varying disabilities and the more abstract conceptualization of Models of Disability. In Chapter Two, these factors in the disability were introduced and more information on each of these was provided. However, in this chapter, more specific information is provided about different types of disability, including counseling techniques, but with the proviso that all of these techniques must be based on a strong, empathic client-counselor relationship that incorporates the CWD's idiosyncratic conceptualization of the disability. Some of these evidence-based and widely used counseling practices include cognitive behavioral theory, refining decision-making skills, values clarification, and developing ego strength. All counseling specialties offer knowledge and skills and have something to offer IWDs. However, before any counseling technique can be ethically applied, counselors should understand disability stereotypes and misconceptions and, in addition, frequently examine their own unconscious biases toward disability and IWDs.

Factors of the Disability That Affect the Individual's Response

Disabilities are culturally determined, including symptom recognition, labeling and diagnosis, and determining the treatment/management. Disabilities are also defined in terms of governmental systems. Normalcy/disability, in addition to being defined as a biological, organic condition, is also legally described and enforced. Therefore, in the United States, Canada, the United Kingdom, and western Europe, labeling disabilities and determining both the type and level of support and treatment of IWDs, varies due to different types of governmental systems, the structure of helping agencies, and the level of support provided to citizens with disabilities. Nonetheless, it is possible, and necessary, to initiate an understanding of the factors that constitute a disability. These are the time of onset; type of onset; severity of the disability; the course of the disability; the functions impaired; the degree of societal stigma; the visibility of the disability, including any disfigurements, degree of incidence, prognosis and treatment/management required. Viewing disability (or any other human characteristic) as a simple dichotomy, such as "yes" or "no" or "severe" or "mild," is an oversimplification that does not recognize anyone's reality of experience. Nonetheless, it is important to obtain some type of preliminary understanding. It is also important to point out that many individuals experience more than one disability. In both self-identity and service provision, the response of individuals with more than one disability can be complex.

This chapter discusses several factors of the disability. Following is a list of the nine factors in the disability discussed in this chapter. Most people conceptualize disability as a visible, stable-course physical disability and there are many individuals with these types of disabilities. Nonetheless, the disabilities of many IWDs are invisible, with fluctuating or episodic courses, and are categorized as cognitive or psychiatric disabilities and the response demands, including societal perceptions, are much more difficult and complex. Some of these difficulties and complexities are discussed here.

Factors in the Disability

1. A silent transition, i.e., the birth of a baby with a congenital disability
2. The effects of a long pre-diagnosis period
3. Social support for individuals with disabilities
4. Role models and "disabled heroes"
5. Dating
6. Marriage and acquisition of a disability

Included in the discussion of the response to disability are suggestions for counseling practices, such in which counseling specialties apply, appropriate techniques, and theoretical orientations which guide applications.

Counseling Theoretical Orientations and Techniques

1. Values clarification
2. Decision making skills
3. Assertive training
4. Building ego strength

5. Social efficacy
6. Marriage and family counseling
7. Personal control counseling
8. Sexual concerns
9. Cognitive behavioral techniques
10. Social justice

Silent Transition: The Birth of a Baby With a Congenital Disability

Response Demands of Congenital Disabilities

1. Many congenital disabilities are low-incidence disabilities.
2. Without a prognosis, parents may feel that there is no future.
3. For newborns with congenital disabilities, it is the parents who undergo the process of response/adaptation.
4. Parents of infants with disabilities experience a silent transition, often neither recognized nor acknowledged by society.
5. The need for an explanatory cause often is important.
6. Bioethical concerns present questions that may not have been considered.

Once considered rather rare, congenital disabilities occur in one of every 16 births in the United States, and these growing numbers of newborns with disabilities represent a demographic change for societies and governments. The medical advances of neonatal medicine has resulted in lower infant mortality rates, leading to corresponding higher rates of congenital disabilities. Some types of congenital disabilities include gene-linked abnormalities (cystic fibrosis, Huntington disease, Tay-Sachs disease) chromosomal abnormalities (Down syndrome, Turner's syndrome, Fragile X syndrome, and Klinefelter's syndrome), hearing loss, vision loss, cerebral palsy, and spina bifida. Many of these disabilities co-occur.

> The incidence of blindness in children with multiple developmental disabilities is more than 200 times that found in the general population. One third of children with partial sight and two thirds of children with blindness have other developmental disabilities, hearing impairments, seizures disorders, and cerebral palsy.
>
> (Miller & Menacker, 2007, p. 152)

While congenital disabilities now occur more frequently, most are low incidence, meaning that the prevalence, or incidence, of each type of disability is rare. There are, however, many, many different types of congenital disabilities, each with a rather low incidence. The following excerpt illustrates this relationship—"hundreds of different conditions," but most of these conditions are rare. J. M. Patterson (1988) explained:

> The prevalence of each of the hundreds of different conditions in children is relatively rare.... Except for a few common disorders such as mild asthma, the prevalence of any condition is less than 1 per 100 children. This low incidence rate of many types of disabilities in children means that many families must seek treatment in large metropolitan hospitals. Frequent travel, or perhaps moving the family residence, may be necessary in order to obtain treatment and services for a child with a disability.
>
> (Patterson, 1988, p. 70)

For some congenital disabilities, accurate prenatal testing for the disability is available. However, many parents (and others) are stunned, confused, and uncomfortable with the birth of a baby who is not the one whom they had imagined or planned for. In the following example from the 1970s, a mother of a child with a congenital intellectual disability related:

> When the baby was born, they said, "Oh God, put her out." This is the first thing they said, "Oh my God, put her out" . . . and the next thing I remember was waking up in the recovery room . . . I had my priest on my left hand and my pediatrician on my right hand . . . and they were trying to get me to sign a paper . . . I just couldn't believe that this was happening to me and I said to my priest, "Father, what's the matter?" and he said, "You have to sign this release. Your daughter is very sick." And I said to the pediatrician, "What's the matter with her?" and he said, "Don't worry honey, she'll be dead before morning. . . ." He said that she had something that was too much to talk about, that I shouldn't worry myself. . . . Nobody was telling me what this was. . . . I was very depressed.
>
> (Darling, 1983, p. 130)

The medical professions deal with congenital disabilities, including communication with the parents, in much more sensitive, ethical, and effective ways than is apparent in this excerpt. This example seems to illustrate the ways in which two types of professionals struggled with the responsibility for dealing with disabilities: the priest (religion) and the pediatrician (medicine).

It is the parents and the extended family who must negotiate the emotional responses to the disability and, the combination of a lack of role models, the lack of prognosis, and little social support create a unique constellation of response needs. Low incidence disabilities often perplex physicians because, unless they practice in a large, university-affiliated teaching hospital, they may never have encountered a particular disability or, as is often the case with congenital disabilities, the co-occurrence of disabilities. Occasionally, there is a long pre-diagnosis period, further adding to the stress. Some parents feel that without a diagnosis, perhaps there is no disability or that the disability will not be permanent. Without a definitive diagnosis, there is no prognosis. A low incidence disability also adds stress because of the medical ambiguity. In addition, individuals responding to low-incidence disabilities are likely to have fewer role models to help them reduce the ambiguity, give emotional support, and share experiences. Counselors understand the importance of role models and can help parents and family members seek out and build alliances with such role models.

Often, parents are faced with many demands and decisions while they, themselves, are recovering from a difficult pregnancy and coping with shock and grief. Another demographic shift that interacts with these demands is the decline of the two-parent family with grandparents and other extended families nearby. These demands are difficult for a financially stable, two-parent family with extended family members nearby. Nonetheless, the increasing numbers of single parents and the geographic mobility of the United States make it far more common for an infant with congenital disability to be born to a single mother without any supportive family nearby. Simple demographic changes (geographic mobility) and social changes (increasing numbers of single parents, most often mothers) combine to make a medical concern (the congenital disability) more difficult.

The response required by a congenital disability is often amplified by its lack of a known cause. In the following excerpt, grandparents and great-grandparents try to prove their "purity."

> [The baby's diagnosis] was a multisyllabic disease, very rare and genetic. Grandparents and great grandparents gasped! The diagnosis set both sides of the family busy rattling skeletons and trying to prove that each was pure and not responsible for the present suffering.
>
> (McPhee, 1982, p. 13)

It is a short leap from determination of the cause to blaming a supposed guilty party. It is often difficult to definitively determine cause for three reasons: 1) the cause is simply unknown; 2) there are multiple causes; and 3) the theory of causation changes. The best example of a causation theory which was widely accepted and ultimately discarded as totally without merit or scientific proof is Autism Spectrum Disorder (ASD). From the 1940s until recently, ASD was thought to be caused by poor parenting, most often mothers. Now, it is known to be a neurocognitive disability. Reading the excerpt about the grandparents trying to prove their genetic purity shows the short leap from the need to determine a cause to placing blame.

Pat Furlong is a nurse married to a physician and they are the parents of two sons born with Duchenne muscular dystrophy, a genetic disorder. Both her sons died in their teenage years. Furlong related a doctor's visit in which the physician tried to blame and shame her. The doctors repeated attempts resulted in an atypical and angry response from Furlong.

> The doctor upbraided her, she says, for having had a second boy. "You should have known about this," she recalls him telling her. "This is a familial disease, it's genetic, you have it in your family." I said, "I don't." (She learned later that she was among the one-third of cases in which the mutation appears spontaneously.) The doctor insisted, "You could have prevented the second pregnancy, or you could have aborted the second pregnancy." Patrick, then four, was sitting on Furlong's lap. "Before that day, I was relatively mild-mannered," Furlong says. She remembers grabbing the doctor's tie and pulling him up to her nose. I said, "If someone should have been aborted today, you're the one."
>
> (Colapinto, 2010, p. 65)

The birth of a child with a disability is often a silent transition, a transition that is neither socially recognized nor supported. For the parents and babies, most likely there will not be baby showers, casseroles and flowers delivered, or "coos" from strangers. Crystal's mother wrote to the newspaper advice columnist, Ann Landers, telling of her frequent experiences and asking Ann to "to alert the boneheads."

> I gave birth to my first child last April. Crystal was 12 weeks premature and weighed less than 2 pounds. We were afraid that she would die or have severe handicaps, but we were blessed with good fortune as her only remaining requirement is the extra oxygen she receives through a nasal tube worn 24 hours a day.

> Because the nasal tube makes her look different, I have received a lot of unsolicited and rude comments. People ask, "What's wrong with her? Was she born that way? What's her problem?" I do not wish to discuss my daughter's medical condition with strangers, and considering the handicaps she might have had, my husband and I feel that there is nothing wrong with Crystal at all.
>
> Ann, please alert the boneheads out there that if they see a child who is "different," to coo over the baby the way they would a "normal" child.
>
> (Green, 2003)

Baby showers are socially sanctioned rites of passage, helping individuals and their families move to another stage of development and assume important new roles. Rites of passage also signal that others will support the individual in their new role and responsibilities. Often part of one's spiritual or religious belief system, these rites of passage assist people in finding their place in the world. When important, major life transitions are ignored, it could be inferred that others do not consider these parents or their child to have a place in the world. Reading Crystal's story, the attention of onlookers seems to be entirely negative and, moreover, implies that strangers/onlookers are entitled to a full and complete answer to their questions. Nonetheless, the birth of a child with a congenital disability can be considered a developmental task in which the parent(s) assume new roles, identities, and responsibilities. This societal-wide silence or negative responses to babies with congenital disabilities can be considered a structural lag in which society has not caught up with medicine. This can be seen in Crystal's mother explanation that she and her husband had expected Crystal to have more severe disabilities and that, to them, Crystal is "normal," shows the disconnect between society's response and medical advances.

A pediatrician, Dr. Rosen, who had practiced for 18 years and has cared for "thousands of children with all sorts of conditions," and "I try to connect with each and every one of them in a special way." Dr. Rosen described one patient who was ignored or stared at, especially when the little boy attempted "to express himself" or "interact" or "show his humanity."

> He was 3 and unable to walk or talk, and when I caught his eye, his face broke open into a huge smile, accompanied by the grunting and rhythmic thrusting of his torso and arms that he uses to express himself.
>
> Shortly after he was born, he was found to have a genetic variance about which, unfortunately, little is known. My patient has an unusually small head, widely spaced eyes, seizures, feeding and digestive problems, and a wide range of developmental delays.

[the mother] said, "I like the people in health care. People in health care, they don't stare at my son like he's some kind of freak, you know? They see him for who he is."

She took a deep breath and continued, "It's different when I'm around other people. Either they make faces because they think he is too big to be in a stroller, or when starts making sounds and throwing his body around, they just stand there and stare. I feel like they don't want either of us around and just wish we would go away."

The pediatrician's conclusion and recommendations follow:

> Perhaps this is why I was so shaken by what I had just heard, about a mother and son being shunned by others who were unable to see the son she loves as a child instead of as a condition or disease. I couldn't help recognize the cruel irony of these strangers withdrawing from this child because of the very sounds and movements that he uses to try and interact with them, undeniable expressions of his humanity.
>
> Faced with such a child in the park or at a restaurant, too many of us just stand there and stare. Instead, notice the twinkle in the child's eyes, even if they are half hidden behind smudged, thick-lensed glasses. Return the smile, even if it twists unusually. . . . Wave back at him when he jerks his arms towards you, and say hello, even if it's hard to understand exactly what he's saying.
>
> (Rosen, 2014)

At times, it is not the child's physical appearance that elicits negative responses from onlookers; instead, it is the behaviors of the child. In the following excerpt, strangers, instead of trying to understand, openly express disapproval of mother and son. Perhaps they are thinking, "Why can't this mother control her son's temper tantrums?" or "I wouldn't tolerate this sort of behavior in my children!" But, the son is not displaying temper tantrums or bad behaviors, but, rather, symptoms of a neurocognitive disability.

> Social isolation may be an adaptive mechanism for families with a child who has an unobservable disability. In my family's situation, my son looks and usually acts like a child who is developing typically, yet this mirage can easily be blown away by loud noises, small spaces containing several people or a busy street with too much traffic. I protect my son from these possible threats with great care. As a result, I am often the recipient of disapproving glances. The label of "helicopter mom" might apply to me—*if* my son didn't actually require that level of care.
>
> (Smith, 2010, p. 55)

Most parents, and others with acquired onset disabilities, report that after an initial emotional adjustment period and medical treatment and stabilization, they return to a "new normal." The developmental psychologist, Erik Erikson (1968) posited that progression to higher developmental stages was motivated by "crises." "Crises" would perhaps be better defined as decision points and, at each of these decision points or crises, the individual experiences "emotional disequilibrium," in which they are uncomfortable, face important decisions, and gradually accept a new identity. Often these crises are considered times of great vulnerability and times of great potential. Eventually, according to Erikson, the individual progresses to the next developmental stage and emotional equilibrium is re-established. Individuals who acquire disabilities, or parents of children with congenital disabilities, may be considered to be experiencing a decision point with the accompanying emotional disequilibrium, but eventually regain their equilibrium, often terming it, "finding a new normal." For friends, family members, and strangers, the emotional equilibrium achieved by parents is difficult to understand since family and friends are unable to relinquish the idea that disability is an unending tragedy. Many parents have tried to tell others, "We're not sad. We're exhausted," in this way underscoring the demands of responding to their child's disability, but stating that they have achieved emotional equilibrium. One feminist disability scholar (Saxton) considers raising a baby with a congenital disability as "everyday" life and the women who raise these children as "ordinary."

> Women sometime conclude, "I'm not saintly or brave enough to raise a disabled child." This objectifies and distorts the experience of mother of disabled children. They're not saints; they're ordinary women, as are the women who are for spouses or their own parent who become disabled. It doesn't take a "special woman" to mother a disabled child. It takes a caring parent to raise any child. If her child became disabled, any mother would do the best job she could caring for that child.
>
> (Saxton, 2006, p. 112)

Another feminist disability scholar (Hubbard, 2006) is clear in stating that women should understand the choice of abortion for fetuses with known disabilities:

> So let me clear: I am not suggesting that prenatal diagnosis followed by abortion is similar to euthanasia. Fetuses are not people. And a woman must have the right to terminate her pregnancy whatever her reasons.
>
> (p. 99)

Medical science has created the accompanying bioethical concerns, including the increasing numbers of infants with congenital disabilities, some of which are severe and multiple. However, it is not the responsibility of medicine to resolve these ethical concerns; rather it is society that should seek answers to these questions. In the case of congenital disabilities, the questions of prenatal testing, abortion, and euthanasia arise. The lack of answers or solutions to these bioethical issues can be considered a societal structural lag and, indeed, resolution is the responsibility of society. While individuals, and their families are considered the primary decision makers, it does become a broader societal issue is affected when large numbers of people are faced with these types of decisions. For example, there is accurate prenatal testing for some disabilities, such as Down syndrome and some types of deafness, and in the future there may be far fewer individuals with these disabilities due to more women deciding to terminate these pregnancies (which is their choice to make). Nonetheless, there is a positive correlation between numbers of individuals with a certain type of disability and the availability of services provided. Therefore, the fewer individuals with Down syndrome, the fewer number of services available for those with Down syndrome.

On a family level, counselors trained in marriage and family counseling and skilled in values clarification might be particularly helpful and could assist families through the decision-making process, and they are much more likely to be helpful if thoroughly educated in disability issues. Skilled and empathic counselors could help pregnant women determine choices and support them in these choices. Society, on the other hand, must support women with the resources necessary. It is important to assist parents, not only in the decision making, but also in acknowledging that these choices are made in a highly prejudicial and blaming society. Reviewing the excerpts of Pat Furlong's physician and the onlooker who accosted Crystal and her mother, it becomes clear that women feel assured of their right to make decisions about their pregnancies and the births of their children. Mothers, fathers, grandparents, and siblings should be encouraged to express their feelings and opinions and, moreover, but it should be clear to all that the family is not obligated to go into detail or provide answers to those who insensitively ask about the cause of a disability. Looking at the "here-and-now" is valuable, but counselors can also assist clients in understanding that, regardless of their choices, there will be a "new normal," and discuss ways in which this new emotional equilibrium can be achieved. Counseling techniques such as building ego strength, assertiveness training, and establishing clear boundaries in which women feel confident in their right to make decisions about their pregnancies and the births of their children.

The simple process of universalizing the experience of congenital disability and the associated bioethical concerns may be considered "psychoeducation" and the importance of psychoeducation should not be minimized because of the importance of countering common misconceptions and prejudicial attitudes toward congenital disabilities. Psychotherapy can be therapeutic. Helping women to understand that there are many others who, due to medical advances, face these same types of dilemmas often leads to a reduction of stress and loneliness. Helping pregnant women understand that, regardless of the choices they make, there will be others who challenge and criticize their decisions, thus making psychoeducation values clarification particularly helpful in countering these criticisms.

Finally, it is crucial to understand that all bioethical questions about disability arise from the Biomedical Model of Disability in which individuals (including fetuses) are defined solely by the disability. Consideration of other Models of Disability, which take into consideration the family, the environment, and available resources and services can improve and enlarge the range of choices. Topics to be explored in counseling may include: How much help and support will be available? Are there assistive technologies which could help my baby? How have others coped with this disability? Will my child have access to services? Are there other parents to whom I could speak? Can role models be identified? Are there support groups available? Counselors who have a broad view of the disability experience and, at the same time, perceptively refuse to simplify the disability experience by applying a single model, can open many possibilities for consideration.

Response Demands of a Long Pre-Diagnosis Period

A long pre-diagnosis period is much more typical of insidious-onset disabilities in contrast to acute onset disabilities in which a definitive diagnosis is rendered quickly. Leading to a lengthy pre-diagnosis period is the following combination: 1) insidious onset; 2) a fluctuating (or episodic) course; 3) an invisible disability; 4) a low-incidence disability; and 5) a progressive, gradual sensory loss. Each of these five factors creates stress, anxiety, and ambiguity for individuals, their families, and the attending physicians. At times, families, friends, and physicians, and the individual himself or herself, question the individual's rationality. On the other hand, diagnosis means clarity, facilitates planning, and includes a prognosis.

> **Disability Factors Which May Lead to a Long Pre-Diagnosis Period**
> 1. An insidious onset
> 2. A fluctuating (or episodic) course
> 3. An invisible disability
> 4. A low-incidence disability
> 5. A progressive sensory loss, such as blindness

An insidious onset is subtle, and symptoms develop gradually before becoming apparent. Often, symptoms are not acknowledged or noticed. For acute onset disabilities, the time of the onset is referenced while for insidious-onset disabilities, the time of diagnosis is referenced. People who experience insidious-onset disabilities may remark, "something wasn't quite right for a long time." In the same way that most individuals with acute onset disabilities remember the exact circumstances of the beginning of their disability, most people with insidious onset remember receiving their diagnosis. A college professor with multiple sclerosis described the day of her diagnosis: "Every [person with] multiple sclerosis can remember the moment of diagnosis. It is one of those events which can be forever recalled in the most exquisite detail" (Toombs, 1995, p. 4). Many chronic illnesses, especially autoimmune illnesses, including multiple sclerosis, lupus, and rheumatoid arthritis, have insidious onsets.

> **Results of Many Insidious-Onset Disabilities**
> - Those with insidious-onset disabilities are less likely to receive treatment.
> - Many are given negative labels, such as irrational, lazy, attention-seeking, hypochondriacal, or thought of as attempting to escape the demands of life.
> - It is difficult for others to change their expectations and perceptions of the individual.
> - Less social support is given to individuals with insidious-onset disabilities.

The symptoms of many chronic illnesses include fatigue, loss of energy, sleep problems, muscle weakness, numbness, vision problems, and pain, all of which are difficult to diagnose and measure. With the episodic nature of many insidious-onset disabilities, family members say such things as "You were just fine yesterday" and cannot understand why their family member cannot get out of bed. It is difficult to communicate the seriousness of the symptoms and for others to change their expectations of someone with a disability that is fluctuating, invisible, with an insidious onset, and has symptoms which are difficult to detect. One woman reported:

> It's hard to justify my fatigue to friends and relatives; my husband often asks, "Why are you so tired?" It took an article in the *National Arthritis News* to finally help me to convince myself and him that my fatigue was real, physiologically, as well as emotionally.
> (Kohler, Schweikert-Stary, & Lubkin, 1998, p. 124)

Two important points are found in this excerpt: first, she herself had doubts about her fatigue, and second, the fatigue is both biological and emotional.

Clare, an Englishwoman, was stunned to learn that, before her diagnosis of multiple sclerosis, her friends had assumed that she was simply lazy and "work-shy." Note her feelings of hurt, anger, and betrayal.

> One interesting piece of information that came to light after I told people that I had MS was the opinions that they and others had had of me. I guess I was both hurt and mildly angry to discover that I had been seen as a lazy and work-shy person. . . . I was just left feeling betrayed by friends of many years.
> (Morris, 1991, p. 181)

Many individuals have described the process of seeking a diagnosis, for themselves or family members, as "diagnostic odysseys." Often, there are misdiagnoses and the misguided treatment plans are undertaken. One expert in family issues and psychiatric disabilities reported the "epiphany" of learning the diagnosis of mental illness which had presented "troublesome and oppressive behaviors" for a long time. Note the feelings of family members as "anger, fear, confusion, and concern."

> After long periods of chaos and confusion, the nature of the problem suddenly seems clear. Family members, sometimes equally go for months or

years of feeling anger, fear, confusion, and concern about a loved one's oppressive behaviors without being able to name them as illness. The point at which a person's troublesome behavior is transformed into a disease, via the pronouncements of medical experts, is typically a moment of epiphany. Such a moment of epiphany, is however, only the beginning of an ongoing interpretative process.

(Karp, 2001, p. 49)

Tosca Appel (1988) was diagnosed with multiple sclerosis at an early age, during her teenage years. The typical age of onset is about age 20. In the following excerpt, she described her pre-diagnosis period. Note that the severity of her symptoms resulted in her parents taking Tosca to emergency rooms of hospitals. It is interesting that Appel remembers exactly when she experienced her first symptom, at age 11 years and nine months. Note also that she was misdiagnosed several times and the negative labels were given to her.

> I was eleven years, 9 months old when my first symptom appeared. My first attack of MS took the form of a lack of motor coordination in my right hand. I was unable to holds utensils and my hand turned inward; my parents in their concern rushed me to the emergency room of the hospital. The intern who saw me at the emergency room told my parents, without any exam, that I had a brain tumor. . . . I was admitted to the hospital, where I stayed for 12 days. Ten days after the initial attack the symptoms abated. . . . The doctors had put the blame of the attack on a bad case of nerves. . . . The second attack occurred when I was 16 years old and in the 11th grade. . . . One day . . . my history teacher asked me a question. I stood up to answer and my speech came out all garbled. I was unable to string the words into a sentence. I was unable to even utter words. All that came out were sounds. I clutched my throat to help the words come out easier. . . . I remember the teacher's look. He looked at me in utter surprise and a little bit helplessly. . . . Again, my parents rushed me to the emergency room where another intern did his initial workup on me. . . . The intern, in his wisdom, thought this behavior was an attention-getter. He thought I was faking the whole thing.
>
> (pp. 253–254)

When a diagnosis is given, the individual is often relieved and happy, in spite of the fact that the chronic illness or disability is serious, and brings many functional limitations. Diagnosis ends "a frightening array of possibilities" (Goodheart &

Lansing, 1997). Finally, there is an explanation for years of symptoms. Note the surprise of others in this excerpt when a diagnosis of a severe disability results in "one of the best days of my life."

> I'll tell you one of the best days of my life was when I got a phone call from the hospital telling me what they decided was wrong with my husband, and they couldn't understand why I was so excited or happy.
>
> (Karp, 2001, p. 50)

Most insidious-onset disabilities are severe, lifelong disabilities with many functional limitations requiring lifestyle changes. Further, many of these types of disabilities are degenerating, often leading to an early death. In this section, only the emotional and social responses required of insidious-onset disabilities are discussed. Elliot Kubla (2018, January 10) described the suspicion with which physicians viewed him, the various "treatment" plans suggested, and the sudden ("overnight") downward change in status:

> By then, I had discovered that I was no longer trusted by my doctors about my own body or experiences. I reported, odd, terrifying, and sudden physical changes; they recommended cognitive behavioral therapy and Weight Watchers. I felt exiled from the world of the well, isolated by thick walls of suspicion....
>
> I went from doctor to doctor looking for answers, but overnight I had gone from being a trusted rabbi and chaplain (who worked with seriously ill and dying people on hospital medical teams) to a "hysterical" chronically ill person. Though I had seen it happen to my clients, I now understood firsthand that being disbelieved is nearly universal for people with chronic illnesses, especially those that are largely invisible or hard to diagnose or both. I had believed that as a health care professional, equipped with skills and advocates to navigate the system, I would be treated differently. I soon learned how hubristic that was.

Autoimmune diseases, in addition to having an insidious onset with symptoms that are difficult to diagnose, are also episodic disabilities, with periods of remission alternating with symptom exacerbation. Many IWDs feel that their bodies or minds have betrayed them and feeling of betrayal is often increased in autoimmune diseases, and stated as "it's my own body destroying me." Nancy Mairs (1997) described the virus which caused her multiple sclerosis as "alien invaders" which resulted in feeling "haunted by a capricious and mean-spirited ghost."

I have known that I have multiple sclerosis for about seventeen years now, though the disease probably started long ago. The hypothesis is that the disease process, in which the protective covering of the nerves in the brain and in the spinal cord is eaten away and replaced by scar tissue, "hard patches," is caused by autoimmune reaction to a slow-acting virus. Research suggests that I was infected by this virus, which no one has ever seen and therefore, technically doesn't even "exist," between the ages of four and fifteen. In effect, living with this mysterious mechanism feels like having your present self, and the past selves it embodies, haunted by a capricious and mean-spirited ghost, unseen except for its footprints, which trips you even when you're watching where you're going, knocks glassware out of your hand, squeezes urine out of your bladder before you reach the bathroom, and weights your whole body with a weariness that no amount of rest can relieve. An alien invader must be at work. But, of course, it's not. It's your own body. That is, it's you.

(Mairs, 1997, pp. 52–53)

Note the way in which Mairs expresses the insidious nature of the onset of her disability in the first sentence. The need for a definitive cause of her disability is thwarted because the cause is a virus which "technically doesn't even exist."

Early intervention programs, state-funded and provided during infancy, preschool, and elementary school, provide mass screenings in which deafness or blindness can be detected. These early intervention programs identify infants and young children with sensory losses and then provide medical care, family interventions, and educational services. In the same way, that rehabilitation services for adults with disabilities are considered cost-effective for society, early intervention programs for children with disabilities have been found to be good investments of public funds and resources. Before the introduction of early screening and early intervention programs in the 1980s, many children, and parents, were unaware they had hearing or vision impairments, especially with progressive losses. An English poet and professor, David Wright, contracted an illness when he was 7 years old. The illness destroyed his auditory nerve. David's doctors, parents, and David himself did not realize that he was deaf. As an adult, he remembered the exact moment when he became aware that he was deaf:

"How was I to know? Nobody told me." He had to "deduce the fact of deafness through a process of reasoning." He heard guns, motorbikes, lorries (trucks), crowds, and drills by touch: "There can't be much I miss of the normal orchestration of urban existence." He could appreciate music too, resting his finger on a piano or a loud speaker. And in a room with a wooden floor h would listen to drums and string instruments through his feet.

(Wright, 1994, p. 22)

Brenda Premo became progressively blind, but did not discover this until the second or third grade, labeling the recognition of her disability as an "aha" moment. She assumed that the other students saw it as she did.

> The first time I remember understanding that my vision was different from other people was in the second or third grade when I realized that the other students could read the blackboard. Before then, I couldn't understand why the teacher would bother to write on the board. When it dawned on me that other kids could read the board and I couldn't, it was one of those "aha" moments in my life. It was a new discovery.
>
> (Mackelprang & Salsgiver, 1999, p. 140)

In Wright's excerpt, the onset of his deafness was not gradual, but the diagnosis/discovery of the deafness was prolonged, much of this due to his compensating strategies, which hid his deafness from himself, teachers, and parents. In Premo's excerpt, her disability does have a gradual, insidious onset and the course is progressive.

Wright's and Premo's experiences would be unusual today, due to the introduction of universal screening the 1980s. Nonetheless, in a few cases, such as disabilities with episodic courses, screening is not always helpful. Screening tests are typically quick, short, inexpensive, and do not require a great deal of professional expertise. Diagnostic tests, in contrast, are time-consuming, expensive, and requires the services of a highly trained and skilled diagnostician. The rationale behind universal screening is to discover a few disabilities among very large groups of people. These few children with possible disabilities are then sent to a skilled diagnostician and, many times, the diagnostician finds that many of these referrals, do not have disabilities. Nonetheless, if only one or two individuals are definitively diagnosed with a disability, the process is deemed a success and services for these one or two individuals are initiated immediately.

When counselors collaborate with medical providers, both clients and physicians are able to recognize that, without a diagnosis, there are impairments and symptoms that can be very life-disrupting. Excellent communication, both in what to say, how to say it, and to whom is important and, finally the important skills of information gathering must be reinforced. Marriage and family counseling could offer a safe environment in which everyone is allowed to express their feelings, including negative emotions, in a complete and honest manner. As every counselor knows, the relationship between the client and counselor is a fundamental aspects of counseling, including empathy. For those who have been discounted and implicitly criticized for imagining illnesses, an empathic counseling relationship in which the client feels truly validated can be healing. Many individuals whose symptoms have been viewed with suspicion by other professional caregivers, need to find a safe and accepting professional environment.

Social Support for Individuals With Disabilities

Social Support
- Often, the lack of social support when an individual acquires a disability, is both surprising and disappointing.
- Social support contributes to a positive response to the disability.

On the one hand, social support is an important component of responding positively to a disability. However, segregation, isolation, and marginalization have increased physical distance between IWDs and IWODs, and stereotyping, prejudice, and discrimination have created social distance. Perhaps the greatest cause of this social gap is the existential angst of IWODs. Simply stated, the presence of IWDs remind IWODs of their possibility of acquiring a disability.

Following are two examples of the lack of social support with the commonalities of 1) surprise and disappointment of the IWDs and 2) the feeling that the abandonment was undeserved. In the first, Randy Souders reacts to becoming paralyzed as a teenager, the result of a diving accident in a swimming pool. He uses the word "drifts" three times in order to emphasize the gradual process of losing friends.

> Initially, everyone rallies around you, you know—they're supportive. All of the friends I had at the time of the accident were right there—right at the beginning. Then, as time went on, one by one they kind of drifted away, slowly. I think it was because they obviously didn't know how to react to me—I certainly didn't know how to make things easier on them. I was having a hard enough time trying to figure out what was happening to me. I don't know if I pushed them away or if they felt that I wasn't the same person. It was a very gradual thing, but most of them just kind of drifted off. And I drifted off into myself.
>
> (Souders, 1993, pp. 153–154)

Note that Souders questions if he is at fault, that somehow, he had pushed his friends away or wonders if he could have made it easier for his friends to accept his disability and the disabled Randy. Then, he answers his own question, "I was having a hard enough time trying to figure out what was happening to me."

The sister of a man with a traumatic brain injury (TBI) reported:

> The hardest thing for me to see is the way his friends and girlfriends treat him. Once the center of attention, now nobody wants to be around him. Inside, he's the most friendly, kind-hearted, and loving person I know. I guess it pisses me off when people that used to love him have completed deserted when being with takes more effort than it did before. I'm afraid he's lonely, and that he always will be somewhat lonely because of something he can't control.
>
> (Degeneffe & Lee, 2010, p. 32)

In the next excerpts, friends were a major part of both the physical and emotional rehabilitation. Meaningful, individually defined goals were important. In the first excerpt, a young man with a spinal cord injury resulting from a motorcycle accident described the importance of attending a Grateful Dead concert:

> My friends came up to visit as usual and said that [my favorite group] the Grateful Dead were playing there in November. My mind was back, but I had to get my strength. The doctors said I would have to sit 4 to 5 hours straight if I were to go to the concert. Every time I got into the wheelchair, I blacked right out. Each day for only a short time, I would sit in a semi-reclined position determined to reach my goal. After a couple of days I was up to three hours. The day of the show I reached my goals and was psyched. The concert was the first time I had been out of the hospital. I had reached my destination.
>
> (Scherer, 1993, p. 22)

For a teenager with severe burns, ping pong with friends was part of a teenager's rehabilitation.

> When I got burned at age 18, I found out who my real friends were: They were the ones who came to see me and they still are my friends. They (friends) made me use my burned hand to play games like ping-pong, so it wouldn't get stiff.
>
> (Holaday & McPhearson, 1997, p. 349)

In a national survey (Stefan, 2001), individuals with psychiatric disabilities were asked, "What are some examples of the worst discrimination you have experienced?" One respondent was succinct, "no job, no friends," another wrote, "I'm sick of losing friends" while another responded, "friends who have abandoned me" (p. 14).

In the same survey, one woman described the social support she received as "worth years of therapy."

> A few years after my illness I met someone who permitted me to talk about my hospitalization. As I described the experience, I cried. A gentle touch that said, "It doesn't matter; we can still be friends," was worth years of therapy. The moment was an emotional breakthrough for me.
>
> (p. 14)

Perhaps the false idea that IWDs are incapable of contributing to others creates the assumption that relationships between IWDs and IWODs are asymmetrical or unbalanced. In these types of asymmetrical relationships, IWDs are always the beneficiaries of services or of pity, rather than being considered work colleagues, or friends, or romantic partners. Many times, IWDs are thought to be burdens. Some disabilities are more stigmatizing than others and this is termed the hierarchy of stigma. Those with physical disabilities, generally, find it easier to enter into equal social status relationships while those with cognitive, intellectual, or psychiatric disabilities have more difficulties. Perceived cause of the disability also influences the degree of social support given. For example, someone with AIDS stated, "I wish I had cancer because then I could go home." Other characteristics of the IWD interact with the disability that can promote or hinder social support including perceived social class and education, attractiveness, and prestige.

If individuals are thought to obsess 24/7 about their disabilities, IWODs might think that they have no interests, activities, or values in common with IWDs. But IWDs do not obsess continuously about their disabilities; most are not continuously depressed, angry, or bitter; and IWDs have multiple identities, experiences, interests, values, and roles. In fact, for most IWDs, the disability is not their primary identification. Remember, earlier in the book, when intersectionality was discussed, one woman stated that when she went to women's rights meetings, the other participants' first question was "What's wrong with you?" rather than the question asked of everyone else, "Who are you?"

Role Models and "Disabled Heroes"

> **Role Models for Individuals With Disabilities**
> 1. Bandura's theory of social efficacy can be applied to IWDs.
> 2. IWDs often have few role models due to three factors.
> 3. "Disabled heroes" are IWDs with extraordinary resources, achievements, and fame.
> 4. "Disabled heroes" are occasionally derisively termed "super crips" by IWDs.

Albert Bandura's (1977) social efficacy theories included the idea that humans master new competencies throughout the lifespan, continuing to learn and grow including the period of physical decline and aging, and although Bandura did not specifically discuss disabilities, his theories do apply to IWDs. Bandura's theory can be summed up in a single sentence: He believed that humans learn through social interaction. Social efficacy includes the components of self-regulating, self-evaluation, social comparison, and observational learning. Rather than viewing the individual's environment as the principal determinant of behavior, Bandura believed that humans possess the ability to control and change their own behaviors. He considered role models to be either real or what he termed "symbolic models," meaning fictional characters in books, television, and the internet. In order to gain access to role models who are meaningful to the individual, they must gain access to different types of environments and Bandura considered the expanding environments of teenagers and adults to facilitate access to a greater number of appropriate role models.

Role models, Bandura posited, can be "symbolic," in which the individual does not have a personal relationship with the role model. Symbolic role models can be historical figures, such as George Washington, Eleanor Roosevelt, and Dr. Martin Luther King, or fictional characters such as Robinson Crusoe, or famous individuals or celebrities. In these types of role models, the individual will never meet these role models, ask them questions, or observe them in daily, routine life. Moreover, a lack of personal interaction and the distance in time and place, all contribute to make it difficult to judge or evaluate the achievements of the symbolic role model. Bandura did not discount the importance of these types of symbolic role models, but he maintained that having a personal relationship with a role model was typically more satisfying and effective.

He also theorized that "observational learning" or "vicarious learning" eliminated the need for a great deal of trial and error learning. By watching others, including reading or hearing about others, we can learn new behaviors. In the same ways, we can learn what *not* to do. He also maintained that the individual's perceptions of their abilities are often more important than actual abilities. Two developmental scholars (McLeod & Almazan, 2004) also emphasized the importance of the individual's perception in both the conceptualization and evaluation of "constraints" and "their abilities to surmount them." Interestingly, the first words in the following excerpt are "bodily alterations." Note that McLeod and Almazan considered transitions as starting points to open up new opportunities while, at the same time, creating stress.

> Bodily alterations, transitions, and turning points have the potential to open up new opportunities, alter life goals, and create stress. Their influence on the life depends on how individuals interpret them and respond to them, as well as the constraints that limit those responses (Elder, 1997; Rutter, 1998). Although constraints are often conceptualized as structurally based, people differ in their perceptions of the limitations imposed by similar structural contingencies and in their perceptions of their ability to surmount them (Bandura, 1986). As a result, different persons faced with the same situation will assert different types and levels of effort to change it, creating diverse life pathways.
>
> (p. 395)

Access to appropriate and meaningful role models for IWDs may be limited by three factors: 1) IWDs often live isolated and segregated lives and may not have the same capability to expand their environments as IWODs; 2) the number of role models is small because many of the traditional avenues of achievement have been closed to IWDs or IWDs have been forced to hide or minimize their disability in order to enter into educational, social, or occupational opportunity structures; and 3) IWDs have been exposed to years of "symbolic" role models in the media, which are typically shown as tragic, lonely, and incompetent individuals.

Rod Michalko (2002) remembered reading about characters who were blind and seeing blind people on television as a teenager. These type of characters were the fictionalized imaginations of writers and producers, but nonetheless, the characters are, in Bandura's phrase, "symbolic role models."

> They were all portrayed as victims of a misfortune.... When I saw blind people in the movies or on television and even when I saw the "real" ones,

> I saw incompetence, sadness, and poverty. And I saw misfortune. Whether my perception was accurate or not is irrelevant; that's just what I saw. What I did not see when I saw these blind people is just as significant as what I did see: I did not see me. Still, when I saw them, I experienced a nebulous fear that I later understood was the fear of seeing myself.
>
> (p. 24)

On the one hand, Michalko does not identify with these fictional characters ("I did not see me"), but on the other hand, he was afraid that he *was* seeing himself. No one thinks of "victims of a misfortune" as role models.

In the next excerpt, a woman has reached young adulthood before she meets a role model with whom she can identify. The meeting seems accidental, in a routine job interview. Perhaps the ordinary nature of the encounter, a job interview, probably contributed to its influential impact. Harilyn Rousso (1993) a woman with cerebral palsy, recounts her surprise at meeting Betty, a woman economist with cerebral palsy. At age 22, this encounter "made me question for the first time the negative assumptions that I had made about my social potential."

> When I was about twenty-two, I had an unexpected, important experience. I worked one summer for a prominent women economist who happened to have cerebral palsy. I can't tell you my surprise when I met her at the job interview. It was a bit like looking at myself in the mirror. Betty had a powerful effect on me. I was impressed that a woman with cerebral palsy, not a very socially acceptable disability in our culture, could become so successful in her career, particularly in a "man's field," anti-trust economies. I was even more impressed that she was married. . . . It never occurred to me that I had any alternative, that I could have *both* a career and a romantic life. Betty's lifestyle, her successful marriage to an interesting, dynamic man made me question for the first time the negative assumptions that I had made about my social potential.
>
> (p. 2)

The title of Rousso's book is *Disabled, Female, and Proud!* and it illustrates an intersectionality comprised of two different disadvantaged statuses. It is apparent that Rousso identified with Betty because she states "It was a bit like looking at myself in a mirror." She had probably attended numerous "career days" at school; however, it is most likely that professionals with disabilities had never been invited to present.

The following excerpt features a 7-year-old French deaf girl, Emmanuelle, who had never seen Sign Language. When she meets an adult, Alfredo, who was deaf and used Sign Language; she was amazed. Emmanuelle was so ill-informed about her disability that she thought she was destined to die as a child.

> Alfredo comes up to me and says, "I'm deaf, like you, and I sign, that's my language."
>
> So Alfredo is deaf, but doesn't wear a hearing aid. What's more he's an adult. I think it took me a while to grasp the threefold oddity.
>
> What I did realize right away, however, was that I was not alone in the world. It was a startling revelation. And a bewildering one because, up till then, I had thought, as do so many deaf children, that I was unique and predestined to die as a child. I discovered that I could have a future because Alfredo was a deaf adult!
>
> The cruel logic about early death persists as long as deaf children haven't encountered a deaf adult. They need to be able to identify with an adult. It's crucial. Parents of deaf children should be made aware of the importance of having their children come in contact with deaf adults as soon as possible, right after birth. The two worlds need to blend—the world of sound and the world of silence. A deaf child's psychological development will be quick and much better, and the child will grow up free of the pain of being alone in the world with no constructed thought patterns and no future.
>
> Imagine that you had a kitten and never showed it a full-grown cat. It might spend its entire life thinking it was a kitten. Or imagine the little cat lived only with dogs. It would think it was the only cat in the world and wear itself out trying to communicate in dog language.
>
> (Laborit, 2010, pp. 615–616)

The "threefold oddity" that Emmanuelle discovered included 1) Alfredo was an adult deaf person; 2) Alfredo did not wear hearing aids; and 3) Alfredo used Sign Language. She was 7 years old when she met Alfredo and, up until then, she did not have a language in which to think.

Using "disabled heroes" as role models can be counterproductive; nonetheless, these IWDs are becoming more visible because disabled heroes are individuals with extraordinary resources or accomplishments, which are not available to most IWDs, or indeed, to most IWODs. Most of these individuals acquired their fame, achievements, and resources before the onset of their disability. Therefore, it is particularly unusual to see many disabled heroes with congenital disabilities.

Some examples of disabled heroes include President Roosevelt, Helen Keller, Beethoven, Stephen Hawking, Albert Einstein, Temple Grandin, and the American film actor Christopher Reeve. President Roosevelt was paralyzed due to polio, Helen Keller was blind and deaf, Stephen Hawking had a degenerating neuromuscular disability, Albert Einstein is thought to have had a learning disability, Beethoven was deaf, Temple Grandin has high functioning ASD, and Christopher Reeve sustained a spinal cord injury in a horse-riding accident.

In misguided attempts to make disability appear more normal, there are posters of these disabled heroes. The message to IWDs is, "If they did it, you can too." And the message to IWODs is "IWDs are high achievers and disabled heroes are all around us." IWODs are unaware of the functional limitations of IWDs and, therefore, are in no position to evaluate the accomplishments of IWDs, dead or alive. For example, experts in learning disabilities question if Einstein did indeed have a learning disability (Huston, 1987). Therefore, in an attempt to reduce prejudice and discrimination against IWDs, these posters actually *increase* the stigma toward disabilities. Such posters plant in the minds of the general public, a "typical" picture of IWDs. Further, many IWDs are offended by these posters, often thinking "why can't I be an average, typical IWD?" or "In order to be identified as an individual with a disability, you must do and be extraordinary things."

In spite of some negative reactions by IWDs, disabled heroes can be excellent role models and provide incentives and motivations to others with the same disability. In the *Time* magazine article (1997) on the protests of IWDs at the proposed Roosevelt sculpture/monument in Washington, DC, which did not show Roosevelt's wheelchair, a small group of IWDs protested. Eventually, these protestors were successful and the monument was re-done to include Roosevelt's wheelchair. In the final outcome, many protestors recounted the importance of Roosevelt as a life-changing role model. For example,

> Mick Countee, sensed the emptiness because after he broke his neck in a diving accident, while he was a Harvard student, his mother told him, "Son, if Franklin Roosevelt could be President, you can finish your education." Countee, who is black, not only finished but also went on to get a law degree from Georgetown and an M.B.A. from Harvard. "Not a day went by," he said last week, "that I did not think of Roosevelt and Roy Campanella." Campanella was the Brooklyn Dodgers catcher who was paralyzed in a car accident but never despaired in public.
>
> Jim Dickson, the man organizing the demonstration, stood nearly sightless along the huge monument walls and imagined how a statue of Roosevelt

in a wheelchair at the entrance would bring the stone to life. When Dickson was seven he was told by his doctor that he had juvenile macular degeneration and would soon be blind. As he walked with his parents out of the doctor's office, his mother told him, "If Franklin Roosevelt who had polio and was in a wheelchair, could be President, then you can do what you want." He never forgot.

For these two men, Franklin Roosevelt was a daily reminder, throughout their lives, that they could also achieve. In both cases, it was their parents who drew their attention to Roosevelt, and it can be assumed that Countee's mother and Dickson's parents supported and encouraged their sons in their accomplishments. Nonetheless, it does not appear likely that either Countee or Dickson met with Roosevelt or had a personal relationship and therefore, Roosevelt would be considered a "symbolic role model," according to Bandura's theory.

In the following excerpt, a man in the hospital, draws a distinction between a symbolic role model (Christopher Reeve) and a real life role model, his mentor. It may seem somewhat incongruous that he refers to himself as an "average spinal cord injured person."

> And then [the hospital staff] are showing people [with a spinal cord injury] in a $2 million yacht or on farms with 40 horses, you know; I mean that was for real? . . . [My mentor] is a real guy, you know, who lives a real life that's not easy and that's different than it was before. . . . Most of the things [in the video] are way out of reach for the average spinal-cord injured person. . . . It's not many Chris Reeves.
> (Veith et al., 2006, p. 294)

Because professional hospital staff produced and used a video of individuals with SCIs with yachts and horse farms, this appeared to be both insensitive and ineffective.

IWDs have derisively named these disabled heroes "super crips." Covington, an IWD, explained the resentment of many IWDs toward "super crips."

> Super Crip is usually a character struck down in the prime of life who fights to overcome insurmountable odds to succeed as a meaningful member of society. Through strength of will, perseverance, and hard work, the disabled individual achieves a *normal* life. . . . Too often, the news media treats an individual with disabilities who has attained success in his life field

or profession as though they were one-of-a-kind. While this one-of-a-kind aspect might make for a better story angle, it perpetuates in the mind of the general public how rare it is for the citizen with disabilities to succeed.

(1997, p. 292)

The late Irving Zola was a sociologist and a college professor. He was also a polio survivor who used a wheelchair. He mentions by name two individuals who are polio survivors. Wilma Rudolph contracted polio at age 4 and became an Olympic athlete, winning a bronze medal in 1956 and three gold medals in 1960. In the 1960s, Rudolph was considered the fastest woman in the world, in spite of the fact that her physician told her mother that, because of the polio, she would never walk again.

It is the . . . message that I have recently begun to abhor. It states that if a Franklin Delano Roosevelt or a Wilma Rudolph could OVERCOME their handicap, so could and should all the disabled. And if we fail, it's *our* problem, *our* personality, *our* weakness. And this further masks what chronic illness is all about. For our lives or even our adaptation do not center around one single activity or physical achievement but around many individual and complex ones. Our daily living is not filled with dramatic accomplishments but with mundane ones.

(Zola, 1982, p. 161)

Zola draws attention to the fact that most IWDs live "mundane" lives and, that by comparing IWDs to these super achievers may lead to illogical conclusions.

On page 1 of a book entitled, *Blind Rage: Letters to Helen Keller* (Kleege, 2006), the author expresses her anger in letters to Helen Keller, whom she probably never met. She never sent the letters.

Dear Helen Keller,

Allow me to introduce myself. I am a writer and part-time English professor. I am American, married, middle-aged, middle-class. Like you, I am blind, though not deaf. But the most important thing you need to know about me, and the reason for my letter, is that I grew up hating you. . . . I hated you because you were always held up to me as a role model, and one who set an impossibly high standard of cheerfulness in the face of adversity. "Why can't you be more like Helen Keller?" people always said to me.

I am not alone in this. Many disabled people think you did our cause a lot of harm. Your life story inscribes the idea that disability is a personal tragedy to be overcome through an individual's fortitude and pluck, rather than a set of cultural practices and assumptions, affecting many individuals, that could be changed through collective action.

(p. 1)

As we have learned, Helen Keller had remarkable resources, such as lifetime financial support from the American Federation of the Blind, income from several American millionaires, and also earned money on the lecture circuit. However, most remarkable of Keller's resources was the services of her companion of 49 years, Anne Sullivan.

Like IWODs, the best role models for IWDs are "normal," average IWDs with whom they can identify and, most important, with whom they have a relationship. In the next excerpt, a woman with spinal cord received practical advice on specific concerns from a woman with a longstanding SCI. Note that the more she learns from her mentor, the less frightened she becomes.

[H]ow [the mentor] got around and what had happened to her and how she dealt with cooking and how she dealt with her kids, how she had sex and what kind of bed she had. Lots of different questions [about] life and living . . . Spasticity and, oh God, just everything . . . And the more I learned, the less scared I got.

(Veith et al., 2006, p. 291)

Another type of "disabled heroes" includes high-functioning individuals with disabilities that are measured on a spectrum or dimension. Individuals with lower functioning and more severe disabilities are represented on the lower end of the spectrum and those with high functioning and fewer deficits are considered to be at the high end of the spectrum. As we have discussed, one of the results of dimensional measurement is the fact that higher functioning individuals represent (to the public) the entire spectrum, including whose with the same type of disability, but on the lower end of the spectrum. Therefore, both these high-functioning and low-functioning individuals have the same disability, but they are very different from each other. These high functioning individuals portray an unrealistic picture of the entire disability group. For example, Dr. Temple Grandin is perhaps the most well-known individual with Autism Spectrum Disorder. Nonetheless Dr. Grandin is a remarkable person, a best-selling author, authority on cattle raising, and university professor.

Those on the higher end of the spectrum tend to *celebrate* their disability; however, those on the lower end of ASD are often non-verbal, engage in repetitive self-stimulating motions, and are not toilet trained. Therefore, many consider these types of disabled heroes trivialize and minimize the experience and limitations of the disability. One mother of a son with ASD explained the far-reaching effects of these types of super heroes. Note that this mother states that there are few individuals of high functioning ASD individuals, "a handful."

> Please don't write about them [high functioning individuals with ASD]. They're a handful of noisy people who get a lot of media attention. They're trivializing what autism really is. It's like stealing money from the tin cup of a blind man who you say that it's not an illness; you're getting people who should be making political and social change to think that's it not a problem.
> (Solomon, 2012, p. 280)

Polio poster children could be considered disabled heroes which were utilized by savvy public relations professionals. Poster children were used, only after the death of President Roosevelt. Up until then, Roosevelt was the "public face" of the polio fundraising/charitable organizations. The decision was made to use beautiful, white children, with relatively mild lower limb paralysis. The combination of children and polio was a big money maker. Children elicit a great deal more sympathy than adults. Only white children were poster children and they were chosen for their attractiveness. Teenagers were thought to be too old to elicit sympathy. Obviously, these poster children did not show a representative view of polio.

Dating for Individuals With Disabilities

Dating can be an exciting, novel experience, and a source of status among one's peers (Smart, 2012). Dating can also increase self-esteem, stimulate social growth, and create stronger self-identity. Affiliation, attachment, and sexual gratification are part of dating. For some, however, dating is a source of frustration and disappointment and can lead to decreased self-esteem. A great deal of dating and other types of sexual interaction are based on physical attractiveness.

Dating for IWDs

- Dating is often a source of self-esteem and status among one's peers.
- For many IWDs, dating is frustrating and can lead to decreased self-esteem.

- The social isolation of many IWDs makes dating difficult.
- The emphasis upon physical attractiveness makes dating difficult for many IWDs.
- Dating requires an equal social status relationship, which is often difficult to achieve in a culture saturated with images of IWDs as tragic, pitiful, dependent people.

One female teenager experienced a therapeutic amputation due to cancer. She worried about her dating possibilities:

> I know young men, especially, really pay a lot of attention to looks and physical attractiveness. I wonder—will a boy accept me just the way I am. You hear them talking about a girl's really built, or how she looks in a bathing suit and I hope they understand that they just amputated my leg, they didn't take my heart and soul and personality. I don't know if they'll ever accept me.
>
> (Darling, cited in Blumberg, Lewis, & Susman, 1984, p. 141)

Nancy Mairs was diagnosed with multiple sclerosis (MS). In the following excerpt, she explained that, before the exacerbation of her symptoms, "I was never a beautiful woman." She also quantifies the number of women "who fall short." The result is feeling shame.

> I was never a beautiful woman, and for that reason, I've spent most of my life (together with probably at least 95 percent of the female population of the United States) suffering from the shame of an unattainable standard. . . . When I first noticed the symptoms of what would be diagnosed as MS, I was probably looking my best. . . . The beginning of MS wasn't too bad. The first symptom, besides the pernicious fatigue that had begun to devour me, was "foot drop," the inability to raise my left foot at the ankle. As a consequence, I'd started to limp, but I could still wear high heels. . . . My self-esteem diminishes further as age and illness strip from me the features that me, for a brief while anyway, a good-looking, even sexy, young woman. . . . No more lithe, girlish figure.
>
> (Mairs, 1997, pp. 55–56)

Robert Neumann (1988) described the way in which his treatments for rheumatoid arthritis limited his contact with girls.

> During my high school days, my social life was virtually nonexistent. Because I received physical therapy at home in the afternoon and because my stamina was poor in any event, I only attended school until about 1 p.m. This eliminated any possibility of interacting with peers in extracurricular activities. . . . Meanwhile, I unsuspectingly continued to . . . dream of the day I would start college and the active love life I had fantasized about for so long. Finally the big day arrived. Armed with a body of knowledge about women derived solely from TV, James Bond movies, and the *Playboy* magazines my younger brother smuggled in, I arrived at a small Midwestern college. . . . It took only a short while before I noticed my actual accomplishments with women were falling far short, not only of my expectations but also of the experiences of my friends. . . . There was no need for me to call on social-sexual skills I had never learned.
>
> (p. 159)

Note that Neumann also compared his lack of success with "the experiences of my friends," thus illustrating that dating can be a source of status among one's peers. These excerpts illustrate two obstacles to dating for IWDs with visible disabilities: the importance of physical attractiveness and the relatively isolated lives of many IWDs. Nonetheless, these experiences pre-date the Americans with Disabilities Act, which was passed in 1990. As an indirect result of the ADA, there are more dating opportunities for IWDs simply due to their greater presence and visibility in the classroom, the workplace, and the professions. This is not to say that the issues of physical attractiveness and isolation have been totally resolved, but they have been decreased.

Like many other social relationships, dating has changed, with online dating sites emerging as a way to meet prospective dates. However, when IWDs refer to their disability in their profile or their photo shows a disability, there are few, if any, responses. Abby Kovalsky explained, "I joined a dating service a year and a half ago. All I hear from the agency is that anyone who reads my profile and then sees my photo is not willing to meet someone with a disability" (Mackelprang & Salsgiver, 1999, p. 17). These types of experiences illustrate the fact that the disability is the master status of the individual and any achievements, interests, shared experiences and values, or attractiveness is cancelled out by the disability.

Friendship and group dating are social opportunities which are increasingly becoming available for IWDs; however, one woman with a disability stated, "Everybody respects and admires me but I don't have a single friend." A man with a disability explained that when men and women got together for an evening out, a type of group date, everyone was happy to have him along. However, when the same men and women began couples' dating, he was left out. His explanation was, "No woman wants to be identified as *my* date."

> On the romantic side, women have a tendency to move away from me.... It's like "see ya later." I mean, it's easy to find someone to say, "Okay, let's go out," but when it comes to the romantic side of it, they're not sure of what to do, what to expect. Too, it's hard to approach someone when you're in a wheelchair, as opposed to the way it was before, I mean, what do you say? "Can I buy you a drink and, by the way, would you help me with mine?"
> (Scherer, 1993, p. 9)

George Covington was Special Assistant for Disability Policy in the office of the Vice-President and was born legally blind. He is a graduate of the University of Texas Law School.

> In my teen years, I was frustrated because I couldn't drive a car and pick up attractive young women and take them out to the park to do all the things in the back seat that everybody else was getting to do. But that was overcome when I got to the University of Texas; you didn't need a car for a date. I discovered nirvana.
> (Covington, 1997, p. 33)

Olkin labeled dating for IWDs as Mount Everest, thus describing the difficulty, whereas Covington thought dating was "nirvana."

> For people with disabilities, dating is Mount Everest. Disability discrimination is most felt in the romantic realm. Studies of attitudes toward disability repeatedly show that people's attitudes become more and more negative as the relationship with the disability gets closer. Those who indicate that they would be fine with the idea of a neighbor with a disability draw the line at their children dating a person with a disability and most people indicate that they would not marry a person with a disability.
> (Olkin, 1999, p. 223)

Perhaps the greatest obstacle to dating and sexual intimacy for IWDs is not their disability but rather the difficulty in establishing equal social status relationships in a society with a media that shows IWDs as pathetic, deviant, and as objects of charity. Most of us are not aware of the extent to which we subconsciously believe in these images and it is often a surprise when IWODs meet IWDs and learn that IWDs do not think of themselves as pathetic, deviant, and needing pity and charity.

Marriage and the Acquisition of a Disability

Marriage and Disability

- Marriage is often the longest relationship experienced and is considered one of the most important relationships in life.
- There is evidence that the marital happiness is the greatest source of overall life satisfaction.
- Married couples will spend more time caring for aging parents than for caring for their children.
- Mid-life is the time of "peak achievement" and "peak earning" and the acquisition or onset of a disability carries the potential to cause significant losses.
- Marriage between an IWD and IWOD is considered an asymmetrical relationship, with the IWD thought to be a "burden" and the IWOD a "saint" or a "loser."
- Losses also include the stability of the relationship and the social threats of others.
- The costs incurred for disability expenses are high.
- Often the partner with a disability must relinquish a job or career.
- Women tend to have more midlife disabilities, most often chronic illness.
- Caregiving is considered to be "women's work" and, while this is changing, men are more often cared for by partners or other family members while women are cared for by paid strangers.
- One successful response is role flexibility.

Developmental stages, including marriage, help define and shape the disability experience. At the same time that the rates of disabilities are increasing, demographic and social changes have changed the definition and experience of marriage, with the Pew Research Center reporting that most Americans agree with this statement, "There are several ways to have a successful family life." Today, parents who have never married, same-sex couples, interracial couples and blended families are considered to be marriages. While the rate of "traditional" marriage is declining in the United States and the average age of first marriage is increasing, the rates of other types of long-term relationships are increasing. In spite of the evolving definition of marriage, marriage (and other types of long-term relationships) is for many people their longest and most important relationship. Nonetheless, a developmental psychologist (Rice, 1998) stated, "data from six national studies conducted in the United States revealed that marital happiness contributed more to personal global (overall) happiness than did any other kinds of satisfaction, including satisfaction from work" (p. 568). Marital satisfaction is the single greatest source of happiness while the opposite is also true: marital dissatisfaction often has negative effects in other parts of life.

Another way in which social and demographic changes have modified marriage includes the definition of "dependents." Historically, dependents of a marriage have been children, but this definition has expanded to include the aging parents of the couple and, with the twin realities of the declining birthrate and increasing lifespans, many married couples invest a greater number of years caring for elderly parents than they do raising children. For example, if each couple has four parents and two children and these children leave home at 18 or 20, the couple may spend a span of 25 or 30 years caring for four parents. One woman did not want to give up her career in order to care for her husband's parents: "I never cared for your parents before. How can you expect me to have them live with us when they are elderly disabled? Do you really expect me to quit my job and take care of them?" At times, every choice and plan are unsuitable.

Mid-life is also the time of "peak" achievement and "peak earnings," with planned competence and good decision-making made early in life, coupled with hard work, expensive and increasing necessary higher education, and other types of sacrifices literally paying off in mid-life. The onset of a disability or the diagnosis of a chronic illness seems a random and unpredictable event with the potential to completely disrupt the individual's life and the lives of the partner and dependents.

Intimate, sexual relationships between an IWOD and an IWD are viewed as asymmetrical, or unbalanced, and therefore stressful. The IWOD is viewed as either a "saint" or a "loser," both negative identities, "or forced into a default position" (Fine & Asch, 1988, p. 247). The IWD is consistently viewed as a burden. One woman in the 1950s, a polio survivor in a wheelchair was told by her mother to "marry anyone who will sink low enough to marry you." This woman was smart enough to ignore her mother, but many other IWDs internalize these false stigmatizations, thinking that "no one would marry me because of my disability." A professor of English with multiple sclerosis (Toombs, 1995) related that many people have said to her, "How *lucky* you are to have your husband," falsely thinking that her marriage is asymmetrical because her husband who does not have a disability is viewed as the contributor while she is thought to be a passive recipient of his kindness and charity. Unbalanced marriages, for any reason, are often stressful because the contributor may become resentful and the recipient may feel insecure, fearing that their partner will leave. Ms. Toombs answers these individuals by saying, "It's my husband who is lucky. I have financially supported him since we married."

The often-used marriage vows of "in sickness and health" does suggest the possibility that one (or both) of the partners may acquire a disability; in spite of this, most couples do not consider the possibility of a disability until they approach old age. The acquisition of a disability or diagnosis of a chronic illness often causes couples and families to re-evaluate their value systems. Twenty years ago, a developmental theorist (Rice, 1998, p. 570) listed 12 marital adjustment tasks, all of which are demanding and continuous, but disability was not included. The possibility of one member acquiring a disability is rarely considered. Some of these marital tasks include coordinating and resolving issues of personal habit, sex roles, power and decision making, family and relatives, and moral values and ideology, and work, employment and achievement. Most couples do not consider the possibility of disability and contributing to this lack of preparation is the reality that the effects of the disability can never be completely ameliorated. Add the demands (and the resulting costs of disability) to this list of marital adjustment tasks and it becomes apparent that marriage can require great resources of love, flexibility, and stamina

Thinking in terms of disability prevalence and speaking generally, men tend to have more traumatic injuries, such as spinal cord injuries and traumatic brain injuries while women tend to experience more chronic illnesses. Of course, there are women who experience traumatic injuries and men with chronic illnesses, but the preceding statement is speaking of large groups of people. Also, the rate of traumatic injuries in men tends to decline after adolescence or the early twenties and following marriage. It is speculated that the "thrills and chills" risky behaviors end as men become older or take on family responsibilities. Demographers (Richards, Kewman, & Pierce, 2000) spoke about the gender prevalence and age prevalence of spinal cord injuries (SCIs):

> A great deal of what is known about the demographics and etiology of SCI comes from the collaborative database . . . funded by the National Institute on Disability and Rehabilitation Research. From that source, we know that more than half of all injuries occur in the 16–30 year old group and that

men make up 82% of the cases. . . . This percentage has changed little in the more than 20 years that the database has been in operation.

(p. 11)

If men tend to "age-out" of traumatic onset disabilities, women tend to "age in" to chronic illnesses. Chronic illnesses tend to occur in middle age; thus women diagnosed with these types of disabilities are often married or in other long-term relationships, frequently with responsibilities for family care and nurturing. Typical chronic illnesses diagnosed during mid-life include amyotrophic lateral sclerosis, multiple sclerosis, rheumatoid arthritis, systematic lupus erythematosus, and post-polio syndrome.

In the following excerpt, a psychiatrist summarizes some of the response demands when one partner acquires a disability. Note that both biologically (chronological time) and socially, disability in midlife is considered "out of phase" and "untimely."

> When a disabling or life-threatening disorder occurs earlier, it is out of phase in both chronological and social time. When such events are untimely, spouse and family lack the psychosocial preparation and rehearsal that occur later, when peers are experiencing similar losses. The ill member and the family are likely to feel robbed of their expectation of a normal life span. . . . As one young women explained whose husband had metastatic cancer confided, "As long as Jim has cancer, we have no future," Suffering is compounded for couples when peers distance themselves from them because they want to avoid facing the possibility of a similar loss of spouse of child.
>
> (Rolland, 1994, p. 186)

Pace-of-life issues and achievement needs are two areas requiring compromise in all marriages. Individuals in marriages with differing "activity levels," have the potential to disagree. An example might be a woman caring for small children, elderly parents, with a demanding career, while her partner might be more laid-back, "live in the moment," and "we'll cross that bridge when we come to it." This partner is obviously not a planful individual, with a long to-do list while the wife might feel that careful (maybe even rigid) planning is a necessity and there is little time for spontaneity. The partner values fun while the wife values achievement. Two women whose husbands have an episodic course psychiatric disability explain that the disability has exaggerated their pace-of-life issues. In the second excerpt, the wife reports that the inability to plan ahead has been "the biggest thing that has changed my life." In the first excerpt, note the wife's "tons of anger" and, while at first, she denies that her anger is directed toward her husband, in the next phrase she concedes that she her anger is toward her husband. She probably feels guilty for a very "normal," common feeling—anger.

> Our entire life together has been one big adaptation! I like things organized and planned. Life with mental illness has too many ups and down with inability to concentrate on planned activities.
> (Mannion, 1996, p. 22)

Mark O'Brien, whose arm was amputated due to an infection, clearly illustrated pace of life issues with a disability. Moreover, both his personality and work demands as a freelance journalist, were based on excellent time management and "multitasking." He summarizes the result of the slower pace of life, "This makes me cranky."

> Besides the pain, the biggest inconvenience about being one-armed isn't any individual task, but in the aggregate. I had a very busy, overbooked life before I lost my arm. Now each thing I do takes longer—sometimes much longer. I could tell you about toasting a bagel, opening a new box of cereal, or changing the trash bag, but you get the idea. A morning routine that used to take 30 minutes now lasts more than an hour. At the end of the day, I have always done less than I expected to. This makes me cranky.
> (O'Brien, 2014, p. 37)

Another wife feels that she, also, has been deeply affected when she asks, "Why did this happen to me?" when it is her husband who has the disability.

> I guess I'm okay with it, but . . . I have tons of anger, not really to him—sometimes to him—but more to you know, "Why me? Why did this happen to me? Why did my husband happen to be the one who got ill?" Because when we got married, we were the perfect little couple. . . . So yes, I've had to revise a lot. . . . I can't think far in advance any more. This is probably the biggest thing that has changed my life because I used to be a planner, all the time planned—ten years ahead. . . . With an illness like this that runs in cycles . . . I just think it's too much to put on yourself to expect things when you don't know what's going to happen.
> (Karp, 2001, p. 143)

Compassion fatigue, or burnout, experienced by partners, family members, and professional care providers is more common with episodic course disabilities than with stable-course disabilities because everyone feels out of control, bewildered, and somewhat helpless. For some disabilities, the episodes or relapses can be predicted by warning signs (prodromal symptoms) or reduced or prevented by avoiding stress and fatigue. Further, most chronic illnesses tend to be episodic. A husband who provides care for his wife with amyo lateral sclerosis explained: "My wife is very important to me. Even though she is not what she used to be, she was once a great wife and mother. ALS can never change that!" Another husband whose wife experienced a stroke stated, "This is not my wife! I did not plan on living my life with someone I do not know or care about any more. Before the stroke, I was thinking about a divorce—now I am planning one!"

The disability may disrupt the intimate, sexual aspects of the relationship. In the next excerpt, the husband is grateful for his wife's "Oscar-winning performance," allowing him to feel, "I am the man." Note also the typical demands of pregnancy combined with the atypical demand of a traumatic injury. His wife understands that she is gaining two dependent individuals almost simultaneously—a newborn baby and a 27-year-old husband with a spinal cord injury.

> After drinking beer . . . I got into my car to drive home. Halfway home, I fell asleep and struck a utility pole while sitting atop my seatbelt. My life was instantaneously altered. As my pregnant wife entered the hospital emergency room at 4:00 a.m., the neurosurgeon blasted her about my high alcohol reading and prognosis. If I survived, I would need constant attention.
>
> After 6 months in the hospital, I was allowed to go home for the weekend. . . . My foremost thought was to resume sexual activity with Valerie and provide for both our needs. At 27, I had serious doubts about being a person or a man and felt the only way to prove my virility was in the bedroom. Valerie was very patient and empathic to my needs. My hygiene was terrible, a tracheostomy was down my throat, my bladder and bowel needed to be emptied prior to commencing intimacy, and there was always the chance of having an accident. To this day, I will always be indebted to her for allowing me to believe that "I was the man." I told her she gave Oscar winning performances when I needed them.
>
> (Collins, 2007, p. 721)

Partner caregiving is often more difficult because of the power issues, gender roles, and the sexual needs of the couple. Importantly, caregiving may interfere with sexual attraction. Further, to my knowledge, the only disability for which there is available information on sexual performance is spinal cord injuries. Sex, in all its forms of expressions, is physical, emotional, and mental, thus calling for case collaboration between physicians, marriage and relationship counselors, and sex therapists.

In the preceding excerpt, there is also an element of self-blame: "after drinking beer" and "sitting atop my seatbelt." Another wife clearly expressed her feelings of anger:

> What a living hell! My husband is one case where we would have been better off if the doctor let him die on the highway. They actually put his brain back into his head and now I must live with a partial person who is killing me emotionally, just as he did before the accident.

Note that this wife feels her husband's traumatic brain injury resulted from his pre-disability lifestyle.

In another type of blame, at times, partners are blamed, explicitly or implicitly for their mate's psychiatric disability. One man avoided his in-laws because they told him that he had caused his wife's (and their daughter's) depression. Occasionally, young children mistakenly think that they did something (or did not do something) which resulted in their parents' disability. If the topic of blame is not introduced and permission granted to discuss it in an accepting and honest environment, it is very difficult to uncover deep emotions. For young children, when there is a temporal relationship between their naughty behavior and the onset of parental disability, these children assume that their naughtiness caused the disability. Children's counselors know that it is often difficult for very young children to understand and articulate their emotions. Without direct and open discussion with all family members, destructive feelings of guilt often continue for years simply due to the fact that the services of a counselor, skilled in communicating with children was not used.

The response/adjustment process is illustrated in the short excerpt which follows. At first, the loss is great, the husband changes from being "the strength of the family who makes everyone proud" to "this person who scares everyone with his temper." At the end, the wife expresses satisfaction, "Sometimes I even like the fact that my husband is around all the time."

> One day I have a family member who is the strength of the family, who makes everyone proud, and the next, I have this person who scares everyone with his temper and who thinks everything is fine when it's a sorry

mess. But life is getting better. The two of us get along. Sometimes I even like the fact that my husband is around all the time. He can be good company.... I guess we'll be a good old twosome until the day we die.... Life is hard. I'm a survivor.

(Dell Orto & Power, 2007)

One woman expressed the pain of losing her job, emphasizing that hobbies (such as painting) were not as satisfying as an actual job:

Weekdays when I see other young women leaving for or returning home from work I feel quite apart from the outside world. Whatever activities you take up, like painting, aren't the same. Nobody can convince you it's the same as being active without a normal work situation.

(Hillyer, 1993, p. 16)

There is a wide array of services that could benefit couples dealing with a disability, including benefits planners, respite care, and vocational rehabilitation. Benefits planners are government workers who help IWDs navigate the financial elements of disability, having been trained in the intricacies of Social Security Disability Insurance (SSDI) and Supplemental Income. Other types of financial planners can help develop trust plans and college trusts for children. Marriage and family counselors, after training and experience in disability issues, can support gender role change and flexibility. Grief counseling might be appropriate, especially with IWDs, who have a degenerating course disability, thus experiencing the need to grieve and respond to each decrement of functioning and additional loss. Anger management and stress management, together with the provision of state-supported respite care, are interconnected and, therefore, can be considered a "package of services." Expressing negative emotions, such as stress, fatigue, and anger in the safe environment of couples counseling is healthier than simple silence and repression.

Caregiving for husbands and men has been viewed as "women's work," although this is changing. Men with disabilities are more likely to be cared for at home by their wives. In contrast, women with disabilities are more often cared for by paid strangers in public facilities. There are demographic reasons for this: 1) women tend to live longer than men and 2) more women are divorced or widowed and, therefore, have no male partner to provide care. However, social explanations appear to outweigh the demographic reasons. Socially, "the role of women [has been] as sources of support for vulnerable people" (G. H. S. Singer, 1996, p. 13). For example, daughters or daughters-in-law, rather than sons or sons-in-law, are known to provide care for elderly parents; the eldest hearing daughter of deaf parents is more likely to act as their interpreter; and when a baby or child acquires the disability, it is the wife who most often quits her job to provide care. The concept of caregiving as "women's work" is gradually changing due to greater role flexibility for both men and women. Perhaps now more gender-balanced, 25 years ago, an interview study reported that ties of obligation and love:

> Represent a defining aspect of femininity. Nurturing and connecting with others ... evoke feminine associations. Many informants spoke of needing to be adaptable, invisible, and even subordinate. ... These characteristics coincide with the generally tentative or inferior status traditionally available to women and, as such, contrast with the more fixed, visible, and dominant roles available to men.
>
> (Preston, 1994, p. 101)

A psychiatrist whose specialty is marriage and family counseling (Rolland, 1994) described the traditional, "stereotyped expectations" of women as caregivers as "skewed" and "rigid."

> Most men tend to tackle the practical or instrumental aspects of coping, avoiding the emotional side of their partner and themselves. Women are typically expected to tend to the emotional needs of their husbands, child, and others and to stifle their own needs. At the time of the initial illness crisis, couples tend to divide up coping tasks according to habitual patterns or stereotyped expectations. ... This division of psychosocial labor can become skewed and rigidified depending on who is the patient and who the caregiver is and on role assignments according to gender. ... A chronic disorder gives couples an opportunity to reexamine habitual role constraints; this should be done with an understanding of the psychosocial demands of the disorder over time.
>
> (p. 254)

Rolland (1994) discusses three aspects of spousal caregiving, describing it as 1) "psychosocial labor," and therefore, automatically considered to be the role of women; 2) pointing out that women are typically required to "stifle" their own feelings; and 3) the caregiving roles should be continuously reexamined, especially in light of the changing nature of the disability.

In the next excerpt, Rolland (1994) described the difference between men and women in receiving care.

Men, socialized to be tough and invulnerable, often feel that being nurtured and dependent is acceptable, if at all, only when they are ill and injured. For many men their early memories of being nurtured with mothering in times of illness . . . powerful voices describe dependency and disability as evidence of infantilism, and failure to fulfill the dominant male role of self-reliant provider for one's family.

(p. 254)

In episodic disabilities, with unpredictable relapses, "control therapy" should be considered. As previously discussed, first-person accounts in which IWDs with episodic disabilities describe the experience as "a roller coaster" or "riding in a speeding car," illustrating a profound sense of lack of control. Episodic course disabilities assault the IWD's and their families' sense of control. "Intentionality" as a coping mechanism to increase feelings, thoughts, and behaviors which are planful associated with an episodic disability, in addition to thought-out action plans developed in times of remission, are recommended as therapeutic interventions. Lack of control, for any cause, leads to stress, ambiguity, and emotional distress and gaining personal control is a strong, universal human motivator. The example of "relapse drills," (much like fire drills) was explained in the section on Intentionality can be applied to marital and family counseling settings. After the relapse, the response plan can be reevaluated; perhaps tweaked; and the IWD and family members led to discuss what they have learned from a particular relapse. In counseling, each family member is asked for an assessment, including their feelings, on the efficacy of their relapse response. This type of control intervention, or intentionality, often reduces the number of relapses or shortens the duration and intensity of relapses. An example of intentionality counseling is seen in the case of a mother and wife with multiple sclerosis who often fell and, in response, every family member was assigned a job, from the husband and older children helping her to her feet, to the three year old getting packages of frozen peas from the freezer to ice the injuries. This family did not *eat* many peas, but there were always lots of peas in the freezer in preparation for possible injuries from falls. Such types of relapse plans and control therapy could be greatly enhanced if counselors, trained in disability issues, were included in the treatment team. This type of control therapy emphasizes maintenance of functioning, including family functioning, and regulation of anticipated loss.

Much of the academic literature on marriage and disability counseling tends to be negative and, indeed, many families have felt that they have been implicitly blamed for not coping well. With limited resources, the complexity of the demands, and the lack of professional support, families and couples are put at emotional risks. The following counseling practices can build coping skills in couples with disability concerns.

> **Suggested Methods in Counseling Couples With Disabilities**
>
> 1. Recognize that the words "family therapy" are often interpreted by the family as blame or shame. Perhaps a better label would be "family psychoeducation."
> 2. Assist the couple to comprehend a new, unexpected, and ambiguous reality.
> 3. Assess the pre-disability level of marital success and emotional functioning as a basis for post-disability coping.
> 4. Recognize that the disability has a differential impact on each family member.
> 5. Remember that negative emotions, such as anger, are "normal." Do not jump to label the family as "dysfunctional."
> 6. Integrate counseling with case management with medical service providers in order to provide information and practical suggestions.
> 7. Focus therapy on problem solving, skill building, and planning to anticipate relapses or secondary conditions.
> 8. Deal directly with feelings rather than "hidden shame or blame."
> 9. Focus on current day-to-day transactions rather than a long and complicated family history.
> 10. Assist the couple to lower their expectations to more realistic goals. Often termed the "Goldilocks Effect," the expectations are neither too low or too high.
> 11. Focus on building communication skills.
> 12. Encourage compliance with medical treatments and therapies. It may not be an issue of simple compliance but of increased compliance.

Marriage counseling, when dealing with a disability, can help couples interpret and understand the disability and redefine a new normal. In the first stages of response, it is important to examine role expectations of each partner, including the way in which each feels about the disability, and respond to immediate demands, rather than focusing on long term insight therapy.

Marriage and family counselors are rarely trained in disability issues, while at the same time, they live in a culture which falsely exaggerates and pathologizes disability. As with any other type of counselors providing services to IWDs, marriage and family counselors will be required to examine and question their own unspoken assumptions about disability. Counseling will become more effective if counselors can provide practical suggestions for the medical management of the disability, including the couple's feelings and perceptions about these treatments. Compliance with medical treatment is necessary; however, increased compliance is even better. Couples require a "safe," warm, and accepting environment in which to discuss their feelings about the disability and marriage and couples' counseling can provide this. In order to provide this foundation of acceptance and empathy in the counseling relationships, counselors need to have informed and accurate information about disability.

Conclusion

Counselors consistently upgrade their skills and seek new understandings. Moreover, counselors do not avoid difficult and complex information and, in these ways, they are able to gain mastery and, in turn, allow their clients with disabilities to gain control and mobilize strengths and resources. However, in order to accomplish these types of goals, a therapeutic alliance must be formed.

In this chapter, counseling theoretical orientations and techniques which can be used with CWDs were introduced, including values clarification, developing decision-making skills, assertive training, building greater ego strength, developing more social efficacy, providing personal control counseling, and using cognitive behavioral techniques. Of course, all of these techniques are used with both with CWODs and CWDs. These counseling techniques, and others, can be implemented within the counselor's area of expertise and agency setting, such as marriage and family counseling, career counseling, academic counseling, and sexual issues counseling. The combination of the counselor's understanding of the disability experience, the counselor's area of specialization, and skillful use of these specific techniques can result in effective counseling outcomes.

Six specific issues were introduced and described. The first issue was "the silent transition of the birth of a baby with a congenital disability," emphasizing that many families, after a period of adjustment, regain emotional equilibrium, expressing this equilibrium and stabilization as reaching a "new normal."

The second issue concerned the impact of a long pre-diagnosis period and the results. Obviously, disabilities and chronic illnesses with type of pre-diagnostic periods are often disabilities with an insidious onset, have a fluctuating course, and are often invisible.

The last four issues discussed in this chapter are related to social relationships, including the availability of appropriate role models, friends, and romantic partners. Equal social status relationships with IWODs are often difficult for IWDs because, first, they may not have a great deal of access to interaction with IWODs and, second, relationships between an IWD and an IWOD are often thought to be asymmetrical.

References

Appel, T. (1988). Personal statement: Living in spite of multiple sclerosis. In P. W. Power (Ed.), *Family interventions throughout chronic illness and disability* (pp. 253–257). New York, NY: Springer.

Bandura, A. (1977). *Social learning theory.* Englewood Cliffs, NJ: Prentice Hall.

Bandura, A. (1986). *Social foundations of thought and action: A social cognitive theory.* Englewood Cliffs, NJ: Prentice-Hall.

Blumberg, B. D., Lewis, M. J., & Susman, E. J. (1984). Adolescence: A time of transition. In M. G. Eisenberg, L. C. Sutkin, & M. A. Jansen (Eds.), *Chronic illness and disability through the life span: Effects on self and the family* (pp. 133–163). New York, NY: Springer.

Colapinto, J. (2010, December 20, 27). Medical dispatch: Mother courage. The Duchenne campaigner. *The New Yorker,* New York.

Collins, C. (2007). For better or for worse. In A. Dell Orto & P. Power (Eds.), *The psychological and social impact of illness and disability* (6th ed., pp. 719–723). New York, NY: Springer.

Covington, G. (1997). The Americans with Disabilities Act. In F. Pelka (Ed.), *The ABC-CLIO companion to the disability rights movement.* Santa Barbara, CA: ABC-CLIO.

Darling, R. B. (1983). The birth defective child and the crisis of parenthood: Redefining the situation. In E. J. Callahan & K. A. McCluskey (Eds.), *Life-span developmental psychology: Nonnormative life events* (pp. 115–143). New York, NY: Academic Press.

Degeneffe, C. E., & Lee, G. K. (2010). Quality of life after traumatic brain injury: Perspectives of adult siblings. *Journal of Rehabilitation, 76,* 27–36.

Dell Orto, A., & Power, P. (Eds.) (2007). *The psychological and social impact of illness and disability* (6th ed.). New York, NY: Springer.

Elder, G. H. Jr. (1997). The life course and human development. In R. M. Lerner (Ed.), *Handbook of child psychology: Volume 1: Theoretical models of human development* (pp. 939–991). New York, NY: Wiley.

Erikson, E. H. (1968). *Identity and crisis.* New York, NY: Norton.

Fine, M., & Asch, A. (1988). *Women and disabilities: Essays in psychology, culture, and politics.* Philadelphia, PA: Temple University.

Goodheart, C. D., & Lansing, M. H. (1997). *Treating people with chronic disease: A psychological guide.* Washington, DC: American Psychological Association.

Green, S. E. (2003). "What do you mean 'what's wrong with her?'": Stigma and the lives of families of children with disabilities. *Social Science and Medicine, 57,* 1361–1374.

Hillyer, B. (1993). *Feminism and disability.* Norman, OK: University of Oklahoma Press.

Holaday, M., & McPhearson, R. W. (1997). Resilience and severe burns. *Journal of Counseling and Development, 75,* 346–356.

Hubbard, R. (2006). Abortion and disability: Who should and who should not inhabit the world. In L. J. David (Ed.), *The disability studies reader* (2nd ed., pp. 93–103). New York, NY: Routledge.

Huston, A. M. (1987). *Common sense about dyslexia.* New York, NY: Madison.

Karp, D. A. (2001). *The burden of sympathy: How families cope with mental illness.* Oxford: Oxford University.

Kleege, G. (2006). *Blind rage: Letters to Helen Keller.* Washington, DC: Gallaudet University.

Kohler, K., Schweikert-Stary, T., & Lubkin, I. (1998). Altered mobility. In I. M. Lubkin & P. D. Larsen (Eds.), *Chronic illness: Impact and interventions* (4th ed., pp. 122–148). Sudbury, MA: Jones and Bartlett.

Kubla, E. (2018, January 10). In my chronic illness, I found a deeper meaning. *New York Times.* Retrieved 02-24-2018 www.nytimes.com/2018/01/10/opinion/in-my-chronic-illness-i-found-a-deeper-meaning.html?mtrref=query.nytimes.com&assetType=opinion Retrieved 02-26-2018

LaBorit, E. (2010). Selections from *The Cry of the Gull.* In L. J. Lennard (Ed.), *The disability studies reader* (3rd ed., pp. 599–618). New York, NY: Routledge.

Mackelprang, R., & Salsgiver, R. (1999). *Disability: A diversity model approach in human service practice.* Pacific Grove, CA: Brooks and Cole.

Mairs, N. (1997). *Waist-high in the world: A life among the nondisabled.* Boston, MA: Beacon.

Mannion, E. (1996). Resilience and burden in spouses with mental illness. *Psychiatric Rehabilitation Journal, 20,* 13–24.

McLeod, D. J., & Almazan, E. P. (2004). Connections between childhood and adulthood. In J. T. Mortimer & M. J. Shanahan (Ed.), *Handbook of the life course* (pp. 391–411). New York, NY: Springer.

McPhee, N. (1982, June). A very special magic: A grandparent's delight. *Exceptional Parent, 36,* 13–16.

Michalko, R. (2002). *The difference that disability makes.* Philadelphia, PA: Temple University.

Miller, M. M., & Menacker, S. J. (2007). Vision: Our window to the world. In M. L. Batshaw, L. Pellegrino, & N. J. Roizen (Eds.), *Children with disabilities* (pp. 137–156). New York, NY: Routledge.

Morris, J. (1991). *Pride against prejudice: Transforming attitudes towards disability.* London: The Women's Press.

Neumann, R. J. (1988). Personal statement experiencing sexuality as an adolescent with rheumatoid arthritis. In P. W. Power, A. E. Dell Orto, & M. B. Gibbons (Eds.), *Family interventions throughout chronic illness and disability* (pp. 156–163). New York, NY: Springer.

O'Brien, M. (2014, July 18). My new life with one arm. *This Week,* 36–37.

Olkin, R. (1999). *What psychotherapists should know about disability.* New York, NY: Guilford.

Patterson, J. M. (1988). Chronic illness in children and the impact upon families. In C. S. Chilman, E. W. Nunnally, & F. M. Cox (Eds.), *Chronic illness and disability* (pp. 69–107). Beverly Hills, CA: Sage.

Preston, P. (1994). *Mother father deaf: Living between sound and silence.* Cambridge, MA: Harvard University.

Rice, F. P. (1998). *Human development: A lifespan approach* (3rd ed.). Upper Saddle River, NJ: Prentice Hall.

Richards, J. S., Kewman, D. G., & Pierce, C. A. (2000). Spinal cord injury. In R. G. Frank & T. S. Elliott (Eds.), *Handbook of rehabilitation psychology* (pp. 11–27). Washington, DC: American Psychological Association.

Rolland, J. S. (1994). *Families, illness, and disability: An integrative treatment model.* New York, NY: Basic.

Rosen, D. (2014, July 24). Seeing the child, not the disability. *New York Times.* Retrieved from https://well.blogs.nytimes.com/2014/07/24/seeing-the-child-not-the-disability/ Retrieved 02-26-2018

Rousso, H. (1993). *Disabled, female and proud! Stories of ten women with disabilities.* Westport, CT: Bergin Garvey.

Rutter, M. L. (1989). Pathways from childhood to adult life. *Journal of Child Psychology and Psychiatry, 30,* 23–51.

Saxton, M. (2006). Disability rights and selective abortion. In L. J. David (Ed.), *The disability studies reader* (2nd ed., pp. 105–116). New York, NY: Routledge.

Scherer, M. S. (1993). *Living in the state of stuck: How technologies affect the lives of people with disabilities.* Cambridge, MA: Brookline.

Singer, G. H. S. (1996). Introduction: Trends affecting home and community care for people with chronic conditions in the United States. In G. H. S. Singer, L. E. Powers, & A. L. Olson (Eds.), *Redefining family support: Innovations in public-private partnerships* (pp. 3–38). Baltimore, MD: Paul H. Brookes.

Smart, J. F. (2012). *Disability across the developmental lifespan.* New York, NY: Springer.

Smith, S. (2010, July). Distress and hope in families raising children with special needs. *Counseling Today, 52,* 54–56.

Solomon, A. (2012). *Far from the tree: Parents, children, and the search for identity.* New York, NY: Scribner.

Souders, R. (1993). Randy Souders. In J. K. Smith & G. Plimpton (Eds.), *Chronicles of courage: Very special artists* (pp. 147–155). New York, NY: Penguin Random House.

Stefan, S. (2001). *Unequal rights: Discrimination against people with mental disabilities and the Americans with disabilities act.* Washington, DC: American Psychological Association.

Time Magazine. (1997, April 28). A monumental mistake: The F.D.R. Memorial misses the essence of the man. *Time, 149,* 17.

Toombs, S. K. (1995). Sufficient unto the day. In S. K. Toombs, D. Barnard, & R. A. Carson (Eds.), *Chronic illness from experience to policy* (pp. 2–23). Bloomington, IN: University of Indiana.

Veith, E. M., Sherman, J. E., Pellino, T. A., & Yasui, N. Y. (2006). Qualitative analysis of the peer-mentoring relationship among individuals with spinal cord injury. *Rehabilitation Psychology, 51,* 289–298.

Wright, D. (1994). *Deafness: An autobiography.* New York, NY: Harper Perennial.

Zola, I. K. (1982). *Missing pieces: A chronicle of living with a disability.* Philadelphia, PA: Temple University.

Ten

RESPONDING TO SOME UNIQUE DEMANDS OF DISABILITY

Counseling Practice Guidelines

In this chapter, some difficult aspects of disability are presented, but with the understanding that all of these are quite rare. In previous chapters, we discussed aspects of disability that are very common to IWDs, some of which are universal among IWDs. In contrast, this chapter focuses on chronic pain, physical disfigurements, the "try harder" syndrome, and substance abuse and alcoholism. With each of these, counseling applications are suggested.

> **This Chapter Includes:**
> - Chronic pain among individuals with disabilities
> - Physical disfigurements
> - The "try harder" syndrome
> - Substance abuse and alcoholism among IWDs

Chronic Pain

Chronic pain is very different than acute pain, both physically and socially. Further, the individual's experience of chronic pain differs from the experience of acute pain. Both types of pain are invisible, difficult to quantify, are part of many disabilities; yet, very little is known about chronic pain. Much more is known about acute pain. Physicians try to establish a baseline, asking patients to rate their pain on a one-to-ten scale, and asking about possible triggers, and the type of pain—stabbing, throbbing, burning, and so forth. Nonetheless all of this information gathering is subjective and it is impossible to fully describe the experience of pain. One person's "six" may be another person's "ten."

The most common cause of pain in the United States is low back problems. Many disabilities require frequent hospitalizations, surgeries and, painful treatments. Frequent hospital stays are typical for many IWDs and physical therapy is often painful. Many types of neuromuscular disabilities and types of arthritis are painful.

Acute pain is a "protective physiological mechanism that informs us when something is wrong with our bodies" (Jeffrey, 2006, p. 68). Often, in acute pain, there is an identifiable pathology and when this pathology is resolved, the pain remits. Individuals, as well as physicians, and family members understand this cause-and-effect relationship. Since everyone understands that when the cause of the pain is resolved, the pain will stop and therefore, the pain is time-limited. For these reasons, acute pain is usually easier to tolerate than chronic pain. Acute pain, most often, can be controlled by medication. Individuals with acute pain are not blamed for their pain.

Chronic Pain

- Is different from acute pain, physically, emotionally, and socially.
- Is intractable and invades every aspect of the individual's life.
- Often, there is no cause-and-effect relationship in chronic pain.
- Is not socially supported; people with chronic pain are avoided because these individuals remind others of the possibility of pain for everyone.
- There are false societal stereotypes that chronic pain can be reduced or eliminated by force of will.
- Chronic pain and depression form a circular relationship; chronic pain often causes depression and depression often causes chronic pain.
- Individuals who experience chronic pain can teach others about the experience of pain.

Chronic pain often has no identifiable cause, does not typically respond to medication, and includes muscle weakness and overwhelming fatigue. In order to be labeled as "chronic pain," the pain must persist for a period of time, typically three to six months. Without an identifiable pathogen or lesion, physicians render the cause as "musculoskeletal in origin." The individual in chronic pain becomes to identify with the pain and often the pain becomes the focus of their life. Individuals who were once active and achievement-oriented, now sit at home, alone. Since the pain is invisible, others may blame the individual for their chronic pain; consequently, depression is very common among those with chronic pain and has a somewhat circular relationship with the pain because depression lowers the pain threshold.

No one wants to hear about someone's chronic pain; rather we like to hear about heroes and "overcomers" who have been able to surmount their pain. In the following example, an Olympic athlete literally surmounted pain.

> Athletes are repeatedly praised by the media for overcoming extreme pain, like the astonishing Olympic gymnast from Japan who completed his dismount with a broken leg. Yet such praise and its implicit meaning (to overcome pain is heroic) leave a difficult legacy for chronic pain patients, who cannot surmount their affliction in a supreme moment of glory, but live with it, unpraised and often unobserved day after day.
> (Morris, 1998, p. 129)

Zachary is a man with a spinal cord injury. Note that, despite his efforts at being "the perfect quad," the rods in his back dissolve and the focus of the last five years of his life "has been staying alive."

> The rods in my back were dissolving through a process of electrolysis. My doctor had no explanation—he said the metal was turning into bubble gum and axle grease. When we redid the rods, I was playing the perfect quad—I wouldn't get a glass of water; I wouldn't put any stress on them at all, and the second set still broke. The third set was actually a double operation, first anterior and then a week later, posterior.... The last five years has been "staying alive." On April 11, I've been a quad for as many days as I was able-bodied. Right now I have no goals in my life other than I want to leave this life consciously.
> (Crewe, 1997, p. 36)

Chronic pain elicits existential angst in others and the way in which they distance themselves from this possibility is to blame the individual for their chronic pain. Of course, others are not consciously aware of this existential angst nor the defense mechanism of blaming the individual. Simply stated, chronic, unremitting pain is a possibility for everyone and most people do not want to be reminded of this reality and, therefore, it is easier to avoid the individual who is in chronic pain and fabricate a way in which to blame the individual. Moreover, others offer advice such as "buck up, forget about the pain," or "think positive thoughts," "drink spinach smoothies," or "go shopping for a new hat."

> If someone tells me she is in pain, she reminds me of the existence of pain, the imperfection and fragility of the body, the possibility of my own, the

inevitability of it. The less willing I am to accept all these, the less I want to know about her pain. If I cannot avoid it in her presence, I will avoid her. I may even blame her for it. I may tell myself that she *could have* avoided it, in order to go on believing that I *can* avoid it. I want to believe that I am not like her; I cling to the differences.

(Wendell, 1997, p. 268)

Ironically, it is people who are in chronic pain who can teach us about the experience of pain.

In one case, a woman with arthritis (Hovey, 2017) believed that others blamed her for her pain and implied that she could manage the pain better. These attitudes did nothing to alleviate her physical pain, but it caused her "self-esteem to be as thin" as her joints.

> I used to think of pain as hurdle that if I were a less selfish creature, I would be able to athletically leap over with grace and poise, throwing in some charity work as I soldier on, casually inspiring those around me to admire my stunning fortitude. I believed that, were I a better, brighter person, I would manage pain silently, prise myself out of my pyjamas move my backside in the direction of a fulfilled life.
>
> You think there's some generously spirited individual who would handle pain better and probably in a smaller dress size. You make too much fuss; you're weak; whereas another in the same situation is strong. There are so many ways to batter yourself, wearing your self-esteem as thin as your joints.
>
> www.e-bility.com/articles/arthritis-pain-managment.php
> retrieved March 12, 2018

A novelist and professor of English at Duke University, Reynolds Price, described his pain. The following is an excerpt from his book, *A Whole New Life*. Price had spinal cancer and underwent three surgeries, radiation treatment, and eventually lost the use of his legs. (This does not meet all the criteria for chronic pain since the cause of his pain was known—the spinal cancer; but he does mention "mysterious reasons.")

> The pain was high and all-pervading from the neck to the feet; it generally peaked in blinding storms late in the day if I was tired. It intensified in conditions of low barometric pressure; and for dozens of other mysterious reasons, by now it had seized frank control of my mind, my moods, and my treatment of friends. Patience had ebbed to its lowest reach.
>
> (Price, 1994, p. 151)

While there is little to be done to alleviate or reduce chronic pain, counseling, especially in groups, can reduce the social stigma, isolation, and the blame from others. Building ego strength and simply having the opportunity to speak about the pain can be therapeutic. Rather than being met with blame and suspicion, a supportive and accepting group provides a sense of normalization and unity. Others experience chronic pain and listening and understanding others' perceptions and interpretations of pain can be helpful. Counselors can assist clients in forging an identity, in spite of the pain and helping the client understand the importance of social relationships which are positive and accepting, rather than blaming. Therefore, it may be necessary for clients to reduce or avoid negative and blaming friends and family members. Social skills training is often helpful as the size of the individual's social group begins to contract. Case collaboration with physicians and physical therapists is recommended because counselors can help other professions to understand the individual's interpretation of their chronic pain. Referral to pain management clinics that utilize meditation, cognitive-behavioral techniques, and hypnosis can result in a productive case collaboration, with counselors complementing the services of these clinics, such as restoring a sense of control can be achieved (somewhat) through goal attainment and a sense of planful competence will help to combat the pain, the losses, responding to the negative and suspicious responses of others. Realistic expectations, including seeking services from appropriate professionals and agencies, might appear undemanding and unchallenging, but realistic expectations are more likely to be met. Training family members to ask, "What can I do to make this better for you?" For example, many individuals, including Reynolds Price, recognized that his pain increased when he became tired. Simply asserting oneself and informing others of their need to rest (and other pain-decreasing treatments) is helpful, but difficult especially when others react so negatively to the pain. Group members have often devised and implemented successful stigma management techniques. On a practical level, individuals who live with chronic pain are the best source of guidance, direction, and information. Obviously, someone who has not lived with chronic pain is not in a position to understand the experience or the social reaction to chronic pain.

Physical Disfigurements

As a child, Ben Mattlin never looked forward to Halloween. He was born with spinal muscular dystrophy. As an adult, he wrote:

> I never thought about a connection between disabilities and Halloween until I learned of the once-common fear of deformities—the limping, hunchbacked,

hook-handed or one-eyed monsters of ancient fairy tales and old horror movies. Even the word "creepy" comes from the same word as the oldest term for folks like me, the politically incorrect "cripple." ... For people Halloween is an *escape* from conformity, but for those of us who don't quite fit the norm, that's nothing special. In fact, demonstrating that you're not exactly what people expect is pretty much what disabled folks do every day.

(Mattlin, 2016, Oct. 28)

Mattlin understands that while he could neither understand nor articulate his dislike of Halloween, the costumes and masquerades of Halloween mimicked and mocked people with disfigurements, some of which are disabilities. Additionally, an entire genre of film, horror movies, features individuals with disfiguring disabilities and, further, filmmakers imply that their unusual appearance has led to disfigured minds. This is often referred to as "the twisted body, twisted soul" idea. Horror movies conflated the idea of disfigurements with tortured, bitter, and lonely lives. Clearly, those with any type of unusual appearance were thought to be sinister, dangerous, and evil.

Disfiguring Disabilities

- Not all disabilities are disfiguring.
- Disabilities, including their treatments, can result in disfigurements.
- Often, disfigurements are more limiting than the functional limitations of the disability.
- Individuals with disfiguring disabilities experience less privacy.
- Disfigurements invoke existential angst in individuals without disabilities.

While many disabilities do not involve disfigurement, other disabilities, their symptoms, and, at times, their treatments do involve unusual appearances. An attractive appearance and projecting physical health, energy, and vitality are frequently thought to be an accurate evaluation of an individual and these ideas do not appear to be diminishing. Amputations, facial disfigurements, hooks for amputated arms and hands, and burns are examples of disfigurements. The symptoms of other disabilities, such as the drooping eyelids of myasthenia gravis, the swollen and misshapen joints of rheumatoid arthritis are also thought to be disfigurements. Some treatments result in disfigurements, especially medications for psychiatric disabilities, some of which result in perioral tremor, commonly referred to as "rabbit syndrome." Those with perioral tremor involuntarily moves their lips in movements that mimic a rabbit while those with tardive dyskinesia involuntarily rock, twist, or jerk. Some disfigurements result when the individual's appearance seems asymmetrical. Prostheses and assistive technology, however, are becoming more acceptable, rather than being considered unattractive. One example of this was formerly labeled the "hearing aid effect" in which individuals refused to wear their hearing aids in public, thinking that they were markers of a defect. Nowadays, hearing aids are often considered in the same way as eyeglasses, assistive technology used by many in order to improve a sensory function. Prostheses, in the past, were pink plastic and nonfunctional; but, their design was never intended to improve functioning but, rather, to replicate an amputated limb and make IWODs more comfortable around them.

Often, disfigurements are thought to be more a social disability, rather than a physical disability. For example, an upper limb amputation typically involves fewer functional limitations than a lower limb amputation. Nonetheless, an upper limb amputation is considered more impairing simply because the loss of an arm or hand is considered more disfiguring than the loss of a leg. Facial scars have few, if any, functional limitations and yet they are considered to be disabilities. Individuals with disfigurements were thought to have experienced "social death" and were described as "closet people" due to their isolation at home. It was commonly thought that "people like that" should not appear in public and no one wanted to be greeted with the "spectacle" of "the maimed and mutilated." A 1911 city ordinance in Chicago stated, "It is hereby prohibited for any person who is diseased, maimed, mutilated, or deformed in any way so as to be an unsightly and disgusting object to expose himself to public view" (Fries, 1997). According to Imrie (1996), these types of ordinances were still on the books in Columbus, Ohio, and Omaha, Nebraska. Regardless of their accomplishments, individuals with disfigurements were not allowed to participate in public life. Also, many with disfigurements self-isolated in order to maintain their self-identity and avoid public scorn.

A woman interviewed by Wright (1960) described the way in which her disfigurement was not part of her self-identity, but only "my disguise that had been put on me without my consent or knowledge" (p. 157). She thought of her appearance as only a mask, having very little to do with "personal beauty." However, as the following excerpt shows, she explained the difficulty of maintaining her self-identity when she looked in the mirror.

> Over and over I forgot what I had seen in the mirror. It could not penetrate into the interior of my mind and become an integral part of me. I felt as if it had nothing to do with me; it was only a disguise. But it was not the kind of disguise which is put on voluntarily by the person who wears it, and which is intended to confuse other people as to one's identity. My disguise had been put on me without my consent or knowledge like the ones in fairy tales, and it was on me for life. It was there, it was there, it was real. Every one of those encounters was like a blow on the head. They left me dazed and dumb and senseless every time, until slowly and stubbornly my robust persistent illusion of well-being and personal beauty spread all through me again.
>
> (p. 157)

The age and the developmental stage of the individual when the disfiguring disability is acquired greatly impacts the response of the individual and of others. During adolescence, disfigurements are very difficult because the teenage years are the time when body image is most important while disfigurements acquired in old age are not as difficult because elderly individuals typically place less importance on their physical appearance.

Joanne Rome was born without a left hand below the elbow. During the developmental stage of childhood, she was teased and tormented by schoolmates. Note the number of adjectives she used to express the nature of her feelings.

> I used to believe I owed an explanation to whomever demanded one. I felt fearful, intimidated, ashamed, out of control, and outraged, yet "what happened to your arm?" was not a question that I could choose to answer or not. I was a freak, an outside, an "other" and the world made it very clear that I owed them an explanation. I was also a little girl who was chased home from school with taunts of "Captain Hook!" ringing in my ears, the object of whispers, stares and laughter.
>
> (J. Morris, 1991, p. 28)

Molly McIntosh was burned as a child and has scars on her face and upper body. She calls her facial scars "my mask," perhaps not incorporating these scars into her self-identity. Ms. McIntosh describe the way in which she responded throughout her life.

> I have horrible scars on my face. What I mean by that is that people react to them with horror. Forty years ago, when I was in my twenties, and also when I was a child, I so hated the way that I looked. I tried not to think

about it but every time I went out in the street I would be reminded about how I looked because of the way people reacted to me. As I walked down the street and someone was coming towards me, they would look and then drop their eyes or move their heads, as if the horror was too much. But then they could never, every time, resist looking again. I used to have bets with myself about the second look. I would promise myself a treat if they didn't look again, but they always did.

(J. Morris, 1991, p. 24)

Some disfigurements are the result of an asymmetrical appearance. For example, a unilateral upper limb amputation (loss of one arm) is considered to be more asymmetrical than a unilateral lower limb amputation (loss of one leg). The more apparent lack of symmetry in the upper body results in greater stigma and isolation, in spite of the fact that both are asymmetrical. An English disability scholar (Marks, 1999) wrote of a man who had cosmetic surgery which reduced his functioning, but was considered "cosmetic."

One speaker at the Sheffield MA Programme explained that he had been born with one thumb. This thumb was surgically removed in order to give his hands "symmetry."

(p. 67)

It is fear, anxiety, and the dread of a possible disfigurement that makes IWODs uncomfortable in the presence of those with disfiguring disabilities. Lucy Grealy (1997) had several surgeries in order to treat her sarcoma (cancer). These life-saving surgeries resulted in facial scars. As a teenager, she loved horses and obtained a part-time job at a horse stable that provided birthday parties, or pony parties, for children from upper-class families. Grealy felt that her disfigurements allowed her "an exotic sense of power" because of the existential angst of these parents.

While the eyes of these perfectly formed children swiftly and deftly bored into the deepest part of me, the glances from their parents provided me with an exotic sense of power as I watch them inexpertly pretend not to notice me. After I passed around the swing sets and looped around to pick up the next child waiting near the picnic table littered with cake plates, juice bottles, and party favors, I'd stand confrontationally, like some Dickensian ghost, imaging that my presence served as an uneasy reminder of what might happened. What had happened to me was any parent's nightmare, and I allowed myself to believe that I was dangerous to them. The parents obliged me: they brushed past me, around me, sometimes even smiled at me.... They were uncomfortable because of my face. I ignored the deep hurt by allowing the side of me that was desperate for any kind of definition to staunchly act out, if not exactly relish, this macabre status.

(p. 19)

The Try Harder Syndrome or "The Trouble With Challenge"

- No amount of motivation or hard work will overcome the functional limitations of a disability, such as telling a blind person "to try harder to see."
- Therefore, rewards or punishments do not act as motivators.
- Challenging someone is based upon the assumption that behavior change is possible and the individual has all the necessary resources to meet the challenge.
- The "Try Harder" syndrome is more common in invisible disabilities and episodic disabilities.
- When IWDs fail to achieve, often negative character traits are attributed to them.
- Some IWDs "challenge" themselves or expect that great effort, interest, and motivation will help them achieve despite the functional limitations of their disability.

IWDs have a derisive label for the false idea of IWODs, that with motivation and sustained effort, IWDs can "overcome" their disability, labeled, "the try harder syndrome." Everyone likes to think that motivation and hard work are the sole determinants of achievements; that if we only work hard enough and want something enough, we will achieve or obtain whatever it is. Most of the time, this "can-do" attitude works, however, with disabilities that have functional limitations no amount of motivation or effort will overcome these limitations. For example, Franklin Roosevelt, the American President who was a polio survivor, stated that he would someday walk and he did expend tremendous effort in order to achieve this goal. But, walking was impossible for Roosevelt because the polio virus had destroyed his hip and leg muscles. For Roosevelt, this example of "try harder" might have been comforting, but for many other IWDs, such an insistence on doing the impossible is useless and, moreover, harmful.

In the following excerpt a man with a central nervous system lupus, an autoimmune disease that attacks the brain and central nervous system, described the try harder syndrome. Note that in the beginning, Kubla believed in the outmoded two outcomes of medicine, total recovery or death.

> Like most of us, I had been raised to see illness as something temporary; a stopover on the way to recovery or to death, not a place to live. But weeks, months and then years passed, and I did not get better. My doctors, and even some friends and family members, suggested that I could get better if only I tried harder, relaxed more deeply, thought more positively. I became a lightning rod for others' fears of disability, dependence, and fragility. In a political moment where health care is treated as a luxury . . . an ethic of personal responsibility reigns. But sometimes, sick people just stay sick. And there's no meditation, medication, positive outlook, exercise or smoothie that can fit it.
>
> (Kubla, 2018, January 10)

In some developmental disabilities, such as Attention Deficit Disorder and Hyperactivity Disorder (ADDHD) the child is viewed as oppositional, lazy, stupid, or all of these when, in reality, the child does not have the ability to concentrate or focus. Adults tell the child to sit still, concentrate, write neatly and legibly, and focus on their schoolwork, all of which the child is not able to do because of the functional limitations of the disability of ADDHD.

Edwina Fairchild was a young girl in England with degenerating vision. Perhaps trying to deny the possibility of their child's blindness, the parents chose to view Edwina as sighted.

> "Sighted" meant hope, rationality, capability, life. Given these choices, the adults tried to force me into the sighted mold. They did this partly by taking me to eye doctors who might be able to "cure" me, but mostly by simply denying that I could be anything but sighted.
>
> (J. Morris, 1991, p. 89)

When Edwina was unable to see, her parents reasoned, "she sees what she wants to see," in this way attributing her lack of vision to lack of motivation. Even as a young child, Edwina knew she was being judged unfairly.

> Some deep part of me must have known it was wrong to be humiliated and punished for something that was a natural and unchangeable part of me. . . . Since I did not fit the acceptable category of "sighted," or even the less acceptable but still comprehensible category of "blind," I threw those who came into contact with me into confusion. I was a creature that

> existed between two concepts, and they strove to get me to fit into one of the other.
>
> (J. Morris, 1991, p. 89)

Edwina's loss of vision was both degenerating and inevitable.

With the exception of Roosevelt's polio, these excerpts are about invisible, episodic, or degenerating disabilities, and individuals with these types of disabilities are often encouraged to "try harder."

At times, especially during the early stages of medical stabilization, IWDs try to challenge themselves. Chuck Close, the New York artist who became quadriplegic, described his efforts. Note Close's social comparison with another IWD who "whined and sat in the corner."

> I thought that if I had a good attitude and worked really hard—I'm someone who's used to being an achiever—I'd overcome problems. So I went into this program and I thought, "Get out of my way. I'm really going to set this world on fire. I'm going to be the hardest working patient they've ever had. I'm going to have the best attitude." I never skipped a therapy session. I never cut out early. But then I would see someone next to me with the worst attitude in the world—wouldn't go, didn't care, whined, sat in the corner. And they got better and walked out of the place. And I didn't get better and I was stuck there. Then I realized that your body gets better when your body wants to get better, and it doesn't when it doesn't. Attitude doesn't make up for everything. And working hard doesn't make up for everything. And you cannot just will yourself where you want to go.
>
> (Close, 1993, p. 19)

The try harder syndrome might also relieve society of responsibility. One author summarized, "Thinking of IWDs as challenged relieves society of the responsibility to dismantle long-term institutionalized prejudice and discrimination, and, furthermore, when the IWD *appears* to fail, he or she is considered lazy or 'chicken'" (Smart, 2016, p. 58). An IWD did not like the euphemistic phrase, "physically challenged."

> I don't like it, though. It ignores a crucial fact—the reason we can't do lots of things is not because we're lazy, or because we won't accept a challenge (isn't it implied when you won't accept a challenge that you're "chicken?") but because many things are simply beyond our control. That's admitting a political truth. Admitting a truth is the first step toward changing it.
>
> ("The Problem with Challenge," 1985, para. 5)

Others have described the problem of challenge by stating, "No amount of a good attitude or smiling will turn a staircase into a ramp." Some IWDs also believe in the false idea of the try harder syndrome. In the following excerpt, a woman asks, "when are we going to truly believe" that many of the problems of IWDs are not due to the disability nor the individual who has the disability. Occasionally, society has convinced IWDs to believe the false idea of challenge and "try harder."

> When are we ever going to truly believe, in our hearts—truly believe—that our problems are not things we are given by God, to solve ourselves, but are things that we have a right to require our society to change—because the problem isn't our disabilities but an inaccessible environment which society built in the first place.
> ("The Problem with Challenge," 1985, para 12 http://www.raggededge-magazine.com/blogs/edgecentric/media/003033.html

Substance Abuse Among Individuals With Disabilities

Substance dependence and abuse includes drugs, improper use of prescribed medications, and alcohol dependence. One source (Substance Abuse and Mental Health Services Administration [SAMHSA], 2016) defines substance abuse as:

> Substance abuse usually means using any substance in a way that leads to a failure to fulfill major responsibilities at work, school, or home, or to substance-related legal or interpersonal problems. It also includes using substances in situations that put one's physical safety at risk. Substance abuse usually manifests as a continued use of a substance despite negative physical or psychological effects, inability to cut down or control the use of the substance tolerance (using more of the substance to get the same effect, and withdrawal symptoms when the substance is no longer consumed.
> (p. 1)

Contrary to public opinion, substance abuse is considered a disability and is categorized as a psychiatric disability. It is true that all types of substance abuse were among the most recent disabilities to be legally and medically defined as disabilities. Defining substance abuse as a disability has the double advantage of providing funding and support for treatment and management. Once considered a moral failing or lack of self-control, defining substance abuse as a disability allows a more compassionate view of individuals who are substance abusers. Nonetheless, consumption of some drugs is the only disability which is illegal.

> **Substance and Alcohol Abuse in Individuals With Disabilities**
> - Prevalence rates are difficult to estimate.
> - Nonetheless, many health demographers believe that the rate of substance abuse in IWDs is twice that of the general population.
> - It is difficult to separate the symptoms of psychiatric disabilities from drug or alcohol psychosis.
> - Very few addictions counselors are trained in disability issues, despite the high prevalence rate of IWDs with substance abuse problems.

While it is hard to find definitive statistics of the number of IWDs with substance abuse, it is generally agreed that substance abuse among IWDs is much higher than in the general population. One author stated, "Data from a number of clinical studies suggest that as many as 20% of individuals with physical disabilities may have concurrent substance abuse problems, a rate twice that of the general population" (SAMHSA, 2016, p. 2). Helwig and Holicky (1994) provided some prevalence estimates of substance abuse among individuals with physical disabilities:

> Studying a small sample of individuals with spinal cord injuries, O'Donnell, Cooper, Gessner, Shehan, and Ashley (1981–1982) reported that 68% of the patients resumed drinking while undergoing rehabilitation hospitalization. Heinenmann, Donohue, Keen, and Schnoll (1988) observed alcoholic symptomatology in 49% of persons with spinal cord injuries. Vocational rehabilitation facility clients reported symptoms of alcohol abuse at a 62% rate (Rasmussen & DeBoer, 1980–1981). Of a sample of clients who were physically impaired 53% reported alcohol or other drug problems as a "substantial" or "great" concern (Thurer & Rogers, 1984). More recently, Boros (1990) estimated that 8% of individuals who were physically disabled have problems with substance abuse.
>
> (p. 227)

These estimates must be considered with caution, since some of these data were collected almost 40 years. These figures relate only to those with physical disabilities (primarily spinal cord injuries), while it is estimated that those with intellectual disabilities report higher rates. Canadian health demographers estimated the rate of substance abuse among those with intellectual disabilities, stating:

Studies on prevalence of substance abuse on this population [individuals with IDs] are urgently needed. An association between the severity of ID and substance abuse does seem to exist (Sturmey, Reyer, Lee, & Robek, 2004). Mild to borderline ID populations have a higher risk of substance abuse (Chapman & Wu, 2014). However, substance use has also been observed in lower categories of ID. Data suggests all types of substance use to be linked to all categories of ID (To, Neirynck, Vanderplasschen, Vanheule, & Vandevelde, 2014. Among all types of substances substance the use and misuse of alcohol has been found to be highest among people with ID (VanDerNagel, Kiewik, Buitelaar, & DeJong, 2011). In Ontario's [Canada] population cohort study, the prevalence of substance-related and addictive disorders among adults with ID was found to be 6.3% as compared to 3.5% in the people without ID.

(Lin et al., 2016)

Further clouding the picture is the inclusion of tobacco use in the definition of substance abuse by some agencies, but not by others. In this chapter, tobacco use is not included. A clarification of prevalence rates is needed due to the fact that various categories of disabilites are affected by the frequency of substance abuse.

Up to this point, prevalence rates have been discussed in terms of *category* of disability, i.e., physical disabilities or intellectual disabilities. Many disability scholars also posit relationship between factors in the disability including, level of severity, visibility, and an episodic course. In Lin's excerpt, it was suggested that individuals with mild or borderline IDs tend to have higher rates of substance abuse and this makes sense because often these individuals are not thought to have a disability and therefore, accommodations are not provided nor are expectations placed at an appropriate level. Individuals with mild disabilities, of all types, experience more prejudice and discrimination for the same reasons. Individuals whose disabilities are invisible also have higher rates of substance abuse due to the greater stigma and prejudice experienced because of the ambiguity of their disability. Those with episodic disabilities, rather than stable course disabilities, report higher rates of substance abuse due to response and coping demands required at each level of loss. All three types of disabilities, mild, invisible, with an episodic courses creates ambiguity, both for others and for the individuals themselves.

Difficulties in determining rate of prevalence and in providing appropriate treatment are often related to complexities of diagnosis. For example, acute episodes of substance and alcohol abuse can mimic many psychiatric disabilities. Indeed, the possibility of a substance abuse disorder must be ruled out before a diagnosis of a psychiatric disability can be made, or stated differently, drug psychosis must be distinguished from a psychiatric disability. In addition to presenting with the same symptoms of many psychiatric disabilities, substance abuse often exacerbates the symptoms of psychiatric disabilities. Finally, there is the problem of making a primary and secondary diagnosis. One source stated "that as many as 40% of persons with a psychiatric diagnosis also have serious drinking problems and should be considered as having a dual diagnosis of psychiatric disability and substance abuse." Such dual diagnoses raise important questions. Which of the two, the psychiatric disability or the substance abuse, should be the primary disability? Which should be treated first? Which agency should be responsible for providing treatment? At times, individuals are refused services at several agencies, each agency thinking that another should be responsible. Perhaps the greatest problem is the lack of trained counselors, counselors who understand disability issues and are trained in addictions counseling. Typically, there are few, if any training programs that educate addictions counselors in disability and, correspondingly, there are no agencies which provide counseling for IWDs with substance abuse disabilities. A possible solution to should dilemmas would be case collaboration; however, this may also prove problematic because many clients present themselves differently in different settings. For example, when approaching an agency that provides funds and services based on documented disabilities, an IWD with a substance abuse problem may present differently than in a counseling/treatment agency which does not require proof of a disability.

With physical disabilities, there is no question of which disability is the primary disability as the physical disability is (almost) always the primary diagnosis. For example, due to the fact that seizures can be fatal, the seizure disorder would be considered the primary disability in an individual who has a seizure disorder and a substance abuse disability. Nonetheless, alcohol and substance use lowers the seizure threshold.

Age is an important factor in recognizing IWDs with substance abuse problems because the younger the IWD, the more likely they are to have substance abuse problems. One prevalence estimate concluded that 41% of individuals with spinal cord injuries (SCIs) experience substance and alcohol abuse. This high prevalence rate is related to the high number of young people who acquire SCIs. In traumatic brain injuries (TBIs), it is estimated that 60% to 70% of these types of injuries are the result of alcohol or substance abuse.

> **Some Possible Causes of the High Prevalence Rate of IWDs With Substance Abuse Disabilities**
>
> - The enabling of families and professionals
> - Frustrations in dealing with chronic pain, spasticity, and increased limitations
> - Decreased tolerance for drugs because of their disability
> - An increase in leisure time and boredom
> - Underemployment or part-time employment
> - Easy access to drugs and medications from medical professionals
> - A sense of societal prejudice and discrimination and the resulting isolation
> - Lower resistance to peer pressure
> - Frequency of a pre-disability substance/alcohol abuse problem which may have contributed to the acquisition of the disability
> - Atypical childhood experiences

In earlier chapters, the insidious and pernicious effects of sympathy, pity, and lowering standards for IWDs were discussed. Enabling behaviors is related to these attitudes and emotional responses. Misguided attempts by both family members and medical providers to accept and/or ignore the substance abuse often results in numerous prescriptions for sleep, anxiety, and pain. Schaschl and Straw (1990) reported that friends, families, and service providers feel that they do have the "right to deny persons with disabilities their own choices, even if those choices are self-destructive." Nurses have stated, "I thought he deserved something" or "It's (the drugs) all he has." One mother rolled marijuana joints for her son "because it calms him down and he doesn't throw himself out of his [wheel]chair." (With the legalization of medical marijuana in many states, perhaps this mother is no longer breaking the law.) In addition, when the substance is discovered (or acknowledged), IWDs often face fewer consequences than IWODs, again a type of enabling behavior. Often, IWDs feel that they are "entitled" to use alcohol and drugs "because I need help dealing with my anger, or anxiety, or depression."

Often, medications are prescribed in order to decrease pain and spasticity, and, therefore, many IWDs have access to many different types legal drugs. For many types of disabilities, such as IDs which are congenital, individuals may not have had many friends and, therefore, may be particularly susceptible to peer pressure to abuse drugs and alcohol. For anyone, with or without a disability, unemployment, part time employment, or underemployment are known factors in substance abuse and IWDs are less likely have employment that fully utilizes their education and potential. Sitting home alone, being socially isolated, bored, and frustrated can lead to self-destructive behaviors. Finally, for many individuals with congenital disabilities, childhoods may have been very unusual, lived out in hospitals in the company of adults. One boy said, "I grew up in a hospital and my parents were my best friends." Several other individuals with congenital disabilities have summarized their childhoods as, "Other children played. I had therapy." In many long-term care facilities, adult caregivers changed shifts every eight hours and children had few opportunities for sustained relationships. In the past, residential schools for children who were deaf or blind (or both) were in wide use and these children enjoyed little privacy and were never alone. One houseparent of a school for deaf children stated his philosophy of childcare: "You have to break deaf kids when they're young" (Evans & Falk, 1986, p. 100). This houseparent beat the children with a large leather belt when they "misbehaved" and the misbehavior was often only a very minor infraction of school rule. Higher rates of substance abuse are associated with childhood sexual abuse and it is known that IWDs experience much higher rates of sexual abuse than the general population, and children with disabilities, especially children with IDs, experience prolonged abuse by several perpetrators.

Psychiatrists have understood the relationship between self-medication and substance abuse. Stated differently, drugs of choice are not chosen randomly. Those with schizophrenia abuse opiates in attempts to mute their rage, disorganization, and aggression. Alcohol is often used by those with anxiety issues and cocaine relieves depression, hypermania, and hypomania.

Ways in Which Substance Abuse Interacts With Disabilities

- Psychological and emotional coping responses are less complete and require more time when the IWD chooses drugs and alcohol as defense mechanisms.
- Physical, cognitive, and social rehabilitation are impaired when the IWD uses alcohol and drugs.
- Alcohol and drugs may interfere with seizure medication.
- Alcohol, cocaine, and amphetamines lower the seizure threshold of those with seizure disorders.
- Alcohol and many other drugs affect all organ systems, including vascular damage to the eyes.

- Some of the deficits of TBIs are deficits in planning, lack of verbal fluency, and motor coordination, difficulties in concentration, attention, memory, and information-processing. Alcohol and drugs exacerbate these deficits.
- Alcohol and drugs may predate the acquisition of the disability or may have contributed to causing the disability.

Practice Applications for Counselors Who Work With IWDs

- Probe and screen for alcohol and substance abuse.
- Gather collaborative information from friends and family (with written permission).
- Determine if the substance abuse predated or postdated the acquisition of the disability.
- Counselors should explore their feelings of blaming an IWD who knowingly engaged in dangerous behavior which resulted in the disability.
- The use of alcohol and drug may cause an IWD to be required to leave group apartments or other supported community living situations and return to long-term care facilities.

Considering the list of interactions of alcohol and drugs with disabilities underscores the need for addictions counselors to learn about disabilities and the various interactions of drug/alcohol and disability. With greater accessibility, both social and physical, the prevalence rates among IWD perhaps will fall. Isolation, social threats, unemployment, and lack of friends and sexual partners are factors in causing many IWDs to turn to drugs/alcohol. Emotional support and counseling, immediately following the acquisition of the disability, allowing IWDs to express their feelings, including negative feelings will also help to lower prevalence rates.

Drug and alcohol treatment often differs based on the time of onset of the substance abuse problems. Especially for spinal cord injuries and traumatic brain injuries, there is a high probability that the use of drugs or alcohol contributed to the acquisition of these disabilities. For others, the beginning of drug and alcohol problems was a response to dealing with the acquisition of disability or the diagnosis of a chronic illness. When people sit home alone, without educational pursuits or employment requirements, drug and alcohol problems are not only possible, but there will be few consequences if the substance abuse problem is discovered. Therefore, to many, including IWODs, this type of drug and alcohol abuse is a "victimless" crime or, at minimum, they are thought to be hurting only themselves.

Many addictions counselors consider pre-disability drug and alcohol abuse to be difficult to treat simply because the abuse (and the associated difficulties) has a longer history. Both spinal cord injuries and traumatic brain injuries are age-skewed, gender-skewed, and are more often related to alcohol use. Of course, the gender-skewedness is changing as more women and girls participate in dangerous activities. There is a term for this type of sensation-seeking, impulsivity, and need for risk, danger, and excitement, "thrill-seeking" as expressed in the following excerpt:

> Especially for males, the years of adolescence and emerging adulthood are a time when sensation seeking, impulsivity, and seeking out unduly dangerous recreational activities are common. After people reach adulthood, many of these behaviors cease, or individuals enter professions that have the possibility of danger, such as the military or police. The "thrills and chills" personality describes someone who is easily bored, is competitive, seeks out new and difficult adventures.
>
> (Smart, 2012, p. 342)

Goma-i-Freixanet (2004) further described the activities of thrill seekers:

> [Thrill seekers] engage in "extreme" sports that provide unusual sensations of speed or defiance of gravity, such as parachuting, scuba diving or skiing. . . . They continue seeking sensation through social activities like, parties, social drinking, and sex.
>
> (p. 187)

The use of alcohol and drugs during dangerous activities serves to decrease inhibitions and risk perception. Alcohol and drugs also cloud judgment, often increasing one's sense of infallibility and immortality. The optimistic bias that tells thrill seekers that injuries happen to other people also includes the idea of risk perception. Simply stated, as individuals enter their twenties and thirties, they become more aware of the probabilities of risk. However, one national sample of motorcyclists (Rutter et al., 1989) showed the perception of risks did predict future behavior, but *not* in the direction of precaution or adoption of safety procedures. The researchers found that the *greater* the perceived risk at one point in time, the *more frequent* the risky behavior at time two (one year later) (Goma-i-Freixanet, 2004, p. 1986).

Obviously, thrill seekers are not content to spend Saturday night studying at the library. Most individuals "outgrow" sensation seeking through a combination of social learning and brain growth, including changes in structure and changing levels of hormones and neurotransmitters. Social learning such as divorces, job losses, incarceration, and school failure, also decreases thrill seeking. Also, adults tend to think more relativistly, being able to weigh risk more accurately.

Thrill and chills seeking presents disability questions. Is everyone supposed to change their entire personality and lifestyle simply to avoid disability? Does the government have the right to mandate the use of helmets and seat belts and prosecute drunk and buzzed driving? Should the public purse (insurance premiums and tax dollars) pay for treatment costs of disabilities which resulted from dangerous behavior? Do counselors have unexamined feelings of blame for clients with disabilities whom we believe knowingly contributed to the cause of the disability?

Conclusion

This chapter discussed four issues: chronic pain, physical disfigurements, the "try harder" syndrome, and substance abuse and alcoholism. None of these is limited to IWDs and, indeed, most IWDs do not experience any of these. Nonetheless, IWDs experience these issues *more frequently* than IWODs. Moreover, when chronic pain, disfigurements, or substance abuse affects IWDs, these conditions interact with the disability.

In order to describe chronic pain, it was necessary to define its counterpart, acute pain. When interacting with individuals who are in pain, either chronic or acute, others feel existential angst, having been reminded of the very human possibility of pain. Most individuals do not be reminded of pain and often avoid those who are in pain. This social rejection is not part of the *physical* condition of pain, but it does intensify the physical experience of pain.

Individuals with disfigurements most often lived isolated, home-bound lives. Indeed, the pernicious idea that "twisted body means twisted soul" was directed toward individuals with disfigurements. However, describing the difficulties of physical disfigurements may soon be obsolete simply because disfigurements will be corrected by surgeries, including facial transplants. Throughout this book, both the *type* of medical improvements and the rapid *pace* of these advances have been considered. Physical disfigurements may soon be only of historical interest.

Substance abuse and alcoholism is more common among IWDs (than IWODs) and many of the predisposing factors of disability were discussed. Moreover, substance abuse and alcoholism exacerbates both the disability and the necessary treatments. Screening and probing for substance abuse should be part of all types of counseling and, certainly, counselors trained and skilled in addictions should be given disability training.

> **Practice Applications for Counselors Who Work With IWDs**
> - Probe and screen for alcohol and substance abuse.
> - Gather collaborative information from friends and family (with written permission).
> - Determine if the substance abuse predated or postdated the acquisition of the disability.
> - Counselors should explore their feelings of blaming an IWD who knowingly engaged in dangerous behavior which resulted in the disability.

References

Boros, A. (1990, March). Barriers to treatment. Paper presented at Breaking Down the Barriers Conference, San Mateo, CA.

Chapman, S. L., & Wu, L. T. (2012). Substance abuse among individuals with intellectual disabilities. *Research on Developmental Disabilities 32,* 1147–1156.

Close, C. (1993). Chuck close. In J. K. Smith & G. Plimpton (Eds.), *Chronicles of courage: Very special artists* (pp. 14–28). New York, NY: Penguin Random House.

Crewe, N. M. (1997). Life stories of people with long term spinal cord injury. *Rehabilitation Counseling Bulletin, 41,* 26–42.

Elder, G. H., Jr. (1997). The life course and human development. In R. M. Lerner (Ed.), *Handbook of child psychology: Volume 1: Theoretical models of human development* (pp. 939–991). New York: Wiley.

Evans, A. D., & Falk, W. W. (1986). *Learning to be deaf.* Berlin: Mouton de Gruyter.

Fries, K. (Ed.) (1997). *Staring back: The disability experience from the inside out.* New York, NY: Plume.

Goma-i-Freixanet, M. (2004). Sensation seeking and participation in physical risk sports. In R. M. Stelmack (Ed.), *On the psychology of personality* (pp. 185–201). Amsterdam: Elsevier.

Grealy, L. (1997). Pony party. In K. Fries (Ed.) (1997). *Staring back: The disability experience from the inside out* (pp. 13–21). New York, NY: Plume.

Heinemannm A. W., Donohue, R., Keen, M., & Schnoll, S. (1988). Alcohol use by persons with recent spinal cord injuries. *Alcohol Health and Research World, 13,* 110–117.

Helwig, A. A., & Holicky, R. (1994). Substance abuse in persons with disabilities: Treatment considerations. *Journal of Counseling and Development, 72,* 227–233.

Hovey, C. (2017). Retrieved from www.e-bility.com/articles/arthritis-pain-managment.php retrieved 03-12-2018

Imrie, R. (1996). *Disability and the city: International perspectives.* New York, NY: St. Martin's.

Jeffrey, J. E. (2006). Chronic pain. In I. M. Lubkin & P. D. Larsen (Eds.), *Chronic illness: Impact and interventions* (6th ed., pp. 67–104). Sudbury, MA: Jones and Bartlett.

Kubla, E. (2018, January 10). In my chronic illness, I found a deeper meaning. *New York Times.* Retrieved www.nytimes.com/2018/01/10/opinion/in-my-chronic-illness-i-found-a-deeper-meaning.html?mtrref=query.nytimes.com&assetType=opinion. Retrieved 02–24–2018

Lin, E., Balogh, R., McGarry, C. et al. (2016). Substance related and addictive disorders among adults with intellectual and developmental disabilities (IDD): An Ontario population cohort study. *BMJ Open, 6,* e011638. doi:10.1136/bmjopen-2016–011638 P. Retrieved from http://bmjopen.bmj.com/ 02–26–2018

Marks, D. (1999). *Disability: Controversial debates and psychosocial perspectives.* London: Routledge.

Mattlin, B. (2016, October 5). A disabled life is a life worth living. *New York Times.* Retrieved from www.nytimes.com/2016/10/05/ . . . /a-disabled-life-is-a-life-worth-living.html Retrieved 02–26–2018

Morris, D. B. (1998). *Illness and culture in the postmodern age.* Berkeley, CA: University of California.

Morris, J. (1991). *Pride against prejudice: Transforming attitudes towards disability.* London: The Women's Press.

O'Donnell, J. J., Cooper, J. E., Gessner, J. E. Shehan, I., & Ashley, J. (1981–1982). Alcohol, drugs and spinal cord injury. *Alcohol Health and Research World, 5,* 48–56.

Price, R. (1994). *A whole new life: An illness and a healing.* New York, NY: Atheneum.

Ragged Edge Online. (1985). *The problem with "challenge."* Retrieved from www.raggededgemagazine.com/archive/challenge.htm

Rutter, M. (1989). Intergenerational continuities and discontinuities in serious parenting difficulties. In D. Cicchetti & V. Carlson (Eds.), *Child maltreatment: Theory and research on causes and consequences of child abuse and neglect* (pp. 317–348). Cambridge, UK: Cambridge University.

Rasmussen, G., & DeBoer, R. (1980–1981). Alcohol and drug use among clients at a residential vocational rehabilitation facility. *Alcohol Health and Research World, 5,* 48–56.

Schaschl, S., & Straw, D. (1990). Results of a model intervention program for physically impaired persons. *Aid Bulletin, 11*(2), 1–8.

Smart, J. F. (2012). *Disability across the developmental lifespan.* New York: Springer.

Smart, J. F. (2016). *Disability, society, and the individual* (3rd ed.). Austin, TX: PRO-ED.

Substance abuse and mental health services administration (SAMHSA). (2016). Retrieved from www.ncbi.nlm.nih.gov/books/NBK343537/ Retrieved 02–26–2018

Thurer, S., & Rogers, E. S. (1984). The mental needs of physically disabled. *Hospital Community Psychiatry, 38,* 282–286.

To, W. T., Neirynck, S., Vadenplasschen, W., et al. (2014). Substance use and misuses in persons with intellectual disabilities (ID): Results of a survey in ID and addiction services in Flanders. *Research on Developmental Disabilities, 35,* 1–9.

Van Duijvenbode, N., VanDerNagel, J. E. L., Didden, R., et al. (2015). Substance use disorders in individuals with mild to borderline intellectual disability: Current status and future directions. *Research on Developmental Disabilities, 38,* 319–328.

VanDerNagel, J. E. L., Kiewik. M., Postel, M. G., et al. (2014). Capture recapture estimation of the prevalence of mild intellectual disability and substance use disorder. *Research on Developmental Disabilities, 35, 808–813.* Wendell, S. (1997). Toward a feminist theory of disability. In L. J. Davis (Ed.), *The disability studies reader* (pp. 260–278). New York, NY: Routledge.

Wright, B. (1960). *Physical disability: A psychological approach.* New York, NY: Harper & Row.

Eleven

NEW HORIZONS FOR THE COUNSELING PROFESSIONS

A combination of factors has resulted in the transformation of the lives of individuals with disabilities (IWDs). Each of these factors has improved the experience of disability; but, the combination has brought about a revolution. These factors include: greater medical advances, the provision of civil rights and protection under the law, and greater accuracy and realism in the portrayal of IWDs in the media. Building upon these societal advances, professional counselors and social workers will provide services to IWDs, using their expertise, knowledge, and skills. However, these professionals will be required to learn about the disability experience in order to provide ethical and effective services to IWDs.

It is hoped that this book will be a small start to a transformation in the helping professions, mirroring medical and societal advances. A single book cannot begin to encompass the entire disability experience or all of the ways in which services can be extended to IWDs. In order to bring about the necessary changes in the helping professions, training, including supervised clinical experience, accreditation guidelines, and licensing and certifying requirements, include practice guidelines for serving IWDs will expand. Such a transformation in the way in which professionals are trained, supervised, licensed, and eventually practice, will require time. Transformation and enhancement of the helping professions will require a shift in the way in which IWDs, and their service needs, are viewed.

I have seen the progress of IWDs through my own training, having received my PhD in Rehabilitation Counseling in 1988, predating the Americans with Americans with Disabilities Act. Since 1988, there have been many medicals advances and the proliferation of assistive technology. Most important, however, I have seen a transformation in the way in which IWDs are viewed, which includes the language used to describe those with disabilities.

In Chapter One, the need for the various types of helping professionals, such as counselors and social workers, to provide services to IWDs was advanced.

Counselors of all specialties and theoretical orientations will provide services to IWDs. Some of these specialties include school counseling, military counseling, career counseling, children and adolescent counseling, university counseling and advising, multicultural counseling, LBGTQ counseling, spiritual, ethical, and religious counseling, group counseling, family and marriage counseling, and many more.

Chapter One provided six reasons for the increasing number of IWDs and, perhaps, counterintuitively, we learned that these increases are considered advances, both for society and for individuals. While it is always best to avoid and prevent disabilities, when the choice is the death of the individual or the acquisition of a disability, generally, disability is preferred. It is medicine, science, and technology, which have brought about these higher numbers of disabilities and, therefore, it is incumbent upon the other helping professions to collaborate with the medical professions and contribute to the lives of IWDs. The helping professions will follow the lead of the medical professions, supporting and enhancing the quality of life of IWDs.

Most demographers either were unaware or ignored the indications that the number of IWDs would expand and grow and the helping professions, much like all of society, were not prepared or trained to serve these growing numbers of IWDs. It is now time to address these inconsistencies and deficiencies in the helping professions.

Chapter Two described and defined disability and, importantly, discussed the large, standardized diagnostic manuals which counselors and social workers can access in order to learn detail and depth about particular disabilities. Does everyone have a disability? The motive behind this question is the need to universalize or normalize disability. However, while the numbers of IWDs have increased, most people do not have disabilities. Furthermore, there is no need to universalize the experience of disability because it is the humanity of IWDs which is common to everyone. Another way in which disability can be universalized involves the consideration that everyone has the possibility of acquiring a disability or receiving a diagnosis of a chronic illness.

If the intended audience for this book is counselors, social workers, and other helping professionals, why include Chapter Two, with its clear medical orientation, in this book? Good question. Some understanding of the disability is necessary and this understanding will hopefully result in respect for the disability and the individual with the disability. Of course, it is the IWD's perception, interpretation, and understanding of their disability which is paramount, and helping professionals are skilled in forming a therapeutic alliance which includes the client's self-image. Further, many times, the disability is not an issue and certainly, the disability is not always the presenting problem.

The message of Chapter Two is somewhat contradictory. On the one hand, the clear message is to respect the individual and respect their disability and, on the other hand, the message is to view the IWD as a complete individual with the same motivations, emotions, and life tasks as everyone else. How should this contradiction be addressed? In the same way as any other issues are addressed, by allowing clients to set an agenda which meets their needs.

Chapter Two may be frustrating to some readers. These readers may want a more complete and detailed description of the various disabilities, which they will not find in Chapter Two. Chapter Two is an introductory, broad overview and introduction and there are many books available more complete information. Nonetheless, the definition of disability must be addressed and clarified before any discussion of providing services to IWDs can be initiated. Chapter Two defines disability and also defines what disability is not.

Chapter Three talks about abstractions, Models of Disability. Models of Disability are more than theories because, typically, theories are postulate only causes of phenomena. These models do ask the question of cause, "what is the etiology, source, or pathogenesis of this disability?" but they also ask and attempt to answer nine other questions. So Models of Disability are far more encompassing than theories of disability. Some authors advocate the use of a combination of models, such as the bio-psycho-social model, but this book strongly asserts that separate consideration of each model will result in better case conceptualization and more effective treatment, and, importantly, lead to collaboration with other types of professionals. Separately considering each model will facilitate viewing the client as a complete individual and assist the service provider in seeing some of the problems and the resolution of these problems to lie outside of the client.

Interactional models more completely reflect the reality of disability and interactional models, as the name suggests, consider factors in the environment, the individual' functions, and government laws and policies to interact with the IWD and their disability. Interactional models open up an entire range of case conceptualization and practice applications. Incorporating Models of Disability in practice will also lead to more professional collaboration since each model asks the question, "Who is responsible for the professional needs of IWDs?"

Chapter Four describes six ways of the evolving ways in which to view IWDs and disability, in general. Many paragraphs begin with the words, "somewhat counterintuitively" suggesting that false ideas can persist for long periods of time and make life difficult (or even impossible) for the subjects of these myths. Strong feelings often contribute to false beliefs and, for many, examining their feelings is difficult. No one enjoys learning that their beliefs are wrong and the attitudes and actions springing from these false ideas are hurtful to others. Surely, these false, hurtful myths "have stood the test of time" and, moreover, many people have subscribed to them. Time and numbers are powerful arguments. While Chapter One suggested that helping professionals will be required to *un-learn* some well-accepted beliefs, Chapter Four described some beliefs which need to be changed. Only after un-learning, can accurate, information be acquired.

The remaining seven chapters discuss practice applications for counseling IWDs and they refer only to IWDs, taking into consideration the unique issues of the disability experience.

This book defines disability and, in defining disability, it is necessary to define the concept of normality. After teaching and studying about disability and IWDs, and providing services to IWDs, I have come to the conclusion that in defining disability, we are defining humanity.

CASE STUDIES

Case Study #1

Jorge Garcia is a 42-year-old man with a "bad back." He has had two surgeries to correct this disability and can no longer return to work as a farm laborer. He is a third generation American who considers himself Hispanic and, after his two sons left home to join the military, he and wife have returned to speaking only Spanish. The intake interview was conducted in English, showing Mr. Garcia to have a fluent command of English. Mr. Garcia reports that he "has done a man's job since I was 12 years old."

Mr. Garcia wants counseling in order to explore job and work options. He has a strong work ethic. He sustained his first back injury by lifting heavy irrigation pipe on the farm and, after recovering from his first surgery, he returned to farm work against medical advice. Following his re-injury and second surgery, Mr. Garcia understands that he cannot return to heavy physical labor. He has worked for the same farmer for 25 years, living in a house on the farm, and driving a farm truck. Mr. Garcia reports that he and his employer did not have any disagreements throughout his long span of employment. Mr. Garcia says that he enjoys working outdoors, year-round, in all kinds of weather. He says working in an office "would kill me." He says that he has lost more than his job stating, "I have lost my life, my home, and my wife." He and his wife have moved into town, a part of town that is predominantly Spanish-speaking.

When asked if he experiences pain, Mr. Garcia said, "Only when I'm changing the sheets on the bed." Since his wife has returned to work, Mr. Garcia has undertaken many of the household tasks. His wife is a cook at a residential facility for elderly people and Mr. Garcia drives her to work at 4:00 a.m. and returns at noon to take her home. Mr. Garcia is expecting his wife to leave her job when he finds employment. Mrs. Garcia loves her job and does not want to quit. The residents at this care center are mostly Spanish-speaking, as are the workers. The residents prefer to eat Mexican food and Mrs. Garcia enjoys cooking this type of food and, even more important, she likes interacting with both staff and residents. Because Mrs. Garcia has been a homemaker her entire marriage (until Mr. Garcia acquired his disability), this is her first employment outside the home. However, Mrs. Garcia does not have, and never has had, a driver's license and there is no public transportation available at 4:00 a.m. Due to the fact that the Garcias need her wages, Mr. Garcia has reluctantly agreed to allow his wife to work. Therefore, the question becomes, does Mrs. Garcia continue to work and how would she get to work if her husband could not provide transportation?

Mr. Garcia has a long work history, but not a varied one, and he never graduated from high school. It seems as if he cannot read either English or Spanish, which is a great embarrassment to him. His stated goal for seeking counseling is "Just get me a job. I want to work."

Also of note: Mr. Garcia's eyes appear watery and red and he blinks frequently. Therefore, a complete examination is recommended. Prolonged exposure to farm pesticides may have damaged his eyes.

Case Study #2

Louisa is a 23-year-old woman who has been diagnosed with a moderate intellectual disability. Her first statement is "I want to die." Louisa presents as fairly high functioning and is extremely attractive. She cried throughout the first session, making it difficult to understand her speech at times. She is a graduate of a high school special education program and is having difficulty in transitioning from children's services (public schools) to adult services. Her parents and siblings appear to be highly protective of Louisa, fearing that "boys would do terrible things to me." Louisa wants to date boys, but her parents are adamant, "That's not going to happen."

Another statement made three or four times throughout the first session is "I have tried so hard." Her failure to learn to drive has been particularly defeating. Her older brother has taken her out driving and has accompanied her to take the written test. She failed the written exam three times, which were major disappointments. Her large family of siblings, all older than she, have had jobs, dated, and gone to college. Her oldest sister and her husband recently had their first baby. Louisa very much wants to care for her newborn niece but is not allowed to be left alone with the baby. In Louisa's opinion, the achievements of her siblings have magnified her failures.

There is some tension between professional providers at the Center for Independent Living and her parents. Louisa attends day activities at this center, which she finds very enjoyable. However, the professionals at the Independent Living Center are encouraging Louisa to move out of the family home and move into a support group apartment, stating that leaving the parental home is an age-appropriate task. In this type of an apartment, support workers would help Louisa with finances, shopping, and household maintenance. Louisa's parents are very much against this plan and have argued with the people at the center, feeling that these professionals have overestimated their daughter's level of functioning, thinking that Louisa functions at a much higher level than she actually does. The professionals told Louisa's parents that they were overprotective and limiting Louisa's progress. Louisa was very disappointed with her parents' decision. Further, Louisa's parents have refused to allow her to attend the Independent Living Center. Her parents have expressed some hesitation about allowing Louisa to come to your counseling office.

Louisa has attempted some preliminary vocational exploration with the Office of Vocational Rehabilitation, but this has not been successful because Louisa insists that she wants to become a doctor. In the intake session today, when asked why she wanted to become a doctor, Louisa said that no one had ever asked this question. Teachers and counselors had simply (repeatedly) told her how impossible it would be. Gently probing in today's counseling intake session, Louisa gave her reason as "I want to wear a white coat." The intake counselor told Louisa that there many jobs in which she could wear a white coat and for which she would be competent. For the first time in the session, Louisa stopped crying.

Louisa's parents came into the intake session during the final ten minutes while Louisa waited in the outer office. Her parents stated that they are beginning to think about Louisa's living, care, and financial arrangements following their deaths. Louisa is the youngest in a family of six children and none of the siblings have a stated a willingness to care for Louisa. A more immediate problem is the fact that Louisa must be driven everywhere and, in the past, most of this transportation was provided by older siblings. Now that these siblings have left home for marriage or to attend university, more of these responsibilities have fallen on the parents. The parents refuse to allow Louisa to take the bus. To Louisa's parents, the solution is simple. Louisa should stay home most of the time, stating that they were very concerned about her safety.

Case Study #3

Matt and Elizabeth state their purpose in seeking counseling is "stress reduction" and to gain some understandings and appropriate responses to extended family members. They reported, "We're not sad; we're exhausted." The couple reported that despite the difficulties of having a child with multiple disabilities, they have learned to manage the many, unceasing demands. Matt and Elizabeth feel that their greatest problem is the response of others to their baby Heather, especially extended families.

Matt and Elizabeth married as teenagers and they had a baby less than two years later. Before the birth of the baby, Elizabeth worked at a fairly high-paying job and Matt attended university and worked at a part-time job. They lived in a one-bedroom apartment on campus in a small university town. While the pregnancy was not planned, both felt that "we were on the right track." Advised by both families to not marry at such a young age, Matt and Elizabeth felt that they made the correct decision. They considered themselves to be "very happy and we're making it." Family members had agreed to help with childcare so that Elizabeth could return to work following the birth of their baby.

The baby was born three months early and was immediately life-flighted to a neonatal care unit at a large children's hospital. Doctors could not diagnose Heather's disability with any precision, referring to it only as a type of neuro-cognitive muscular disability. None of the physicians had treated a newborn (or child) with such extensive disabilities. Heather has never spoken, moved on her own, or breathed. She has always been fed through a tube in her stomach, used a respirator, and is not toilet trained. In addition, she is blind and has a severe intellectual ability. The physicians warned Matt and Elizabeth that Heather would probably die a few days after her birth. Heather stayed in the neonatal unit for more than five months while Matt returned to his university studies. Elizabeth stated that the most difficult part of the baby's hospitalization was being separated from Matt.

When Heather reached the weight of five pounds and Elizabeth and Matt had mastered all the procedures for caring for her, the family returned to the one-bedroom apartment. Heather breathed with a ventilator, equipped with an alarm system to warn if the ventilator stopped working. The sound of the alarm signaled that Heather's life was in immediate danger. A nurse, who was funded by the state, arrived at the apartment at 10:00 every night and left at 6:00 in the morning, allowing the parents to sleep. A few of these nurses did not learn the correct functioning of the ventilator and, therefore, the alarm occasionally sounded, awaking everyone. Nonetheless, the couple reported that the night nurses "saved our lives, our sanity, and our marriage." Matt and Elizabeth formed very close relationships with these nurses, partly because they understood that these nurses loved their baby.

One set of grandparents expressed willingness to babysit Heather, which necessitated learning many complicated medical procedures. The other grandparents refused to help saying, "Heather could die while we're babysitting her and WE DON'T WANT THAT!" Matt and Elizabeth responded that Heather could die while she was with them. These grandparents also implied that Matt and Elizabeth were responsible for solving their own problems since they had advised against the early marriage.

Elizabeth quit her job and Matt reduced his load of coursework at the university in order to work full-time. Church members and fellow students helped with food preparation, housework, laundry, and running errands. The most helpful assistance was the loving acceptance of Heather and emotional support for the parents.

Physicians did not expect Heather to live for very long and were astounded that she survived up to this point. Heather was now 5 years old and she had two younger brothers.

Still without a definitive diagnosis, Matt and Elizabeth feel grateful for Heather. However, they wonder how long Heather will live.

Case Study # 4

Dennis Pepperhoff brought paper and pencil to the intake interview, stating that he has a poor memory since he acquired his traumatic brain injury (TBI). He was injured three years ago in a car accident when he was 42 years old and could not return to his work as a doctor and surgeon. When asked why he wants counseling he replied, "Two reasons: the antidepressants didn't work and I'm really angry at God." Dennis reported that he tried counseling on two previous occasions, but counseling was not helpful. Notes from a previous counselor stated, "Dr. Pepperhoff gains new insights in one counseling session and then forgets them at the next session." This counselor also wrote, "I may have been too sympathetic with this client. I could not find the appropriate level of support to help him. I think I was stressed when Dr. Pepperhoff seemed to regress, especially after particularly successful sessions." Notes from another counselor state, "His lack of cognitive abilities, especially abstract thinking, presents difficulties for counseling."

Presenting as a reserved and emotionally controlled individual, Dennis began crying at the end of the session. The initial impression of this client is his overriding deficit identity. Dr. Pepperhoff spent considerable time relating his many educational and professional achievements, including his high salary. Expecting 20 more years of working and earning a high salary, he is very discouraged about his financial losses and lack of professional status. Neurologists told him that after one year post-injury that there would be little further recovery. Most of the weakness and paralysis has been alleviated, but Dr. Pepperhoff states that, for the first time in his life, he is very clumsy and uncoordinated. Laughingly, he stated, "That's not very good for a surgeon."

His wife has had to find a job, which makes Dr. Pepperhoff angry with himself and with her. He deeply loves his wife and understands that she is only trying to help, but he thinks she is too bossy and completely commandeers the family and the household. His teenage children often pointed out his mistakes, memory lapses, and faulty reasoning. Dr. Pepperhoff is shocked to be reminded of his disability by his children. He seems to stay at home accomplishing little; however, he began to weep when he stated, "I'm a failure as a husband and a father."

Dr. Pepperhoff stated that he has lost many of his physical skills, stating that he can no longer ride a horse. He was raised on a cattle ranch and reported that he learned to ride a horse at the age of three. After graduation from medical school and completing his surgical residency, he purchased horses for recreational riding. The loss of his main recreational activity (and part of his identity) is devastating. He does not understand how he could possibility forget to ride a horse. Pre-disability, he enjoyed camping and outdoor life. Now Dr. Pepperhoff reports, "I can't even put up a tent."

His memory loss is extensive and pervasive, stating "Losing my keys is a crisis and it panics me" and "When I get in the car, I can't remember where I was going, which probably doesn't matter because I wouldn't remember how to get there." He is overwhelmed by the paperwork to apply for disability benefits and admits some embarrassment in asking for government assistance. He stated, "I never thought I would be so reduced." He traveled to a large city to see a neuropsychologist once a week for a period of more than a year and summarized, "That was a total waste." Dr. Pepperhoff sought out the services of naturopathic physicians, but felt that these, too, were ineffective.

Dr. Pepperhoff loves his wife and children, but he is afraid they will leave him. He also loves his church and, on several occasions, has sought spiritual counseling, but this did seem to help. Extended family members, friends, former colleagues, and his wife tell him that he is easily frustrated, often becoming angry. Most of the time, he stays at home, feeling depressed and helpless.

Case Study #5

Christine is a 23-year-old graduate student and is blind, having had retinitis pigmentosa. She was articulate, attractive, and well dressed. Also, she interacted appropriately and pleasantly throughout this intake interview. She is actively gay and has a large circle of friends and colleagues. At this point in her life, she states that she is ready for a long-term romantic relationship but fears that no one would want a blind partner. She is estranged from her birth family since they belong to a very conservative church and do not approve of her sexual orientation. Her parents interpreted her choices as ingratitude for their sacrifices and support during her childhood and adolescence. Christine was sent to an expensive residential school for a few years which allowed her, while she had some remaining vision, to learn Braille, orientation and mobility (O&M), and other life skills. Her mother was required to find employment in order to pay the tuition to this school for blind teenagers.

Christine reported that she considers her type of blindness to have many advantages, stating that since she knew at a young age that she would become blind she had time to prepare emotionally. She has worked at a telephone call center and considers herself to be socially skilled and to be self-disciplined, organized, and planful. Her graduate studies in English literature, she believes, will eventually result in a teaching job. Christine spends a great deal of time in this session speaking about her love of literature.

She reported that following her parents' refusal to accept her as a gay person, she used street drugs for a short period of time. By her own account, during this period of drug use, "my life was out of control." She felt "ping-ponged" between professional service providers. Drug rehabilitation agencies would refer her to disability services while disability services told her that she should seek services from drug rehabilitation agencies. After some time, she did receive services from a public drug rehabilitation hospital. Christine is now clean and sober, stating laughingly, that inpatient drug treatment was easy for her because she had attended a residential school for years!

She is confident and pleased about her progress and eventual success in her chosen career path, and she is financially self-sufficient with three sources of income: her work as a college teaching assistant, a scholarship, and disability benefits. She is happy with her circle of friends and has had some satisfying short-term sexual relationships. Feeling enormously empowered by leaving her parents' conservative church, she considers herself a feminist. Christine feels that her life is fulfilling but with only one lack, albeit a very important lack. Christine stated that she wants a long-term partner, but wonders if this is possible because she is blind, stating that it is not the blindness itself, but the false perceptions others have of blindness.

Christine stated that she is proud of her independence and financial, professional, and academic success. She says that she does not want to be an object of pity or to have her partner considered some sort of saint for choosing a blind partner. Christine admitted that she had "played the blind card to get what I wanted and I knew at the time it was wrong." When asked what she meant by this, Christine said that she emphasized her blindness in order to receive several scholarships, explaining "the interviewing panels always felt sorry for the poor blind girl."

Christine has insight into her past behavior, both the results and her motivations. She also stated that leaving her parental home and long-time church had "freed me and now I don't care what anybody thinks of me—as a disabled person or as a gay woman or as both. I can deal with all that." She felt that she delayed coming out to her parents because "I thought, wrongly, that I owed them for taking care of me and my disability. I am SO amazed at how freeing it is to be away from my family."

Case Study #6

John Swensen appeared for this intake interview as an attractive and well-groomed 28-year-old. He is a veteran of the Iraq wars. He has double lower limb amputations and uses prostheses. He has recently been discharged from a veterans affairs hospital after a suicide attempt. John tried to shoot himself, but survived when his roommate found him. When asked about this suicide attempt, John became angry and stated that two men, who he thought were his friends, saved his life on two different occasions. One was a fellow Marine who saved him in Iraq and the other was his roommate. John reports that he is angry at both of these men, saying "they should have left me to die. Both of them are a—."

Asked why he was interesting in counseling, John stated, "My best friends are my dogs and I can't seem to figure out what to do next" and "I've been in and out of the VA hospital so many times that I've lost count," and "I can't seem to do anything and when I do do something, I do it wrong, including trying to kill myself." He has been married twice and divorced twice, admitting that at times he had been emotionally abusive. Today, he presented as extremely angry and agitated. At times, he appeared to be threatening. John repeated the phrase, "What's the point?" several times throughout this session.

He reported that the happiest he had been since coming home from Iraq was the time spent at the large rehabilitation center in Denver where he finished recovering and learned to use his prostheses and other life skills. When asked why he thought he had been happy at this time, John had difficulty answering and after a long pause, said, "I guess because I saw so many other people more f—ed up than me."

John lacked motivation and did not show any orientation toward the future. A considerable length of time was spent on discussing the meaninglessness and stupidity of the war. He stated that he feels estranged from his family. His father and brother flew out from the East Coast to visit him when he was in the hospital after the suicide attempt, but less than 24 hours later they returned home. John referred to his father and brother in profane terms. He also stated that his former wives "hate my guts and they're probably right." He does say that his dogs love him, "probably because they're dumb dogs."

John has had counseling on several occasions and did not consider these various types of counseling to have been helpful. He reported that one counselor advised him "to get a hobby." Another counselor told him he might have obsessive-compulsive disorder and one of the results of his perfectionistic tendencies is his inability to begin career exploration. When I asked him if he thought he were OCD, John only smiled and laughed.

When asked if he was dating or involved in a romantic relationship, John appeared uncomfortable, answering after a considerable pause, "No, what woman would want me—the legless wonder? Two women divorced me when I had legs!" When asked if he had any sort of educational or career plans, he said "Not a clue." When asked if he contemplated another suicide attempt, he did not answer.

John presented as experiencing feelings of hopelessness and helplessness.

Case Study #7

Jerry Smith was court ordered to attend counseling due to an arrest for shoplifting, his first arrest. Jerry is 20 years old, well-groomed, and presents as highly intelligent. He had a flat affect and spoke in a low monotone. Immediately upon graduation from high school, he enlisted in the Army. He found the military to be stressful and "intellectually boring." During basic training, Jerry reported hearing voices telling him he was Jesus Christ. Occasionally, the voices told him that he was a dog. These hallucinations were very real, frightening, and crippling. The Army hospitalized him and the military psychiatrist diagnosed him as having schizophrenia. Eventually, he was discharged from the Army. Throughout this intake interview, he kept stating, "I need to repent. If I don't, I will go to hell." When asked if he continued to take his medications, the reply was a big smile with "Hell, no!"

During the history-taking intake interview, Jerry reported that he had been in "gifted and talented" courses throughout elementary and junior high school. In high school, he had completed several "concurrent enrollment" courses, which granted him university credits. Jerry stated that he spoke French, German, and Spanish, having taken these courses in school. He was proud of his intelligence and linguistic abilities. In the Army, he replied to his drill sergeants in French which served to make the drill sergeants angry.

Jerry stated that he was a "loner" and "I have no idea what a friend is." According to school records, Jerry had refused counseling from school counselors in spite of the fact that teachers had referred him because he appeared to be somewhat depressed, eccentric, and disengaged from others. Today, when asked if he had had a favorite teacher or class, he appeared surprised at these questions. After some pause, he answered, "No." Jerry had attempted to work part-time jobs while in high school, but he was quickly terminated from all of them. When asked about his family, he appeared noncommittal, stating that "they're all right." Further probing revealed that he did not feel affection nor antipathy toward his parents, although he stated that he understood that they were greatly concerned about him. Jerry reported that he did not have any type of relationship with extended family members.

The only positive Jerry discussed was his relationship with the Army psychiatrist. Jerry reported that, for the first time in his life, he was allowed to talk at length about being Jesus Christ and the great responsibility he felt. The psychiatrist encouraged examination of Jerry's hallucinations and did not seem to be surprised or shocked. Nor did the psychiatrist try to convince Jerry that these hallucinations and beliefs were not real. Also, in the hospital, he was medicated with antipsychotic medication, and within a few weeks his psychotic symptoms remitted. Jerry felt safe in the hospital and understood by the psychiatrist. Other than his hospitalization, Jerry thought the Army was a "bunch of shitheads" who demand "crazy-ass shit." He regarded his fellow recruits as "idiot loser redneck hillbillies."

Jerry felt extremely guilty about going to hell. In contrast, when asked about his shoplifting, arrest, and court appearance and asked if he felt any remorse or guilt, he shrugged his shoulders and replied, "Not really." Throughout this session, Jerry kept asking the intake counselor, "How can Jesus Christ go to hell?"

Jerry's parents were asked to speak with the intake counselor without Jerry. The background history they gave paralleled the history Jerry gave. His parents worried about Jerry's "weirdness" and lack of friends, but expressed pride in his intelligence and academic achievements. His parents had encouraged Jerry to join the Army, thinking that the discipline and structure would be helpful. They also thought that living with other young men would lead to Jerry's social acceptance and friendships. The parents are very disappointed and somewhat ashamed of Jerry's failure to complete basic training. Jerry's older brother, whom they described as "more normal," attended an out-of-state university and lived in the dorm on campus. At Christmas, this brother came home, relating how well his college studies were going. In June, the parents discovered that, although he had registered for coursework, he failed all the courses, both fall and spring semesters, because he stayed in his dorm room playing video games and never attended class. The following year, this older son lived at home and attended community college and received passing grades.

When asked what they would like to see happen, the parents responded, "Make him take his meds so he won't have to go to jail." The mother appeared to be unaware of the serious nature of Jerry's hallucinations.

As the parents were leaving, the father stated casually, "You know, when I was a kid, I was diagnosed with schizophrenia."

INDEX

Note: *Italic* page references indicate boxed text.

abbreviations in discussing disabilities 3
abnormality, defining 90
abortion of fetuses with known disabilities 12, 88
abuse of IWDs, screening for *258–259*, 259–263, *261*
academic accreditation 28
acceptance of disability, theories of 297, *297*; *see also* cognitive restructuring; stage theory
acceptance needs 268
Access-Ride system 119
accommodations for disabilities 11, 25, 28, 97, 101, 171–174, *171*
achondroplasia 243
acquired disabilities 43–46, *43, 44*
acquisition of disability: as developmental task 325–329, *328*; marriage and 364–375, *364, 374*
activism, disability *263*, 264–267
actual number of disabilities 18
acute care 26–27
acute onsets 42–43, *42*
acute pain 380
adaptive behaviors *263*, 264–267
addiction *see* substance abuse
adolescence and disability *44*, 45
advances in medicine 13–14, 112
advocacy, disability 117, *263*, 264–267
affective intentionality 323–324, *323*
affiliation needs 268
age and substance abuse 394
aging of IWDs 17, 21
alcohol abuse *see* substance abuse
Almazan, E. P. 353
ambiguity and disability 43, 47–48, 59, 61, 136, 200, 257, 293, 336, 393

Amendments to the Americans with Disabilities Act (ADAAA) 10, 21, 25–26, 101, 267
American Counseling Association (ACA) 168, 185, 210
American Medical Association 19
American Psychiatric Association (APA) 1, 19, 66, 68
Americans with Disabilities Act (ADA): accommodations for IWDs and 97, 202; amendments to 10, 21, 25–26, 101, 267; as civil rights law 18; definition of disability in 10, 18; disclosure of disability and 202; enforcing 118; generational effect of 25–26; increases in number of IWDs and 21–26; justice concept and 23–24; lives of IWDs and, changing 267; media's changing view of disabilities and 245; perception of IWODs about 23; person-first language in 3–4; protections under 10–11, 21, 23; resistance to 22–23, *22*; surveys on 101; Title IV of 112; titles in 21, 112; violations, examples of 171–172
American Sign Language 58–59; *see also* Sign Language
amputations 27, 95, 131, 387, 413–414
amyotrophic lateral sclerosis (ASL) 47, 292, 302
anger about disability 310–312, 368
anger management 371
Appel, Tosca 345
apraxia 236
Asch, A. 247
Ashley, J. 392
Asperger's syndrome 69
assisted suicide 88, 244

assistive or adaptive technology (AT) 50–51, 53, 93–96, 99, 112, *216*, 217–223, *221*
Attention Deficit Disorder and Hyperactivity Disorder (ADDHD) 109, 389
autism, infantile 65
Autism Spectrum Disorder (ASD) 19, 46, 61, 65, 71–72, 255, 337, 359–360
autoimmune diseases 346
automatic assisted suicide 88

Bach-y-Rita, Paul 96
Baltes, P. B. 325
Bandura, Albert 322–323, 352
Barnes, C. 243–244
Batshaw, M. L. 309
behavioral intentionality 323–324, *323*
Beisser, Arnold 303–304
Bettelheim, Bruno 65
Bickenbach, J. E. 86, 91
Binet Intelligence Test 108
Biomedical Model of Disability: bioethical questions raised by 342; counseling services and 284–285, *285*; counselors and 285–286, *285*; critics of 88; defining disability in *82*, 91–92, 191, 242; description of 82–90, *82*; disability-awareness training and 31; disability as deviance and 117–118; focus on 78; Gawande and 84–85, 89; helping concept in 179; individual's response to disability practice guidelines and 284–285, *285*; intra-psychic approach and 164; Moral/Religious Model and, supplanting of 83; as non-interactional model 91; physician as authority in 87, 92, 166, 276; self-esteem of IWDs and 230; training in counseling and, outmoded *28*, 31
bio-social-environmental model 2
birth weight and disability rate 13
blame for disability 295–296, 382
blindness 58, 95–96, 133, 180, 243, 389–390, 411–413
Blind Rage (Kleege) 358–359
Boros, A. 392
BrainPort 96
British National Health Service (NHS) 273, 316
Bronfenbrenner, Urie 107–109
bureaucracy, burden of *204–205*, 205–208
Burgdorf, Robert 22
burnout of caregivers 369
Buys, N. 321

Canadian Bill of Human Rights 91
caregivers 252–258, *252*, 369–370
case management 87, 278–279
case studies: Christine (blindness) 411–413; Garcia, Jorge (physical disability) 406–407; Louisa (intellectual disability) 407–408; Matt and Elizabeth (stress of child with disability) 408–410; overview 4; Pepperhoff, Dennis (traumatic brain injury) 410–411; purpose of 4; Smith, Jerry (schizophrenia) 414–416; Swenson, John (amputation) 413–414
categorical measurement of disability 70–71
categories of disabilities 5–6, *5*, 38–39, *38*; *see also* cognitive disabilities; physical disabilities; psychiatric disabilities
Cate, I. M. P. 146
cause of disability, need for 63–65, *63*
cerebral palsy 233, 261
certification, professional 28
challenges versus disability 37
charity 81–82, 140
chemical abuse *see* substance abuse
Christmas Carol (Dickens) 242
chronic conditions and illness 6, 27, 367
chronic pain 379–383, *380*
Churchill, Winston 193
Civil Rights Law (1964) 22, 117
civil rights law for IWDs 3–4, 9–10, *10*, 22–23, *22*, 81, 117–118; *see also specific law*
Civil Rights Model of Disability 77, 91–92, *115–116*, 116–121, 226
Cleland, Max 267
client change 159
clients with disabilities (CWDs): accommodations in counseling office and 171–174, *171*; ambiguous 167, *174*, 175; biases and misconceptions of counselors and 175–177, *175*; characteristics of 163–164, *163*; considerations in counseling 167, 168–169; counselors' past commitment to, lack of 280; counselors' understanding of disability and 180–182, *180*; counselors and, view of 159, 170–171, *170*; disidentification and 176; environment and, limiting 187–189, *187*; history-taking with 187–189, *187*; over-identification with 176–177; paradoxes in counseling 163–164, *164–165*; pathologizing disability and, avoiding 189, 190–193, *191*, *193–194*; pre-disability period, avoid idealizing 194–195, *194*;

rapport building with 182–183, *182*, 217; relationship with counselors and 126–127; respecting *177–178*, 178–182, *180*; self-identities of 174–175, *174*, 231–234, *232*, *234*; sexuality and self-identity of 231–234, *232*, *234*; sympathy versus empathy for 208–210, *208–209*; "testing" behavior of 183; understanding 2, *180*; *see also* individuals with disabilities (IWDs)
clients without disabilities (CWODs) 163
Close, Chuck 290, 304, 390
Code of Ethics (ACA) 168, 210
cognitive disabilities 5–6, *5*, 39; *see also specific type*
cognitive intentionality 323–324, *323*
cognitive restructuring 284, 297–303, *297–298*, *299*
Cohen, Richard 48, 203–204, 284, 300–301, 305–306
communication violence 263
compassion fatigue of caregivers 369
conceptualizing disability 123; *see also* Models of Disability
congenital disabilities 13, 43–44, *43*, 55, 334–342, *334*, 375
containment of disability effects 300–301
continuum or spectrum diagnoses/measuring 60–63, *60*, 71
contributing to others by IWDs, importance of 224–226, *224*
Cooper Hewitt Design Museum 99
Cooper, J. E. 392
core beliefs about disability, counselors': aspects of counseling and, important 126–127, *126*; disability as deviance or diversity 147–150; individual is not the disability 128–131, *128*; IWDs don't long to be "normal" or "cured" *128*, 131–135, *131*; IWODs are responsible for their own discomfort *128*, 135–139, *135*; "little acts of degradation" toward IWDs *128*, 143–146, *143*; overview 2, *128*, 159–160, 404–405; past 126; well-intentioned, nice people can cause discrimination and prejudice *128*, 139–143, *139*
Corey, G. 126
cosmetic surgery 214–215, 387
cost-benefit analysis of disclosing invisible disability *199–200*, 200–204, *201–202*
counseling services: aspects of, important 126–127, *126*; Biomedical Model and 284–285, *285*; factors influencing profession of 28; limitation of training and education in 28–32, *28–29*; Models of Disability and 123, *123*; new reality for counselors and new demand for 5–9; overview 402–403; paradoxes in providing 163–164, *164–165*; in past 6; providing to IWDs 27–28; *see also* counselors; practice guidelines
counselor change 159
counselors: aspects of counseling and, important 126–127, *126*; biases and misconceptions of, questioning own 175–177, *175*; Biomedical Model and 285–286, *285*; change in 159; client change and 159; client's disability and, understanding 180–182, *180*; considerations in counseling CWDs and *167*, 168–169; couples with disabilities and 373–375, *374*; CWDs' view of 159, 170–171, *170*; duty to report abuse and 263; ethics of 28, 127; language and 159–160; new horizons for 402–405; past commitment to CWDs and, lack of 280; rapport with CWDs and 182–183, *182*; relationship with client and 126–127; skills of, upgrading 159, 375; theoretical orientations and techniques for 333, *333–334*, 375; tips for 185–186, *186*, 211, 374, 397; *see also* core beliefs about disability, counselors'; new reality for counselors; practice guidelines; *specific issue*
Countee, Mick 356–357
counting and reporting disability, more accurate 17–18
couples with disabilities, counseling 373–375, *374*
course of disability 47–49, *47*
Covington, George 58, 363
Crawford, D. 232–233
Crenshaw, Kimberle Williams 246
crises 340
cross-disability perspective 32, 158, 226, 266
curing disability, IWODs belief about *128*, 131–135, *135*

dating for IWDs 360–364, *360–361*
Deaf culture 111–112, 157, 263
Deaf joke 174
deafness 43–44, 58–59, 130, 216, 347–348
Deegan, Patricia E. 306, 312–313
deficit breeds growth belief 325

deficit and disability 39–40, *39*, 87–88
defining disability: in Americans with Disabilities Act 10, 18; in Biomedical Model *82*, 91–92, 191, 242; categories of disability in 5–6, *5*, 38–39, *38*; cause of disability and, need for 63–65, *63*; characteristics of disabilities and, overview 41–42, *74, 74*; complexity of 36, 74; elasticity and 121–123; in Environmental Model *106*; in Functional Model *93*; as inability to work 106; individual's meaning of their disability and 37; in Interactional Models 91–92; liberalization of 19; loss or deficit and 39–40, *39*; in Moral/Religious Model *77*; multifaceted experience of IWDs and 37–38; overabundance or excess of functions and 39; overview 1–2, 73, 403–404; points in considering 37; in Social Model *112*; for Social Security Disability Insurance 18; substance abuse and 19
degenerating disabilities 47, *47*, 88
degenerating and episodic disabilities 47–48, *47*
degradation of IWDs, little acts of *128*, 143–146, *143*
deinstitutionalization movement 16–17, 24–25, 253–254
Deland, Mike 193
demeaning images of IWDS in general culture 241–245, *241*
denial of disability 211–216, *211, 212, 213, 215*, 278, 305–309
depression 52, 309–310
Design Meets Disability (Pullin) 94
developmental delay 309
developmental disabilities 19, 389
developmental stage of individual at time of onset 44–46, *44*
developmental task, acquisition of disability as 284, 325–329, *328*
developmental theorists 45, 269, 328; *see also specific name*
deviance, disability as 117–118, 147–150, 248
deviant or atypical behavior 110
diabetes 19, 27, 63, 248
diagnosing disabilities: ambiguity and 59; on continuum or spectrum 60–63, *60*, 71; course of disability 47–49, *47*; diagnostic inflation and 72–73, *72*; diagnostic masking and *40*, 41; "diagnostic odysseys" and 344–345; diagnostic overshadowing and 41; DSM-5 and *72, 73*; functions impaired and 49–51, *49*; language in communicating 67; medications and 52; overview 1–2, 73; physical 40; pre-diagnosis period and, long 43, 342–349, *343*, 375; psychiatric 40–41, 59; self-identity of IWD and 38; severity of disability and *51*, 52; standardized systems of 52, 66–69, *66*, 73; threshold and, raising 61; time of onset and 43–46, *43, 44, 46*; type of onset and 42–43, *42*; visibility of disability and 52–53, 53–54
diagnostic inflation 72–73, *72*
diagnostic masking *40*, 41
"diagnostic odysseys" 344–345
diagnostic overshadowing 41
Diagnostic and Statistical Manual of Mental Disorders (DSM) 83, 92, 121
Diagnostic and Statistical Manual of Mental Disorders-5 (DSM-5) 1, 18–19, 36, 46, 52, 66–69, 72, 152
diagnostic terms, medical 152
Dickens, Charles 80, 154, 242
Dickson, Jim 356–357
dimensional measurement of disability 70–71
disability activism *263*, 264–267
disability advocacy 117, *263*, 264–267
disability-awareness training 30–32
disability blindness 179–180
Disability History Project (NPR) 81, 137, 291
disability knowledge, incorporating into society 147–150, *147*
disability language *see* language, disability
Disability Rag 29, 231
disability rights movement 24–25, 81
disability role *112*, 114, 134, 211–216, *211, 212, 213*; *see also* Social Model of Disability; social role demands of IWDs practice guidelines
Disability Through the Lifecourse 65, 277
disability transcendence *see* transcendence, disability
Disabled Americans Act *see* Americans with Disabilities Act (ADA)
Disabled, Female, and Proud! (Rousso) 354
"disabled heroes" 352–360, *352*
"Disabled Life Is a Life Worth Living, A" 99
disabled role *see* disability role
disclosure of invisible disability *199–200*, 200–204

discomfort of IWODs, responsibility for *128*, 135–139, *135*
discrimination against IWDs 8, 10–12, 23–24, 26, 81, 113, 132, 240, 248
disenfranchised groups other than IWDs 245–246, 246–251, *247*
disfiguring disabilities *44*, 45, 318–319, 383–388, *384*
disidentification 176
dissonance 204
diversity, disability as 147–150, 248
Donohue, R. 392
Down syndrome (DS) 16–17, 56, 207–208, 214–215
drug abuse *see* substance abuse
duty to report abuse or neglect 263
duty to warn of abuse or neglect *258*, 259
dwarfism 243
dyslexia 109

Economic Model of Disability *77*, 100–106, *100*
EEG measures 265
elderly and disabilities 15–16, 44–46, *46*, 57
Elephant Man, The (film) 318–319
Elliott, T. R. 253
emergency medicine advances 14, 218
emergency services 21, 26–27, 49, 112, 122, *261*, 263
Emerman, Anne 140
emotional disequillibrium 293
emotional shock of disability 304–305
empathy versus sympathy 208–210, *208–209*
employment and disability 101, 105–106, 188
Encyclopedia of Counseling (ACA) 185
environmental effect on disability 187–189, *187*, 284; *see also* Environmental Model of Disability; *specific type*
Environmental Model of Disability *77*, 92, *106–107*, 107–112, 219
epidemics, polio 84–85
epigenetic developmental theories 328
epigenetic growth and disability 328–329
episodic disabilities 47, *47*, 88, 373
Erikson, Erik 269, 326, 340
esteem needs 268
"eternal children" concept 235–236
ethical practice guidelines: avoid confusing normalcy with ideal 184–186, *184*, *186*; avoid idealizing pre-disability period of CWD's life 194–195, *194*; avoid pathologizing disability *189*, 190–193, *191*, *193–194*; basis for 195–196; caveat about 167; considerations in counseling CWDs and *167*, 168–169; establish rapport with CWDs 182–183, *182*; overview 3, 163, 167, *170*; professional collaboration and, need for wider 196; provide accommodations in counseling office 171–174, *171*; question if environment is limiting CWDs' achievement 187–189, *187*; recognize that CWDs view counselors as IWODs 170–171, *170*; recognize that working with CWDS requires questioning own biases and misconceptions 175–177, *175*; resist urge to simplify CWDs identity or to categorize with disabilities 174–175, *174*; respect client and respect disability *177–178*, 178–182, *180*
ethics of counselors 28, 127
ethnic minorities and disabilities 246–247, 249–251
euphemisms 154–155, 157
Evans, Pam 132
existential angst of disability 136–138, 176, *384*
expectations for IWDs, lowered 141–142
"Expect Delays" (podcast) 118–120
experience of disability practice guidelines: avoid confusing denial of disability role with deniability of disability 211–216, *211*, *212*, *213*, *215*; avoid confusing sympathy with empathy 208–210, *208–209*; encourage mutual support 226–231, *226*, *227*; overview 3, 199, 236–237; recognize burden of bureaucracy *204–205*, 205–208; recognize cost-benefit analysis of disclosing invisible disability *199–200*, 200–204, *201–202*; recognize infantilization experienced by PWDs 235–236; recognize sexuality as important aspect of client's self-identity and self-esteem 231–234, *232*, *234*; respect assistive technology of client *216*, 217–223, *221*; understand importance of contributing to others 224–226, *224*

facial scars 385
Fairchild, Edwina 389–390
Far From the Tree (Kent) 133, 265
fear of acquiring a disability 136–137
Fine, M. 247
foot-binding of Chinese girls 113

Freudian theorists 65; *see also specific name*
Freud, Sigmund 269
Frieden, L. 267
Functional Model of Disability 77, 92, 93–100, *93*
functions impaired by disability 49–51, *49*
Furlong, Pat 337, 341

Garland-Thomson, Rosemarie 141, 145, 248
"gateway disability" 27
Gawande, Atul 8, 14, 27, 84–85, 89
Gehlen, A. 325
general public 36, 41–42
Gessner, J. E. 392
Gill, Carol 9
"gimp pride" or "gimp humor" 155–156
Goeke, J. 215
Goffman, E. 215
Going Back to Civvy Street 219
Golden Age of Employment for IWDs 105–106
Goma-i-Freixanet, M. 398
Goodman, J. 166
Graf, N. M. 85
Grandin, Temple 61, 71, 359
Grealy, Lucy 387–388
grief counseling 371
Groopman, Jerome 67

Hadden family 55–56
Hahn, H. 110
Hall, Robert David 154, 244–245
Harris, R. W. 209
Harris, S. P. 73, 82
Hawking, Jane 255–257
Hawking, Stephen 49, 154, 184, 255, 292, 302
health insurance 26–28, 85–86, 88, 105, 174
Health Insurance and Portability and Accountability Act (HIPPA) 174, 205
hearing aid designs 99
Heinenmann, A. W. 392
Heller, T. 73, 82
Helwig, A. A. 141, 392
Henley, M. 287
Herlihy, B. 259
Herr, Hugh 94–95
Hettler, W. 190
hierarchy of needs 180–181, 268, *268*
hierarchy of stigma 58–60, *58*, 62–63, *62*, 219
high-incidence disabilities 54, *54*, 57

history-taking with CWDs 187–189, *187*
Hockenberry, John 148
Hofsiss, Jack 276, 290, 318
Hoirup, Laurie 98
Holicky, R. 141, 392
Howe, Samuel Gridley 291–292
"How I Lost My Hand and Found My Life" (Weisskopf) 279–280
Huemann, Judith 230, 264–265
humanist theorists 45, 181, 268–269; *see also specific name*
humor, value of 294

identity politics 24–25
Iezzoni, Lisa 104
Imrie, R. 385
increases in number of IWDs: actual number versus reported number of disabilities and 18; advances in medicine and 13–14; American with Disabilities Act and 21–26; medical causes for 12–17, 20–21, *20*; outcomes of 20–28, *20*; overview 403; statistical causes for 17–19; structural lags and 20; survival rates of traumatic injury and 20; training and education programs for counselors and 26–27
incremental care 85, 88
individual is not the disability belief 128–131, *128*
individuals with disabilities (IWDs): abuse of, screening for *258–259*, 259–263, *261*; accommodations for 11, 25, 28, 97, 171–174, *171*; adaptive behaviors of *263*, 264–267; aging of 17, 21; Americans with Disabilities Act and changed lives of 267; assisted suicide and 244; assistive or adaptive technology and 50–51, 93–96, 99; bureaucracy and, burden of *204–205*, 205–208; caregivers of 252–258, *252*, 369–370; civil rights laws for 3–4, 9–10, *10*, 22–23, *22*, 81, 117–118; contributing to others and, importance of 224–226, *224*; control of own life and 8; counseling needs of 8; counseling services for 5–9; dating for 360–364, *360–361*; demeaning images of, in general culture 241–245, *241*; developmental theorists and 45; discomfort around, responsibility for *128*, 135–139, *135*; discrimination and prejudice against 8, 10–12, 23–24, 26, 81, 113, 132, 240, 248; dissonance and 204; elderly 17, 21; employment and

101, 105–106, 188; engagement with life and 293; expectations for, lowered 141–142; functioning of, public view of 96; general public and 36; Golden Age of Employment for 105–106; as high achievers 356; humanist theorists and 45; idiosyncratic function of 94; individual is not the disability belief and 128–131, *128*; infantilization experienced by 235–236; inferior public services and 116–117; "inspiration porn" and 142–143; institutions for 260; IWODs' understanding of experience of, challenge of 37, 138; jokes about, toleration of 240; LBGTQ 117, 247–249, 251; "little acts of degradation" toward *128*, 143–146, *143*; longevity for 16–17; medical abandonment and 169; medical services and 7; multifaceted experience of 37–38, 202–203; national laws protecting 21–26, *22*; other disenfranchised groups and, belonging to *245–246*, 246–251, *247*; physiognomy and 300; pity of 81, 141; political identity of 247; post-ADA generation 25–26; quality of life and 7; questions posed to 144; response to disability and beliefs of 292–293; self-esteem of 230; self-identity of 1, 4, 6–7, *7*, 20, 38, 42, 88, 141, 284, 385; self-naming and, defiant 155–156; social perceptions of 10–12; social role expectations and 211–216, *211, 212, 213*; stereotyping 7, 139–143; stigmatized diagnoses and 7; stigma toward 58–60, *58, 62*, 63, 351; substance abuse in 391–396, *392, 395*, 399–400; transcendence for *270–271*, 271–275; voice in treatment and 83; well-intentioned, nice people creating discrimination and prejudice of *128*, 139–143, *139*; *see also* clients with disabilities (CWDs); increases in number of IWDs; *specific issue and disability*

individual's response to disability practice guidelines: acquisition of disability as developmental task and 284, 325–329, *328*; Biomedical Model and 284–285, *285*; cognitive restructuring and 284, 297–303, *299*; commonalities between cognitive restructuring and stage theory and *297–298*, 298; deficit breeds growth theory and 325; factors of disability affecting 332–342, *333–334*; focus in 284; individual factors facilitating positive responses and *291*, 292–293; intentionality and 322–324, *323*; lifelong process of 288; Models of Disability and 284–287, *285*; Moral/Religious Model and 285; overview 3, 284, 329; paradoxes of 288–290, *288*; poor responses to 295–297, *295, 297–298*; positive responses and 291–294; Price and 287–288; response term and 287; stage theory of responding to disability and 284, 303–322, *303, 313–314, 319–320*; theories of acceptance of disability and 297, *297*

individuals without disabilities (IWODs): accommodations for IWDs and 97, 172; Americans with Disabilities Act and, perception of 23; assistive technology for IWDs and 220; civil rights laws for IWDs and 117–118; counselors viewed as 159; disability civil rights and 117; disability role and 114; discomfort of, responsibility for 111, *128*, 135–139, *135*; disfigurements and, fear of possible 387; employment of IWDs and 101; experience of disability and, challenge of understanding 37, 138; higher end of spectrum diagnosis of IWDs and 71; invisible disabilities and 200; "little acts of degradation" toward IWDs and, unawareness of *128*, 143–146, *143*, 173; misunderstanding of IWDs and 53–54; Moral/Religious Model and 79; names for, by IWDs 155–156; perceived cause of disability and 62; political identity of IWDs and 247; self-identity of IWDs and 1; self-identity of 149; separation from IWDs and, need for 64; skepticism and suspicion toward IWDs and 49; stigma toward IWDs and 59; wish of IWDs to be "normal" or "cured" belief of *128*, 131–135, *131*

Industrial Revolution and disabilities 109–110

infanticide 88

infantile autism 65

infantilization experienced by IWDs 235–236

infant mortality 13–14

insidious onsets 42–43, *42*, 343–344, *343*

"inspiration porn" 142–143

institutions for IWDs 16–17, 260

intellectual disability (ID) *40*, 41, 52, 107–109, 309, 407–408

intentionality 322–324, *323*

Interactional Models of Disability *90*, 91–93, 121

International Classification of Disease (ICD) 83
International Classification of Disease-10 (ICD-10) 1
International Classification of Functioning (ICF) 36, 66, 68
International Classification Statistical Classification of Diseases and Related Health Problems–Tenth Revision, Clinical Modification (ICD-11) 66, 68
interpreters, Sign Language 173–174, 263
intersectionality of disability with other disenfranchised groups *245–246*, 246–251, *247*
intra-psychic approach 164
invisible disabilities *199–200*, 200–204
IQ scores 52, 107–108
"It's Not All About My Legs" 131

Johnson, A. G. 116
Johnson, Harriet McBryde 132, 146
Johnson v. Thompson (1992) 249
jokes about disability, toleration of 240

Kaier, Anne 137
Keen, M. 392
Keller, Helen 291–292, 358–359
Kendall, E. 321
Kent, Deborah 133
Kiger, G. 29
kindness, misguided *128*, 139–143, *139*, 209
Kleege, G. 150
koans, Zen Buddhist 272, 315
Kovalsky, Abby 362
Kriegel, Leonard 24, 150
Kubla, Elliot 346, 389

Laborit, Emmanuelle 308
Lamm, Richard 103
Landers, Ann 337–338
Langer, Elana 99
language, disability: counselors and 159–160; diagnosing disabilities and, communicating 67; emotional 153–154; euphemisms 154–155, 157; "gimp pride" or "gimp humor" and 155–156; guidelines 152–154; overview 151; person-first 3–4, 156–159, *156*; power of 151–152; results of inappropriate 150, *150*; sensational 153–154; Sign 44, 58–59, 112, 173
late-life deafness 44
LBGTQ IWDs 117, 247–249, 251
learning about disability 149–150
learning disabilities 19
Lefly, H. P. 327

Levine, Anne 107–108
Lewis, Alex 272–273, 315–316
licensing laws 28
life spans 15–17
Life Spent in the High Latitudes, A (Perkins) 304–305
Lin, E. 393
Linton, S. 31, 102–103, 131, 155, 214
literature and disabilities 80–81, 154, 242
Living in a State of Stuck 297
longevity 15–17
Longmore, Paul K. 121–122, 172, 207, 225–226
long-term care 26–27, 85–86, 88
Loots, G. M. P. 146
loss and disability 39–40, *39*, 87–88
low-incidence disabilities 54–57, *54*

McIntosh, Molly 386–387
McLeod, D. J. 353
Mairs, Nancy 346–347, 361
Marks, D. 242
marriage and acquisition of disability 364–375, *364*, *374*
marriage counseling 86, 373–375, *374*
Marsh, D. T. 327
Martin, Lee 145
Maslow, Abraham 180–181, 267–269, *267*, *268*, 313
Mattlin, Ben 383–384
measuring disabilities: categorical 70–71; on continuum or spectrum *60*, 61–63; dimensional 70–71; hierarchy of stigma and 58–60, *58*, *62*, 63; high-incidence 54, *54*, 57; low-incidence 54–57, *54*; nomenclature changes and 69–70; overview 1–2, 73; perceived cause and 62–63, *62*; qualitative 70–71; quantitative 70–71
media and disabilities 242–245
Medicaid 105
medical abandonment 169
medical advances 13–14, 112
medical care coverage 26–28, 85–86, 88, 105, 174
medical profession, self-transformation of 26–32
medical providers, collaborating with 275–280, *275*
medical response to disability 48, 84, 122
medical services and IWDs 7
medical versus sociopolitical aspects of disability 11
Medicare 105, 205

Mee, Charles 91, 195, 310–311
mental illness *see* psychiatric disabilities
"mental rehabilitation" concept 296–297
mental retardation term 309
Merrick, Joseph Carey 318
Michalko, Rod 134, 243, 295–296, 353–354
middle age and disabilities *44*, 45, 365
Mind's Eye, The (Sacks) 51
Minority Group Model of Disability *see* Civil Rights Model of Disability
minority groups 117
Miracle Worker, The (film and stage play) 292
Models of Disability: Biomedical *53*, 77, 78, 82–90; Civil Rights 77, 78, 91–92, *115–116*, 116–121, 226; collaborating with medical providers and 275–280, *275*; conclusions about 121–122, 275–276; considerations in discussing 78; counseling services and 123, *123*; disability-awareness training and 32; Economic 77, 100–106, *100*; Environmental 77, 91–92, *106–107*, 107–112, 219; Functional 77, 91–92, 93–100, *93*; functions of 77, *77*, 285; individual's response to disability practice guidelines and 284–287, *285*; integration of 286; Interactional *90*, 91–93, 121; Moral/Religious 77, *78–79*, 79–83, 87, 91, 92; non-interactional 91–93, 121; overview 2, 76–78, 121–122, 404; perceived cause of disability and 80; purposes of 89, 99; Social 77, *112*, 113–115, 143; social role demands of IWDs practice guidelines and 332; understanding 76; value of 76; *see also* Biomedical Model of Disability
Mooney, Jonathan 109, 153
Moral/Religious Model of Disability 77, *78–79*, 79–83, 87, 91, 92
moratoriums, social 326–327
Morris, Jenny 50, 64, 94, 122, 132, 192, 242
mourning a disability 309
Ms. Wheelchair Florida (2014) 262
multiple sclerosis 203, 343–345
Murderball (film) 95, 213
Murphy, Robert 289
mutual support groups 226–231, *226*, *227*
Myers, J. E. 190
"My Supercharged, Tricked Out, Bluetooth Wheelchair Life Force" 222

National Alliance on Mental Illness (NAMI) 254
National Organization of Disability (NOD) 101
National Public Radio (NPR) programs 81, 118–120, 137, 291

Naugle, R. I. 308
Navarro, Mireya 154, 244–245
Nazi Germany's mass murder of people with disabilities *100*, 101–102
neglect of IWDs, screening for *258–259*, 259–263, *261*
Neumann, Robert 361–362
neurodevelopmental disabilities 46; *see also specific type*
NeuroTribes (Silberman) 71, 101
"Never Enough Time" (Yoels and Clair) 276
new horizons for counselors 402–405
new reality for counselors: counseling services for IWDs and, new demand for 5–9; increases in number of IWDs 12–21, *20*; medical profession self-transformation 26–32; national laws protecting IWDs 21–26, *22*; overview 1, 5, 32–33, 402–403; paradox of disability and 9–12; three realities combined and 12
"No Arms, No Legs—No Worries" 274, 317
non-interactional Models of Disability 91–93, 121
normalcy (absence of disability) as ideal belief, avoiding 184–186, *184*, *186*
normality, concept of 7, *7*, 46, 134, 149, 185
nursing home lobby 105

O'Brien, Mark 368
O'Brien, Miles 307
Obsessive Compulsive Disorder (OCD) 61
O'Donnell, J. J. 392
old age disabilities 15–16, 44–46, *46*, 57
Olkin, R. 363
Ostrove, J. M. 232–233
overabundance of functions 39
Owen, Robert 299

pain management 383
paradox of disability 9–12
paralysis 14, 16, 274, 292, 296–297, 309–311, 317, 397–398
Paralyzing Fear (PBS) 260
Paris, J. 59
partner caregiving 369–370
paternalism 83, *90*, 92, 139–140, *139*, *167*, 168–169, 196, *209*, 210, 236, 286
pathologizing disability, avoiding *189*, 190–193, *191*, *193–194*
Patterson, J. M. 55, 335
perceived cause of disability 62–63, *62*, 80
Perkins, Roberts 304–305
Perlman, Izak 7
personal care attendant (PCA) 262

person-first language 3–4, 156–159, *156*
persons with disabilities (PWDs) *see* individuals with disabilities (IWDs)
persons without disabilities (PWODs) *see* individuals without disabilities (IWODs)
Pew Research Center 364
phantom limb sensation 307
physical disabilities: case study 406–407; category of 5–6, *5*; defining 38; diagnosing 40; loss or deficit and 39; as primary disability over substance abuse 394; *see also specific type*
Physical Disability (Wright) 298
physical disfigurements *44*, 45, 318–319, 383–388, *384*
physiognomy 300
physiological needs 268
pity of IWDs 81, 141
polio 12, 50, 84–85, 133–134, 164, 289, 310–311, 360
political identity of IWDs 247
poor response to disability 295–297, *295*, *297–298*
positive response to disability: factors facilitating 291–293, *291*; first-person accounts of 294–297; humor and 294; IWODs beliefs and 292–293; requirements for 293–294
postlingual deafness 44
Post-Traumatic Stress Disorder (PTSD) *72*
practice guidelines 3, 284, 405; *see also* ethical practice guidelines; experience of disability practice guidelines; individual's response to disability practice guidelines; social role demands of IWDs practice guidelines; societal issues practice guidelines; unique demands of disability practice guidelines
pre-diagnosis period, long 43, 342–349, *343*, 375
pre-disability period, avoiding idealizing 194–195, *194*
prelingual deafness 43–44
Premo, Brenda 141–142, 173, 186, 348
prenatal testing 12
Price, Reynolds 287, 382
Pride against Prejudice (Morris) 50
Privilege, Power, and Difference (Johnson) 116
proactive reaction to events 303
prostheses 14, 94–95, 218, 385
psychiatric disabilities: category of 5–6, *5*; continuum or spectrum diagnoses and 60, *60*; defining 39; diagnosing 40–41, 59; diagnostic masking and 41; DSM and 121; intellectual disabilities and 41; prevalence of 40; responding to diagnosis of 312–313; stigma of 59–60, 63; stress and 41; transcendence and 274–275, 317–318; *see also specific type*
psychotherapy 342
Public Television Service (PBS) program 260
Purdy, Amy 131, 195, 218–219
Putnam, M. 224

qualitative measurement of disability 70–71
quality of life (QOL) 7
quantitative measurement of disability 70–71
questioning in responding to disability, personal 310–311

race and disabilities 246–247, 249–251
rapport building with CWDs 182–183, *182*, 217
rate of disability 46, *46*
reactive reaction to events 303
Reed, P. G. 268–269, 271, 314
Reeve, Christopher 292, 357
Rehabilitation Act (1973) 58
Reichman, Frieda Fromm 65
Remley, T. P., Jr. 259
reported number of disabilities 18
"Representations of Disability and the Interpersonal Relationships of Women with Disabilities" (Crawford and Ostrove) study 232–233
Resch, J. A. 207
response demands of IWDs *see* social role demands of IWDs practice guidelines
response to disability *see* individual's response to disability practice guidelines; poor response to disability; positive response to disability
Rethinking Disability in Social Work (May and Raske) 116
Robinson, Margaret 236
Robison, John Elder 69
Rogers, Carl 166, 182
role models 352–360, *352*
Rolland, J. S. 372–373
Rome, Joanne 386
Roosevelt, Eleanor 251
Roosevelt, Franklin Delano 50, 62, 193, 200, 202, 218, 250–251, 292, 305, 356–358, 360, 388
Rosen, D. 338
Rousso, Harilyn 354
Rudolph, Wilma 62, 358

Sabi Roam cane 100
Sacks, Oliver 6, 39, 51
safety needs 268
Schaschi, S. 395
Scherer, M. 223
Schindler, A. 73, 82
schizophrenia 45, 65, 130, 414–416
"schizophrenogenic mother" 65
Schnoll, S. 392
Scribner, Charles 51
self-actualization 267–270, 314
self-blame 295–296
self-definition 24–25, 129, 151
self-esteem 230
self-naming, defiant 155–156
self-reliance 97
sensory substitution 96
service laws 9–10, 18; *see also specific law*
severity of disability *51*, 52
sexuality and CWDs' self-identity 231–234, *232, 234*
Shehan, I. 392
Shell, Marc 308
Shewchuk, R. M. 253
Sign Language 44, 58–59, 112, 173
Sign Language interpreters 173–174, 263
Silberman, S. 51, 71, 101
silent transition of congenital disability 334–342, *334*, 375
simulation exercises 29–30, 32
Singer, Pete 146
"six-hour retardates" concept 109
Smart, J. F. 322
Smith, Susan 176–177
Sobsey, D. 157, 260
social inequalities and disabilities 115; *see also specific type*
socially constructed disability 113
Social Model of Disability 77, *112*, 113–115, 143
social moratoriums 326–327
social oppression 320–321
social perceptions of disability 10–12; *see also specific type*
social relationships and disability: dating 360–364, *360–361*, 376; marriage 364–375, *364, 374*, 376; role models 352–360, *352*, 376; social support 349–351, *349*, 376
social role demands of IWDs practice guidelines: congenital disability and 334–342, *334*, 375; dating 360–364, *360–361*, 376; "disabled heroes" and 352–360, *352*, 376; factors of disability affecting individual's response and 332–342, *333–334*; long pre-diagnosis period and, demands of 342–349, *343*, 375; marriage 364–365, *364, 374*, 376; Models of Disability and 332; overview 3, 332, 375–376; role models and 352–360, *352*, 376; support groups and 349–351, *349*, 376; *see also* social role expectations of disability
social role expectations of disability 211–216, *211, 212, 213*; *see also* social role demands of IWDs practice guidelines
Social Security Administration (SSA) 207, 225
Social Security Disability Insurance (SSDI) 18, 89, 106, 174, *205*, 225, 371
societal issues practice guidelines, integrating counseling with: availability of, lack of 280; collaborate with medical providers 275–280, *275*; look for transcendence 267–275, *267, 268, 270–271*; overview 3, 240, 280; recognize activism and advocacy as adaptive behaviors *263*, 264–267; recognize demeaning images of IWDs in general culture 241–245, *241*; recognize IWDS may be members of other disenfranchised groups 245–246, 246–251, *247*; screen for abuse and neglect *258–259*, 259–263, *261*; support and acknowledge caregivers 252–258, *252*
Sociopolitical Model of Disability *see* Civil Rights Model of Disability
Solomon, Andrew 55, 65, 138, 192
Souders, Randy 301–302, 349–350
spina bifida 13–14, 249
spinal cord injuries (SCI) 14, 16, 26, 274, 292, 296–297, 309–311, 317, 397–398
spinal muscular atrophy (S.M.A.) 98
stable course disabilities 47–48, *47*
stage theory 284, *297–298*, 303–322, *303, 313–314, 319–320*
standardized systems of clinical diagnostic criteria 52, 66–69, *66*, 73; *see also specific name*
standardized tests 186
staring at disability, avoiding 145
Stefan, S. 48–49, 103, 107, 249
stereotyping IWDs 7, 139–143
Sternberg, Louis 306
Stigma (Goffman) 215

stigma of disabilities 52, 58–60, *58*, *62*, 63, 114, 219
Straw, D. 395
stress of disability 41, 43, 86, 111, 136, 138, 176, 228, 257, 278, 336, 353, 365–366, 408–410
stress management *189*, 190, *227*, 257–258, 288, 298, 322, 369, 371
Strong at Broken Places (Cleland) 267
structural lags 20, 253
Stuart Karten Design 99
substance abuse: age and 394; defining 391–392; defining disability and 19; effects on disability *396–397*, 397–399; in IWDs 391–396, *392*, *395*, 399–400; practice guidelines for counselors and 397–399, *397*; prevalence of 392–393; as psychiatric disability 391; self-medication and 396; stigma toward 60
Substance Abuse and Mental Health Services Administration (SAMHSA) 391
Sullivan, Annie 292, 359
"super crips" 357–358
Supplemental Security Income (SSI) 89, 106
support groups for disabilities: in Environmental Model *107*, 110–111; mutual 226–231, *226*, *227*; self-advocacy and 266; social role demands of IWDs practice guidelines and 349–351, *349*, 376
survival rates of traumatic injury 20
sympathy versus empathy 208–210, *208–209*

technology, disabilities and new 112
therapeutic amputation 27
"This American Life" (NPR) 118–120
threshold for diagnosing disability, raising 61
time of onset 43–46, *43*, *44*, *46*
Tollifson, Joan 110–111, 133, 149, 228, 271–272, 294, 314–315
transcendence, disability: discrimination and prejudice juxtaposed with 240; hierarchy of needs and 268, *268*; for IWDs *270–271*, 271–275; looking for 267–275, *267*, *268*, *270–271*; Maslow's theory of 267–270, *267*; psychiatric disabilities and 274–275, 317–318; self-actualization and 267–270; stage theory and *313–314*, 314–319; Vash's concept of 303, 325
traumatic brain injury (TBI) 14, 318, 350, 397–398, 410–411

try harder syndrome 388–391, *388*
type of onset 42–43, *42*

Undercoffer, Martha 145
unique demands of disability practice guidelines: chronic pain 379–383, *380*; overview 3, 379, *379*, 399–400, *400*; physical disfigurements 383–388, *384*; substance abuse among IWDs 391–399, *392*, *395*, *396–397*; try harder syndrome 388–391, *388*
universal health care coverage 26–27
universal irreversible physical transitions 178
US Census 12, 16, 24
US Congress 118
US Supreme Court 22, 103, 118

Vash, Carolyn 164, 270, 295, 303, 313, 325
visibility of disability *52–53*, 53–54
Vujicic, Nick 273–274, 294, 316–317

Weihenmayer, Eric <or Erik?> 95–96, 155, 184, 188, 225, 264–265, 312
Weisskopf, Michael 202–203, 220, 222, 279–280, 312
well-intentioned, nice people creating prejudice and discrimination *128*, 139–143, *139*
Wendell, S. 149
"We're All Little John Waynes" 262
wheelchair athletes 95
wheelchairs, evolution of 50–51, 218
Whitt, J. K. 201
Whole New Life, A (Price) 382
Wildman, S. M. 23
Will <or Well?>, Madeline 8–9, 113
Wilson, Brittany 118–120
Wilson, D. J. 85
Wolfensberger, W. 235
World Health Organization (WHO) 1, 18, 36, 66
Wright, Beatrice 284, 298–299, *299*, 385
Wright, David 347–348

Young, Stella 138, 142–143

Zen Buddhism 272, 315
Zola, Irving K. 242–243, 358
Zon hearing aid design 99